MARK

God's Word *for the* Biblically-Inept™ SERIES

Scott Pinzon

CARTOONS BY

Reverend Fun
(Dennis "Max" Hengeveld)
Dennis is a graphic designer for Gospel Films and the author of *Has Anybody Seen My Locust?* His cartoons can be seen worldwide at www.reverendfun.com.

STARBURST PUBLISHERS®

P. O. Box 4123, Lancaster, Pennsylvania 17604

To schedule author appearances, write:
Author Appearances
Starburst Publishers
P.O. Box 4123
Lancaster, Pennsylvania 17604
(717) 293-0939

www.starburstpublishers.com

CREDITS:
Copyedited by Chad Allen
Cover design by David Marty Design
Text design and composition by John Reinhardt Book Design
Illustrations by Mark Ammerman and Melissa A. Burkhart
Cartoons by Dennis "Max" Hengeveld

Unless otherwise noted, or paraphrased by the author, all Scripture quotations are from the New International Version of The Holy Bible.

Scripture taken from the HOLY BIBLE: NEW INTERNATIONAL VERSION® (NIV®). Copyright © 1973, 1978, 1984 by International Bible Society. Used by permission of Zondervan Publishing House. The "NIV" and "New International Version" trademarks are registered in the United States Patent and Trademark Office by International Bible Society.

Reverend Fun cartoons ©Copyright Gospel Films Incorporated.

To the best of its ability, Starburst Publishers® has strived to find the source of all material. If there has been an oversight, please contact us, and we will make any correction deemed necessary in future printings. We also declare that to the best of our knowledge all material (quoted or not) contained herein is accurate, and we shall not be held liable for the same.

First Printing, August 2001

ISBN: 1-892016-36-2
Library of Congress Number 20-01090816

Printed in the United States of America

READ THIS PAGE BEFORE YOU READ THIS BOOK . . .

Welcome to the *God's Word for the Biblically-Inept*™ series. If you find reading the Bible overwhelming, baffling, and frustrating, then this Revolutionary Commentary™ is for you!

Each page of the series is organized for easy reading with icons, sidebars, and bullets to make the Bible's message easy to understand. *God's Word for the Biblically-Inept*™ series includes opinions and insights from Bible experts of all kinds, so you get various opinions on Bible teachings—not just one!

There are more *God's Word for the Biblically-Inept*™ titles on the way. The following is a list of available books. (See page 350 for ordering information.) We have assigned each title an abbreviated **title code**. This code along with page numbers is incorporated in the text **throughout the series**, allowing easy reference from one title to another.

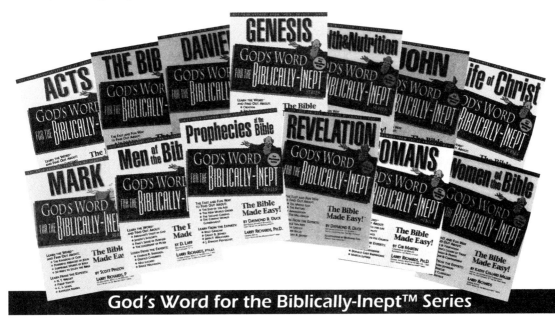

God's Word for the Biblically-Inept™ Series

Title	ISBN	Code	Price
Acts by Robert C. Girard	ISBN 189201646X	**GWAC**	**$17.99**
The Bible by Larry Richards	ISBN 0914984551	**GWBI**	**$16.95**
Daniel by Daymond R. Duck	ISBN 0914984489	**GWDN**	**$16.95**
Genesis by Joyce Gibson	ISBN 1892016125	**GWGN**	**$16.95**
Health & Nutrition by Kathleen O'Bannon Baldinger	ISBN 0914984055	**GWHN**	**$16.95**
John by Lin Johnson	ISBN 1892016435	**GWJN**	**$16.95**
Life of Christ, Volume 1 by Robert C. Girard	ISBN 1892016230	**GWLC**	**$16.95**
Life of Christ, Volume 2 by Robert C. Girard	ISBN 1892016397	**GWLC2**	**$16.95**
Mark by Scott Pinzon	ISBN 1892016362	**GWMK**	**$17.99**
Men of the Bible by D. Larry Miller	ISBN 1892016079	**GWMB**	**$16.95**
Prophecies of the Bible by Daymond R. Duck	ISBN 1892016222	**GWPB**	**$16.95**
Revelation by Daymond R. Duck	ISBN 0914984985	**GWRV**	**$16.95**
Romans by Gib Martin	ISBN 1892016273	**GWRM**	**$16.95**
Women of the Bible by Kathy Collard Miller	ISBN 0914984063	**GWWB**	**$16.95**

JUST FOR TEENS!

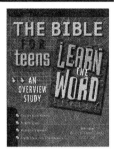  

● **Learn more at www.learntheword.com** ●

The Bible for Teens—Learn the Word™ Series

Who says Bible study has to be boring? Finally, there is a Bible commentary that meets the needs of today's teens by explaining biblical principles and Scripture in a fun, informative, and entertaining format. Adapted from *The Bible—God's Word for the Biblically-Inept™*.

(trade paper)   ISBN 1892016516 $14.99

Bible Bytes for Teens: A Study-Devotional for Logging In to God's Word

Teens can focus on byte-sized Scripture passages and related teaching to get clear spiritual direction for their day. Also included are reflective study questions and a power-packed design that teens will love.

(trade paper)   ISBN 1892016494 $13.99

What's in the Bible for . . .™ Teens

By Mark Littleton and Jeanette Gardner Littleton

Written to teens, this book explores biblical themes that speak to the challenges and pressures of today's adolescents, such as relationships and peer pressure. Helpful and eye-catching "WWJD?" icons, illustrations, and sidebars are included.

(trade paper)   ISBN 1892016052 $16.95

AND FOR WOMEN . . .

Bible Seeds: A Simple Study-Devotional for Growing in God's Word

Especially for women, this book combines Bible study, devotional readings, word studies, practical application, and room to write. Make this book your very own portable garden for growing in God's Word.

(trade paper)   ISBN 1892016443 $13.99

CHAPTERS AT A GLANCE

ILLUSTRATIONS

INTRODUCTION

Welcome to **Mark—God's Word for the Biblically-Inept**™. This is just one book in a whole series of books that makes understanding the Bible fun and easy. This is not a traditional Bible study or commentary; it's a REVOLUTIONARY COMMENTARY™ that will permanently change your outlook on the Bible. You'll not only Learn the Word™ . . . you'll learn the basics of how to teach yourself the Word!

Let's Get Started
(Let's Get Started)

To Gain Your Confidence

Mark—God's Word for the Biblically-Inept™ is for you if you want to know more about Jesus, but don't get much out of sentences like, "A parallel to the epistemological ramifications of the pseudepigrapha suggests the heuristic vocabulary word yada yada yada."

I love the scholars and what they've given us, but scholars tend to write to scholars. This book is for the rest of us. In it I'll explain Mark to you in simple, vivid terms that bring the book to life. I know you're a smart person (unlike that other publishing company that thinks its readers are dummies). You just haven't been exposed to some of this stuff before. Well, relax; none of it is too hard for you, and I'm not taking a single step through Mark without stopping to make sure you're still with me. So come along . . . Mark will rock your world!

> **John 1:1** In the beginning was the Word . . .

(Verse(s) of Scripture)

What Is The Bible?

The Bible looks like one big book, but it's actually sixty-six books by many authors, written over a span of roughly 1,600 years, gathered into one collection. If you look at your Bible's table of contents, the books listed under "Old Testament" were written before Jesus Christ walked on earth (see GWBI, page 1). The books listed under "New Testament" were written after Jesus visited earth (see GWBI, page 147). And that one blank page between the Old Testament and the New Testament? That represents a four-hundred-

☞ **GO TO:**

Matthew, Mark, Luke (other books)

(Go To)

year gap. (And you thought you'd waited a long time for the Star Wars sequel!)

How did these books end up together? Jews of ancient times wrote the books of the Old Testament to record the history of their nation and its relationship with the Jewish God, Yahweh. Their nation and their God produced Jesus, and the New Testament tells of his birth, death, resurrection, ascension to heaven, and how people lived once they decided to follow Jesus' teachings. The New Testament ends with references to a time when Jesus will physically return to earth. In a sense the Bible became the Bible because it gathered together one continuous, epic story of how God reached out to humans.

Henrietta C. Mears: The Old Testament is an account of a nation (the Hebrew nation). The New Testament is an account of a Man (the Son of Man). The nation was founded and nurtured of God in order to bring the Man into the world (Genesis 12:1–3). God Himself became a man so that we might know what to think of when we think of God (John 1:14; 14:9). His appearance on the earth is the central event of all history. The Old Testament sets the stage for it. The New Testament describes it.[1]

What Is A "Gospel"?

The word "gospel" comes from an Old English word meaning "good story." What is this good story about? We would call it a biography, but the New Testament Gospels (Matthew, Mark, Luke, and John) were written during the first century, when the concept of a biography was different than ours.

Generally, the goal of an ancient biography was to give the reader insight into the character of a person. In Wendy's hamburger commercials decades ago, Clara Peller kept demanding, "Where's the beef?" To the ancient Roman audience, the "beef" was the grown man's words and deeds. Anything else was just bun. So, the Gospels focus heavily on the sayings and actions of Jesus. First-century biographies commonly left out where a person was born, or how their parents met. That was considered irrelevant. This is why none of the Gospels describe the full life of Jesus.

Instead, the gospel accounts were selective. Back then, no one assumed that a biography included the whole sweep of someone's life, for one very practical reason: writing materials were precious. The gospel writers could not drive to Kinkos and pick up a ream of paper. They had serious space limitations; the entire story had to fit on one standard-length scroll. John 21:25 says of Jesus' deeds, "*If every one of them were written down, I suppose that even the whole world would not have room for the books that would be written."* That means the Gospels were written with this thought in mind: "I can only tell about a few of Jesus' deeds and sayings. Which will give the clearest picture of who he was? Which are the best ones?"

To put it in *Biblically-Inept* style, the Gospels are a collection of Jesus' Greatest Hits.

A Capital Idea!

Throughout this book and the *God's Word for the Biblically-Inept* series you'll notice "gospel" is sometimes capitalized ("Gospel") and sometimes lowercase ("gospel"). This could cause some confusion, but there is a reason for the difference. The word is capitalized when it refers either to a book of the Bible ("the Gospel of Mark") or to the salvation message of Jesus Christ ("Spread the Gospel."). It is lowercase when used as an adjective ("the gospel account") or when it is quoted from a source that lowercases it. In addition, we'll keep it lowercase when we're simply discussing the term. If you get confused, my advice is to pay no attention to the capitalization and keep on reading.

Why Study A Gospel?

Hey, who *is* this guy, Jesus? What did he teach, what did he say about himself? How do you know it? There is no better, purer, more reliable information available about him than the gospel accounts. That's one reason to study them—to go straight to the source when learning about the man who is often referred to as the central figure in history.

Though the Gospels resemble ancient biographies, they broke the ancient concept of a biography by adding an extra element: religious purpose. The authors of the Gospels intentionally wrote to provoke readers to believe in Jesus Christ.

Does this mean the Gospels are unreliable propaganda? Actually, it means the opposite. Yes, the gospel writers are die-hard advocates of Jesus, but they didn't start that way. They came by it honestly. When they tell you that his sacrifice changed them to their core, they're not being manipulative; they're being authentic. The Gospels repeatedly demonstrate that when neutral people met Jesus, he shattered their preconceptions and transformed their lives. To leave that out would be a lie.

Each of the four Gospels asserts that, despite the way things appeared, Jesus wasn't merely a victim. He died purposely, as a sacrifice to pay for the wrongdoings of everyone else, including

(Wayback Machine)

POWER TOOL
Check the Old Testament cross-references.

(Power Tool)

Something to Ponder

(Something to Ponder)

KEY POINT

The Gospels are ancient biographies with a religious purpose.

you and me. The greatest reason to study the Gospels is so you can personally evaluate whether that message is true. In fact, if you've never studied the Gospels firsthand, you're letting someone else tell you what to think about one of the most important topics in all of life. On a subject this significant, you don't want to depend on secondhand information. So another reason to study the Gospels is, you owe it to yourself!

If your reading of the Gospels convinces you they are true, you then have another great reason to study them. If you want to obey the teachings of Jesus Christ—to be his disciple and imitate him—you need all the information about him you can get. The Gospels provide that information; they provide the inspiration to help you keep following him—one more good reason to study the Gospels.

Why Study Mark's Gospel?

Because this upstart first-century reporter scooped all the other apostles, that's why. Most scholars believe Mark was written down first (perhaps around A.D. 60), while John's Gospel was written last and probably did not begin circulating until A.D. 90 or later. For a period of years believers found everything they needed to know about Jesus in Mark's account alone. His was the most immediate—the closest to the actual deeds.

Mark is a great place to get acquainted with Jesus for another reason: Mark's Gospel is the shortest of the four and the easiest to understand. If you think back to the last biology textbook you had to drag around, sometimes shorter is better, right?

Who Wrote The Gospel Of Mark?

Surprise! Not Mark. Most scholars believe that a guy named John Mark traveled as an assistant to the apostle Peter. He heard Peter's firsthand, eyewitness accounts about Jesus over and over, in many different locales. Eventually Mark wrote down Peter's teachings.

Better Late Than Later

Critics of the Gospels love to point out that stories of Jesus existed only in oral form for decades before being written, as if that proves these accounts became exaggerated. Today we consider spoken accounts inferior to written accounts because the printed word can be checked and verified. But this view is a modern invention. The Hebrew culture saw it the opposite way. People attached greater authority to eyewitnesses than to written material. Think about it: if you were trying to judge whether a person is lying, would you rather read their story from paper, or stare them in the eyes as they spoke? To first-century Hebrews, papyrus was dead compared to the "living voice."

Besides, without public libraries, photocopiers, and newspapers, ancient peoples were forced to excel at passing along verbal information reliably. They structured stories in memorable fashion. They memorized better than we do because they valued it more than we do. Only as the apostles aged and were martyred was their knowledge captured in writing, but this is better than losing it entirely.

We are two decades farther from World War II than Mark was from the deeds of Jesus when he wrote them down, yet our accounts of Pearl Harbor are accurate. In historical terms one generation is not enough time for lies to creep in; too many survivors remember what really happened. That makes the gospel accounts some of the most dependable documents in all of history.

What Others are Saying:

Josh McDowell: After trying to shatter the historicity and validity of the Scriptures, I came to the conclusion that they are historically trustworthy. If one discards the Bible as being unreliable, then he must discard almost all literature of antiquity.[2]

That Explains So Much!

Why do scholars link Peter with John Mark? Besides an unbroken line of tradition dating all the way back to their lives, we have some scriptural evidence. Have you ever read the story of how an angel busted Peter out of jail? When Peter went to the home where the believers were praying for him and knocked on the door, at first they were so stunned that their prayers had been answered, they forgot to let him in! That was Mark's mom's <u>house</u>. (Some traditions place the Last Supper in the upper room of Mark's house, too.) And in one of his letters, Peter refers to *"my <u>son</u> Mark."*

The Gospel of Mark reads like the kind of book Peter would write. Here are several reasons to believe the Gospel of Mark was a transcription "as told by Peter":

- Its tone is rough and blunt and its language is crude. Peter was a relatively uneducated fisherman; compared to people who were in urban centers of power in his day, he grew up as a country hick!

- The disciples seem dense. I'll explain this more later, but compared to the stories in Matthew and Luke, in Mark the disciples look extra dumb. This may reflect the way Peter felt when Jesus repeatedly asked <u>questions</u> like, "Do you *still* not understand?"

☞ **GO TO:**

Acts 12:12 (house)

1 Peter 5:13 (son)

Mark 8:21 (questions)

- The pace is brisk. Every anecdote about Peter shows him being as direct and to the point as the Gospel of Mark is.

- Jesus is presented as a man of power. Peter was the kind of bold personality who jumped right into things. When Jesus walked on water, Peter said, "Oh yeah? Me too!" and jumped ship. When he didn't like what Jesus said, he tried to correct Jesus. When backed into a corner, he whipped out his sword and chopped a guy's ear off. No namby-pamby philosopher would impress Peter, but a man whose strong words were matched by his strong deeds would.

For these and other reasons we'll discover, it seems the content of Mark originated with Peter. This story of Jesus comes from a big man who was no pushover, but was a firsthand eyewitness. If you hate phony baloney and love authenticity, you'll enjoy the Gospel of Mark.

How To Use *Mark—God's Word for the Biblically-Inept*™

It doesn't get much simpler than this:

- Sit down with this book and your Bible.

- Start the book at chapter 1.

- As you work through the chapter, read the specified verses in your Bible.

- Use the sidebar loaded with icons and helpful information to boost your knowledge and your interpretive skills.

- Answer the Study Questions and review with the Chapter Wrap-Up.

- Go on to the next chapter.

- Repeat seventeen more times.

That's it! Oh, one final step: enjoy knowing Jesus better than you did before you started.

This book contains a variety of special features to help you learn. We've peppered them around in the outside column of this introduction so you can get used to them. Here's a brief explanation of each.

Sections and Icons	What's It For?
CHAPTER HIGHLIGHTS	*the most prominent points of the chapter*
Let's Get Started	*a chapter intro and warm-up*

KEEP IT REAL

(Keep It Real)

Study Questions

(Study Questions)

CHAPTER WRAP-UP

(Chapter Summary)

Bible Quote	*what you came for: the Bible*
Commentary	*my thoughts on what the verses mean*
GO TO:	*other Bible verses to help you understand better (underlined in text)*
What?	*definition of a word (bold in text)*
KEY POINT	*major point of the chapter*
What Others Are Saying	*if you don't believe me, listen to the experts*
Wayback Machine	*interesting, relevant historical background*
It's Greek to Me	*a closer look at the meaning of a passage in its original language*
Power Tool	*a study technique you can use in all Bible study, not just Mark*
Illustrations	*a picture is worth a thousand words*
Something to Ponder	*interesting points to get you thinking*
Remember This . . .	*don't forget this*
Keep It Real	*ways the passage may apply to your daily life*
Study Questions	*something to get you discussing, studying, and digging deeper*
CHAPTER WRAP-UP	*Recap of the most prominent points*

A Confession And A Tip

I confess: I'm not as smart as I look. (And if you've ever seen me, pity is flooding your heart right now.) What I mean is, when it comes to the eternal majestic almighty God, *none* of us are as smart as we think we are. In fact, I distrust Bible teachers who are absolutely certain about everything, because that means their God is so teeny he fits entirely within their understanding. Please remember as you read this book that all humanity's best scholarship can only suggest what we *think* God is up to.

So in these pages, I do not intend to tell you what to think. I'll tell you what *I* think, but for your own sake you must train yourself to rely on God as your primary teacher. Toward that goal I'll show you techniques you can use to understand the Bible without going wild and starting your own Heaven's Gate Branch Davidian cult. But the conclusions are up to you and prayerful interaction with God. To put it another way, instead of telling you *what* to think, I hope to show you *how* to think.

That was the confession. Now here's the tip: To get the maximum personal benefit, you can do one thing each time you sit down with this book: Pray and ask Jesus to reveal himself to you. As you read about what he did two millennia ago, ask him to show you what he's doing in your life today.

☞ **GO TO:**

1 Corinthians 3:18 (smart)

1 Corinthians 8:2 (certain)

Bible Quote: This is where you'll read a quote from the Bible.

James 1:5 If any of you lacks wisdom, he should ask God, who gives generously to all without finding fault, and it will be given to him.

Commentary: This is where you'll read commentary about the biblical quote.

Decisions, Decisions: In Or Out?

James, the brother of Jesus, is writing to the new believers who were scattered about the Roman world (see GWBI, pages 213–214) when they fled from persecution. James knows that godly wisdom is a great gift. He gives a simple plan to get it: if you n~~~~ wisdom, ask for it. God will give it to us.

Up 'til now we've concentrated on finding the wind ~~ sails of your drifting marriage and overcoming marital prob~~ But you may be the reader who is shaking her head, thinking that I just don't understand what you're going through. You can't take the abuse any longer; you've forgiven the **infidelity** time after time; and in order for you and your children to survive, you see no alternative but divorce.

So let m~~ husband ~~~ [**Go To:** When you see a word or phrase that's underlined, go to the sidebar for a biblical cross-reference.] your get out a~~ ~~nues, abuse sec~~ ~~p the ing to you; they are also harmful to your children's physical and emotional state.

When you feel you've depleted all of your options, continue to ask God for wisdom in order to have the knowledge to make the right decisions. Wise women seek God. God is the <u>source</u> of wisdom and wisdom is found in Christ and the Word.

"What?": When you see a word in bold, go to the sidebar for a definition.

in fidelity: *sexual unfaithfulness of a spouse*

☞ **GO TO:**

Psalm 111:10 (source)

Remember This . . .

Gary Chapman, Ph.D.: Is there hope for women who suffer physical abuse from their husbands? Does reality living offer any genuine hope? I believe the answer to those questions is yes.[6]

What Others are Saying:

Give It Away

You don't have to be a farmer to understand what the Apostle Paul wrote to the Corinthian church (see illustration, page 143). A picture is worth a thousand words, and Paul is painting a master-piece. He reminds us of what any smart farmer knows: in order to produce a bountiful harvest, he has to plan for it.

What Others Are Saying: This is where you'll read what an expert has to say about the subject at hand.

MEN OF POWER LESSONS IN MIGHT AND MISSTEPS 9

127

Feature with icon in the sidebar: Throughout the book you will see sections of text with corresponding icons in the sidebar. See the chart on pages xvi–xvii for a description of all the features in this book.

Part One

CELEBRITY JESUS

© Copyright Gospel Films, Inc. * www.reverendfun.com

"Hey honey, my best friend is here and he says I have to drop everything and go fishing."

Getting Started: A Ground Rule

As we study Mark, how do we interpret what he (or any Bible writer) says? Over the centuries people have interpreted the Bible in many different ways, usually reflecting the culture of their times. For example, scholars from the Middle Ages liked to interpret

Bible passages allegorically. Medieval scholars took the story of Noah and the ark symbolically, claiming Noah represented Christ; the dove represented the Holy Spirit; and the olive branch, which the dove brought to Noah, represented divine mercy. If this was the meaning, did an actual flood ever occur? Who could say? Anyone could make up any symbolic interpretation for any passage, so the meaning of Scripture was uncertain.

Today we usually interpret Scripture literally. This approach also has weaknesses if taken too far. The Bible says God gathers the sea into <u>jars</u>, and that trees can <u>clap</u> their hands, yet no one says, "I won't believe the Bible until I see God's giant sea jars!" No one listens for the applause of pines. That's because those passages are **figurative**, not meant to be taken literally.

How can we tell the proper way to interpret a passage? Which parts should be taken literally, and which parts figuratively? Very good questions. And here's a good answer, the Golden Rule of biblical interpretation: *find out what the passage meant for the first audience to hear it or read it.*

God set his Word in a specific cultural setting. He used stories and people and definite times and places. No Bible passage can mean something today it never meant before.

Our job, then, is to face each scripture passage with the question, What did this teach its first hearers about God? We then take that timeless principle and carefully apply it to our current situation. That's why we spend a lot of time in each *God's Word for the Biblically-Inept™* book explaining history and Bible times. Understanding what God was saying to his people back then prevents us from making wacko, way-off interpretations now.

With this Power Tool in mind, we realize that to understand Jesus better, first we have to grasp some of the mindset of the people he spoke to: the inhabitants of first-century **Palestine**.

☞ **GO TO:**

Psalm 24:7 (jars)

Isaiah 55:12 (clap)

figurative: metaphorical; symbolic

POWER TOOL

Find out what the passage meant to its first audience.

Palestine: Israel and surrounding territories

What Others are Saying:

John Bright: Only a fool would come to his Bible as if he were the first to do so, as if all the labors and minds in the church past had nothing to teach him.[1]

Gordon D. Fee & Douglas Stuart: The concern of the scholar is primarily with what the text *meant*; the concern of the layperson is usually with what it *means*. The believing scholar insists that we must have both. Reading the Bible with an eye only to its meaning for us can lead to a great deal of nonsense as well as to every imaginable kind of error—because it lacks controls. . . . Our concern, therefore, must be with both dimensions. The believing scholar insists that the biblical texts first of all *mean what they meant*. That is, we believe that God's Word for us today is first of all precisely what his Word was to them.[2]

Palestine: A Political Football

Poor Israel. Whomped into submission by the Babylonians in 586 B.C., successful in revolting in 164 B.C., then captured by **Pompey** a century later (63 B.C.), God's chosen people lived in one of the most hotly contested chunks of real estate the ancient world knew. The maps on pages 4–5 show why: tiny Israel sat at the cross-roads of every major invasion route. Over the centuries, as the Egyptians, the Babylonians, the Assyrians, and the Persians wrestled each other for world dominance, little Israel sat in the middle like a beetle in the ring during a WWF wrestling bout. When the Romans conquered the world, they ran over Israel with very little effort. Unlike most of the conquered nations, however, Israel refused to accept her fate.

Pompey: (106–48 B.C.) a great Roman general and statesman

Philip Yancey: Palestine, the one lump the anaconda could not digest, exasperated Rome to no end. Contrary to Roman toler-ance for many gods, the Jews held tenaciously to the notion of one God, their God, who had revealed to them a distinct culture as the Chosen People.[3]

What Others are Saying:

William Barclay: It is the simple historical fact that in the thirty years from 67 to 37 B.C. before the emergence of Herod the Great, no fewer than 150,000 men perished in Palestine in revolutionary uprisings. There was no more explosive and inflammable country in the world than Palestine.[4]

What Did The Jews Expect?

While exiled in Egypt, Babylon, and various other nations, the Jews heard from numerous prophets (such as Isaiah, Jeremiah, and Ezekiel) that God would some day bring them back to the Holy Land, make them prosperous, dwell with them, cause them to lead the other nations, and write his law upon their <u>hearts</u>. By the first century those things had simultaneously come true and not come true.

☞ **GO TO:**

Jeremiah 31:33–34 (hearts)

THE WAYBACK MACHINE

If you want to understand the perspective of a first-century Jew, you should know about four national symbols that most Jews embraced with fierce devotion: Temple, Territory, Torah, and Tribe.

Maps of Israel's Place in Four World Empires

The shaded areas indicate the territory of the empires and the small blackened areas indicate Israel's place within each empire. From an outsider's viewpoint, Israel played a bit part in world history. From Israel's viewpoint, the Jews were God's chosen people, determined to hang on to their identity. That's why this teeny country became a persistent annoyance to mighty Rome.

Assyrian Empire, 720 B.C.

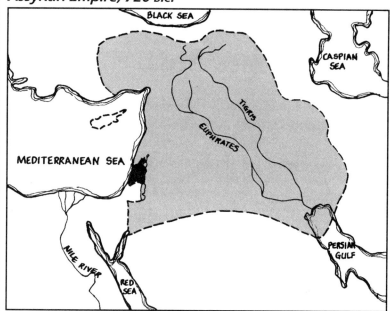

Babylonian Empire, 586 B.C.

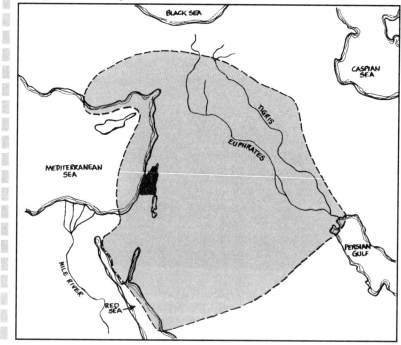

Persian Empire, 450 B.C.

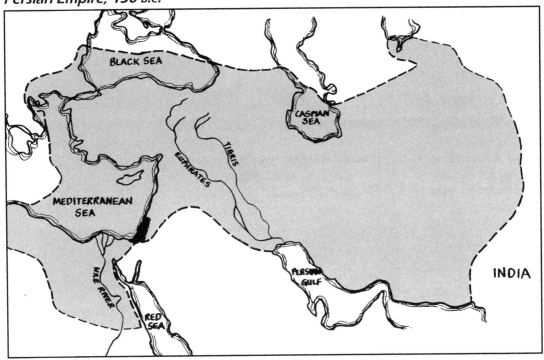

Roman Empire, A.D.

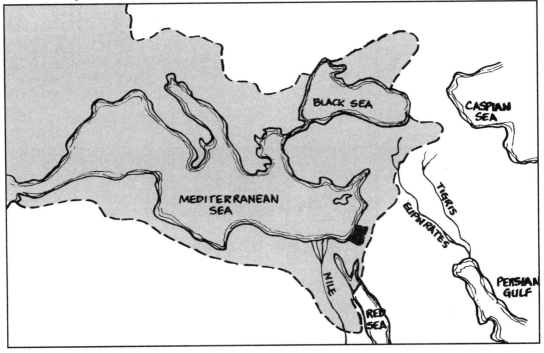

Temple

The Temple in Jerusalem was the central symbol in the mental world of a Jew. With hundreds of thousands of pilgrims flowing into the Temple on feast days and holy days, then flowing out again when each holiday ended, the Temple acted like the pulsing heart of Judaism. The Temple was the God-designated spot where heaven met earth, where God met his people. If you said, "God will dwell among us again," most Jews would automatically assume you meant that God's cloud of glory would fill the Temple again. (They would never picture God coming as a human.) This is why Jews in the Old Testament books of Jeremiah and Nehemiah felt devastated when conquerors destroyed the Temple. It meant they could not communicate with God at all, because the one place to meet him was the Temple. Without the Temple—no access to God. We'll have much more to say about this later (including a picture of the Temple, on page 219).

Territory

The Territory of the Jew was the land of Israel, because it was land God had promised to the Jews' ancestor, Abraham. To first-century Judaism, Israel was the garden of God, the holiest and most important region on earth. The Jewish concept of the world involved diminishing degrees of holiness. Morally speaking, the center of the universe was the Holy of Holies, a room deep inside the Temple. The outer courts of the Temple were less holy; outside the Temple walls, a bit less holy; outside Jerusalem, a bit less holy; and at Israel's border, holiness ended. This concept played so strongly in the Jewish mind that some Jews referred to other races as "dogs." (See illustration, page 7.)

Torah

Yahweh: Hebrew word for Jehovah (God)

The Torah was the written law of Israel, and much more; Jews thought of it as the revealed will of **Yahweh**. The Torah contained instructions on the treaty between Israel and God, and told how the Jews could enjoy God's blessing and stay in the Territory. The Torah enjoyed such high regard that Jews who didn't live near Jerusalem came close to considering it a "portable Temple." If you followed its instructions, you created a holy place for Yahweh in your own life. A quote from the **mishnah** reads, "Where two or three are gathered to study the Torah, there is the **Shekinah**."

mishnah: rabbinical commentary on the Torah

Shekinah: radiant glory of God's presence

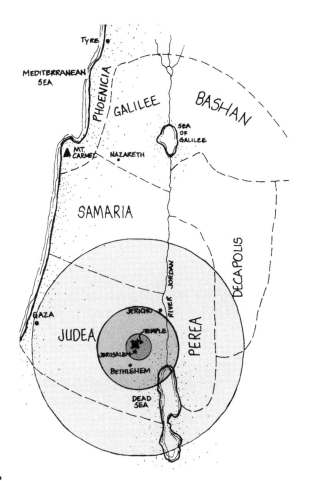

Israel's Geographical Concept of Holiness

The Temple and Jerusalem were as central to the Jewish story as Gilligan and the Skipper were to Gilligan's Island. In the Jew's mind, every other nation on the globe was less important to God—sort of like in Gilligan's original theme song, when the Professor and Mary Ann were simply "and the rest."

Tribe

The Tribe of the Jews was, of course, Israel. Being a Jew made you the living fulfillment of God's promise that Abraham would have innumerable descendants. Driven to keep their racial identity, most Jews tried not to intermarry with other races.

National Treasures

The importance to the Jews of Temple, Territory, Torah, and Tribe cannot be overstated. Imagine the Chinese have conquered the United States and reduced all fifty state capitols to rubble. Cantonese and Mandarin are the official languages of what used to be your country. The USA no longer exists, except in your memories and in the symbols of the American flag and the Constitution. How would you feel if someone then jumped up in front of a crowd and mockingly shredded the American flag? If you can understand why that would drive you to rage or despair, you have glimpsed what Israel's symbols meant to the oppressed Jew.

KEY POINT

Remember the four symbols of the Jews: Temple, Territory, Torah, Tribe. Jesus is about to do outrageous things to them!

You Mentioned Confusion?

With that background established, I can explain why the Old Testament prophecies seemed both fulfilled and unfulfilled to first-century Jews.

"Hallelu Jah!"	"Oy Vey!"
The exiled Jews were now back in their land.	Though they were in their land, Romans oppressed them.
The rebuilt Temple allowed Jews to worship God.	The Romans could stop the worship at any time, and sometimes did in hideous ways.
Jews were allowed to have a high priest.	The Romans picked the priests, who often bought the office illegally.
The Jews were still God's chosen race.	He had not spoken to them for almost five hundred years.

Can you see why Jews were divided about whether or not their exile had truly ended? The Jews at the top of the social heap benefited from the status quo. The majority of people did not. Faithful Jews knew God's presence did not fill the land.

If you've heard many sermons at all, you've heard a pastor say, "Here is what the Jews believed in Jesus' day." No matter what he says next, the pastor is probably right: *some* Jews believed it! There was almost nothing all Jews stood united on. They were deeply divided on how to interpret all the prophecies, including the ones about the Messiah. As my friend, Rabbi Joseph Hilbrandt, says, "Two Jews? Three opinions!"

What did the Jews expect? Everything from a mighty military king to nothing at all. And even with all those options, no one expected what they actually got.

What Others are Saying:

N. T. Wright: Christianity, as we shall see, began with the thoroughly Jewish belief that world history was focused on a single geographical place and a single moment in time. The Jews assumed that their country and their capital city was the place in question, and that the time, though they did not know quite when it would be, would be soon. The living God would defeat evil once and for all and create a new world of peace and justice.[5]

What Did the Non-Jews Want?

Gentiles: *non-Jewish people or nations*

worldview: *a comprehensive way of seeing the world*

The **Gentiles**, of course, had a completely different **worldview** than the Jews. What did Gentiles expect? They expected Jews to shut up, calm down, and accept their conquerors. Many of the countries Rome conquered actually appreciated coming under a powerful regime that enforced peace, brought prosperity, created the first-ever worldwide network of roads, and brought culture and a limited amount of democracy. If the price for all this was to mouth the idea that Caesar was God, well, why not? You knew in your heart you didn't mean it.

Obviously, with the might and arrogance of a worldwide empire running on one track, and the Jews' centuries-long zeal and passion for the one true God running down another track, the intersection of those two tracks could only mean a collision of historical proportions. And into that intersection stepped a peasant construction worker with a few odd ideas. I'll let Mark take it from here, because this is where his story begins.

MARK 1:1–13
WHAT IF GOD WAS ONE OF US?

Let's Get Started

I love Mark because it was written to an audience unfamiliar with Jewish customs—like us. The Roman mind appreciated men of action and had no time for quiche-eatin' sissies; Mark's Gospel has narrative edge, even blood and guts. Consider these aspects of Mark's account.

- Jesus shows up suddenly as a take-charge guy and gets right down to business—none of that "Away in a Manger" baby stuff you get in Matthew and Luke.

- In Mark 1–6:6 especially, Jesus is virtually a Galilean rock star. He's the center of lots of clamor and urgency and attention, and he's hipper than the establishment.

- Pompous bureaucrats plot against Jesus and he slams them every time, winning conflicts that feel like the kind of macho arguments in action movies such as *Crimson Tide* and *A Few Good Men*.

- Jesus has a secret identity! Cool!

- The action-packed narrative rushes us from one startling incident to the next. Mark paints emotions in neon, not pastels. People are amazed, outraged, thrilled, hateful; nobody in Mark's Gospel just scratches their beard and says, "Hmm." Mark depicts Jesus as a gutsy man who knows anger, frustration, and fear.

- I identify with Mark's portrayal of the disciples. My own experience in following Jesus has been turbulent, confusing, full of low lows and high highs. Reading about these clods who went on to make good, I know I am not a hopeless case.

Compared to Matthew's highly footnoted account and Luke's polished, literary Gospel, Mark seems rough-and-tumble; hard-edged and ironic; each bit of glory purchased with grit. It feels *real*, and on those days when I think I'm the only Christian who hasn't taken a Sappy Pill, "real" is all I want. I call Mark "special" because, of all the Gospels, Mark's style is best suited for short-attention-span, cynical us.

So let's get started. Mark's surprisingly subversive opening is just one verse ahead.

OF BEGINNINGS, BAPTISMS, AND BEHALFS

> **Mark 1:1** The beginning of the gospel about Jesus Christ, the Son of God.

What If Joan Osborne Was One Of Us?

Singer Joan Osborne's 1995 hit, "One of Us," asked some great questions: What if God was one of us? If seeing God's face meant you had to believe, would you still want to see his face?

Mark's answer to Joan is yes. He has not only seen God's face and believed, now he wants us to see that face too. The opening phrase of Mark's Gospel, which serves as his title for the entire book, tips us off to Mark's purpose in two ways: one implicit, one explicit.

Subversive Wordplay

The **implicit** tip-off is his use of the word "gospel." In the introduction I told you *gospel* means "good story," but the word implied much more to Mark's audience.

The word we translate "gospel" is, in Greek, **evangelion** (ee-van-JEL-ee-on). Mark borrowed the word from the **imperial cult**, who used it when proclaiming milestones in the emperor's life. The emperor's accomplishments were treated as royal holidays, with heralds proclaiming the good news throughout the empire. This proclamation of royal good news, usually tied to a national day off, was known as an *evangelion*.

Mark's use of that word would startle a first-century audience. If there were an *evangelion* about Jesus, it meant he had to be royalty—a king. In fact, this is exactly what Mark intends to imply: Jesus is king, and so much more.

What's An "Anointed One"?

The **explicit** tip-off of Mark's purpose is the phrase, "*Jesus Christ, Son of God.*" A lot of people assume that "Christ" is Jesus' last name, but it isn't. It's actually a title. What does "Christ" mean? The full context requires a little explaining.

The Jews of the first century viewed themselves as descendants of Abraham, God's <u>chosen</u> people (see GWGN, pages 94–95, 253). Most Jews also believed God allowed Rome to conquer them because he was punishing them for <u>disobeying</u> him in years past (see GWDN, pages 15, 20–21).

The Jews had clung, however, to one hope for hundreds of years: God had promised them a powerful king who would someday restore their glorious status as God's most favored nation. This king, combining religious and political power, would <u>speak</u> on God's behalf as powerfully as Moses did; would <u>descend</u> from the lineage of Israel's best and strongest king, David; and would <u>establish</u> a kingdom that would last forever.

This prophet is predicted and described hundreds of ways in the Old Testament. The main streams of thought depict a king coming to defeat God's enemies, restore the land of Israel to the Jews, restore the Jews to God, and restore the presence of God to the Jews by rebuilding the destroyed Temple.

This heroic figure came to be called, in Hebrew, **meshiach**. The term came from the ancient Hebrew practice of **anointing** a king on the day of his coronation, as a symbol of God's power and presence resting upon the king. In English we pronounce the word "Messiah." In Greek, the equivalent term was "Christos," which we call "Christ."

What you called the expected king didn't matter. What mattered was that he was the only hope the Jewish race had for regaining sovereignty in their own land; almost every Jewish heart keenly sought any sign of the highly anticipated <u>Anointed One</u>. By Jesus' day, they had been expecting their hero for several hundred years.

explicit: stated, expressed

THE WAYBACK MACHINE

☞ **GO TO:**

Deuteronomy 10:15 (chosen)

Jeremiah 35:15, 17 (disobeying)

Deuteronomy 18:15, 18 (speak)

2 Samuel 7:12 (descend)

2 Samuel 7:13–16 (establish)

Daniel 9:25–26 (Anointed One)

meshiach: *literally, "anointed one"*

anointing: *applying oil in a sacred rite*

Philip Yancey: It would be impossible to exaggerate the import of the word *Messiah* among faithful Jews. The Dead Sea Scrolls discovered in 1947 [see WBFT, pages 14–15] confirm that the Qumran community imminently expected a Messiah-like figure, setting aside an empty seat for him each day at the sacred meal. Audacious as it may be to dream that a tiny province wedged in among great powers would produce a worldwide ruler, nonetheless Jews believed just that. They staked their future on a king who would lead their nation back to glory.[1]

Not-So-Great Expectations

☞ **GO TO:**

Psalm 2:7–12; 2 Samuel 7:14 (Son)

Most Jews thought of the Messiah as a super-king and *representative* of God, but not as *being* God. In popular Jewish expectation, the Messiah was not necessarily divine, which is why Mark hastens to add after the word Christ, *"Son of God."* However, if the Jews had read their Scriptures carefully and with an open mind, they would have known the Messiah was God's <u>Son</u>.

Something to Ponder

The phrase "Son of God" is important here, because the rest of Mark's Gospel treats Jesus' divine identity as some kind of secret. As we'll see, people do not recognize who Jesus is *until he dies.* God knows who Jesus is; demons know who he is; even animals seem to know—everyone but the people Jesus came to save. That's why Mark wants you, the reader, to know right from the start: Jesus is God.

David E. Garland: The prologue briefly lets the readers in on what are otherwise secrets that will remain hidden in various degrees to all of the characters in the drama that follows. It contains what Mark knows and believes about Jesus as he allows his readers a fleeting glimpse into Jesus' identity and mission from a "heavenly vantage point."[2]

KEY POINT

Mark believed Jesus embodied God.

> **Mark 1:2–4** It is written in Isaiah the prophet:
> "I will send my messenger ahead of you,
> who will prepare your way"—
> "a voice of one calling in the desert,
> 'Prepare the way for the Lord,
> make straight paths for him.'"
> And so John came, baptizing in the desert region and preaching a baptism of repentance for the forgiveness of sins.

If God Came, We'd Have To Get Ready

Since Mark 1:1 is really the title of his book, you could say the very first thing Mark does in his Gospel is quote the Book of Isaiah. This indicates the importance of Old Testament references. These references reach even deeper than first meets the eye, because the phrases Mark attributes to Isaiah actually come from <u>three</u> different scripture passages. (Some scholars say Mark started his book with a mistake by doing this, but writers of his era commonly blended texts together. Remember, Mark wrote before footnotes or bullet points were invented.)

In this Gospel John (and Jesus) seem to appear from nowhere. The Old Testament quotations indicate that in reality, they showed up because of God's long-term plan. The Greek tense Mark uses for *"It is written"* has this sense: "it was written and still is." In other words, these ancient Scriptures apply today. The three Scriptures he quotes combine to say:

* The powerful Messiah is coming.
* A messenger will come before Messiah to prepare his coming.
* Any smart person who hears the messenger will get ready for Messiah *now*.

How do you get ready for the Lord? The word "prepare" was used in Isaiah 40:3 with the idea of "removing obstructions." Roll the boulders to the side, fill in the pot holes, and shove the tumbleweeds out of the way, because the king is coming in royal procession. Mark follows this quote, however, by saying John came *"preaching a baptism of **repentance** for the forgiveness of **sins**,"* so we know he means this king wants us to remove spiritual obstructions.

Billy Graham: If repentance could be described in one word, I would use the word *renounce*. "Renounce what?" you ask. The answer can also be given in one word—"sin." . . . Only the Spirit of God can give you the determination necessary for true repentance. It means more than the little girl who prayed, "Make me good—not real good, but good enough so I won't get whipped."[3]

☞ **GO TO:**

Exodus 23:20; Malachi 3:1; Isaiah 40:3 (three)

repentance: *sorrow causing a turn from wrong*

sins: *disobedience, whether willful or passive*

What Others are Saying:

> **Mark 1:5–6** The whole Judean countryside and all the people of Jerusalem went out to him. Confessing their sins, they were baptized by him in the Jordan River. John wore clothing made of camel's hair, with a leather belt around his waist, and he ate locusts and wild honey.

Recycling In The Bible: Is John Elijah?

If you felt God had given you a prophetic message that all of America must hear, where would you go to spread this message as far and fast as possible? To the television studios of Hollywood? To the book publishers of New York? To the Internet geniuses of Silicon Valley? Probably the *last* places you'd go would be to the South Dakotan Badlands or Death Valley in California's brutal Mojave Desert. How would you ever muster an audience in those harsh, isolated spots?

Yet this is essentially what John the Baptizer did. Instead of heading into Jew Central (Jerusalem), or Pagan Control (Rome), he took his stand in the Judean desert . . . and *"all the people of Jerusalem went out to him"*!

Jerusalem is at least twenty miles from the Jordan River and about four thousand feet above it—a tough hike going out and a tougher one coming back. What would make thousands of otherwise-sane people trek across miles of blistering hills just to hear a man in retro duds insult their integrity? John had tapped into two powerful themes of Jewish thought: *salvation comes from the wilderness*, and *the return of Elijah*.

Salvation Comes From The Wilderness

As a race the Jews witnessed incredible displays of God's power when he miraculously freed them from slavery in Egypt. This act is known as the *Exodus*. After they escaped Egypt God led them through the desert and entered into a **covenant** with them.

God structured this covenant exactly like the peace treaties that **suzerains** entered into with their **vassals** in that time and place. These desert treaties typically included a list of blessings the vassals would enjoy for obeying the treaty, and a list of curses that would fall upon them if they broke the treaty. God led Israel out of the desert into a lush land, as promised, but Israel violated their treaty with God persistently, until God had no choice but to activate the curses clause. The Israelites lost their country and went back into slavery again.

In your Bible the **Prophets** describe facets of the Jewish long-

☞ **GO TO:**

Exodus 20–24
(covenant)

Deuteronomy 28
(list of blessings)

covenant: binding legal agreement

suzerains: feudal overlords, or dominant states

vassals: persons protected by a lord

Prophets: OT books Isaiah through Malachi

ing to return to full status as God's beloved people. A major theme threaded through these books (especially Isaiah) is the image of a "new exodus," when God will redeliver his people from bondage. The old exodus brought Israel from the desert into **Canaan**, so Jews reasoned the new exodus would begin in the desert and end in the Promised Land. One group of devoted religious Jews, called the Qumran community, believed this so strongly they moved out into the desert to be the first to welcome the Messiah when God began the new exodus.

This is why Mark begins his gospel with *"the voice of one crying in the wilderness,"* and this is one reason Jews flocked to see John. He was in the right place, saying right words—words that could indicate the end of their exile.

Canaan: the land God promised the Jews

William L. Lane: The summons to "turn" basically connotes a return to the original relationship with the Lord. This means a return to the beginning of God's history with his people, a return to the wilderness. . . . As the people heed John's call and go out to him in the desert far more is involved than contrition and confession. They return to a place of judgment, the wilderness, where the status of Israel as God's beloved Son must be re-established in the exchange of pride for humility. The willingness to return to the wilderness signifies the acknowledgment of Israel's history as one of disobedience and rebellion, and a desire to begin once more.[4]

What Others are Saying:

The Return Of Elijah

People in Jesus' time did not dress just like people in the Old Testament, and in particular, city dwellers did not dress like people of the wilderness. Mark deliberately mentions, *"John wore clothing made of camel's hair, with a leather belt around his waist,"* to show that John dressed like a prophet—specifically, Elijah. Because of Old Testament prophecies, Jews believed Elijah had to return before God would restore their fortunes. (To learn all about Elijah, see GWMB, pages 130–140.)

According to Scripture Elijah never died, so a few Jews probably thought John really was Elijah. The majority of them, however, would have understood John was a contemporary man representing a message and a spiritual authority like Elijah's.

John strengthened this image by his revolutionary purity. Mark mentions John's strange diet because it was **kosher**. Roasted locusts were not only a common wilderness survival food, but a clean food. (The honey may have been made from bees, or may

☞ GO TO:

2 Kings 1:8 (Elijah)

Malachi 4:5–6 (return)

2 Kings 2:7–14 (died)

Leviticus 11:20–23 (clean)

kosher: sanctioned by Jewish law; ritually fit

have been the syrup of carob pods. See GWHN, page 135.) John's primary activity, baptizing, was a radical symbol of holiness; no one had baptized Jews in this manner before! When a non-Jew converted to Judaism, Jews sometimes immersed them in water as a religious symbol of new purity. John was treating the Jews as if they were so sinful, they had ceased being God's people. He was making them come to God the same way Gentiles did. By the thousands, they obeyed.

KEY POINT

John's prophetic message made him a virtual Elijah.

Why did so many Jews flock to the desert to hear John? If it walks like a prophet, talks like a prophet, looks like a prophet, and acts like a prophet . . . it must be a prophet! They expected Elijah, and they got him, as Jesus will affirm in Mark 9.

What Others are Saying:

Life Application Bible Commentary: John baptized, but he only baptized people who humbly repented of their sins and sought *forgiveness of sins*. Baptism did not give forgiveness; baptism was a visible sign that the person had repented and received God's forgiveness for his or her sins. Matthew recorded that some of the Jewish religious leaders (Pharisees and Sadducees) came to be baptized and John angrily turned them away, for he knew there was no humble repentance in their hearts (Matthew 3:7–9).[5]

> **Mark 1:7–8** And this was his message: "After me will come one more powerful than I, the thongs of whose sandals I am not worthy to stoop down and untie. I baptize you with water, but he will baptize you with the Holy Spirit."

Drowned By The Most Powerful One

In Middle Eastern culture slaves untied the sandals of arriving guests and washed their feet. John is saying he is not even worthy of being a slave to the Coming One. Jews had tremendous respect for Elijah; they would have been startled to hear an Elijah figure take such a lowly stance. When you combine this with John's previous references to being the forerunner of a king, his meaning is that the Coming One is not merely powerful; he is the *most* powerful. This language would have intrigued his audience, because it predicts the Messiah without using any of the customary messianic language.

☞ **GO TO:**

Isaiah 11:2–3 (linked)

Isaiah 44:3; Ezekiel 36:26–27; Joel 2:28–29 (Spirit)

What would John's listeners make of, *"he will baptize you with the Holy Spirit"*? They did have some frame of reference, for many Hebrew Scriptures linked the coming of God's Spirit with the arrival of the Messiah. A good first-century student of the prophets understood that the Messiah would be accompanied by a dose of God's Spirit that would help all of God's people live in victorious obedience to God.

What generosity! The believer would be submerged in a virtual river of the Spirit. In the past God's Spirit had rested on people like Samson, Elijah, and others, but this language implied something fuller, more permanent, more internal. The promise of Holy Spirit baptism became fulfilled years later, on the Day of **Pentecost**, when Jesus sent the Holy Spirit to the disciples in the form of tongues of fire.

John was saying that although he was the forerunner of a king, the messenger of victory was not comparable to the victor. The victor was coming soon, however, so they'd better get ready. The Anointed One would do some anointing of his own, unprecedented in its transforming power.

John's message helped people *get ready* to meet the Savior, but that message in itself did not save people. Only Jesus had the message of salvation.

> **Mark 1:9–11** At that time Jesus came from Nazareth in Galilee and was baptized by John in the Jordan. As Jesus was coming up out of the water, he saw heaven being torn open and the Spirit descending on him like a dove. And a voice came from heaven: "You are my Son, whom I love; with you I am well pleased."

Pop Quiz

What? It's only part way through Mark 1 and already we're having a *pop quiz*? Yep. But trust me, you'll have fun with this, and it'll give you insight into the culture and times of Jesus. Read the list of pop culture phrases below. Each phrase might come from TV, a movie, a song, literature—you know, pop culture! Try to name the source of each. (The first one's already done for you, as an example.)

1. "I'm giving 'er all I can, Cap'n, but I'm goin' ta need more dilythium crystals!"—Chief Engineer Scotty, *Star Trek*

2. It was the best of times, it was the worst of times.

3. It was 20 years ago today Sergeant Pepper taught the band to play.

☞ **GO TO:**

Jeremiah 31:31–34 (obedience)

Acts 2 (Pentecost)

IT'S GREEK TO ME

Pentecost: *Jewish feast fifty days after Passover*

Remember This . . .

4. "To be, or not to be; that is the question."

5. "And I would have gotten away with it, too, if it weren't for you pesky kids!"

6. Just do it.

7. "Help me, Obi-Wan Kenobi; you're my only hope."

8. ". . . able to leap tall buildings in a single bound . . . "

9. Today's program has been brought to you by the number 3.

10. "Toto, I don't think we're in Kansas anymore."

How did you do? (The answers are in the back, in the appendix called "Answers.") Odds are you could identify most of them, perhaps even all of them. That's because these quotes permeate our culture; in some cases they are literally hanging in the air. For the ones you knew, didn't they generate a flash of images, music, or emotion far beyond the short phrase on the page?

Here's the point. Old Testament Scriptures saturate the Gospel of Mark. Just as each of us are steeped in certain touch points of American culture, the Jews of Jesus' day intimately knew the Hebrew Scriptures. The Jewish male went to school daily to learn the Scriptures inside and out. The Jewish love for Yahweh led to endless discussions of his ways in the home and marketplace. The merest snatch of a few words could trigger an entire rich context of associations in a Jew's mind.

That brings us to the Power Tool for this chapter: *check the Old Testament cross-references*. The New Testament anchors its roots in Old Testament bedrock. If you don't notice the Old Testament allusions as you read, you miss layer upon layer of meaning that was obvious to the hearers of John the Baptist and Jesus. This is especially evident in the account of Jesus' baptism.

Be sure to inspect all the references in the chart below. Then you can add the habit of checking cross-references to your toolkit of interpretive skills!

POWER TOOL

Check the Old Testament cross-references.

From Mark . . .	From the Old Testament . . .
". . . he saw heaven being torn open . . ." (1:10)	Isaiah 63:17–64:1
". . . the Spirit descending on him like a dove . . ." (1:10)	1 Samuel 16:13; Isaiah 61:1–2
"You are my Son, whom I love; with you I am well pleased." (1:11)	Psalm 2:7
The Spirit on him, plus God's approval (1:10–11)	Isaiah 42:1

Jesus? Repent?

John was baptizing people who had repented of their sins, so an obvious question arises: why did Jesus need to be baptized? (The

Bible teaches Jesus <u>never sinned</u>.) The Old Testament verses in the previous table suggest some answers. Some of these passages attribute powerful kingly characteristics to the Messiah; others show him as a holy servant God approves. Would a servant king make his subjects do something he wouldn't do himself?

Jesus insisted on being baptized partly to be an **exemplary** model and partly because it was a strong symbolic action. (We'll learn much more about prophets and symbolic actions in the chapters on Mark 3:13–35, Mark 11:1–25, and Mark 11:27–12:44.) In the Old Testament the Messiah is treated as representing all of Israel. Jesus had to be baptized to symbolize how all of Israel needed to become clean before God again.

> Jesus was baptized on behalf of all his people, which should not be a strange notion to Christians today. It is the same kind of representative act as his death: he died for all of us. You could say the earthly ministry of Jesus was bookended by two representative acts: his baptism and his crucifixion.

> Mark creates another bookend with his use of the unusual word "torn." Instead of saying heaven "opened," he said, in Greek, that it was *schizo*—torn, or split (a violent word). Mark's only other use of this word in the whole book is at the death of Jesus. The moment he died, the veil in the Temple that separated people from God's holy presence was *schizo*—<u>ripped</u> from top to bottom. Jesus' first deed as Messiah foreshadows his final deed.

Overview Of Jesus' Baptism

When Jesus came to earth, he <u>emptied</u> himself of the privileges of being God. He needed this anointing of the Holy Spirit to carry out his ministry, which is probably why he doesn't do any miracles until after his baptism. Here is a final overview of Jesus' baptism to give you more to think about.

☞ **GO TO:**

Hebrews 4:14–15
(never sinned)

exemplary: worth imitating

Something to Ponder

IT'S **GREEK** TO ME

☞ **GO TO:**

Mark 15:38 (ripped)

Philippians 2:5–8
(emptied)

John 1:32–34 (sign)

What Happened?	What'd It Mean?
Heavens tore open	• This suggests access between God and humans is now possible. • It permits the Spirit to descend.
Spirit descends	• "Messiah" means "Anointed One"; this is the anointing.
In the form of a dove	• Doves were used in the Temple as a blood sacrifice for sins. • John the Baptizer had been told to watch for this as the <u>sign</u> of the Messiah.
Voice from heaven	• What it says brings together important messianic texts combining kingship and servanthood.

What Others are Saying:

Luci Shaw: Even sinless Jesus, who needed no cleansing for himself, came to John the Baptizer for this ritual of water, perhaps as a model—a living metaphor of the need for human cleansing.[6]

A. B. Simpson: He had to be baptized. Why? There was no sin in him. There is a very deep and tender lesson here. He was baptized not because He needed it, but because we needed it. He was baptized that He might be made identical with us. . . . They went down in the Jordan because of their sin. He went down in the Jordan because he took sin upon Himself.[7]

HAND TO HAND IN THE SAND

> **Mark 1:12–13** At once the Spirit sent him out into the desert, and he was in the desert forty days, being tempted by Satan. He was with the wild animals, and angels attended him.

If God Came, He'd Have To Get Ready

It's easy to understand the idea that humans need to get ready before meeting God. It takes more effort to grasp the idea that God needed to get ready to serve us. Yet the Bible teaches that Jesus needed preparation for his ministry. For example, he was God before coming to earth, so he didn't have any experience in obeying God the Father; he had to <u>learn</u> how.

Mark shows us two ways in which God the Father prepared Jesus the Son for ministry: first, by equipping him with the Holy Spirit at his baptism; and second, by leading him into the desert to have a showdown with the enemy. Now that the Messiah had been anointed with the Spirit's power and God's authority, would he use his power appropriately?

Compared to the other Gospels, Mark tells us almost nothing of the battle between Jesus and Satan. He doesn't even say who won! He *does* tell us implicitly, however, because for the rest of his Gospel, Mark shows that demons were terrified of Jesus, did everything Jesus told them to do, and acknowledged Jesus was the Messiah. This could never have happened if Jesus had given in to their boss. (For more on who Satan is, see GWBI, pages 170–172, and GWRV, pages 127–128 and 175.) In addition, for the rest of the Gospel Satan himself never shows up again. Apparently, Jesus whipped him so bad, Satan didn't want a rematch.

☞ **GO TO:**

Hebrews 5:8 (learn)

KEY POINT

Jesus and Satan are not peers. Jesus is vastly superior to Satan.

God did not lead Jesus into a test to *find out* if Jesus was ready for ministry. He led Jesus into the desert to *demonstrate to others* Jesus was ready.

Remember This . . .

Billy Graham: Satan offered Jesus power and glory if he would forsake God . . . Jesus Christ resisted the temptation! . . . He completely triumphed over the Tempter to reveal to all people of all succeeding generations His sinless character.[8]

What Others are Saying:

KEEP IT REAL—In this first chapter I've focused mostly on helping you understand the first-century setting of Mark. But, as Paul wrote, *"All Scripture is . . . useful for teaching, rebuking, correcting, and training in righteousness"* (2 Timothy 3:16). As we study together, I hope your reading of Scripture will take you beyond an intellectual exercise, into the heartfelt realm of *"training in righteousness."*

In each chapter I'll share areas where I felt God was teaching, correcting, and training my own heart as I studied Mark. I've also included some of my prayers (which are in italics). I hope these personal entries will encourage you to tune in to the many unique, intimate lessons God wants to show you in Mark's pages. They could be the same as mine, but they'll probably be different. Happy listening!

• Mark 1:1. The Gospel is literally a "happy proclamation." When was the last time I portrayed the Gospel as a "happy proclamation" to my unbelieving friends? (Ouch!)

• Mark 1:3. Am I daily preparing the way for the Lord in my heart, by removing rebellious obstacles to him? Not even close! For some reason, I think I'm safer holding back certain areas of my life from his control. How totally futile. *Lord, help me obey and reverence you as the king you are.*

• Mark 1:11. *God, you spoke your favor of Jesus before he had done a single thing to earn your approval. Help me remember that you love me because I am in Jesus. Because of him, and like him, I don't have to do anything to earn your approval.*

Study Questions

1. What is the main element that Mark's first audience probably had in common with us today?
2. What does the Greek word *evangelion* mean, and what is its relationship to the English word "gospel"? Why would the use of the word *evangelion* startle or intrigue Mark's readers?
3. What are some of the titles of the person whom Jews were counting on to rescue their nation from slavery and exile?
4. Why would thousands of Jews go into the desert to hear John the Baptizer?

5. What does the Greek word *schizo* mean, and where are the two places it appears in Mark?

CHAPTER WRAP-UP

- Mark is the shortest of the four Gospels and moves at a faster pace than the others. He wants you to know, right from the start, that Jesus is not only the Christ, but is also God in human form. (Mark 1:1)

- Old Testament Scriptures predicted that when the Messiah was ready to appear, a prophet similar to Elijah would precede him to prepare the way. John the Baptizer was that prophet. (Exodus 23:20; Isaiah 40:3; Malachi 3:1; Mark 1:2–6)

- One thing the Messiah would accomplish was to give God's people power from the Holy Spirit. (Isaiah 11:2–3; Isaiah 44:3; Ezekiel 36:26–27; Joel 2:28–29; Mark 1:7–8)

- Jesus did not need to be baptized *"for the repentance of sins"* because he never sinned. He allowed himself to be baptized as a representative of all Israel, who did need to repent of their sins. During his baptism, the Holy Spirit came upon him, and numerous signs occurred indicating that Jesus had God's approval and would lead Israel as both a king and a servant. (Isaiah 63:17–64:1; 61:1–2; 42:1; 1 Samuel 16:3; Psalm 2:7; Mark 1:9–11)

- God demonstrated that Jesus was ready to begin his ministry by sending Jesus into the desert, where he was tested and tempted by Satan. We know Jesus won this battle because of the authority he later showed over every demon he encountered. (Mark 1:12–13)

MARK 1:14–45
ACTION-FIGURE JESUS

Let's Get Started

The next time you're in a small group setting and you need an ice breaker, ask people if they've ever had a "brush with greatness." People love to tell of the times when they met a movie star, a famous politician, or an accomplished athlete. (And you'll be impressed to know I once turned down an offer to ghostwrite for Mr. T.)

For some reason it raises our self-esteem to think we are good enough to hobnob with the snobs. We didn't invent the misguided concept of worth by association recently, though. In chapters 1 through 3 of Mark, Jesus launches his ministry, and immediately the common people mob him as if he were a first-century rock star. They clamor for him so much that he doesn't even have time to eat.

Sound like a successful debut? Actually, the frenzy didn't help Jesus achieve his goals. How many in the crowds were there for the right reasons? How would Jesus handle the sudden fame, with its related flatterers and naysayers? How could he impress deep spiritual concepts into a person's heart when that person was yelling, elbowing, and struggling to touch him?

Obviously, there were challenges ahead for Jesus, but in five snapshots Mark's Gospel depicts Jesus beginning his ministry decisively and with power:

1. Jesus commands men to drop everything and follow him. They do it.
2. Jesus teaches about God with such authority people marvel.

3. Jesus rebukes an evil spirit and drives it away.

4. Jesus heals a sick woman.

5. Jesus cures all the sick and demonized people in an entire town.

THE HAPPY SCARY SECRET KINGDOM

> **Mark 1:14–15** After John was put in prison, Jesus went into Galilee, proclaiming the good news of God. "The time has come," he said. "The kingdom of God is near. Repent and believe the good news!"

What Is The Kingdom Of God?

If you ask the average Christian, "What was the main message of Jesus?" odds are you'll get a response such as, "Believe in me and be saved," or "Love God and love your neighbor." Those are things Jesus taught, but the Gospels assert his core message was, *"the kingdom of God is near. Repent and believe the good news!"* In Mark they are the first words Jesus speaks, and they become a recurring theme.

What would the typical first-century Jew understand this message to mean? How should we interpret it?

☞ **GO TO:**

Mark 4:11, 26, 30; 9:1, 47; 10:14–15, 23–24; 12:34; 14:25; 15:43 (kingdom)

THE WAYBACK MACHINE

Ancient non-Jewish religions of Mesopotamia, Canaan, and other areas of the Middle East viewed history as a cycle. The cycle of four seasons repeated year after year, so Middle Eastern religions assumed history ran the same way—in a big circle, with death and fertility taking turns. A circle, of course, has no beginning and no end.

Jews, because of their belief in Yahweh, were the first to believe history is going somewhere. Instead of viewing history as a circle, the Jews thought of it as a line—a line that has to end somewhere. They thought history would end when Yahweh broke in, stopped the natural flow of events, and dealt out judgment. This concept is what the Old Testament means when it uses the phrase, *"the day of the Lord,"* sometimes shortened to *"the day"* or *"in that day."* The Jews packed a lot of meaning into those words. See the table on page 27 to find out several aspects of what the prophets said would happen in "that day."

What Would Happen?

Aspect of "the Day of the Lord"	Reference
God would judge and punish the sins of Israel.	Joel 1:13–15; Joel 2:1, 11; Amos 5:18–20; Zephaniah 1
God would judge and punish the countries who mistreated Israel.	Isaiah 1:24; Isaiah 2:12–18; Isaiah 13:6–9, 14, 19; Jeremiah 46:10; Obadiah 15
God would bring salvation, justice, and forgiveness for the truly repentant.	Joel 2:28–32; Isaiah 12:1–3; Isaiah 25:9
God would end the Jewish exile, return them to their land, and prosper them.	Isaiah 61:1–9; Jeremiah 30:8; Jeremiah 31:10–14; Hosea 2:21–23; Amos 9:13–15; Joel 3:18
A descendant of King David would rule in *shalom* (peace).	Isaiah 11:1–10; 4:2; Jeremiah 30:8–9; Hosea 2:18; Amos 9:11–12
God's active presence would dwell with Israel.	Isaiah 12:4–6; Hosea 2:16, 19–20; Zechariah 2:10–12
Not only Jews, but people of all nations would honor and worship the true God.	Isaiah 2:12–20; Zechariah 14:9; Hosea 2:21–23
Before any of this would happen, first Elijah would return.	Malachi 4:5

Taken in summary, the passages mentioned in the table (and others too numerous to cite) describe *"the day of the Lord"* as a time when God's reign becomes absolute over the entire earth. What characterizes God's reign? It's a time when the bad guys finally get the punishment they should've gotten all along, and the good guys get their rewards. If you're bad, it's scary; if you're good, it's a delight.

When Jesus mentioned *"the kingdom of God,"* first-century Jews would have understood him to mean *"the day of the Lord"* was very close. *"The day"* means punishment for the bad and rewards for the good, so you can understand the rest of Jesus' double-barreled phrase: *"repent"* (so you wind up on the happy side of God's judgment) and *"believe the good news"* (because God's reign means forgiveness, mercy, and prosperity for the good people). (For excellent insights on the meaning of God's kingdom, see GWLC, pages 156–159).

But Jesus' message would also confuse first-century Jews. If you always figured *"the day of the Lord"* meant the instant shattering of Roman power, what have you been expecting? An army, fiery comets from heaven, plagues, **Shekinah** glory—something *big*. What they got instead was a lone construction worker with a country accent saying, "The day is here! Trust me on this, guys!"

> **KEY POINT**
>
> Jesus' core message was that God's kingdom had arrived on earth.

> **Shekinah:** *radiant presence of God*

redemption: *escape by
payment of a price*

Using their Scriptures, the Jews had drawn part of the picture correctly, but Jesus had some innovations up his sleeve.
That's why almost every time he preached, his message began, *"The kingdom of God is like . . ."* He was giving Israel a
Master's Degree in Reeducation.

What was Jesus' startling innovation? That *"the day of the
Lord"* was a two-parter (as shown in the diagram below).
His words told them, and his actions demonstrated, that the
kingdom **redemption** including forgiveness, benefits, blessings, and healing were present *now*. His words and deeds
also showed the kingdom judgment, justice, and punishment
were being saved for the future (in fact, you and I are still
waiting for it; see GWPB, pages 66–67, 114). Later in Mark,
this two-part program for the future is part of what Jesus
means when he refers to *"the secret of the kingdom."* Whenever the Bible refers to a concept as a "secret" or a "mystery,"
it generally means that the concept was not understandable
to previous generations. You and I, however, two millennia
after Jesus' first coming, are privileged to understand. God's
kingdom reign has begun, but is not complete. Some have
compared it to the Allied invasion of occupied France on
D-Day, June 6, 1944. From that point, Hitler's reign was
doomed, but the war didn't end until May of 1945—almost a
year later. You and I are alive during God's mopping-up op-
eration; the enemy has not surrendered yet, but victory is
assured.

The Day of the Lord

*Jews in Jesus' day anticipated
"the day of the Lord," when
the Messiah would suddenly
initiate God's reign; but the
Messiah would come* twice *to
initiate God's reign com-
pletely. Between visits, his
kingdom would begin as a
spiritual reign.*

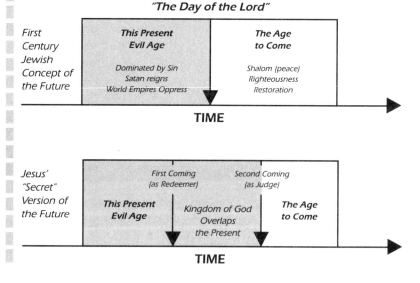

Gordon D. Fee: In place of the totally future, still-to-come end-time expectation of their Jewish roots, with its hope of a coming Messiah accompanied by the resurrection of the dead, the early believers recognized that the future had already been set in motion. . . . However, the End had only begun; they still awaited the final event, the (now second) coming of their Messiah Jesus. . . . They lived "between the times"; *already* the future had begun, *not yet* had it been completely fulfilled.[1]

FIVE SNAPSHOTS OF POWER

Jesus' mission to bring the reign of God to earth has just begun. What should he do first to show Satan's reign is ending? Mark sketches five brief scenarios, rapidly filling us in on Jesus' authority. In the first of these five snapshots of power, Jesus begins to gather a following.

> **Mark 1:16–20** As Jesus walked beside the Sea of Galilee, he saw Simon and his brother Andrew casting a net into the lake, for they were fishermen. "Come, follow me," Jesus said, "and I will make you fishers of men." At once they left their nets and followed him.
>
> When he had gone a little farther, he saw James son of Zebedee and his brother John in a boat, preparing their nets. Without delay he called them, and they left their father Zebedee in the boat with the hired men and followed him.

Snapshot #1: Calling With Command

Writers often depict the disciples as humble, uneducated men. You get the impression following Jesus was a no-brainer for them because they had nothing better to do. This picture isn't accurate.

The Bible refers to fishing often, but never as a recreational pursuit. In first-century Palestine, fishing meant business.

Most fishermen of the day used two kinds of nets, each mentioned in the passage above: a small net that one man could cast, and a larger drag-net that several men lowered from boats. Once fishermen decided the nets had been underwater long enough, they could haul them into their small boats, or drag them to shore to sort the saleable fish from the useless ones. Hauling nets full of fish was physically demanding work. Most fishermen were tough, muscular men.

☞ GO TO:

Matthew 13:48 (shore)

☞ **GO TO:**

Luke 5:5; John 21:3
(night)

☞ **GO TO:**

John 1:44 (Bethsaida)

Mark 1:21, 29
(Capernaum)

Mark 1:30 (married)

POWER TOOL

Notice and study
repeated words.

concordance:
alphabetical list of Bible
word locations

☞ **GO TO:**

Mark 2:14; 8:34; 10:21;
1 Peter 2:21 (follow)

Jeremiah 16:16; Ezekiel
29:4–5; 38:4; Amos
4:2 (fisher)

On the Sea of Galilee fishermen worked the <u>night</u> shift at least as often as the day. The Zebedee crew may have been *preparing* their nets by *repairing* their nets after a hard night's work. Regardless, only wealthier fishermen had a crew at all. Mark tells us James and John *"left their father Zebedee in the boat with the hired men,"* which means these brothers were squarely in the middle class or better. They were operating the family business profitably enough to have employees.

How well off was Simon, to whom Jesus gave the name Peter? It's possible he owned two houses, for he is listed as being "from the town of <u>Bethsaida</u>," but we also know he had a home in <u>Capernaum</u>. He was also <u>married</u>. He owned and operated his own business, had strong community and family ties, and perhaps owned two lakeside homes.

He and his business colleagues could hardly be described as men with no lives. These two pairs of brothers were busy middle-class family men with lives as full as yours and mine. Yet when Jesus summoned them, they jumped at the chance to follow. If they lived today, it would be as though they managed a small auto repair shop or a Taco Bell franchise and walked out on it—employees, equipment, everything—just because Jesus said so. Would you do as much if you heard his call?

Follow The Fisher Of Men

What does Jesus mean when he commands these strong men, *"Follow me"*? He was telling them to accept him as an authority in their lives. To join his group. To imitate his example. To make his cause their cause.

How did I get all of that out of one little word? By using the Power Tool for this chapter: *notice and study repeated words.* When a word shows up a lot in a book of the Bible, it's usually a hint about a theme in the book. Use a **concordance** to find all the places a word appears, and you'll be able to piece together more of what that word means. Peter emphasizes the word "<u>follow</u>." One of the big themes in this Gospel is the pros and cons of following Jesus.

Remember the Power Tool from chapter 1, *check the Old Testament references*? Try combining it with this Power Tool, and see who is the <u>fisher</u> of men in the Old Testament. You'll hear Jesus' invitation to these guys in a way you never did before, but in a way more like how they heard it.

It's important to notice details and ponder, "What did he mean by 'Follow me' and 'fisher of men'?" but notice the bigger picture too. Mark wants us to see the startling power of Jesus. He could walk past people occupied in the day-to-day concerns of their own lives, tell them to drop what they were doing to join his cause, *and they did it.* This is the real point of Mark's first snapshot of power.

We know from the other Gospels that Jesus had <u>met</u> these men before. I don't think this diminishes the power of what Mark depicts here. When people encountered Jesus, they saw something in him they wanted more than they wanted their own comfortable routines. That is a man to watch!

Something to Ponder

☞ **GO TO:**

John 1:35–43 (met)

What Others are Saying:

John R. W. Stott: [Jesus] never lowered his standards or modified his conditions to make his call more readily acceptable. He asked his first disciples, and he has asked every disciple since, to give him their thoughtful and total commitment. Nothing less than this will do. . . . At its simplest Christ's call was "Follow me." . . . To follow Christ is to renounce all lesser loyalties.[2]

> **Mark 1:21–28** They went to Capernaum, and when the Sabbath came, Jesus went into the synagogue and began to teach. The people were amazed at his teaching, because he taught them as one who had authority, not as the teachers of the law. Just then a man in their synagogue who was possessed by an evil spirit cried out, "What do you want with us, Jesus of Nazareth? Have you come to destroy us? I know who you are—the Holy One of God!"
>
> "Be quiet!" said Jesus sternly. "Come out of him!" The evil spirit shook the man violently and came out of him with a shriek.
>
> The people were all so amazed that they asked each other, "What is this? A new teaching—and with authority! He even gives orders to evil spirits and they obey him."

Snapshot #2: Teaching With Confidence

In Mark's five snapshots of power, episode 2 occurs in the **synagogue** at Capernaum, the largest of the many fishing towns surrounding the Sea of Galilee (see illustration, page 33). Commerce related to the sea made Capernaum a thriving town and a logical

synagogue: Jewish meeting place for worship

choice for the local headquarters of Roman troops. The Jews living there had to put up with a lot of heathen sin and evil and decadence.

Mark doesn't clue us in about what Jesus taught. Instead, the story remains tightly focused on Jesus' authority. The word for <u>authority</u> comes from the Greek word *exousia*, used eight other times in Mark. It means freedom and power to act however one wants. In this context it has an added meaning of being sure that what one says is true. In other words, Jesus knew exactly what he was talking about. And you know what? That frightened some people.

Synagogues in Jesus' day had no permanent **rabbi** or teacher, but they did have a leader, who functioned like a master of ceremonies. Whenever a visiting teacher came through town, customarily the synagogue leader asked him to read from the Torah and teach. This is how Jesus could speak in synagogues so often on his travels.

In the introduction to Part 1, I mentioned one of the national symbols of Israel was the Torah (page 6). Jews loved the Torah. I mean, they LOVED the Torah. Many men, called scribes, dedicated themselves to a full-time career of preserving and studying the Torah, learning all the latest thinking on how to interpret it and teaching others about it. Scribes instituted synagogue services out of their reverence for Torah.

As we'll see in Mark 7, however, the scribes became too impressed with themselves. Hebrew writings from the time between the Testaments indicate scribes believed their pupils should reverence the scribes above a pupil's own parents. Over the centuries they also created a massive oral tradition, including complex discussions about the application of Scripture. They thought this oral tradition was more important than the written Scripture itself.

As experts in the law of Moses, scribes were like the lawyers of our day. Just as a lawyer in court may spout off the names of obscure cases to prove her deep knowledge of the law, the scribes of Jesus' time made a point of quoting each other and various rabbis past and present. This is why the crowd was amazed at Jesus' teaching; he skipped all the name-dropping and footnoting and cut right to the heart of things. He had

IT'S
GREEK
TO ME

☞ **GO TO:**

Mark 1:27; 2:10; 3:15; 6:7; 11:28–29, 33; 13:34 (authority)

THE WAYBACK MACHINE

rabbi: *Hebrew for "my great one"*

Something to Ponder

no reason to quote someone else to prove he knew the truth, for who knows the truth better than God?

Charles Spurgeon: Oh, yes, he preached wondrously, he was always preaching, with all his heart and soul he preached! . . . Always a preacher, he was always ready, in season and out of season, with a good word. As he walked the streets he preached as he went along; and if he sought retirement, and the people thronged him, he sent them not away without a gracious word. . . . He lived the Prince of preachers; he died and became the theme of preachers, he lives again and is the Lord of preachers.[3]

What Others are Saying:

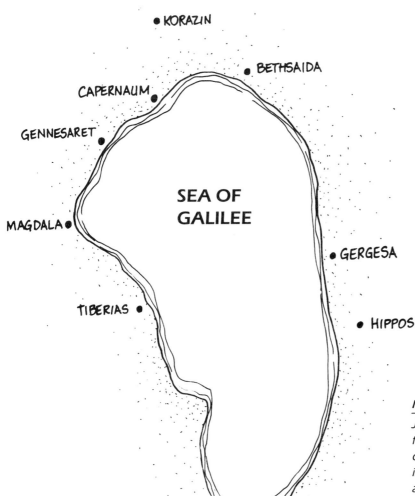

Map of Villages of Galilee

Jesus launched his ministry from Capernaum, the largest of the thirty towns surrounding the Sea of Galilee. He also returned there occasionally. It was the home base of his ministry (Matthew 4:13).

demon: *spirit being hostile to God*

Why Muckdrool Freaked Out

Maybe the best way to figure out why a **demon** disrupted synagogue that day is to look at things through the demon's eyes. Pretend for a second that you're Muckdrool, a squalid spirit who has contentedly lived inside poor Joel ben Joel for a few years. Joel goes to synagogue every Sabbath, but you don't care because no one there really knows what they're talking about, much less about you. For fun you sometimes wreck the service by making Joel shout random curses or stand up and give the ladies a long evil stare.

This week you're sitting in the synagogue, deciding how you'd like to disrupt the service, when this guy comes in who absolutely reeks of heaven. You do a demonic double take and suddenly realize—*you know this guy*. Back when you were in heaven, before you joined Lucifer's rebellion and got kicked out, you served him!

Suddenly you're not so comfortable. What's *he* doing here? You thought you were safe hiding in Podunk. He begins talking, saying the kingdom of God is here now. You're a spiritual being, so you know exactly what that means; your time is up! The reason the Son has come here today is for you!

Hardly able to stand his holy presence, you force yourself to watch a few minutes longer. Gradually you realize to your astonishment that these people have no idea who he is. Can't they sense the Spirit in him? Can't they feel the harsh burning radiance of his virtue? Having been an intelligent, crafty student of human nature for centuries, you decide to throw everyone into confusion and mess up Jesus' agenda; you make Joel ben Joel cry out, *"What do you want with us, Jesus of Nazareth? Have you come to destroy us? I know who you are—the Holy One of God!"* You think this is a smart move, because **conjurers** get control over spirits by naming them properly. Your opening move is to show Jesus you know his entire and proper name, and you have plenty more tactics where that came from.

You never get the chance. Instead of doing what stupider people do, which is to enter into a conversation with a being who lies fluently, Jesus tells you, *"Be quiet!"* Adding to the insult he commands, *"Come out of him!"* Your bluff won't work. You'd hoped that maybe here on earth, his authority would not equal what it was in heaven; but he knows exactly who he is, and you are hopelessly overmatched. With no alternative but to obey the Holy One of God, you flee, screaming with frustration.

conjurers: *one who practices magic arts*

KEY POINT

Jesus has total, complete dominance over demons.

Randy Alcorn: Scripture puts it this way: "You believe that there is one God. Good! Even the demons believe that—and shudder" (James 2:19). Demons see spiritual realities they have no choice but to believe, no matter how much they rebel against them. They hate the incarnation, virgin birth, and resurrection, but they believe them with as much conviction as the most fervent Christian. Demons are atheists in their behavior, but fundamentalists in their beliefs.[4]

> **Mark 1:29–34a** As soon as they left the synagogue, they went with James and John to the home of Simon and Andrew. Simon's mother-in-law was in bed with a fever, and they told Jesus about her. So he went to her, took her hand and helped her up. The fever left her and she began to wait on them.
>
> That evening after sunset the people brought to Jesus all the sick and demon-possessed. The whole town gathered at the door, and Jesus healed many who had various diseases.

Snapshot #3: Healing With Ease

The incredible authority of Jesus got rid of a demon in a few short words. In those days other religious Jews had exorcism rites that sometimes seemed <u>effective</u> in getting rid of demons (and sometimes <u>not</u>), but those rites were **protracted** affairs that left the exorcist exhausted (and probably worked chiefly by boring the demon to death). Had conquering the demon in the synagogue worn Jesus out? Not even close! Mark's third snapshot of power depicts Jesus going directly from the synagogue to Simon Peter's house and instantly healing Simon's mother-in-law.

The Greek word for "fever" in the noun form is also the word for fire; thus, Simon's mother-in-law was burning with an extreme temperature. Yet Jesus healed her in a moment, without uttering a word, and he healed her completely. She not only felt better; she felt energized enough to prepare a meal and serve guests. No one in Capernaum had ever seen a man this powerful.

> **Mark 1:34b** He also drove out many demons, but he would not let the demons speak because they knew who he was.

☞ **GO TO:**

Luke 11:19; Mark 9:38 (effective)

Acts 19:13–16 (not)

protracted: prolonged

IT'S
GREEK
TO ME

Adventures Of The Clark Kent Savior, Episode 1

Verse 21 told us that the events at the synagogue happened on the **Sabbath**. The healing at Simon's house happened *"as soon as they left the synagogue,"* so this happened on the Sabbath too. It was illegal by the scribes' tradition to heal on the Sabbath, because they considered healing a form of work. Most Jews reckoned the Sabbath as extending from sundown to sundown, so as soon as sunset ended, the town flocked to Jesus' door.

I love visualizing Mark's third snapshot of power. Imagine you are one of the villagers bringing your sick spouse to Jesus because you witnessed his astonishing deeds at the synagogue. Dusk has turned the night cobalt blue. You live in a rural society without city lights, so you approach Simon and Andrew's house under millions of sparkling stars. The oil lamps inside shine a golden welcome from the windows. Everyone you know is here, and everyone is being healed. The old lady from next door, no longer lame; your little blind nephew, now able to see. With each healing, your hopes for your own loved one rise. Mark's narrative does not suggest the clamor of later incidents. We've no reason to believe the people were anything but reverent and orderly, with soft cries of relief and praise mingling with the lapping of Lake Galilee. What a beautiful presence Jesus had in this town!

There is one note of conflict. Demons flee from Jesus, who *"would not let [them] speak because they knew who he was"* (Mark 1:34). Jesus is doing the deeds of Superman, but he is silencing the spirits as if trying to remain Clark Kent. Why does he forbid the demons from saying who he is? I'll let you think about it awhile, because we'll have several more episodes with the secret identity Savior later.

> **Mark 1:35–39** Very early in the morning, while it was still dark, Jesus got up, left the house and went off to a solitary place, where he prayed. Simon and his companions went to look for him, and when they found him, they exclaimed: "Everyone is looking for you!"
>
> Jesus replied, "Let us go somewhere else—to the nearby villages—so I can preach there also. That is why I have come." So he traveled throughout Galilee, preaching in their synagogues and driving out demons.

Snapshot #4: Praying With Persistence

So . . . when was the last time you spent the day driving out demons with a single command and calmly healing every sick person that crossed your path? Never? Hey, that's one more thing you and I have in common.

What was the secret of Jesus' limitless spiritual power? Mark gave us a hint when he showed the Holy Spirit resting upon Jesus like a dove. Here's another hint: Jesus prayed.

The words translated *"the morning, while it was still dark"* indicate the last **watch** of the night, between 3:00 and 6:00 A.M. You just read what type of day Jesus had before he got up this early. After ministering all day and late into the night, why wasn't he sleeping in? Obviously, prayer was important to him. And if he, being the Son of God, needed it enough to force it into his schedule, how much more do you and I need it? (For more on the topic, see WBFW, pages 20–21.)

Jesus seems to come out of his prayer time with a renewed sense of focus and urgency. Immediately he leaves the scene of his initial victories to travel throughout Galilee, for, he tells his disciples, *"That is why I have come."*

watch: duty hours of a sentry

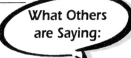

What Others are Saying:

Ronald J. Sider: Jesus himself took time away from his urgent ministry to talk alone with his heavenly Father. Then he made astounding promises to answer our prayers. If we know who Jesus is, how can we not make personal prayer a high priority?[5]

Life Application Bible Commentary: The Romans had divided the land of Israel into three separate regions: Galilee, Samaria, and Judea. Galilee was the northernmost region, an area about sixty miles long and thirty miles wide. Jesus did much of his ministry in this area, an ideal place for him to teach because there were over 250 towns concentrated there, with many synagogues where Jesus could proclaim his message, the Good News. . . . Even the small towns had about fifteen thousand people.[6]

> **Mark 1:40–42** A man with leprosy came to him and begged him on his knees, "If you are willing, you can make me clean."
> Filled with compassion, Jesus reached out his hand and touched the man. "I am willing," he said. "Be clean!" Immediately the leprosy left him and he was cured.

Snapshot #5: Touching With Compassion

As wonderful as this story is to you and me, first-century hearers would have found it even more marvelous. For one thing Jesus' motivation in healing the leper reads differently in some Greek manuscripts than it does in this English translation. Where the NIV has *"filled with compassion,"* some ancient manuscripts read, "moved with anger." An angry healer? Why would Jesus be ticked off at the leper? From what we've seen of him so far, it's safe to say he wasn't. More probably, he was angered at the way Satan had been able to trash God's chosen people.

IT'S GREEK TO ME

THE WAYBACK MACHINE

☞ **GO TO:**

Leviticus 13–14 (law)

The New Testament words for "leper" and "leprosy" could refer to a range of various skin diseases, only a few of which represent the same condition our modern science calls leprosy. It's important to understand, though, that first-century medicine knew of no cure for leprosy. When Jesus healed this poor man, his accomplishment was as astounding to Mark's audience as it would be today if you healed a man dying from AIDS. But you know what? That's not even the best thing Jesus did for this man.

Aren't your friends great? Whether hitting a restaurant together on a payday Friday night, shopping together, belly-laughing at an idiotic inside joke, or hanging out at one another's house in comfy slob clothes, you can hardly compare anything to the rich feeling of companionship you get with people who accept you. If you're a Christian with Christian friends, you can become even closer because you can worship God together—a marvelously ennobling experience to share.

The first-century leper was completely cut off from all of this. According to the <u>law</u> God gave Moses, here was the life of the leper: *"The person with such an infectious disease must wear torn clothes, let his hair be unkempt, cover the lower part of his face and cry out, 'Unclean! Unclean!' As long as he has the infection he remains unclean. He must live alone; he must live outside the camp"* (Leviticus 13:45–46). God, in his wisdom, had created a procedure to prevent the majority of his people from being infected with contagious skin diseases.

Hebrew law said lepers could rejoin everyone if they were ever cured, but remember the huge oral tradition the scribes preserved? It said healing a leper was as difficult as raising the dead. In the Old Testament even God himself had only healed leprosy <u>twice</u>. So imagine the poor folk who *did* get infected. They lived isolated lives, legally obligated to use both sight and sound to warn away all would-be friends. Worst of all, these lepers lived in a society totally centered around the worship of Yahweh, yet the main place to do so—the Temple in Jerusalem—banned them from the premises.

The first amazing thing about Jesus healing the leper is this: *"Jesus reached out his hand and touched the man."* When was the last time this leper had felt any human touch, much less a warm hand of compassion? Jesus, however, was not afraid to make intimate contact with this unclean person.

The next amazing thing is that instead of the leprosy infecting Jesus, the purity of Jesus wiped out the leprosy.

Perhaps the *most* amazing thing is that as soon as the leper showed himself to the priests, he would be back in society. Unclean? No more. Isolated? No longer. He could rejoin his loved ones. He could be a normal man; instead of being a financial burden on his family, he was free to get a job and support them.

Jesus healed the leper physically, but also brought blessing socially, spiritually, and (in potential) financially. This kind of all-aspects miracle is typical of what happens when the kingdom of God breaks into our world. God's reign affects every aspect of our lives, not merely the parts we regard as "spiritual."

> **Mark 1:43–44** Jesus sent him away at once with a strong warning: "See that you don't tell this to anyone. But go, show yourself to the priest and offer the sacrifices that Moses commanded for your cleansing, as a testimony to them."

Adventures Of The Clark Kent Savior, Episode 2

Did the wisest man who ever walked the earth believe for a second the leper could contain himself? Then why make this request at all? Why is Jesus hiding who he is?

One possible reason in this passage is Jesus wants to cool the Jesusmania that prevents him from relating normally to people.

Something to Ponder

The frenzy sweeping Galilee threatened to run out of control. Too much talk of a new leader would bring Roman troops swooping into the midst of things.

Here's another possibility. Jesus may have known how the temple leaders would regard a country healer who had no credentials. When he tells the ex-leper to show himself to the priest *"as a testimony to them,"* perhaps Jesus means "as a **testimony** to them that the holy man in Galilee they've heard about is more than a rabble-rousing kook."

testimony: firsthand authentication of a fact

What Others are Saying:

Gary Smalley and John T. Trent: To touch a leper was unthinkable. . . . Yet the first thing Christ did for this man was touch him. Even before Jesus spoke to him, He reached out His hand and touched him. . . . Think how this man must have longed for someone to touch him, not throw stones at him to drive him away. Jesus could have healed him first and then touched him. But recognizing his deepest need, Jesus stretched out His hand even before He spoke words of physical and spiritual healing.[7]

HERO OF THE FRINGE FOLK

> **Mark 1:45** Instead he went out and began to talk freely, spreading the news. As a result, Jesus could no longer enter a town openly but stayed outside in lonely places. Yet the people still came to him from everywhere.

Outside In Lonely Places

Understandably, the ex-leper cannot contain himself. After all, this is his first chance to interact freely with society in a while. Even though he is praising Jesus enthusiastically, he is also disobeying him. His misguided efforts block what God wanted to do; Jesus can no longer enter the towns. How many other illnesses went unhealed in town because of this man's blundering zeal?

In this first chapter of Mark, the radical love of Jesus would intrigue and startle a first-century reader. Think about who Jesus has ministered to so far. Did he confer with the temple leadership, or summon all the Galilean synagogue leaders together for a summit? No. He dealt with society's outsiders:

- a man possessed with an evil spirit

- Simon's mother-in-law (women had little status in Jewish culture)
- a leper, declared unclean by religious laws.

In the next chapter Jesus helps more of society's dregs: a paralytic, and the lowest of the low—a Jew who collected taxes for Rome.

From the start Mark portrays Jesus as a hero of the fringe folk. Also from the start hindrances block the good news, keeping Jesus outside in lonely places. Yet such was the powerful message of this holy man of action that *"the people still came to him from everywhere."*

Conflict did, too. But that's a story for the next chapter.

Joni Eareckson Tada: Condemned criminals, half-breeds, short guys with too much money, women whose homes you visited only after dark—these were the people he went after. He washed their feet and went to their parties. But you never got the sense that his hands were dirty afterwards. . . . People who were sorry about themselves and sick with how they had acted never met with such mercy.[8]

KEEP IT REAL—Here are a few thoughts that pierced my heart as I studied the second half of Mark 1. How do they compare to things that moved you?

- Mark 1:18, 20. The first four disciples dropped *everything* and followed Jesus *immediately*. Sometimes slow obedience is the same as no obedience. *Jesus, where am I holding back from following you? Help me hold everything lightly—except you.*

- Mark 1:22. The scribes dedicated their lives full-time to studying and teaching God's Word, yet they still didn't know the Scriptures properly, because they valued their own traditions more. When God entered their midst, they missed it completely. *Jesus, help me to know not only the Word of God, but also the God of the Word.*

- Mark 1:32–34. As a follower of Jesus, sometimes I long for more of his power. I don't want it in order to be famous, or to feel high on my own strength. It's just that the world is so heartbreakingly needy. Jesus was able to help almost *everyone*. In contrast, I'm able to help . . . er, let's just say I have a ways to go in that department.

- Mark 1:45. The leper couldn't help but tell people about Jesus and the result was that *"[Jesus] stayed outside in lonely places."* This phrase haunts me. How often has some well-meaning thing we've done hindered the ministry of Jesus, driving his kingdom work out to the edges of our lives? That is not where Jesus belongs.

Study Questions

1. List some concepts that would come to the mind of a typical first-century Jew upon hearing the phrase, *"the day of the Lord"* (also referred to as *"God's reign"*).
2. What was Jesus' startling innovation about *"the day of the Lord"*?
3. Name three or four incidents Mark wrote down in order to give us snapshots of the power and authority of Jesus.
4. What hint does Mark 1:35 give us about how Jesus maintained his ministry focus and his power?
5. Besides being touched, and cured of his physical condition, what was another wonderful aspect of the leper's healing?

CHAPTER WRAP-UP

- The core message of Jesus was, *"The kingdom of God is at hand. Repent and believe the good news!"* The *"kingdom of God"* was written about in the later half of the Old Testament as *"the day of the LORD"* and had a specific meaning to Jews. The most prominent theme was that God's reign would bring punishment for sin and rewards to the righteous. Other main threads of meaning are shown on page 27. (Mark 1:14–15)

- Jesus innovated on the concept of the day of the Lord. His ministry showed that kingdom mercy, healing, and redemption had arrived now. Judgment and God's full reign on earth were put off until later. For now, we live in an overlapping age, where God's kingdom reigns in the hearts of believers, but believers still live in this present evil age. Jesus will return later to finish establishing God's kingdom. (Hebrews 2:8; Philippians 2:8–11)

- Mark begins his book with five quick snapshots of Jesus as a man of powerful action and authority, an image sure to appeal to the Roman mind. (Mark 1:16–34)

- One secret of Jesus' incredible power was his reliance upon his heavenly Father, shown in the way Jesus took time to pray. (Mark 1:35–39)

- When Jesus healed the leper, he not only healed a skin condition, but also brought potential blessing into the social, spiritual, and financial aspects of the man's life. The kingdom of God affects all areas of life, not just the spiritual. Disobeying Jesus, the leper blabbed to everyone about what Jesus had done for him. (Mark 1:40–45)

MARK 2:1–3:12
ANTIESTABLISHMENT JESUS

CHAPTER HIGHLIGHTS

- Who Said Jesus Could Forgive Sins?
- Jesus, Man of Bad Manners?
- The Disciples Party On
- Conflict in a Cornfield
- Mad at Mercy
- Crowding Jesus

Let's Get Started

Mark has shown the undeniable authority of Jesus. Now he introduces a new theme: conflict.

The first-century Jews saw themselves as God's people, not Rome's people. The average Jew felt the real rulers over him (besides Yahweh) were the high priest, the priests of the Temple **cult** in Jerusalem, and the **Sanhedrin** (I'll explain who they were later). There was no separation between church and state. In fact, the state wanted to *be* the church; the Romans taught Caesar was god. Jews didn't buy that, but they got to keep their religion only by permission of the Roman government. This forced the Jewish religious leaders to be careful politicians. In effect, when Jesus went around and healed or forgave without involving the official religious establishment, he was bypassing the local government. To those nervous religious leaders, someone undermining their authority risked getting them all into trouble with Rome.

cult: devoted members of a religious ritual

Sanhedrin: first-century Jewish equivalent of Congress

MARK'S CAVALCADE OF CONFLICT

> **Mark 2:1–7** A few days later, when Jesus again entered Capernaum, the people heard that he had come home. So many gathered that there was no room left, not even outside the door, and he preached the word to them. Some men came, bringing to him a paralytic, carried by four of them. Since they could not get him to Jesus because of the crowd, they made an opening in the roof

above Jesus and, after digging through it, lowered the mat the paralyzed man was lying on. When Jesus saw their faith, he said to the paralytic, "Son, your sins are forgiven."

Now some teachers of the law were sitting there, thinking to themselves, "Why does this fellow talk like that? He's blaspheming! Who can forgive sins but God alone?"

Conflict #1: Hey! Who Gave You Permission To Give Permission?

This account is the first of five consecutive stories showing the conflict between Jesus and Israel's official religious might. Each story features an accusing question that the religious leaders ask. In this first story their question is, *"Why does this fellow talk like that?"*

Jesus' statement seemed out of line in several ways. First, it ignored the obvious need the paralytic came to him for and addressed an issue that seemed completely irrelevant. Second, a normal man must have the ego of a **megalomaniac** to claim the authority to forgive sins. Obviously, the only one who can forgive sin is the one who defined sin: God. By claiming to forgive someone's sin, Jesus is coming as close to claiming godhood as anyone could without explicitly stating it.

Two more facts reveal why this statement was startling. In first-century Jewish law, claiming to be God was **blasphemy**, and blasphemy was a capital offense. For what Jesus just said, the scribes had legal cause to drag him outside the city and have him clobbered with big rocks until he died. So, *"Why does this fellow talk like that?"* is a very good question.

megalomaniac: *one with a mental disorder marked by childish feelings of personal importance*

blasphemy: *misusing God's name or insulting God; also, the act of claiming the attributes of God*

☞ **GO TO:**

Exodus 34:6–7 (forgive)

Leviticus 24:10–16 (capital offense)

Mark 2:8–12 Immediately Jesus knew in his spirit that this was what they were thinking in their hearts, and he said to them, "Why are you thinking these things? Which is easier: to say to the paralytic, 'Your sins are forgiven,' or to say, 'Get up, take your mat and walk'? But that you may know that the Son of Man has authority on earth to forgive sins . . ." He said to the paralytic, "I tell you, get up, take your mat and go home." He got up, took his mat and walked out in full view of them all. This amazed everyone and they praised God, saying, "We have never seen anything like this!"

Healing Godstyle

There are only three possible answers to the teachers' questions: (1) he's joking (showing an unbelievably misguided sense of humor); (2) he's nuts, because he thinks he's God; or (3) he *is* God.

These *"teachers of the law"* (the same as the scribes I defined for you in the chapter on Mark 1:14–45) had been sent from Jerusalem to check on this upstart hick. I doubt discerning their thoughts ranks as Jesus' mightiest miracle. In addition to asking "Who does this guy think he is?" they probably assumed Jesus had "forgiven" the man in order to avoid the fact that he couldn't heal him.

Jesus gave them—and us—an extremely important lesson. He did heal the man, but more important than the healing was the purpose it served. The healing was an external demonstration of how effectively the **Son of Man**, Jesus, can deal with our internal sin. Just as one word from Jesus could end this man's years of exile on a mat, one word from Jesus could end years of exile from God. Once again, the in-breaking of the kingdom of God brought forgiveness and wholeness in <u>one</u> package.

The scribes knew that no one could forgive sins but God alone. Jesus' miraculous deed said to them, "Exactly. Who did you think you were dealing with?"

☞ **GO TO:**

Luke 5:17 (Jerusalem)

Psalm 103:2–3 (one)

Son of Man: *Jesus' favorite designation for himself; used fourteen times in Mark*

What Others are Saying:

C. S. Lewis: Yet this is what Jesus did. He told people that their sins were forgiven, and never waited to consult all the other people whom their sins had undoubtedly injured. He unhesitatingly behaved as if He was . . . the person chiefly offended in all offences. This makes sense only if He really was the god whose laws are broken and whose love is wounded in every sin. In the mouth of any speaker who is not God, these words would imply. . . a silliness and conceit unrivalled by any other character in history.[1]

Act Now, And We'll Throw In A Free Skylight

The paralyzed man got to Jesus because his friends made a hole in the roof. Could you picture this happening at your home Bible study? Your group leader tries to lead a discussion, while from overhead you hear the buzz of a circular saw blade biting into roof tiles, followed by sledge hammer blows that shake the house. The dust of pulverized drywall drifts down while the splintering sound of tearing wood and protesting nails drowns out the leader's voice.

And all that merely gets the paralyzed guy into the *attic*.

adobe: *sun-dried earth and straw, mixed*

thatch: *a matting of reeds, branches, and mud*

First-century Palestinians constructed their houses of stone and a clay-based mortar similar to **adobe**. Typically their houses had just one room and an outside staircase on one wall for easy access to the flat roof. (See illustration below.) In the hot climate of Israel (similar to southern California), the roof served as an extra room. The roof itself was usually made of wooden beams covered with **thatch** and compacted earth. Some homes had clay tiles laid under the thatch, between the beams. These fragile roofs had to be replenished every fall to get ready for winter rains; they were easily repaired.

This means the four industrious friends could break the roof apart with their bare hands. What's impressive is not their act of breaking the roof. What's impressive is Jesus wasn't in the least annoyed by their interruption. In fact, he viewed their persistence as faith, and rewarded them for it.

> **Mark 2:13–14** Once again Jesus went out beside the lake. A large crowd came to him, and he began to teach them. As he walked along, he saw Levi son of Alphaeus sitting at the tax collector's booth. "Follow me," Jesus told him, and Levi got up and followed him.

First-Century Roof

Lionel Ritchie's mid-1980s hit "Dancin' on the Ceiling" could have been written about the huts of first-century Jews. The flat, sun-baked roof (like the one pictured) was used for everything from drying grains and olives to watching the stars.

Jesus Adopts A Traitor

Bearing in mind that Jews viewed the conquering Romans as godless "dogs," how do you suppose the average Jew felt about a fellow Jew collecting money for the Romans? Average people didn't know the precise amount of tax Rome expected, so tax collectors typically <u>overcharged</u> and kept the difference. There was no lower form of pond scum to the Jewish mind. Most synagogues **excommunicated** Jewish tax collectors.

Yet Jesus took one look at Levi sitting in a Roman toll booth, and said, *"Follow me."* Again, Jesus seeks the outcasts of Jewish society. The first four disciples could always return to fishing if things didn't work out. A Roman tax collector who quit could not get his job back, yet Levi (also known as <u>Matthew</u>, the author of the Gospel of Matthew) appreciated the invitation enough to drop his lucrative position and follow.

☞ **GO TO:**

Luke 3:12–13
(overcharged)

Matthew 9:9; 10:3
(Matthew)

excommunicated: *kicked out permanently*

> **Mark 2:15–16** While Jesus was having dinner at Levi's house, many tax collectors and "sinners" were eating with him and his disciples, for there were many who followed him. When the teachers of the law who were Pharisees saw him eating with the "sinners" and tax collectors, they asked his disciples: "Why does he eat with tax collectors and 'sinners'?"

Conflict #2: A Messiah With Poor Table Manners

Remember how important four national symbols—Temple, Territory, Torah, and Tribe—were to the conquered Jews? Mark's second conflict story actually centers around the Torah when the Pharisees ask, *"Why does he eat with tax collectors and 'sinners'?"*

Most Christians do not clearly understand who the Pharisees were. If you think they were nothing but insufferable, self-righteous hypocrites, let me tell you why I love these guys, and why every Christian should be thankful for them.

Scholars do not agree about exactly how or when the Pharisees were established, although some studies indicate they saw themselves as continuing the work of <u>Ezra</u>. We do know the Pharisees, although just a minority, had influence and popular support among the Jews nearly 150 years before Jesus.

☞ **GO TO:**

Ezra 1–10 (Ezra)

THE WAYBACK MACHINE

Many Christians today assume the Pharisees were priests. They were not; 95 percent of them were **laymen**. Pharisees knew the Jews had been forced into exile because they had not followed God's law. Therefore, the Pharisees reasoned, if they could persuade all Jews to observe the commands of Torah, God would end the exile and bring them back to prosperity in Israel. These ordinary men formed as a band of individuals who loved God and wanted to lead exemplary lives to influence their entire nation positively. They were "Promise Keepers B.C." (To find out about the apostle Paul's life as a Pharisee, go to GWRM, pages xvi–xvii.)

Like the scribes the Pharisees devoted themselves to understanding and protecting Torah. In times of war with persecuting nations, Pharisees volunteered for "certain death" missions to delay their opponents so others could scoop up precious Torah scrolls and rush them to safety. Much later, in A.D. 90, Pharisees were the men who determined which Hebrew scriptures God had truly inspired. The result is what Christians call the Old Testament. If there had been Wheaties in their day, the Pharisees would have been on the box. Without Pharisees, we would have no Old Testament, which is why every Christian should thank God for them.

They initiated noble tasks like defining what work was, so they could follow God's rule not to work on the Sabbath. As the decades rolled by and the **halakah** grew, however, the Pharisees took a good thing too far. They invented stricter rules about avoiding work on the Sabbath, just to be on the safe side (see illustration, page 49). This way if they slipped in following their own personal code, they still would be innocent of breaking God's law. They confused people, however, by presenting their own *interpretation* of the law as *being* God's law, and no one could live up to the strict rules they invented.

To preserve Israel's identity as a nation, Pharisees emphasized outward, visible obedience to the laws. This was where the Pharisees got their name, which means "separate ones." They stressed the importance of following kosher dietetic rules to remain personally pure. What began as a sincere desire to lead Israel by holy example evolved into self-righteous display. By the time of Jesus, Pharisees would not eat without practicing elaborate cleansing rituals, and they would not eat with

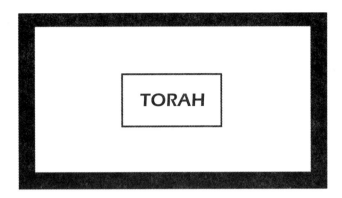

Hedge around Torah

Pharisees wanted to make sure they didn't break God's laws, so if the Torah had a rule like "Don't watch TV on Sundays," the Pharisees would expand the rule to "Don't watch TV ever." This has been referred to as "building a hedge around Torah."

people who didn't observe the **Pharisaical** table customs. Perhaps now you can see why the Pharisees were shocked when a teacher who had fantastic insight into the Torah ate with "sinners" (the Pharisee's term for anyone who didn't follow their rules).

Pharisaical: having to do with Pharisees

> **Mark 2:17** On hearing this, Jesus said to them, "It is not the healthy who need a doctor, but the sick. I have not come to call the righteous, but sinners."

Who's In Jesus' Rolodex

If Levi was a "sinner" in the eyes of the Jewish religion, and probably excommunicated from the synagogue, it's no wonder his friends included *"many tax collectors and 'sinners'"* (Mark 2:15). He could hardly make friends with righteous people who rejected him. In calling Levi Jesus had found a way to introduce God to a whole circle of people who had nothing to do with religion. This concept escaped the Pharisees, who assumed Jesus must be a "sinner" too if he hung out with them. (For another view of Matthew's party, see GWLC, pages 164–165.)

Given the Pharisees' perspective, it's no wonder they asked, "Why does he do that?" Given Jesus' perspective, it's no wonder he answered so easily and concisely. He hadn't come to call the "righteous." (You know that Jesus meant it ironically, because by their very attitude these Pharisees showed they were not righteous.) Luke's Gospel expresses Jesus' mission even more concisely: *"For the Son of Man came to seek out and to save the lost."*

☞ **GO TO:**

Luke 19:10
(Jesus' mission)

David E. Garland: These incidents present for the reader two incompatible religious outlooks, two ways of doing religion that are in inexorable conflict. One leads to death; the other to life. . . . The call of Levi and Jesus' feasting with sinners discloses the contrast between a religious attitude that keeps sinners and the unhallowed at arm's length and one, the good news of God, that welcomes all comers.[2]

> **Mark 2:18** Now John's disciples and the Pharisees were fasting. Some people came and asked Jesus, "How is it that John's disciples and the disciples of the Pharisees are fasting, but yours are not?"

Conflict #3: But, But, But . . . John's Doing It!

Mark's third conflict account is a perfect example of the extremes the Pharisees went to in their misguided quest for holiness. Old Testament law called for one <u>day of **fasting**</u> per year for the mourning of Israel's sins. Building their hedge around Torah, the Pharisees fasted <u>twice a week</u>. Once again people confused pharisaical custom with God's law, leading them to question Jesus. If Jesus was bringing a new and highly spiritual teaching, why were his disciples behaving less righteously than already-existing factions of Judaism?

☞ **GO TO:**

Leviticus 16:29–31 (day of fasting)

Luke 18:10–12 (twice a week)

fasting: refusing food and drink

> **Mark 2:19–22** Jesus answered, "How can the guests of the bridegroom fast while he is with them? They cannot, so long as they have him with them. But the time will come when the bridegroom will be taken from them, and on that day they will fast.
> "No one sews a patch of unshrunk cloth on an old garment. If he does, the new piece will pull away from the old, making the tear worse. And no one pours new wine into old wineskins. If he does, the wine will burst the skins, and both the wine and the wineskins will be ruined. No, he pours new wine into new wineskins."

Shredding Shirts and Bursting Bottles

Jesus' astonishing answer asserts two things that would have mystified or disturbed the questioners. First, he calls himself the "bridegroom," clearly implying that every spiritual person should celebrate because he's here! Although the rabbis sometimes used the image of the wedding feast to express the joy of the messianic era, nowhere in the Old Testament nor in later Jewish literature was the Messiah represented as the bridegroom. His listeners probably have no idea what to make of his veiled statement.

Second, he gives two brief analogies about how new things don't fit with old things. If you've ever used a new patch to repair old blue jeans, you can relate to the first analogy; as soon as you wash cotton, it shrinks and tears away. We have less experience with **wineskins**. They were made from hide, so they turned brittle with age, as any leather does. If you poured new wine into a brittle skin, when the new wine fermented the expanding gases popped the wineskin, and you lost both the skin and the wine.

wineskins: *goat skins, sewn watertight*

The thrust of these analogies is that Jesus' message was not some slight addition to contemporary Jewish practice. His presence changed everything. His teaching sprung from the arrival of God's kingdom on earth—a whole new situation the Torah was never intended to deal with. The truth of who Jesus was and what he came to do was too big to fit inside the structures of ancient Jewish tradition.

Something to Ponder

Jesus' analogies passed over the heads of his listeners. They would have passed over our heads too, had we been there. With the benefit of hindsight, however, we see now that when Jesus began his ministry, the kingdom of God began its reign on earth. Of course it wasn't time to institute mourning rituals (like fasting)! This was the era all earth had longed for! The Savior had arrived!

Yet Jesus said, *"The time will come when the bridegroom will be taken from them, and on that day they will fast."* Many modern Christians think fasting is an ancient custom that is not useful today. This statement of Jesus contradicts such thinking. It says fasting is appropriate for his disciples after he is gone. Jesus is still gone, so fasting is still appropriate. If you've never tried it, you'll be surprised at the benefits it can bring (see GWHN, pages 233–240).

What Others are Saying:

Richard J. Foster: In a culture where the landscape is dotted with shrines to the Golden Arches and an assortment of Pizza Temples, fasting seems out of place, out of step with the times. . . . More recently a renewed interest in fasting has developed, but we have far to go to recover a biblical balance. . . . Fasting can bring breakthroughs in the spiritual realm that will never happen in any other way. It is a means of God's grace and blessing that should not be neglected any longer.[3]

> **Mark 2:23–28** One Sabbath Jesus was going through the grainfields, and as his disciples walked along, they began to pick some heads of grain. The Pharisees said to him, "Look, why are they doing what is unlawful on the Sabbath?"
>
> He answered, "Have you never read what David did when he and his companions were hungry and in need? In the days of Abiathar the high priest, he entered the house of God and ate the consecrated bread, which is lawful only for priests to eat. And he also gave some to his companions."
>
> Then he said to them, "The Sabbath was made for man, not man for the Sabbath. So the Son of Man is Lord even of the Sabbath."

Conflict #4: The Sabbath Isn't Fair Ya See

In this fourth conflict story, the featured question is, *"Why are they doing what is unlawful on the Sabbath?"* Jesus responds with a line of reasoning that is totally original, totally unexpected, and totally irrefutable by the Pharisees.

The Pharisees had established thirty-nine categories of actions that you had to stay away from on the Sabbath, but they based them only partly on God's actual law. The rest came from their interpretations and traditions. The point of the Sabbath was to provide a day of rest and an opportunity to reflect on God. People who followed the pharisaical teaching spent so much time trying not to violate the technical definition of "work" that they couldn't rest at all.

While to our modern sensibilities it looks as if the disciples were committing minor theft (kinda like eating grapes at the grocery store before you have them weighed and paid), on any other day but the Sabbath their behavior was perfectly legal.

The law against harvesting on the Sabbath was meant to give farmers a break. These were fishermen, not farmers, so they weren't doing their occupation on the Sabbath, nor were they trying to make a profit. Basically, the Pharisees wanted to punish them for grabbing a snack. Their question to Jesus

THE WAYBACK MACHINE

☞ **GO TO:**

Deuteronomy 23:24–25 (legal)

equaled first-century trash talk: if your disciples are so ignorant they don't even know the basic Sabbath laws, you must be one worthless teacher.

Jesus did not go around purposely tweaking the Pharisees' sense of right and wrong, nor gleefully pushing their hot buttons. He was leading his normal life. He healed people. He took a walk. He let hungry people have a snack. But when the self-righteous faultfinders attack Jesus repeatedly, he begins to answer in stronger and stronger tones, because his message is not getting through to them. Here, he could have explained, "The Torah allows this," but instead Jesus begins his response with, "Have you never read . . . ?" and then cites a well-known Bible story. Nothing could be more insulting to these specialists in the **minutiae** of the law than to imply they hadn't read the Scriptures.

The <u>story</u> Jesus cites tells of a time God allowed David to set aside religious ritual because the practical need of hunger was more urgent. Jesus' counterquestion had a point. If they had read this passage, they had either missed or forgotten the lesson it taught. Practically speaking, they acted as if they had never read it. Jesus sums up the lesson concisely with, "The Sabbath was made for man, not man for the Sabbath." In other words, "This is a day of rest, guys, not a day to knock yourself out proving you're more legal than the next guy. Lighten up!"

■　■　■

Modern readers often miss one important aspect of this account. When Jesus defends his disciples' actions because they are like David's warriors eating the **showbread**, in the listeners' minds the comparison of the two stories would not stop there. Since David's warriors received special permissions because they were on God's business, Jesus is implying that he and his disciples are also going about God's business in some way the Pharisees are not. The comparison casts the Pharisees in the role of Doeg, the coward slinking off to tattle on the man who should be king.

Further, Jesus compares himself to David. David was Israel's greatest king, but in this story he and his followers had not yet been installed. (For highlights of King David's life, see GWMB, 91–105.) Jesus' answer to the Pharisees invokes an unstated yet clear claim to messiahship.

minutiae: minor, trifling details

☞ **GO TO:**

1 Samuel 21:1–6 (story)

showbread: bread set before the face of God

Jesus brings this to a sharp point, concluding, *"So the Son of Man is Lord even of the Sabbath"* (Mark 2:28). To assert it in such a fashion that he is clearly referring to himself must have outraged the Pharisees. Here is a man who acts as if he is the Messiah, but he never comes right out and says it. He says *"the kingdom of God is at hand,"* and obviously thinks he is king of that kingdom. The Pharisees' frustration, fueled by their own failure to catch Jesus in a nice, juicy, indictable sound-byte, helps explain the extreme reaction that concludes the fifth and final story in Mark's conflict series.

What Others are Saying:

A. W. Tozer: The God of the Pharisee was not a God easy to live with, so his religion became grim and hard and loveless. It had to be so, for our notion of God must always determine the quality of our religion. Much Christianity since the days of Christ's flesh has also been grim and severe. And the cause has been the same— an unworthy or inadequate view of God.[4]

> **Mark 3:1–6** Another time he went into the synagogue, and a man with a shriveled hand was there. Some of them were looking for a reason to accuse Jesus, so they watched him closely to see if he would heal him on the Sabbath. Jesus said to the man with the shriveled hand, "Stand up in front of everyone."
>
> Then Jesus asked them, "Which is lawful on the Sabbath: to do good or to do evil, to save life or to kill?" But they remained silent.
>
> He looked around at them in anger and, deeply distressed at their stubborn hearts, said to the man, "Stretch out your hand." He stretched it out, and his hand was completely restored. Then the Pharisees went out and began to plot with the **Herodians** how they might kill Jesus.

Herodians: *Jewish political party supporting Herod*

Conflict #5: A Rotten Evil Wicked Healing

In this final story in Mark's Cavalcade of Conflict, for once Jesus is asking the questions. He asks, *"Which is lawful on the Sabbath: to do good or to do evil, to save life or to kill?"* The answer is as obvious to the Pharisees as it is to you and me, but they weren't looking for truth. They were *"looking for a reason to accuse Jesus."* They wanted to humiliate this self-styled Messiah, and they would not yield on the smallest point.

Yet Jesus sticks to his mission. When he conflicts with the Pharisees, it's because he's doing what he came to do, not because he let their jealousy get to him. After about the third encounter, I'd get in some Pharisee's face, bump my chest against his and growl, "You got a problem with me, falafel breath?" But Jesus neither descends to their petty level, nor fears them. He knows what they're thinking: that healing is work. But unlike the Pharisees, Jesus focused on people's needs, not on preserving his reputation. He healed the man's hand anyway.

Jesus does something clever first. He asks a question that leaves the Pharisees no way out. They can't say, "God's Sabbath is for killing and hurting!" But the way Jesus phrased the question, they couldn't object to healing on the Sabbath, either. Since they didn't object, that implicated them as collaborators in the healing.

Mark ends the conflict series by showing how misled the Pharisees had become. They pretend concern about which deeds pleased God on the Sabbath, yet spent the Sabbath planning murder.

John Fischer: Few activities in life rival the thrill of passing judgment on another human being. . . . It is our "out-look" that predominates—an outlook that takes great pleasure in scrutinizing the minutest detail of someone else's compromise while overlooking large chunks of our own self-contradiction with nary a blink. . . . For the Pharisee, being the gatekeeper—and therefore controlling who gets in and who stays out—is more desirable than enjoying the fruits of entering in.[5]

THE BEACH GETS CROWDED

> **Mark 3:7–10** Jesus withdrew with his disciples to the lake, and a large crowd from Galilee followed. When they heard all he was doing, many people came to him from Judea, Jerusalem, Idumea, and the regions across the Jordan and around Tyre and Sidon. Because of the crowd he told his disciples to have a small boat ready for him, to keep the people from crowding him. For he had healed many, so that those with diseases were pushing forward to touch him.

I'll Teach; You Keep The Getaway Boat Running

Thousands came to hear John the Baptist; Jesus drew a larger crowd. The list of regions and cities indicate that not only Jews followed Jesus, non-Jews flocked to him too. The crowds grew disorderly enough, however, that Jesus kept a getaway boat ready. Literally translated, the Greek here is *"a small boat should be constantly attending him."*

Maintaining order must have been difficult. The regions listed indicate this crowd would not have had one common language. In addition, you've seen how unruly crowds can get at sports arenas or rock concerts. Imagine the passion there'd be if people believed all their health problems would end if they could touch one individual! The Greek indicates the people literally fell on Jesus.

> **Mark 3:11–12** Whenever the evil spirits saw him, they fell down before him and cried out, "You are the Son of God." But he gave them strict orders not to tell who he was.

Adventures Of The Clark Kent Savior, Episode 3

The demons continue to recognize Jesus as the Son of God, and he continues to silence them. So far in Mark, God the heavenly Father has recognized Jesus as his Son; numerous <u>demons</u> have recognized him; and in a few chapters, we'll see that even <u>nature</u> itself recognizes who Jesus is. In fact, everyone and everything recognizes the Son of God—except the people he came to save. This irony grows sharper as we progress. Have you formed a theory about why Jesus maintains his secret?

Summary Execution

Mark finishes this series of conflict stories with a brief summary of Jesus' ministry (Mark 3:7–12). Summaries occur rarely in Mark, and usually indicate the end of a section of the book. That brings us to our Power Tool for this chapter.

I used to think verse-by-verse commentary was the best way to read the Bible. But when you go verse by verse, you miss larger patterns. In this chapter, for example, we noticed how Mark grouped several conflict stories together. We also observed the way Mark uses summaries to divide his book.

☞ **GO TO:**

Mark 1:11 (Father)

Mark 1:24, 34 (demons)

Mark 4:39 (nature)

KEEP IT REAL—Every time I study the Pharisees, I see myself. I *hate* that! But I'm glad God keeps shining the light on me, or I'd never become more like Jesus. Here's what his light revealed to me in this chapter.

• Mark 2:1–12. The Pharisees watched something wonderful occur, but instead of rejoicing, they criticized and nitpicked. *God, I've done that so many times. Help me see past the surface, past the style issues of ministers I don't agree with, to rejoice when good is done—even if it doesn't happen the way I would do it.*

• Mark 2:13–17. *"I have not come to call the righteous, but sinners."* At times I have gotten so involved in church life that I've lost all my relationships with non-Christians. *Help me to go where you would go, Lord.*

• Mark 3:1–6. Like the Pharisees quibbling about how to do good on the Sabbath, then using the day to plot a murder, I have worked up a sinful attitude while arguing about God stuff. For example, I've battled with others over worship music styles. What could be blinder or stupider than fighting about how to worship God? *When I do your work, Lord, help me to do it in your way, with your heart.*

A great way to understand the New Testament better is to *think in chunks, not individual verses.* The New Testament authors did not write in chapters and verses; those were put in centuries later. So try looking for paragraphs and complete thoughts or, in the Gospels and Acts, notice which episodes sit side by side. Not all of Mark is written in chronological order. The writers **juxtaposed** certain stories to make a point. If you ask, "Why is this story grouped with the next story?" you'll notice themes you never saw before. We'll spend more time on this in the chapter on Mark 3:13–35, where Mark pulls off some masterful literary tricks.

POWER TOOL

Think in chunks, not verses.

juxtaposed: placed side by side unexpectedly

Study Questions

1. Why did the Pharisees have a problem with Jesus forgiving the sins of the paralytic (Mark 2:7)?

2. When the Pharisees were first founded, they had wonderful motives. What did they originally intend to do? What went wrong?

3. Why did Jesus eat with crooked, sinful, and outcast people (Mark 2:16–17)?

4. What was the meaning of Jesus' analogies about new cloth on an old garment, and new wine in old wineskins (Mark 2:21–22)?

5. Explain some of the parallels between what Jesus and his disciples were doing in the cornfield and the story he cited about David and Abiathar. What clear implication would first-century hearers draw (Mark 2:23–27; 1 Samuel 21:1–6)?

- Mark 2:1–3:6 includes five stories that show Jesus in conflict with the established religious authorities of his day. Each conflict story features a question.

- *"Why does this fellow talk like that?"* (Mark 2:7). The Pharisees were offended that Jesus claimed to forgive sins. To prove he had the authority to do so, he healed a paralyzed man. (Mark 2:1–12)

- *"Why does he eat with tax collectors and sinners?"* (Mark 2:16). Jesus violated the pharisaical table laws by eating with people who had been excommunicated from the synagogue. He did this because it was an effective way to reach non-religious, non-churched people with the good news of the kingdom of God. (Mark 2:13–17)

- *"How is it that John's disciples and the disciples of the Pharisees are fasting, but yours are not?"* (Mark 2:18). Jesus introduced a way of relating to God that the ancient Jewish customs had not considered and didn't address. Trying to stuff his message into the Temple customs would be like putting new wine in an old wineskin: the new wine would burst the old wineskin. (Mark 2:18–22)

- *"Why are they doing what is unlawful on the Sabbath?"* (Mark 2:24). Jesus' disciples weren't doing anything wrong; the Pharisees merely thought they were. Superficial human traditions that make it harder to do God's true work deserve to be scrapped. (Mark 2:23–28)

- *"Which is lawful on the Sabbath: to do good or to do evil?"* (Mark 3:4). The Pharisees became so hard-hearted about preserving their view of God and their positions in the community that they would rather kill Jesus than admit the truth that they were misguided. (Mark 3:1–6)

- Mark 3:7–12 is a summary statement about Jesus' ministry. Jesus withdrew from his disciples, and a crowd followed him. The crowd was so large Jesus asked the disciples to keep a runaway boat handy. Jesus delivered people from evil spirits.

Part Two

BAFFLING JESUS

REVEREND FUN

"Say what you will . . . I thought it was way cool how Jesus got those demons to leave that poor fella."

Did He Just Say What I Thought He Said?

Mark began his book by introducing Jesus as a man of power and authority whose **unorthodox** teaching and ministry earned the resentment of local religious figures. In the next few chapters Mark shows how almost no one comprehends what Jesus is really up

unorthodox: *not fitting with established doctrine*

to. We'll see Jesus misunderstood by religious leaders sent from Jerusalem, by people in his own hometown, by his own family, and even by his disciples.

Does this discourage Jesus? Most of the time he seems content to let people misunderstand. He has come to spread the kingdom of God, but apparently it's a kingdom of secrets to those unwilling to stretch their preconceived notions. For those willing to follow him even though they don't fully understand, Jesus offers a precious gift; he <u>explains</u> himself.

☞ **GO TO:**

Mark 4:11 (explains)

KEY POINT

Ordinary thinking says, "Show me and I'll believe." Jesus says, "Believe, and I'll show you."

Jesus has come to a religious community that thinks it has a monopoly on the truth. They think they know it all, while outsiders know nothing. Jesus uses every resource at his disposal—stories, healings, even symbolic actions—to undermine their confident ignorance about God. To a world that says, "Show me, then I'll commit," Jesus says, "Commit, then I'll show you."

Mark conveys all this in the rough-and-tumble style we've come to expect, retaining some raw details the other gospel authors omit. He also uses intriguing literary devices that reflect great craftsmanship.

There are plenty of spiritual treats ahead. Will you be one of the outsiders who doesn't care enough to try for the deeper meaning? Or will you be one of the privileged few who commits to Jesus, and thus earns a behind-the-scenes explanation of *"the secret of the kingdom of God"* (Mark 4:11)? Mark practically dares you to press on.

MARK 3:13–35 SHOCKING WORDS OF JESUS, PART ONE

CHAPTER HIGHLIGHTS

- Why Twelve Disciples?
- Your First Mark Sandwich
- What Is the Unforgivable Sin?

Let's Get Started

Every Christian knows there isn't a more accurate account of who Jesus was and what he did than that of the Gospels. As I pointed out earlier, these ancient Middle Eastern writers had a different concept of reporting than we do today.

Mark got his accounts of Jesus from Peter. In essence Mark had an assortment of true stories about Jesus, each standing independently, and like a kid with Legos, he had to decide how to assemble them into a unified whole. Though some parts of the Gospel are in chronological order, such as the events leading up to Jesus' death, other parts are not. In the passages we've already studied, Jesus probably didn't do five consecutive healings, then have five consecutive arguments. Life isn't that tidy. Mark organized his Jesus stories to convey particular messages.

This brings us to the Power Tool for this section: *watch for literary devices*. A "literary device" is a way of arranging written material to bring out extra meaning. Mark uses a number of them. We easily recognize some, such as the <u>flashback</u>, which interrupts the flow of a story to relate something that happened earlier in time. Other literary devices of Mark seem more exotic to us. In Mark 3:13–35 we'll see the first of Mark's **intercalations**.

Now "intercalation" is a fifty-dollar word, which means you got quite a bargain on this book. All it means is that Mark interrupts his story to tell a second story, then returns to the first story—thus making the two stories comment upon one another. Scholars have referred to this as the "Markan sandwich." I like to think

POWER TOOL

Watch for literary devices.

☞ **GO TO:**

Mark 6:17–29 (flashback)

intercalation: *something inserted between existing layers*

Mark would have loved Oreos. Some of his stories have one kind of beginning and ending, with a different kind of creamy center stuck in between.

If this doesn't make sense to you yet, that's okay. You'll get it once we arrive at Mark 3:20–35. For now I hope I've whet your appetite to see what this is all about.

Before we get to Mark's Oreo, he wants to show what happens when a prophet performs a symbolic action. Ready? Here we go!

Papias (c. 60–130 A.D.): Mark, having become the interpreter of Peter, wrote down accurately, though not indeed in order, whatever he remembered of the things said or done by Christ. . . . He was in company with Peter, who used to offer teaching as necessity demanded, but with no intention of giving a connected account of the Lord's discourses. So Mark committed no error in thus writing some single points as he remembered them. For upon one thing he fixed his attention: to leave out nothing of what he had heard and to make no false statements in them.[1]

TWELVE "TO BE WITH HIM"

> **Mark 3:13–15** Jesus went up on a mountainside and called to him those he wanted, and they came to him. He appointed twelve—designating them **apostles**—that they might be with him and that he might send them out to preach and to have authority to drive out demons.

apostles: literally, "sent-out ones" or "messengers"

12 + 1 = Blasphemy?

In Bible times if your occupation was "prophet," you didn't get the great employee benefits we have today. Prophets had no 401(k) plan, no paid vacation, no company chariot. You didn't even get a written job description, but if you *had* had a job description, one of the items on it would have been, "Perform symbolic actions, as instructed by senior management."

Prophets resorted to symbolic actions when words alone could not penetrate the dull consciences of ordinary people. Symbolic actions were things that the prophets did (often purposely weird or offensive) to dramatize God's message. They were intended to startle people, to grab attention, or to create an extra-powerful presentation of God's message. Here's a table that lists just a few of the symbolic actions prophets performed in the Old Testament.

Symbolic Action	Who Did It	What It Symbolized
Take a bunch of arrows and smack them against the ground repeatedly.	King Jehoash (2 Kings 13:18–19)	It symbolized the number of times Israel would defeat her oppressors.
Leave underwear buried under a rock by the river.	Jeremiah (Jeremiah 13:1–11)	As the underwear had been ruined, God would ruin the pride of Judah.
Walk around town wearing an ox's yoke.	Jeremiah (Jeremiah 27:2–11)	Israel should accept being slaves under the "yoke" of the king of Babylon.
Make a model of Jerusalem under siege, then try to look at it through a frying pan.	Ezekiel (Ezekiel 4:1–3)	God would not pay attention to Israel's cries for help when attacked.
Lie on your left side in public for over a year, eating bread baked over cow manure.	Ezekiel (Ezekiel 4:4–5, 9–15)	God would punish 390 years of Israel's sin by cutting off their food supply.

The Jews of Jesus' day thought Jesus was a prophet because, like the prophets of old, some of his actions had symbolic meaning. Mark gives the first example in this passage. *"Jesus went up on a mountainside,"* Mark tells us. This is symbolic already! Why didn't Jesus pick his disciples on the beach, or lounging around the dinner table? Because the Old Testament presents a rich heritage of mountaintops as the location where revelation occurs. Mountaintops figure prominently in the stories of <u>Noah</u>, <u>Abraham,</u> and <u>Moses</u>. Throughout his Gospel Mark locates Jesus on a <u>mountain</u> when something significant happens.

Once he was up on the mountain, what did Jesus do? *"He appointed twelve"* (3:14). Why not nine, or fifteen? Because the coming of the kingdom of God meant that the Jewish exile was over. Israel had *twelve* tribes, but they had not been visible since the Assyrian invasion scattered them in 734 B.C. No Jew would have missed the symbolism of having twelve key followers; Jesus clearly intended to bring Israel back to wholeness.

Significantly, Jesus was not one of the Twelve. The Twelve had been gathered around a person, just as the twelve tribes of Israel camped around the presence of God. Jesus had cast himself as the central figure of the coming restored Israel. Again, no Jew would miss the implication; Jesus saw himself as Messiah.

Modern times have ushered in the odd phenomenon of politicians running for president of the United States without admitting they are running. A potential candidate forms an "exploratory committee." She might launch a fund-raising

☞ **GO TO:**

Genesis 8:4, 20 (Noah)

Genesis 22:2–14 (Abraham)

Exodus 19:1–6 (Moses)

Mark 6:46; 9:2; 13:3 (mountain)

KEY POINT

Jesus chose twelve disciples as a symbol that he would redeem all twelve tribes of Israel.

Something to Ponder

task force. She applies to get her name on the ballot in all fifty states. The charade is so transparent that eventually she appears on *Larry King Live* and admits, "I'm having a press conference next month to announce that I'm running for president." To anyone with a brain, this person is obviously planning to run for president, but officially she is not a candidate.

In Jesus' day the politics were such that Jesus' actions were just as transparent to informed observers. He could tell the demons not to say anything, but they didn't have to; every action of Jesus clearly spoke, "I am the Messiah."

Remember This . . .

What was the main duty of the twelve privileged men invited into Jesus' inner circle? The answer is the same now as it was then: to *"be with him."* Sure, they had other responsibilities, but those all flowed out of their prime duty, spending time in the presence of Jesus. Is that simple or what? Jesus spent a lot of time teaching them, but he also let them watch his example. Following the theory that "more is caught than taught," it did the disciples as much good to be with Jesus as it did to listen to Jesus.

What Others are Saying:

N. T. Wright: For Jesus to give twelve followers a place of prominence . . . indicates pretty clearly that he was thinking in terms of the eschatological restoration of Israel. . . . his choice of twelve (with himself not being *primus inter pares* [first among equals], but actually calling them into being, and in some sense standing over against them) indicates that he believed himself to be the one through whom the true Israel is being reconstituted.[2]

> **Mark 3:16–19** These are the twelve he appointed: Simon (to whom he gave the name Peter); James son of Zebedee and his brother John (to them he gave the name Boanerges, which means Sons of Thunder); Andrew, Philip, Bartholomew, Matthew, Thomas, James son of Alphaeus, Thaddaeus, Simon the Zealot and Judas Iscariot, who betrayed him.

A Motley Crew

Who did Jesus pick as his core advisers? We don't know as much about them as we'd like to. A few of his twelve disciples aren't mentioned in the New Testament other than in the four lists of the twelve disciples!

Webster defines "motley" as "composed of diverse, often incongruous elements." By this definition Jesus drafted a motley crew indeed, as indicated by the chart below (see also GWLC, pages 185–188).

Name	Affiliation
Simon	Jewish fisherman; brother of Andrew. Jesus nicknamed him "petros" (Peter), meaning "rock." Native of Galilee.
James, son of Zebedee	Jewish fisherman; brother of John and a native of Galilee, from the hometown of Bethsaida. Went on to become the first apostolic martyr (Acts 12:2).
John son of Zebedee	Jewish fisherman; brother of James. Jesus nicknamed James and John "Boanerges" ("sons of thunder"). Known as "the disciple Jesus loved," John took Jesus' mother into his home after Jesus died (John 19:24–27).
Andrew	Jewish fisherman; brother of Simon Peter. However, Mark lists Peter, James, and John first because they had the closest relationship with Jesus. Andrew was originally a follower of John the Baptist.
Philip	An old Macedonian name meaning "lover of horses." Philip was another native of Bethsaida (John 1:44) and also a disciple of John the Baptist. Andrew and Philip are almost always mentioned together, and most likely were good friends.
Bartholomew	Not actually a name. Translated, it means "son of plowman" and may have been the last name of Nathanael. This man may have been a farmer, but we don't really know. His name appears nowhere except in lists of the apostles.
Matthew	This tax collector for Rome was also called Levi. His name comes from a Hebrew word meaning "gift." He became the author of the Gospel according to Matthew.
Thomas	Aramaic word for "twin." Thomas is barely mentioned in Mark, but shows up repeatedly in John's Gospel. Though known as "Doubting Thomas" (John 20:24–25), he was a realist who fully committed to Christ (John 11:16).
James, son of Alphaeus	Unknown apart from this list. Since Matthew is called "Levi, son of Alphaeus" in Mark 2:14, James might have been his brother. He is sometimes called "James the younger."
Thaddaeus	We know little about Thaddaeus because his name appears only in the list of twelve apostles. Some manuscripts substitute the name "Lebbaeus." Luke calls him "Judas, son of James," apparently making him Zebedee's grandson. Disciples named Judas often adopted other names to avoid being identified with Jesus' betrayer.
Simon the Zealot	Jewish freedom fighter. The Zealots believed in using violence to end the Jewish exile. Eventually their rebellious efforts caused Rome to crush them in A.D. 70.
Judas Iscariot	Judas was such a common name that further identification would have been needed. "Iscariot" could mean "from the village of Karioth." Initially Judas was trustworthy, because he served as treasurer for the disciples. However, at some point his heart changed (John 12:6). This is the disciple who betrayed Jesus.

This group may include as many as three pairs of brothers and a pair of like-minded friends (Philip and Andrew). It's easy to picture these Galilean natives getting along, but Simon was associated with the Zealots—a group who believed in the violent overthrow of the Roman government. What were his conversations like with Matthew, a former tax collector for the Romans? How did pessimistic Thomas interact with impulsive, big-mouthed Peter? Why did Jesus nickname James and John the "sons of thunder"?

These tantalizing glimpses of the disciples' personalities reveal little. What we know for sure is that Jesus molded these **factious**, mostly uneducated, sometimes rowdy men into saints whose characters reflected his.

factious: *inclined to form self-centered cliques*

What Others are Saying:

Philip Yancey: I would have puzzled over the strange mixture represented by the Twelve. . . . No scholars like Nicodemus or wealthy patrons like Joseph of Arimathea have made it into the Twelve. One must look hard to detect any strong leadership abilities. . . . it is the very ordinariness of the disciples that gives me hope. Jesus does not seem to choose his followers on the basis of native talent or perfectibility or potential for greatness. . . . Three followers in particular (the brothers James and John, and Peter) Jesus singled out for his strongest reprimands—yet two of these would become the most prominent leaders of the early Christians.[3]

YOUR FIRST MARK SANDWICH

> **Mark 3:20–22** Then Jesus entered a house, and again a crowd gathered, so that he and his disciples were not even able to eat. When his family heard about this, they went to take charge of him, for they said, "He is out of his mind."
>
> And the teachers of the law who came down from Jerusalem said, "He is possessed by Beelzebub! By the prince of demons he is driving out demons."

Make Jesus Stop!

Mark forces the reader to consider Jesus' identity by using a sophisticated "sandwiching" technique. He begins an account of Jesus' family deciding to *"take charge of him,"* because they believe Jesus has lost it. Mark suspends this story while describing how some Thought Police from Jerusalem accused Jesus. He returns to the family account a little later (in Mark 3:31). He did this on purpose and intends for us to consider what the family accusation and the scribal accusation have in common.

Both parties intend to get Jesus to stop his work. Jesus' family is merely mistaken, while the teachers from Jerusalem are actively hostile. Nonetheless, if either group succeeded, the ministry of Jesus would end.

Of all the Gospels only Mark has the guts to include the fact that Jesus' earthly family thought he had <u>lost his mind</u>. We don't know how much of Jesus' message they had heard, but it is reasonable to assume they knew a lot about his ministry. They just didn't understand it. In fact, they thought the way he was caught up in his work was unhealthy. When he couldn't even eat because of his mission, the family decided he was out of control. Thinking of the stereotypical Jewish mother ("Eat! Eat!"), you have to chuckle.

We do know, however, that eventually Jesus' <u>mother and brothers</u> believed in him (unfortunately, we don't have any information on what happened to his <u>sisters</u>).

Reporters From Headquarters

"Teachers of the law who came down from Jerusalem" had come all the way to what is probably Capernaum to check out Jesus, proving the impact of his new but popular ministry had extended to the very pinnacle of the Jewish community. These Jewish lawyers came from Jerusalem, so they might have been members of the Sanhedrin. If so, any average Jew would have been intimidated by their presence.

The Sanhedrin, the highest council in both legal and religious affairs for the Jews, may have started with the <u>seventy elders</u> Moses appointed to help him judge legal squabbles. Out of the multiple millions of Jews in Palestine, only seventy-two could join the Sanhedrin at any time. They were considered the brightest, most educated, most devoted men in the Jewish **aristocracy**—the best of the best.

The high priest of the Temple ran the council, giving it all-encompassing authority over Jews. Functionally speaking, the Sanhedrin had the power of Congress, the Supreme Court, and the papacy, combined. Now that's clout! If they didn't like what they saw, and if they so chose, Sanhedrin representa-

☞ **GO TO:**

Mark 3:21
(lost his mind)

Acts 1:14
(mother and
brothers)

Mark 6:3 (sisters)

THE WAYBACK MACHINE

☞ **GO TO:**

Numbers 11:16–25
(seventy elders)

aristocracy: *small, wealthy privileged class*

tives had the authority to declare Capernaum a "seduced city," off-limits to kosher Jews.

Is Jesus intimidated? Yeah, right! Does your golfing scare Tiger Woods?

> **Mark 3:23–27** So Jesus called them and spoke to them in parables: "How can Satan drive out Satan? If a kingdom is divided against itself, that kingdom cannot stand. If a house is divided against itself, that house cannot stand. And if Satan opposes himself and is divided, he cannot stand; his end has come. In fact, no one can enter a strong man's house and carry off his possessions unless he first ties up the strong man. Then he can rob his house."

Jesus Plays Hardball

When the representatives from Jerusalem claim that Jesus casts out demons because he himself is owned by a more powerful demon, Jesus counters by spotlighting the flaws in their logic. How is it possible for Satan to destroy himself? And why would he irrationally try to do himself in? Is the king of evil really responsible for these massive displays of *mercy*?

Jesus then adds a two-sentence parable about a "strong man," full of implications. With the symbolism decoded, Jesus is saying Satan is like a strong man who has dominated Israel to the extent that Israel is practically Satan's house. Jesus is not an ally of this strong man. In fact, Jesus is a *stronger* man who ties up the strong man and plunders the plunderer—stealing back what the strong man should never have had in the first place. When did Jesus tie up Satan? Probably in the desert, right after his baptism. From then on, with every exorcism, every healing, Jesus is grabbing a treasure—a human life—and returning it to God.

Jesus' brief analogy would remind any first-century Jew schooled in Scripture of Isaiah 49:24–25. Take a second to check it out! And while most Jews would have missed the reference, Jesus may also have been drawing from Isaiah 53:11–12, so look there too. You'll see the know-it-alls again had missed descriptions that should have convinced them Jesus was doing exactly what the Messiah was supposed to do.

KEY POINT

Jesus overpowers Satan.

☞ **GO TO:**

Mark 1:12–13 (desert)

Dean Merrill: After talking frankly about all the false prophets in the world, "the spirit of antichrist," and other dangers of his time, [John] rebounds with this ringing declaration: "You, dear children, are from God and have overcome them, because the one who is in you is greater than the one who is in the world" (1 John 4:4). Do we truly believe this? Are we convinced that our Lord is fundamentally stronger than the devil and his followers? If so, then why all the dismay?[4]

> **Mark 3:28–30** "I tell you the truth, all the sins and blasphemies of men will be forgiven them. But whoever blasphemes against the Holy Spirit will never be forgiven; he is guilty of an eternal sin."
>
> He said this because they were saying, "He has an evil spirit."

Have You Committed The Unforgivable Sin?

Even Jesus' fiercest opponents never questioned the authenticity of his miracles and healings. This powerfully confirms Jesus' ministry. Not even those strongly motivated to discredit him said, "That woman wasn't really healed!" or "You didn't really drive a demon out of him!" They couldn't. They knew Jesus' miracles were real. They were reduced to weak arguments like, "Okay, you're powerful, but the source of your power must be bad."

If you had seen Jesus do the things described in these first few chapters of Mark, what would you have thought of him? Judging from the size of the crowds, the average person believed in his power right on the spot. Even a neutral cynic would have to say, "I don't know what's going on, but this deserves a closer look." These are reasonable responses. The teachers from Jerusalem, however, went to a hostile extreme by "demonizing" Jesus, so Jesus warned them to stay away from the unforgivable sin—blasphemy against the Holy Spirit.

What is this blasphemy against the Holy Spirit? The context helps define it. Israel's religious leaders had seen Jesus do things that puzzled and alarmed them. Jesus had reasoned with them from their own Scriptures and demonstrated in holy power that he was from God. They responded by looking at the Holy Spirit's good fruit and declaring it evil. The point is, *they knew better.* Instead of seeking truth, their resistance to Jesus grew in proportion to his popularity. They weren't merely mistaken about Jesus. They were clinging to their own pride so defiantly that if being

paradox: self-
contradictory statement

"right" meant they had to call God evil, and call evil good, they would.

Jesus' declaration creates a **paradox**. He begins by saying all sins and blasphemies can be forgiven. Then he says the blasphemy of the Spirit can't be forgiven. How can both be true? Simple. Forgiveness of sin comes from no one but God. If you declare that you're not the problem, that God is, that *he's* the evil one . . . where else will you go to get forgiveness?

Rejecting Jesus out of ignorance is fixable; you can be educated. Sinning because you're weak is fixable; you can be encouraged and strengthened. But if you purposely make yourself blind and deaf to the only source of salvation, what can be done? You have cut yourself off from God, so it is not God who makes blasphemy against the Holy Spirit unforgivable. The person who refuses to admit their need for forgiveness makes it unforgivable.

KEEP IT REAL—This sin is not a single action, but a long-term attitude—a continual state of having contempt for the Spirit's work. I've dealt with many young believers who fear they have committed this sin and feel haunted by guilt. They tremble to think they've crossed some line, and God will never let them into heaven now. If you are capable of those feelings at all, it proves you have not committed the unforgivable sin. Those who are committing it don't give one flying flip about what God thinks of them; they're too busy passing judgment on God. So, if you have any concern that you may have called some unusual work of the Holy Spirit satanic, return to Jesus' initial statement: *"all the sins and blasphemies of men will be forgiven them"* (Mark 3:28). Sincerely apologize to God, receive his forgiveness, and move on.

IT'S
GREEK
TO ME

Jesus does not say definitively that these teachers have committed the blasphemy against the Holy Spirit. He solemnly warns them. The phrase *"I tell you the truth"* is unique to Jesus, and in the Greek has the curious appearance of Jesus saying "Amen" to his own statements. This phrase functions like the Old Testament phrase, "Thus saith the LORD," making this a very serious caution indeed. These teachers of the law are dangerously close to committing the unforgivable sin, but they still have time to repent.

What Others
are Saying:

Charles Spurgeon: Satan often comes and says, "You are no Christian; all your supposed Christian experience is false." Very well, suppose it has been false; then I will start afresh; saint or no saint, I will begin over again by trusting Christ to be my Saviour.[5]

> **Mark 3:31–35** Then Jesus' mother and brothers arrived. Standing outside, they sent someone in to call him. A crowd was sitting around him, and they told him, "Your mother and brothers are outside looking for you."
>
> "Who are my mother and my brothers?" he asked.
>
> Then he looked at those seated in a circle around him and said, "Here are my mother and my brothers! Whoever does God's will is my brother and sister and mother."

Redefining Family

By the time Jesus' mother and brothers arrive to take charge of him, he is lecturing a crowd. Did the siblings really think Jesus would cut off a public presentation just because they showed up? Perhaps.

Our modern culture values freedom of the individual above all else. We're taught family and responsibility come after independence. Not so for first-century Middle Easterners. Know why there are so many "**begats**" in the Bible? Because to these folks your family was the basis of social and economic life—the source of your identity. Three or four generations lived in one house together. If you did well, it reflected on your family. If you did poorly, you besmirched the family name. That's why the embarrassed family of Jesus felt they'd better get him under control. It's also why Jesus' response would have been impossibly shocking in the first century. Even by today's standards it's slightly rude. Back then, it was outrageous.

Why wouldn't Jesus meet with his relatives? As usual Jesus had an entirely different agenda than that of everyone else. He was there to found a spiritual kingdom. Those who joined him in radical obedience to God could share intimacy with him. Those who tried to prevent his mission could never be as close to him as his followers.

Who did he see when he looked around that circle? Most likely, the Twelve. But suddenly he throws the door wide open with one profound, powerful word: *"whoever."* That word should make you rejoice. If you and I are willing to obey God, Jesus will be our brother. All of us can join his family. It may cost us everything, but we have a place. We <u>belong</u>.

☞ **GO TO:**

Genesis 10; Matthew 1:1–17 (begats)

begats: *King James era word meaning "gave birth to"*

☞ **GO TO:**

Psalm 27:10 (belong)

Max Lucado: One of the sweetest reasons God saved you is because he is fond of you. He likes having you around. . . . If God had a refrigerator, your picture would be on it. If he had a wallet, your photo would be in it. He sends you flowers every spring and a sunrise every morning. Whenever you want to talk, he'll listen. He can live anywhere in the universe, and he chose your heart. . . . Face it, friend. He's crazy about you.[6]

Cleaning Up Mark's Crumbs

So what do you think of Mark's first sandwich? Do you see why Mark stuck the "blasphemy" story in the middle of the "family" story? Let me try to sharpen the point for you.

Jesus is bringing the kingdom of God to Israel. Look up Mark 8:33, and you'll see very clearly how Jesus views anything and anyone who tries to stop his mission. Anything that resists the kingdom of God is, by definition, fighting for another kingdom. The only other kingdom is Satan's kingdom. There is no neutral ground.

The slanderous scribes intentionally attacked Jesus, but his concerned family was simply misguided, thinking him mad. When Mark sandwiches the stories together, it tells us that whether you're hostile or merely mistaken, if you're trying to control, block, or stop Jesus, you're working for Satan and against God.

KEEP IT REAL—Mark shows Jesus being misunderstood by friend and foe alike. But there were a few places where Jesus' message came through to me loud and clear!

• Mark 3:14. The number one job of a disciple is to be with Jesus. How could I forget such a simple, foundational concept? Yet I do. So often I've run all around town "doing God's work" without leaving any time for prayer, reflection, and simply spending time in God's presence. *Jesus, help me make "being with you" my top priority.*

• Mark 3:13–19. Jesus made apostles out of many different personality types, from men who had no notable accomplishments. *When I fear that I won't fit in with the Christian community or that I haven't done anything impressive enough, Lord, remind me that being a Christian is not about how good I am at following, but about how good you are at leading.*

Study Questions

1. Define what a symbolic action is, and cite as many examples of them from the Bible as you can.
2. Why did Jesus choose twelve disciples? What was their special designation, and what did it mean (Mark 3:14)?

3. What were the three main duties of an apostle (Mark 3:14–15)?
4. What is an intercalation? Why is it important?
5. Based on Mark's context, what does "blasphemy against the Holy Spirit" appear to be (Mark 3:22–30)?

CHAPTER WRAP-UP

- Mark did not record all of Jesus' life in chronological order. Knowing that, we can understand Mark's message better by paying attention to his *literary devices,* or, how he has arranged his material.

- Prophets of Jehovah often acted out his word, in addition to proclaiming it. Jesus probably chose twelve disciples as a symbolic act, showing he would redeem all of Israel, and that he was as central to Israel's hopes as God's presence was to the Jews of the Exodus. (Mark 3:13–19)

- The apostles were a diverse bunch with little to recommend them, yet Jesus molded them into men who reflected his character. That means he can do the same for you and me.

- Mark intentionally grouped together the story of Jesus' family thinking he was out of his mind, and the story of Jerusalem lawyers accusing Jesus of being possessed by the prince of demons. Combined, the stories indicate that anyone trying to stop or control Jesus, regardless of their motive, is working against God. (Mark 3:20–35)

- If you are worried that you may have committed the unforgivable "blasphemy against the Holy Spirit," the very fact that you care proves you have not committed it. (Mark 3:28–29)

MARK 4:1–34
SHOCKING WORDS OF JESUS, PART TWO

Let's Get Started

Suppose that in a freak accident involving your PlayStation2, your remote channel changer, the Clapper, and a lightning bolt, you have been zapped through a worm hole that transported you back in time and relocated you on the island featured in the first season of the TV show, *Survivor*. That show, however, is now centuries in your future. Uppermost on your mind are the primitive warriors eyeing you warily from the jungle.

As it turns out, these friendly tribesmen don't want to eat you. Oddly, they like you! In fact, with one look at your jacket and its incredibly awesome futuristic technology called "a zipper," they become obsessed with knowing *everything* about your world. As day fades into day, they constantly badger you to tell them more of your fantastic kingdom.

Here's the problem. You know about things like electricity, pizza, digital cable television, megachurches, the Internet, leveraged indexed mutual funds, and NASCAR. They know about things like dirt, the sky, water, huts, and rats. How will you bridge the gap? How will you ever get them to understand why it's cool the government has an executive branch, a judiciary branch, and a legislative branch? Heck, in a society that has seen no food except fish, grubs, snakes, and rats, how will you explain something as simple as a burrito?

Jesus found himself in a similar situation. He was the only person on the whole planet who knew, *really knew*, what the king-

KEY POINT

Jesus had the challenging task of communicating to his followers the ins and outs of a world that was completely alien to their own.

parables: truth expressed in tales

What Others are Saying:

POWER TOOL

Use Scripture to interpret Scripture.

dom of God is like. Worse, the people he talked to were under the *false* impression that they knew what the kingdom of God was like.

He bridged the gap by doing the same thing that eventually you would have resorted to on *Survivor.* He told stories—stories that said, "Here's something you do know about. OK? Now, my kingdom is like that thing in this one way. Get it? No? OK, here's something else you're familiar with. My kingdom is like that thing in this particular way. Get it? All right, then let's keep trying. . . ."

More than any of the gospel writers, Mark focuses on Jesus as a man of action. So much so that he often mentions *that* Jesus taught without telling us *what* Jesus taught. In this next chapter, however, Mark strings together several of Jesus' teaching stories, known as **parables**. The word derives from the Greek *parabole*, which means "putting things side by side." Each parable tries to convey what the kingdom of God is like.

C. H. Dodd: At its simplest the parable is a metaphor or simile drawn from nature or common life, arresting the hearer by its vividness or strangeness, and leaving the mind in sufficient doubt about its precise application to tease it into active thought.[1]

STORYTELLER JESUS

Look out! Dodge! *Watch it!* . . . Okay. You can breathe easy now. Whenever the subject of Jesus' parables comes up, the scholars scamper in all directions, and I was afraid you'd get trampled. But the room has cleared now, leaving just you and me. Can we talk?

People have gone hog wild imposing their own views on the parables. Once you get into symbolism, interpreters let their imaginations shift into sixteen-valve overdrive. So let me suggest some guidelines that will keep our interpretations sane. First, let me remind you of the Golden Rule of Interpretation, expressed earlier: find out what the passage meant for the first audience. With any parable it's especially helpful to remember that it couldn't mean now what it never meant before.

My second interpretive guideline is also the Power Tool for Mark 4:1–34: *use Scripture to interpret scriptural symbols.* Here's an example of what I mean. For many centuries Western culture has used the human skull as a symbol for poison or death. Because of those centuries of tradition, a writer is unlikely to use a skull to symbolize happiness and cheer. Scripture works the same way. If the Bible uses "sheep" as a symbol for God's people over and over, you wouldn't assume that in one story "sheep" refers to demons, right? When you encounter an unfamiliar symbol, see how else that symbol has been used in Scripture. Many times, the Bible is its own best commentary.

Oh, and here's a word of caution. Don't press the parables. Most of Jesus' parables made only one major point. An elaborate parable, such as the Prodigal Son, may have two or three main themes. Usually the details of a parable are not symbols in themselves; they merely create a setting so the story can exist. Don't bother looking at a parable like the Prodigal Son and asking, "What does the distant country represent? What does the famine stand for? What do the pigs mean? Is America the fatted calf?" We're on safer ground when we stick to the bigger picture.

With those guidelines in mind, let's tackle a parable that Jesus seemed to think was pretty simple.

☞ **GO TO:**

Luke 15:11–32
(Prodigal Son)

> **Mark 4:1–9** Again Jesus began to teach by the lake. The crowd that gathered around him was so large that he got into a boat and sat in it out on the lake, while all the people were along the shore at the water's edge. He taught them many things by parables, and in his teaching said: "Listen! A farmer went out to sow his seed. As he was scattering the seed, some fell along the path, and the birds came and ate it up. Some fell on rocky places, where it did not have much soil. It sprang up quickly, because the soil was shallow. But when the sun came up, the plants were scorched, and they withered because they had no root. Other seed fell among thorns, which grew up and choked the plants, so that they did not bear grain. Still other seed fell on good soil. It came up, grew and produced a crop, multiplying thirty, sixty, or even a hundred times."
>
> Then Jesus said, "He who has ears to hear, let him hear."

A Very Dirty Parable

What kind of sloppy farmer is this, anyway? He's tossing valuable seed *every*where: On the path. On the rocks. In the thorns. Upstairs. Downstairs. Friends don't let friends drink and sow.

Actually, to think the farmer was sloppy is to misapply modern sensibilities to an ancient story. The broadcasting of seed Jesus describes was perfectly typical in his place and time. Palestinian farmers scattered the seed first, *then* plowed it under along with the thorns, the weeds, and everything else in the field. The ordinary Jewish farmer had little land to work with; he was not about to let a single inch go unused if it could produce part of a cash crop.

> **Mark 4:10–12** When he was alone, the Twelve and the others around him asked him about the parables. He told them, "The secret of the kingdom of God has been given to you. But to those on the outside everything is said in parables so that,
> "'they may be ever seeing but never perceiving,
> and ever hearing but never understanding;
> otherwise they might turn and be forgiven!'"

KEY POINT

Jesus used parables to separate the idly curious from the true seekers.

Your Discipleship Benefits Package

In verse 13 Jesus will explain the sower parable, but oddly placed between the parable and its explanation is this intercalation, which divides the world into two teams—the disciples, and *"those on the outside."* The disciples get a wonderful employee benefit—*"the secret of the kingdom of God."* What do outsiders get? Parables, used here almost to mean riddles. No one is eager to tackle this strange passage because in it Jesus seems to be purposely **obscuring** his message to prevent people from believing.

☞ **GO TO:**

Mark 4:11
(outside, secret)

Mark 4:2, 33; 12:12
(understand)

obscuring: *concealing; making vague*

Frankly, it's a sticky passage, but I'm comforted by a couple of thoughts. First, all of Jesus' miracles and healings were public displays of his power. Clearly he wanted people to believe, or he wouldn't have bothered with a public ministry. Second, many people *did* understand the parables.

Here's another important point. To whom does Jesus explain the parables? Just his twelve favorite guys, right? Wrong. *"When he was alone, the Twelve and the others around him asked him about the parables"* (emphasis mine). This was not an exclusive circle. If you had walked up to listen to his explanations, he wouldn't have stopped and said, "Hang on, Twelve. You! Yeah, you with the big nose! This is private. Beat it!" If you wanted a promotion from outsider to insider, all you had to do was gather around.

Really, two words in 4:12 provide the only sticky point, "*so that.*" These are the words that make it sound like Jesus used parables purposely to confuse people. In Jewish thought, however, those words could indicate a purpose ("I *want* you to miss God's kingdom") or a result ("*and so* they missed God's kingdom"). Jesus quotes Isaiah 6:9, where God was explaining to Isaiah that the people would never believe even though Isaiah preached faithfully. The bad results were because of the unfaith of the people, not because of God's will.

Mark has presented the outsiders as hostile, reviling Jesus and his message. Mark does not portray the insiders as wiser than the outsiders—merely less hostile, more interested. Insiders couldn't understand the parables either, until Jesus explained them. The insiders' only virtue was they sought Jesus out.

The parables worked like the cloud that separated the <u>fleeing Israelites</u> from the pursuing Egyptians. This cloud, which was the presence of God, brought "*darkness to the one side and light to the other.*" The parables, which were the word of God, had the same result. Stories that blinded the hard-hearted, tantalized the soft-hearted and lured them into Jesus' circle.

IT'S GREEK TO ME

☞ GO TO:

Exodus 14:20
(fleeing Israelites)

What Others are Saying:

N. T. Wright: Jesus was articulating a new way of understanding the fulfillment of Israel's hope. He had radicalized the tradition. This . . . is how stories work. They invite listeners into a new world, and encourage them to make that world their own, to see their ordinary world from now on through this lens, within this grid. The struggle to understand a parable is the struggle for a new world to be born.[2]

David E. Garland: There is good news in the misunderstanding of the disciples. If we fail to comprehend perfectly all of the mystery, neither do these first disciples, and Jesus does not discard them for a more insightful lot.[3]

> **Mark 4:13–20** Then Jesus said to them, "Don't you understand this parable? How then will you understand any parable? The farmer sows the word. Some people are like seed along the path, where the word is sown. As soon as they hear it, Satan comes and takes away the word that was sown in them. Others, like seed sown

> on rocky places, hear the word and at once receive it with joy. But since they have no root, they last only a short time. When trouble or persecution comes because of the word, they quickly fall away. Still others, like seed sown among thorns, hear the word; but the worries of this life, the deceitfulness of wealth and the desires for other things come in and choke the word, making it unfruitful. Others, like seed sown on good soil, hear the word, accept it, and produce a crop—thirty, sixty or even a hundred times what was sown."

A Parable Unpacked

Every sermon I've heard on this passage asserts, "The 'word.' You know . . . the Gospel!" But that's not what "the word" would have meant to the disciples. Jesus had not died and risen at this point, so technically there was no Gospel in the sense we use today. To properly interpret *"the word,"* we need to stay in Mark's context.

"The word" was probably shorthand for Jesus' message that the kingdom of God had begun. If so, the point of this story is that the Jews should not expect God's reign to begin with one apocalyptic blast. As mentioned in the chapter on Mark 1:14–45, the idea that *"the day of the Lord"* would come in two installments was Jesus' innovation. Jesus may have told this story to let his listeners know what to expect. Jesus is the farmer; *"the word"* is his message that the kingdom of God has begun; and the good news is that, despite a slow start and lots of obstacles, the kingdom of God will arrive (but not in the way the ordinary Jew expected).

Does this interpretation make sense to you? Before you answer, you might check <u>another parable</u> of Jesus that could make this one clearer.

Jesus' comments indicate we're closer to his meaning when we meditate on how the seed revealed the quality of the soils, and on the fact that fruitfulness is clearly an indicator of God's reign. Those thoughts will also aid us in interpreting other parables in this chapter.

Perhaps you disagree with my interpretation. If so, I'm delighted! It means you are actively thinking about and interacting with Mark's text. That is not only the main goal of this book; as we're about to see, it's also the reaction Jesus intended his parables to provoke.

☞ **GO TO:**

Mark 12:1–12
(another parable)

Philip Yancey: The kingdom of heaven is like a farmer going out to sow his seed. As every farmer knows, not all the seed you plant ends up yielding crops. Some falls among rocks, some gets eaten by birds and field mice, some gets crowded out by weeds. All this seems natural to a farmer, but heretical to a traditional kingdom-builder. Are not kings judged by their power, their ability to impose their will on a populace, their strength in repelling enemies? Jesus was indicating that the kingdom of God comes with a resistible power. It is humble and **unobtrusive** and coexistent with evil—a message that surely did not please patriotic Jews intent on revolt.[4]

unobtrusive: *inconspicuous; not blatant or aggressive*

> **Mark 4:21–23** He said to them, "Do you bring in a lamp to put it under a bowl or a bed? Instead, don't you put it on its stand? For whatever is hidden is meant to be disclosed, and whatever is concealed is meant to be brought out into the open. If anyone has ears to hear, let him hear."

Disguised, Disclosed, Discovered

As with many of the parables, you can read sixteen commentaries on this passage and discover sixteen different opinions. Perhaps Jesus anticipated this; perhaps this is why he repeats the phrase, *"If anyone has ears to hear, let him hear,"* already stated <u>before</u> in this chapter. In his dynamic translation *The Message*, Eugene Peterson translates the phrase, *"Are you listening? Really listening?"*

☞ **GO TO:**

Mark 4:9 (before)

So that it reads easily, the NIV has written the phrase, *"Do you bring in a lamp? . . . "* However, even scholars who differ on how to interpret this short parable agree that the literal Greek forms this odd question: "Does *the lamp come* for the purpose of being placed under the measure? . . . Does it not *come* for the purpose of being placed on the lampstand?" This language narrows the interpretive possibilities, for it makes the lamp appear to have a will of its own—almost as though the lamp is a person.

Is "lamp" ever used in the Bible as a symbol for a person? Sure is; try 2 Samuel 21:17 and 1 Kings 11:36; 15:4. These verses call King David the lamp of Israel, then refer to his descendants using the same term. The Messiah was a de-

IT'S GREEK TO ME

☞ **GO TO:**

John 8:12; 9:5; 12:46
(himself)

scendant of David. Add all this up and Jesus might be speaking of <u>himself</u> in this parable. If so, the parable refers to how the Messiah's presence is a secret.

The word translated "bed" here actually refers to one of the couches that first-century Palestinians reclined on while eating their meals. Jesus seems to be saying *"the lamp of Israel"* has come, but so far has been shoved under the couch—a senseless move, since he is *"meant to be disclosed."* Yet after his death and resurrection, Jesus (and God's full plan) will be *"brought out into the open."*

> **Mark 4:24–25** "Consider carefully what you hear," he continued. "With the measure you use, it will be measured to you—and even more. Whoever has will be given more; whoever does not have, even what he has will be taken from him."

I'm So Broke I Can't Even Pay Attention

Jesus immediately follows Mark 4:21–23 with a caution that says, in very sober tones, *pay attention*; the amount of interest you give God is the amount of interest he'll give you. To express this, he uses the **metaphor** of a measure.

metaphor: symbol

His audience had never once seen a prepackaged retail item. When they went to the market for staples, such as grain or flour, the merchants measured out the requested amount from a large supply. If you asked for four measures of grain, the merchant could weigh out four scant measures. Or, if the merchant liked you, he could weigh out four measures, with each one shaken down, pressed together, and running over. (The only modern equivalent I can think of is when we order popcorn at the movies.)

Jesus is saying that if you love God enough to consider the parables diligently, God will reward you by revealing himself. If you take one glance at Jesus and casually dismiss him as a bumpkin telling pointless stories, you will find yourself equally dismissed by God. If the A-for-effort students persist in pursuing God, God will give even *more* understanding. In contrast, the Jew who ignores Jesus will find that even the little bit he already knew about God's kingdom and the coming Messiah will turn out to be incorrect: *"even what he has will be taken from him."*

Billy Graham: In every phase of life we face this recurring question: "What think ye of Christ?" In youth, too happy to think—I've plenty of time. In manhood, too busy to think—I must make a living. In maturity, too anxious to think—I've more urgent problems. Declining years, too old to think—my pattern of life is set. . . . Death, too late to think—the spirit is flown, the day of opportunity is past, the harvest is gone, and now God's Judgment Day.[5]

> **Mark 4:26–29** He also said, "This is what the kingdom of God is like. A man scatters seed on the ground. Night and day, whether he sleeps or gets up, the seed sprouts and grows, though he does not know how. All by itself the soil produces grain—first the stalk, then the head, then the full kernel in the head. As soon as the grain is ripe, he puts the **sickle** to it, because the harvest has come."

sickle: curved blade with
a short handle

Knock That Crop Off

Of the four gospel writers, only Mark preserved this parable. It features one unusual word, prominent because of its rarity in the Bible. The literal Greek word is *automatos*, from which we derive the word *automatic*. The NIV translates the phrase as *"all by itself."* The seed in this parable grows spontaneously; we might call this passage the Parable of the Automatic Crop.

Two key thoughts make this a simple parable to interpret. First, Jesus has already told us that sometimes he uses "seed" to symbolize *"the word"* (Mark 4:14). Second, the final phrases of the parable, *"he puts the sickle to it, because the harvest has come,"* echo an Old Testament prophecy about the <u>judgment day</u> of God (see GWPB, pages 113–118). This means the parable most likely indicates how God's kingdom will look or act between when it is first announced and when judgment day arrives.

How does this "seed" grow into a harvestable crop? Mysteriously. Gradually. It follows its own rules, which the sower of the word does not fully know. There are definite stages to its maturing (*"first the stalk, then the head, then the full kernel in the head"*), none of which can be skipped. The story concludes with the distinct impression that at the moment the crop reaches its peak ripeness, the harvest will occur.

When we remember that many Jews of the time thought they

☞ **GO TO:**

Joel 3:13
(judgment day)

KEY POINT

Our job is to plant the seed—to spread God's word. God will take care of the rest.

could initiate God's reign by overthrowing Rome and establishing a Jewish police state in Palestine, the point of the parable becomes clear. It says God has a different agenda and a different time table than his people realize. The person who is patient and willing to let God's kingdom come in its own way will be in harmony with God. The person who tries to hasten God's kingdom by following human methods will get the same thing as a farmer who digs up his crop to see if the roots are healthy—nothing.

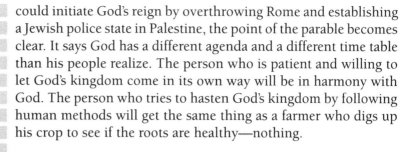

What Others are Saying:

N. T. Wright: [Jesus] would be the means of Israel's God returning to Zion. He was, in short, announcing the kingdom of God—not the simple revolutionary message of the hard-liners but the doubly revolutionary message of a kingdom that would overturn all other agendas, including the revolutionary one.[6]

> **Mark 4:30–32** Again he said, "What shall we say the kingdom of God is like, or what parable shall we use to describe it? It is like a mustard seed, which is the smallest seed you plant in the ground. Yet when planted, it grows and becomes the largest of all garden plants, with such big branches that the birds of the air can perch in its shade."

The Little Kingdom That Could

In the final parable Mark selected for this series, Jesus compares the reign of God to a tiny seed that grows into a startlingly big bush. *"The seed"* seems to be *"the word,"* so the picture is one of Jesus bringing the kingdom of God to earth by his teaching and preaching. One man and his handful of middle-class followers does not seem like much of a kingdom; yet Jesus predicts that when this "seed" has had a chance to grow, it will become rrrrrilly big.

Have you ever seen a mustard seed? It makes a watermelon seed look like an elephant. A mustard seed looks like a grain of sand. When you pick one up, you almost need a magnifying glass to be sure you're holding it. The mustard bush, however, can grow as tall as twelve feet—about twice the height of a man. Even the natives of Galilee who had seen mustard plants all their lives would remain impressed with the contrast between the size of the seed and the size of the shrub, just as those of us in the Pacific Northwest never grow dull to the difference between the size of a pinecone and the size of our towering pines. Jesus is telling his audience, "This kingdom is starting off small, but it will become miraculously huge."

What do we make of the birds in this short parable? As modern Americans (perhaps over-influenced by Disney cartoons like *Bambi*) we read of the birds finding shelter and sigh, "Awww, how sweet." Now I don't want to intrude on any *Bambi* moment you might be having, but Jesus' audience probably didn't hear it that way. If we look at how birds are used as a symbol elsewhere in Scripture, we discover they usually indicate bad news. You get a long list of birds <u>eating</u> the bodies of dead people, birds of prey <u>trying to steal</u> animal sacrifices meant for God, birds offered <u>as sacrifices</u> for sin, birds as a dream <u>symbol of death</u>, and birds as the <u>dimwitted prey</u> of evil. The prophets Ezekiel and Daniel add one more symbolic meaning for birds; <u>birds equal non-Jews</u>, or Gentiles.

Could Jesus be hinting to his disciples that the kingdom of God will grow large enough to incorporate non-Jews? Jesus has told each parable in this chapter to describe the kingdom of God and to readjust Jewish expectations, so it makes sense he would drop such a hint, but we don't know for certain. Don't let my speculation distract you from the main point; when Jesus announced the kingdom of God, it didn't look like much. Now it does, and it still has not completely arrived. How spectacular Jesus' kingdom will be when it is fully present!

☞ **GO TO:**

Deuteronomy 28:26; 1 Samuel 17:46 (eating)

Genesis 15:11 (trying to steal)

Leviticus 1:14; 14:4 (as sacrifices)

Genesis 40:17–19 (symbol of death)

Ecclesiastes 9:12; Jeremiah 5:26–27 (dimwitted prey)

Ezekiel 17:22–24; 31:6; Daniel 4:12 (birds equal non-Jews)

HOW TO JOIN THE INSIDERS' CLUB

> **Mark 4:33–34** With many similar parables Jesus spoke the word to them, as much as they could understand. He did not say anything to them without using a parable. But when he was alone with his own disciples, he explained everything.

All-Access Backstage Pass

When I was a movie and music reviewer during the 1980s, I sure loved getting free tickets. Whether it was a fourth-row seat to a hot band's concert, entry to a prerelease screening of a new movie, or a chair with the press corps at the Grammies, I always felt elite when getting in free.

But there was something even better than a free ticket—a backstage pass. Backstage, past the beefy bouncers, away from the glare of the stage lights, you get something the crowds don't—a sense of the real person behind the performer. Almost every celebrity I met seemed different in person than they did on screen, whether smarter, younger, smaller, or larger. Many of them had intentionally developed a public **persona** that was different from their private person.

persona: an individual's social facade

Jesus did the same thing. To the crowds—laced with the curious, the skeptics, the non-Jews, and the faultfinders—Jesus presented only certain aspects of himself. In private the disciples had the unspeakable privilege of seeing all of Jesus, intimately and at length. In the near future they would endure trauma, religious expulsion, whippings, and slander, all because they had been with Jesus. But no disciple ever concluded the hard times were not worth it.

Do you want to know more of Jesus? All you have to do is keep reading. Mark is about to show us mightier miracles than ever.

What Others are Saying:

A. W. Tozer: To have found God and still to pursue Him is the soul's paradox of love, scorned indeed by the too-easily-satisfied religionist, but justified in happy experience by the children of the burning heart. . . . Come near to the holy men and women of the past and you will soon feel the heat of their desire after God. They mourned for Him, they prayed and wrestled and sought for Him day and night, in season and out, and when they had found Him the finding was all the sweeter for the long seeking.[7]

KEEP IT REAL—By Mark's definition, am I an insider or an outsider? Certainly Jesus has not explained everything to me, but maybe I'll gain insight if I listen to the voice of his Spirit telling me thoughts such as these:

• Mark 4:1–20. When the seed of God's word lands in my heart, what kind of soil does it land in? I have followed Jesus enough years to prove my heart is not the shallow soil, nor the rocky soil, but the thorny soil is the kind where *"the worries of this life, the deceitfulness of wealth and the desires for other things come in and choke the word."* I could become that soil at any time, unless I'm diligent. *Lord, keep me fruitful for you.*

• Mark 4:11. Followers of Jesus get tons of benefits in the world to come, but in this world the primary benefit is getting to spend time with the Savior. *Lord, do I value your words enough? Have I made the effort to leave the crowd, to sit and listen to you closely?*

Study Questions

1. What was the main thing Jesus tried to describe in the parables of Mark 4 (Mark 4:11, 26, 30)?
2. Name the three guidelines I suggest for interpreting parables. Do you agree or disagree with them, and to what extent?
3. What is the probable meaning of *"the word"* (Mark 4:14)?
4. What are two possible meanings of *"the lamp"* (Mark 4:21–23)?
5. What did the man do to make the crop grow in Mark 4:26–29?

CHAPTER WRAP-UP

- Jesus used parables to describe the kingdom of God, partly to shake up the people who thought they knew what the kingdom of God was like. Most parables make one or two main points. Don't try to turn every story detail into a spiritual symbol.

- The Parable of the Four Soils showed that the reign of God would arrive in an unexpected and resistible fashion, not as an apocalyptic blast. (Mark 4:1–20)

- The Parable of the Lamp could refer to Jesus himself, or to his message. Either way, "the lamp" arrived in secret, but would soon be known to everyone. Jesus added that even if the meaning behind his preaching was hard to understand, people who took the time to puzzle it out would be rewarded. (Mark 4:21–25)

- The Parable of the Automatic Crop showed that God would bring about his reign in his own timing, using his own mysterious methods. All humans can do is scatter seed—that is, preach the message of God. He'll bring judgment at the right time. (Mark 4:26–29)

- The Parable of the Mustard Seed illustrated that God planned to make a great kingdom out of humble beginnings. It might also have implied that Gentiles would find rest in his kingdom. (Mark 4:30–32)

- Jesus allowed his preaching to confuse the crowds—not to prevent them from believing, but to see who wanted truth strongly enough to seek him out and ask for more explanation (Mark 4:10–12). Jesus explained more to those who gathered around in private, and explained everything to those who committed to follow him. (Mark 4:33–34)

MARK 4:35–5:20
POWER-RANGER JESUS

CHAPTER HIGHLIGHTS

- Jesus Muzzles the Sea
- Jesus Heals a Madman
- That Secret Identity Thing Again

Let's Get Started

Need your garage rearranged for maximum efficiency? Want your closet systematized, maybe with clothes coordinated by color theme? Too bad Mark's no longer around to help you. He's obviously quite the organizer. We've seen how he arranged Peter's eyewitness accounts of Jesus into five snapshots of power, several consecutive conflict stories, and a thoughtful selection of parables.

The parables served as a gateway to greater intimacy with Jesus. If you didn't care enough about him to try to decipher the stories, or to check with him for the answers, you were an outsider. As a counterpoint to this veiled aspect of Jesus, Mark now presents several stories of Jesus pulling off bold miracles.

In Mark's account so far, we've already seen Jesus as a man of power who reached out to the outcasts. But now, like the first-century forerunner of **Spinal Tap**, Mark turns the volume to eleven. In these miracle stories, Jesus triumphs successively over challenges from nature, demons, disease, and death—just about every major threat of the first-century world. The people Jesus reaches next are *extreme* outcasts, each driven by desperation. His power is *beyond* human—the power of God himself.

Typical of Mark's style, ironies abound. What results from Jesus' repeated displays of breathtaking power and compassion? The disciples still don't know who he really is. As we'll see later, the people of Jesus' own hometown write him off as a conceited weirdo.

In the next few passages you'll see the disciples ask each other in alarm, "Who is this?" Mark leaves the question intriguingly unanswered. Or does he? You'll have to read on and decide for yourself.

Spinal Tap: *a parody rock band known as "world's loudest"*

ACTS OF AN EXHAUSTED GOD

> **Mark 4:35–38** That day when evening came, he said to his disciples, "Let us go over to the other side." Leaving the crowd behind, they took him along, just as he was, in the boat. There were also other boats with him. A furious squall came up, and the waves broke over the boat, so that it was nearly swamped. Jesus was in the stern, sleeping on a cushion. The disciples woke him and said to him, "Teacher, don't you care if we drown?"

Power Nap

Mark's narrative indicates Jesus had spent a full day teaching the crowds, then more time "homeschooling" the disciples. By sundown the Son of David must've felt pretty tuckered. Perhaps that's why he leaves abruptly. In other accounts of Jesus ending a day of ministry, he <u>dismisses</u> the crowds. Here, the quote *"Let us go over to the other side"* indicates haste.

☞ **GO TO:**

Matthew 14:22; Mark 6:45 (dismisses)

Some scholars assessing the Greek for *"leaving the crowd behind"* discern connotations that Jesus practically abandoned his audience. The phrase *"they took him along, just as he was"* means the sailors departed suddenly without checking provisions, planning what clothes to bring, or anything like that. These phrases would make sense if Jesus was too tired to go on one minute more.

IT'S **GREEK** TO ME

The movie *Twister* features some incredibly frightening tornadoes. How did the filmmakers infuse their special effects with such menace? They enhanced the sounds of the tornadoes with savage animal growls—something our psyche responds to on a gut level. Mark writes about this storm in the same way. Where the NIV says *"the waves broke over the boat,"* Mark's Greek says the waves literally "hurled upon" the boat. This wasn't just a storm; it was a *"furious squall."*

Something to Ponder

Do storms really get that severe on the landlocked Sea of Galilee? And does it make sense for successful, lifelong fishermen to miss signs that a storm this large was brewing?

Yes and yes. Mountains surround the Sea of Galilee, placing it in a basin. When cold weather fronts sweep down from above the mountains and collide with warmer air over the water, the resulting churn of air currents has nowhere to go. Tempests can be both sudden and violent. When my friend Richard Brimer toured the Holy Land, he saw Lake Galilee at dusk, absolutely calm, flat as glass. In the morning a German tour bus arrived, and the tourists set up changing tents on the shore, so they could don bathing suits and sun themselves. One of Lake Galilee's trademark storms fell suddenly. The wind tore the tents away, scattered camping utensils all over the beach, and rocked the tour bus so hard it almost turned over! Afterwards, the German tourists mentioned this passage in Mark, which they've probably never forgotten since.

Squalls descended on Lake Galilee unpredictably. Even veteran fishermen couldn't always see them coming. Many of them learned the general time of day when squalls tended to happen and avoided working at those times. This was part of why Peter and his men often fished at night. This trip occurred after sundown, so their knowledge and expertise led them to think they were safe.

At least four disciples were seasoned fishermen, which makes their panic all the more chilling. These weren't sissy-boys intimidated by a false alarm. They had spent their lives in a community of sailors on this lake. They knew exactly what conditions people had survived—and what people hadn't.

Some commentators make fun of the sailors for turning to a landlubber (Jesus) for help, but I doubt they were looking for a sailing lesson. They probably wanted all hands to bail like mad! Only Mark's narrative preserves the exasperated tone of the disciples: "Teacher, don't you care if we drown?" Matthew and Luke <u>smooth</u> some rudeness out.

THE WAYBACK MACHINE

☞ **GO TO:**

Matthew 8:25; Luke 8:24 (smooth)

> **Mark 4:39–42** He got up, rebuked the wind and said to the waves, "Quiet! Be still!" Then the wind died down and it was completely calm.
>
> He said to his disciples, "Why are you so afraid? Do you still have no faith?"
>
> They were terrified and asked each other, "Who is this? Even the wind and the waves obey him!"

Put A Muzzle On It, Wouldja?

☞ **GO TO:**

Mark 1:25 (silence)

None of the disciples could have expected Jesus' response. This dead-tired man got up and spoke to the weather, using the same words he used to <u>silence</u> demons. Mark's Greek uses an unusual tense. The closest English equivalent is, "Put the muzzle on and keep it on!" And the savage weather obeyed!

If they have replays in heaven, I would love to see the expressions on the disciples' faces when the piercing shriek of wind and the boom of crushing waves turned instantly calm. Imagine if you were one of those disciples. One moment, you're scrambling around with a wooden scoop trying to save your life. The next, you're motionless. The only sounds are a creak from the mast and the plinking of drops that fall from your soaked beard into puddles.

Oh, and there's one more sound—Jesus' voice, as he wearily says, *"How can you be such cowards? Don't you have any faith at all?"* (Mark 4:40, *The Message*). Presumably, he lays back down and resumes his nap.

The disciples were terrified and you can imagine why, but there's one part of their belief system that made this moment even more weighty to them than it might be to us. I beg your patience while I explain.

Today we don't have many mysterious frontiers left on earth. If we want to know what's on the other side of the moon, we just toss up a rocket. If we want to know what's on the bottom of the ocean, we plunk a remote-control sub in the water and send it on down with lights and a video camera.

Not so for the ancient mariners. No one knew what was in the depths of the ocean (or, for that matter, the Sea of Galilee). Humans could only swim as deep as a man could hold his breath. A reliable method for determining longitude at sea did not exist until the eighteenth century. Most seafaring con-

THE WAYBACK MACHINE

Yahweh's Awesome Dominion over the Oceans

Churning up the sea and creating fair skies are but a whisper of his power.	Job 26:12–14
Yahweh can still the roaring of the seas.	Psalm 65:5–7
Yahweh can part oceans or turn them into deserts.	Psalm 74:12–14; Nahum 1:34
Yahweh stills surging seas and mighty waves.	Psalm 89: 8–9
Yahweh is mightier than sea breakers.	Psalm 93:4
Waters deeper than mountains flee at his rebuke. He sets the boundaries for the oceans.	Psalm 104:5–9

sisted of skirting the continents, keeping the shore in sight. The ocean was a huge, dangerous mystery.

In Jewish thought the ocean symbolized chaos, the unpredictable realm from where evil comes. Frail humans could do nothing in the face of chaos. Only one entity could—Yahweh. God's power to silence chaos was absolute (see table, page 92).

God's authority over chaos, symbolized by great waters, was such an ancient part of Jewish tradition that Genesis 1:2 ("Now the earth was formless and empty") was often read as, "The earth was chaos." Part of what was so great about creation was that God was powerful enough to seize chaos and make something good and orderly out of it (see GWGN, pages 5–6).

This may help you understand the disciples' reaction to Jesus' miracle. It was completely ingrained into their understanding that *no one could command the sea but Yahweh.*

Perhaps this was the first time it occurred to the disciples the Messiah was divine. The reason they said, *"Who is this?"* is because the evidence they had just witnessed led to an impossible conclusion. Only Yahweh could rule the waters with a word, and yet Jesus had just done so. The only explanation possible . . . was impossible!

Many readers find this miracle so fantastic they don't take the passage literally. They feel more comfortable treating it as a myth or an allegory, but the **myriad** of eyewitness details says otherwise. Mark records the time of day (verse 35); the fact that *"there were other boats with him"* (verse 36)—a useless detail if this is a myth; and the dialog of the disciples (verse 41). This really happened!

Something to Ponder

myriad: *numerous*

Max Lucado: After the storm, they worshiped him. They had never, as a group, done that before. Never. Check it out. Open your Bible. Search for a time when the disciples corporately praised him. You won't find it. You won't find them worshiping when he heals the leper. Forgives the adulteress. Preaches to the masses. They were willing to follow. Willing to leave family. Willing to cast out demons. Willing to be in the army. But only after the incident on the sea did they worship him. Why? Simple. This time, they were the ones who were saved.[1]

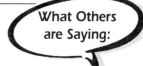

What Others are Saying:

JESUS INVENTS DEVILED HAM

The eventful boat ride begun in Mark 4 ends across Lake Galilee, in Gentile territory. Here, Jesus meets one of the most moving figures in all of Scripture.

> **Mark 5:1–5** They went across the lake to the region of the Gerasenes. When Jesus got out of the boat, a man with an evil spirit came from the tombs to meet him. This man lived in the tombs, and no one could bind him any more, not even with a chain. For he had often been chained hand and foot, but he tore the chains apart and broke the irons on his feet. No one was strong enough to subdue him. Night and day among the tombs and in the hills he would cry out and cut himself with stones.

Man Of The Tombs

demon-possessed:
overruled and controlled
by evil spirit beings

Mark spares no detail in describing a **demon-possessed** man of the tombs, whose existence sounds like pure torture. Tombs in this time and place were caves cut into the rocks, so this wild man probably used an abandoned one like an animal uses a den. Experiencing agonies we can only guess at, he spent night and day terrifying others and mutilating himself. Not even chains controlled his destructive fury, so people probably drove him out of all normal social settings, leaving him nowhere to go except the religiously unclean cemetery.

What would you do if you saw this guy running straight at you?

> **Mark 5:6–10** When he saw Jesus from a distance, he ran and fell on his knees in front of him. He shouted at the top of his voice, "What do you want with me, Jesus, Son of the Most High God? Swear to God that you won't torture me!" For Jesus had said to him, "Come out of this man, you evil spirit!"
>
> Then Jesus asked him, "What is your name?"
>
> "My name is Legion," he replied, "for we are many." And he begged Jesus again and again not to send them out of the area.

Jesus Versus The Legion Of Doom

Jesus stood his ground. In fact, the ensuing conversation indicates the *demons* were the frightened ones. The **demoniac** immediately knew Jesus as *"Son of the Most High God."* That term was most often used by non-Israelites for the Hebrews' god, Yahweh. In other words, the demons in this man instantly recognized Jesus. (For more information on spiritual warfare, see GWDN, pages 259, 265–267, 270–271.)

demoniac: person possessed by a demon

The demons' compulsion to tell Jesus their name demonstrates his total authority over them. Imagine being surrounded by a SWAT brigade who is pointing guns at you, demanding that you throw down your knife; these demons experienced the spiritual equivalent. They give up their name: *"Legion, for we are many."* A Roman legion consisted of 6,000 troops, 120 horsemen, and additional technical personnel. Even if the demons inside this guy were not a numeric equivalent, "many" is right! It's no wonder mere mortals couldn't tame them.

Legion begs Jesus not to send them *"out of the area."* We don't know what this means. With the Messiah standing before them it would have been obvious to the demons that God's reign had begun. Perhaps they were expecting instant judgment. Jesus alludes elsewhere to the restlessness of spirits who leave their human residences: *"When an evil spirit comes out of a man, it goes through arid places seeking rest and does not find it"* (Matthew 12:43). Perhaps the demons wished to avoid this state of restlessness.

> **Mark 5:11–13** A large herd of pigs was feeding on the nearby hillside. The demons begged Jesus, "Send us among the pigs; allow us to go into them." He gave them permission, and the evil spirits came out and went into the pigs. The herd, about two thousand in number, rushed down the steep bank into the lake and were drowned.

Jesus Does Demons A Favor

Legion's strange request yields a strange result. Jesus, King of Compassion, is willing to grant even demons a favor. At their request, he sends them into a herd of two thousand pigs.

The Greek word Mark uses for *"steep bank"* (5:13) can also be translated "cliff," which makes more sense—because the first thing these demons do is run the porkers into the lake, where they drown. I once spent part of a summer on a pig farm, where I learned firsthand that one frightened hog can squeal loudly enough to make your eardrums bleed. *Two thousand* freaked out hogs would've raised a hullabaloo that didn't stop echoing off the Galilean hills until last week. The other thing I learned is that a pig is not a herd animal; each pig does it's own thing. The fact that thousands of them acted as one implies there really were thousands of demons.

> **Mark 5:14–17** Those tending the pigs ran off and reported this in the town and countryside, and the people went out to see what had happened. When they came to Jesus, they saw the man who had been possessed by the legion of demons, sitting there, dressed and in his right mind; and they were afraid. Those who had seen it told the people what had happened to the demon-possessed man—and told about the pigs as well. Then the people began to plead with Jesus to leave their region.

Our Precious Pigs!

A herd of pigs represented a small fortune in the economy of Jesus' day. Jesus clearly believed one man restored to health was worth more than the economic benefits of two thousand pigs. The grateful townspeople felt the same way, and raced to bring other mentally unbalanced and ill people for healing—oops! I must've switched my Revised Version with my Reversed Vision, because that's not what happened.

The pig shepherds would've been in trouble for losing not one piggy, not two, but the *entire flock*. The townsfolk, more concerned about the loss of pigs than the newfound health of a human being, begged Jesus to leave. And despite the incredible power and authority Jesus had just shown, he meekly left.

exorcism: when one is freed from an evil spirit

Mark probably intends this **exorcism** and the muzzling of the storm to be a pair. Why do I think so? For three reasons.

1. One account comes right after the other.
2. He gives the storm and the demons the same ferocious qualities.
3. He uses the same Greek phrase to quote what Jesus said when he calmed the storm and silenced the demons (compare Mark 4:39 and 1:25).

Jesus can control the raging of both storm and demon because in either case, chaos recognizes his superior authority.

Randy Alcorn: We shouldn't take the devil lightly. But we should also realize this roaring lion is on a leash held by an **omnipotent** and loving God. We must neither underestimate nor overestimate his power. Speaking of demons, God tells us, "You, dear children, are from God and have overcome them, because the one who is in you is greater than the one who is in the world" (1 John 4:4). Nothing must be more infuriating to demons than for us to realize that if we've repented of our sins and trusted Christ as our Savior, then the same Lord who evicted them . . . dwells within us. He's infinitely more powerful than they. Through Him we can overcome them. The devil may be big to us, but he is small to God.[2]

omnipotent: *all-powerful*

Big Topic, Little Space

The mysterious workings of demons fascinate many people, and can lead them into spiritually and psychologically dangerous practices. Nonetheless, the topic of demons presents an opportunity to explore a superb way to find out what the Bible says on any subject: *consult a Bible dictionary.* That's the Power Tool for this section.

POWER TOOL

Use a Bible dictionary.

A Bible dictionary contains definitions of terms, places, and proper names found in the Bible. The definitions are long enough that a good Bible dictionary seems more like a one-volume encyclopedia than a regular dictionary.

For example, here are some things I learned by looking up the entry for "demons" in the *Dictionary of Jesus and the Gospels* (InterVarsity Press, 1992):

Demons in Mark's Gospel

Mark uses the word "demon" thirteen times and "unclean spirit" eleven times, often synonymously. These evil spirit beings cause people to:

Twitch, writhe, and shout	1:26
Have superhuman strength	5:3–5
Injure themselves	5:3–5
Throw themselves down	9:18
Foam at the mouth	9:18
Grind their teeth	9:18
Destroy themselves	9:22
Have special insight into who Jesus really is	1:24–25, 34; 3:11–12; 5:7

Here's another example. Mark starts this story by telling us it takes place in the region of the Gerasenes. A quick look in the *New Bible Dictionary* (InterVarsity Press, 1962) gave me some background on this geographical area, including the fact that no other Bible incident is set there.

Wonder how many miracles of Jesus are recorded in the Gospels? Looking in a Bible dictionary is quicker than counting them yourself. Not sure what the Sanhedrin is? Take a quick peek in a Bible dictionary. How did Peter die? Consult a Bible dictionary. Ask your pastor or scholars you respect in your community of faith to recommend a Bible dictionary they endorse; there are plenty of excellent ones.

> **Mark 5:18–20** As Jesus was getting into the boat, the man who had been demon-possessed begged to go with him. Jesus did not let him, but said, "Go home to your family and tell them how much the Lord has done for you, and how he has had mercy on you." So the man went away and began to tell in the Decapolis how much Jesus had done for him. And all the people were amazed.

The Rejected Disciple

Repeatedly, the unpredictable Jesus of Mark's Gospel catches me off guard. When the demons asked for mercy, I'd expect Jesus to say no. He said yes. When the townspeople beg him to leave, I'd expect Jesus to say no. He said yes. And when the poor healed madman begs to accompany Jesus, *of course* Jesus should say yes. But he said no. Why?

"They saw the man who had been possessed by the legion of demons, sitting there, dressed and in his right mind" (Mark 5:15). This is the traditional Eastern pose of a student—a disciple. On top of that, when the healed man of the tombs *"begged to go with him"* (Mark 5:18), Mark uses the exact same Greek words he used to describe the <u>primary responsibility</u> of the twelve disciples: *"to be with him."* This man is not merely bumming a lift across the lake; he is ready to make a full commitment to discipleship. Didn't Jesus want to gather followers? Wouldn't Jesus be doing the right thing by accepting this former man-monster into the community of believers?

Jesus' response provides the answer: *"Go home to your family."* What had given thousands of demons access into this man's heart?

How long had he been in his tormented state? How long had his family been without him? We don't know, but he had been wild long enough to be known throughout the region. Beyond the man's grateful urge to follow, Jesus considered the bigger picture. Did he have elderly parents who needed him? A wife who missed the man she had originally wed? A little daughter who had learned to hide when he came growling? If the man left this Gentile sector, his family would hear rumors that he had been healed, but they wouldn't see it for themselves, and they wouldn't have their son, husband, or father restored to them. Jesus did the right thing for all involved. Actually, it's Jesus' next statement that provides the real surprise.

Adventures Of The Clark Kent Savior, Episode 4

In a reversal of his usual practice Jesus says to the man, *"Tell them how much the Lord has done for you, and how he has had mercy on you."* He sends the guy a-blabbin' into a populous region, the Decapolis. (Decapolis means "ten cities." How do I know that? I looked in a Bible dictionary.)

Why does Jesus seem to reverse his strategy? I'm not telling yet. The explanation of all this secret identity stuff is coming in just a few chapters, but I'm not above dropping a few hints. First of all, look at the geography. Everyone who has been silenced has been in Jewish territory; here, we're in Gentile territory. Second, look at the message; it was not "the Jewish Messiah is here!" It was, "The Lord has had mercy on me." With those two hints, have you guessed yet why Jesus hid his identity in Israel?

Mark finishes this striking account with, *"And all the people were <u>amazed</u>."* Mark uses the word "amazed" a lot. The Power Tool in the chapter on Mark 1:14–45, *notice and study repeated words*, suggests we take a closer look at it. If you examine the contexts where it appears, in each case Mark describes people who are astounded at Jesus' skill, power, or insight, but who fall short of following him.

☞ **GO TO:**

Mark 1:22; 1:27; 2:12; 5:20; 6:2; 6:6; 10:24; 11:18; 12:17; 15:5 (amazed)

Life Application Bible Commentary: Without training or background, without the capacity to explain Old Testament prophecies or to expound on theories of the Trinity, this man simply told his story. . . . When God touches your life, don't be afraid to share the wonderful events with your family and friends. Not everyone can travel as a missionary. Jesus knows the right position for each of us. Sometimes kindness at home and unselfish service means more than becoming a full-time Christian worker.[3]

What Others are Saying:

KEEP IT REAL—Unlike the drenched apostles, I don't have to ask, "Who is this?" I already know. The trouble is, I keep *forgetting*, which is why Mark's powerful portrayals pierced my heart.

• Mark 5:1–5. The description of the crazed man of the tombs sounds just like someone who lives inside of me when I'm depressed or hopeless. Surely the Jesus who saw the man worth saving underneath all that wild self-destruction will not give up on me when I'm emotionally cutting myself with stones of self-loathing. I must remember that the One who mastered literal demons will also conquer my figurative demons.

Study Questions

1. What was unusual about how Jesus departed from the crowd in Mark 4:35–36?
2. How did Jesus save the sinking boat? What was unusual about the language he used?
3. What did the apostles probably believe that made the quieting of the storm even more mind-blowing to them?
4. What did the name "Legion" indicate (Mark 5:9)?
5. Why is it likely that Mark intends the story of the storm and the story of the demoniac to work as a pair?

CHAPTER WRAP-UP

- The account of Jesus stilling a storm on the Sea of Galilee is a real, eyewitness account, not a myth. He quieted the storm by telling it to "put the muzzle on and keep it on," the same language he used to silence demons in Mark 1:25. (Mark 4:35–41)

- Across Lake Galilee, in Gentile turf, Jesus encountered a madman whom no one could tame, living among tombs. He was driven by a legion of demons (perhaps thousands)—evil spiritual entities that somehow overruled the man's will. When Jesus ordered the demons to leave the man, he permitted them to enter a nearby herd of pigs. The pigs immediately drowned themselves. (Mark 5:1–13)

- The townspeople of the area cared more about the financial loss of the herd than they did about the miraculous healing of the demoniac. They feared Jesus and begged him to leave the area. He graciously complied. (Mark 5:14–20)

- Mark probably intends the two stories (the muzzling of the storm and the healing of the demoniac) to go together. In both cases, Jesus shows effortless superiority to raging forces of chaos. He performs acts only God can do.

MARK 5:21–6:6
PARTY-POOPER JESUS

- Mark Sandwich: Dying Girl, Sick Woman
- Why a Sandwich?
- The Homeys Take Offense

Let's Get Started

Mark has just treated us to two momentous encounters with Jesus. Heroically, Jesus stood against the chaotic elements of nature, then healed a tortured man by single-handedly taking on thousands of demons at once. Have these epic accounts whet your appetite for more of Jesus' miracle power? I hope so, because Mark is about to serve up another of his narrative sandwiches.

The following story begins with an urgent request for Jesus to come heal a dying girl. Jesus, his large entourage, and an even larger crowd, hop to it as if Jesus were a guest doctor pushing the crash cart on *ER*. An interruption en route spells glory for one woman and tragedy for the little girl. Did Jesus mess up by allowing himself to be delayed? Are you kidding? As Jesus himself responds, *"Don't be afraid; just believe"* (Mark 5:36).

Mark is about to reveal more fabulous deeds of the Savior, but typical of his gritty, ironic style, he ends this section with a portrait of folks who miss every bit of the miraculous. After the incredible heights of power Mark has shown us, we reel at the blindness of people who should love Jesus the most, but understand him the least.

Ready for high highs and low lows in the career of Jesus? Let's get started!

MARK SANDWICH:
DYING GIRL, SICK WOMAN

> **Mark 5:21–24a** When Jesus had again crossed over by boat to the other side of the lake, a large crowd gathered around him while he was by the lake. Then one of the synagogue rulers, named Jairus, came there. Seeing Jesus, he fell at his feet and pleaded earnestly with him, "My little daughter is dying. Please come and put your hands on her so that she will be healed and live." So Jesus went with him.

Jairus And A Killer Virus

What a startling contrast! Totally rejected by the people on the eastern (Gentile) side of Lake Galilee, Jesus sails back to the western (Jewish) side and draws a huge crowd. They literally (in Greek) "gathered on top of" him. What happens next is surprising; Jairus falls at Jesus' feet and begs for help.

A synagogue ruler like Jairus would have had duties such as arranging who would lead prayer or read from the Torah during Sabbath services. He would've looked after the synagogue building and handled the details of getting the **alms** collected, then distributed appropriately. He had a trusted, prestigious position in the Jewish community. The shock here is that since the conflict stories began back in Mark 2, this is the first time a member of the Jewish establishment shows any respect for Jesus. Admittedly, a dire emergency drives Jairus to do so, but we'll soon see Jairus is as faithful as he is desperate; he hangs in there with Jesus when all seems lost. In contrast to the demoniac of the tombs, who threw himself at Jesus' feet in apparent mockery, Jairus throws himself at Jesus' feet in faith.

Given the size of the crowd, Jesus was obviously not sitting around wishing for something to do. As with the paralytic lowered through the ceiling, however, he doesn't seem put out by the interruption. He simply goes to the rescue.

alms: gifts collected for the poor

What Others are Saying:

Anne Graham Lotz: If you and I are going to meet the needs of others, we must not view people as interruptions. We must be willing to see them from God's perspective, and we must be willing to give up some of our own time to help meet their needs. Jesus gave up His time to Himself, He gave up His "holiday," He gave up His "family" time in order to meet the needs of the crowd. He knew that meeting the needs of others invariably requires some personal sacrifice.[1]

> **Mark 5:24b–28** A large crowd followed and pressed around him. And a woman was there who had been subject to bleeding for twelve years. She had suffered a great deal under the care of many doctors and had spent all she had, yet instead of getting better she grew worse. When she heard about Jesus, she came up behind him in the crowd and touched his cloak, because she thought, "If I just touch his clothes, I will be healed."

Sneaky Healing

Just as we begin the story of Jairus and his daughter, a tragic new character interrupts—a woman who has been bleeding for twelve years. When blood pressure drops, the heart has difficulty pumping oxygen to the brain. Lightheadedness can result, along with a lack of mental clarity and an overall run-down feeling. This would be depressing for a week, much less twelve years. Even more sadly, the ailment had impoverished the woman, for she had *"spent all she had"* only to get worse. If the problem was blood loss and it was getting worse, her condition was life threatening. Just as no one could cure the Gerasene demoniac, no one could cure this woman.

Most commentators believe her condition was related to a uterine or menstrual problem. If so, this woman's situation was pitiable for another reason, unique to ancient Jewish culture.

Disease influenced everyone in the preaspirin, premicroscope, prescientific world. In the big cities of the Roman Empire, where "sewage system" meant open ditches and people jammed together in government housing called *insula* (notorious for collapsing), only 50 percent of the population was over twenty-five years of age. Only 5 percent reached age fifty. You could expect a longer life in the Galilean countryside, but not by much.

In this ancient society how could you tell an infectious blood condition from a noninfectious blood condition? You couldn't. Blood loaded with staph, hepatitis, or rabies looked no different than 100-percent-pure, hearty blood. So Jewish law included <u>rigid methods</u> for keeping the Hebrews safe from blood-borne disease.

If you had the problem this woman had, you experienced the same social curses as lepers. Any time weariness from your disease forced you to rest, whatever you sat or laid on was ceremoni-

☞ **GO TO:**

Leviticus 15:25–31 (rigid methods)

ally unclean. If you touched someone, even a family member, they were unclean until they had taken a bath and washed their clothes. You were not allowed in the Temple. How would you like to take that lifestyle out for a twelve-year test drive?

This woman's mere presence in a crowd made her an outlaw. Her condition must have kept her physically weak, so what is she doing here at all? The answer is obvious. She'd heard of someone who cured the incurable. As with Jairus, she was equal parts desperation and faith.

She reached out to touch the edge of his garment. Mark doesn't specify what Jesus wore. Perhaps she slunk so low that she touched only his robe's hem, down by his heels. My messianic Jewish friends like to suppose that as an observant rabbi Jesus would have worn the traditional Jewish prayer shawl, and the woman touched one of his prayer tassels. Whatever she touched, this lady knew intuitively if she could get the tiniest piece of Jesus, that would be enough.

What Others are Saying:

Andrew Murray: My Lord Jesus is equal to every emergency. My Lord Jesus can meet the wants of every soul. My whole heart says, "He can, He can do it; He will, He will do it!" Oh come, believers, and let us claim most deliberately, most quietly, most restfully—let us claim, claim it.[2]

> **Mark 5:29–33** Immediately her bleeding stopped and she felt in her body that she was freed from her suffering.
>
> At once Jesus realized that power had gone out from him. He turned around in the crowd and asked, "Who touched my clothes?"
>
> "You see the people crowding against you," his disciples answered, "and yet you can ask, 'Who touched me?'"
>
> But Jesus kept looking around to see who had done it. Then the woman, knowing what had happened to her, came and fell at his feet and, trembling with fear, told him the whole truth.

Smells Like God's Spirit

In his breakthrough grunge hit "Smells Like Teen Spirit," Kurt Cobain growled, "I feel stupid, and contagious." Jesus, in contrast, could sing, "I feel righteous, and contagious." Once again, when uncleanness touched Jesus, it did not corrupt him. When uncleanness touched Jesus, it became pure.

I love the moment when Jesus stopped and asked, "Who touched my clothes?" The apostles have no idea why this suddenly matters. You might feel the same way the disciples did if you were a paramedic responding to a life-or-death situation, and your lead medic suddenly stopped to complain, "Hey, my slacks aren't creased!" All the disciples could do was question the question.

At this point in the account the disciples don't know what Jesus and one other person in that jostling crowd know: *"power had gone out from him."* This almost suggests the woman snatched a healing from Jesus without his permission. Certainly this didn't happen every time someone touched Jesus. The secret to understanding it might be found in Jesus' statement that *"the Son can do nothing by himself; he can do only what he sees his Father doing, because whatever the Father does the Son also does"* (John 5:19). Jesus *"made himself nothing"* when he came to earth, *"taking the very nature of a servant"* (see Philippians 2:5–11), which means he emptied himself of the limitless power he held in heaven and entrusted it to the Father. Through the **anointing** with the Holy Spirit, the Father entrusted power back to Jesus, who was free to use it when it served the Father's purposes. (If the concept of the Trinity is new to you, see GWLC, pages 83–84.)

anointing: *literally, "outpouring"; metaphorically, God-given favor for a special purpose*

It appears here, however, the Father remained in control of his own power. The woman was healed through God's free and gracious decision. By an act of sovereign will, God determined to honor the woman's faith. Jesus, ever in tune with the Father, immediately sensed something of what had happened.

What was going on in this poor woman's mind and heart in that moment? On one hand she sensed the bleeding had stopped and she was healed. On the other her illegal attempt to sneak through the crowd was about to be exposed. Not knowing what to expect, she stepped forward, *"trembling with fear."*

> **Mark 5:34** He said to her, "Daughter, your faith has healed you. Go in peace and be freed from your suffering."

Miracle-Making Faith

Jesus wants to complete her healing. His simple-sounding phrases are loaded with blessing for her. First, he calls her a daughter, meaning a daughter of Israel. After twelve years of being excluded from society, she has just been included for the first time. Second,

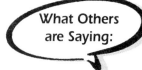
he commends her faith, which had been strong indeed to drive her into such a reckless situation. Third, he wishes her peace, a traditional farewell arising from the Hebrew concept of *shalom*—a profound experience of well-being arising from God's salvation. *Shalom* encompassed wholeness, prosperity, security, and friendship. It was the seal of the kingdom of God upon her new health—an acknowledgment of the miracle's legitimacy (it was given, not stolen) and a promise that the miracle would stick.

If Jesus had not taken time to ferret her out, she may never have known that her faith played an integral role in her healing. Who knows? She may have assumed Jesus was wearing a magic robe. She also would not have known that her healing came with God's full blessing. Jesus had done the right thing in stopping to address her individually.

Or had he? The next moments suggest that the delay cost Jairus an irrecoverable price.

What Others are Saying:

Claus Westerman: The Hebrew word *shalom* is formed from a verb that means to make something complete, to make something whole or holistic. Shalom is this condition of being complete, of fullness or wholeness.[3]

> **Mark 5:35–36** While Jesus was still speaking, some men came from the house of Jairus, the synagogue ruler. "Your daughter is dead," they said. "Why bother the teacher any more?"
>
> Ignoring what they said, Jesus told the synagogue ruler, "Don't be afraid; just believe."

Not A Zero-Sum Kingdom

World War II brought us the phrase "zero-sum game." "Zero-sum" means that there are multiple sides in conflict, and that a gain for one side means a corresponding loss for the other side. Sharing a pie is a zero-sum game. After everyone has divided the pie, one way or another, there will be zero pie left. If I get 40 percent of the pie, you get 60 percent. But if I really like this flavor of pie and stab you with my fork until you give me 60 percent of the pie, you only get 40 percent.

As Jesus finishes speaking with the healed "daughter of Israel," messengers from the house of Jairus inform the rescue team that Jairus's daughter died while the healer was en route. From Jairus's perspective, it looks like a zero-sum game. Because Jesus chose to be with the bleeding woman, he was not there in time for the dying girl.

Jesus knows that the kingdom of God is *never* a zero-sum game. God's power is limitless, his wisdom infinite. His compassion flows into every nook of society. He never blesses one person at the expense of another. This is too much for Jairus to absorb during the shock of his loss, so Jesus boils it down to a sentence: *"Don't be afraid; just believe."* Talk about words to live by!

Max Lucado: Faith is trusting what the eye can't see. Eyes see the prowling lion. Faith sees Daniel's angel. Eyes see storms. Faith sees Noah's rainbow. Eyes see giants. Faith sees Canaan. Your eyes see your faults. Your faith sees your Savior.[4]

> **Mark 5:37–40a** He did not let anyone follow him except Peter, James and John the brother of James. When they came to the home of the synagogue ruler, Jesus saw a commotion, with people crying and wailing loudly. He went in and said to them, "Why all this commotion and wailing? The child is not dead but asleep." But they laughed at him.

Phony Mourners

Ever heard the term "ambulance chaser"? It describes a lawyer who hopes people get hurt, so he can "helpfully" offer to sue whoever hurt them—not because he cares about the suffering person, but because of the fat commission he might win himself.

The "ambulance chasers" in Jesus' day might have been these professional mourners. In first-century Palestine, the more mourners you hired, the more you honored your dearly departed. Pro mourners did more than cry; they sang, played instruments, danced, clapped, and wailed. (Nowadays we call this a "rock band.")

Most professional mourners were women. Customarily, they formed a circle around the leader of the dance of death, and danced rhythmically from left to right with their hair hanging down. Their wildness and volume would gradually increase, intended to reach a frenzied climax just before the dead person's burial. This was the tumult Jesus barged into, but he tossed a wet blanket over the entire performance, saying, *"The child is not dead but asleep."* We see the true depth of these mourners' "sorrow" when they switch instantly from laments to mocking laughter.

> **Mark 5:40b–43** After he put them all out, he took the child's father and mother and the disciples who were with him, and went in where the child was. He took her by the hand and said to her, *"Talitha koum!"* (which means, "Little girl, I say to you, get up!"). Immediately the girl stood up and walked around (she was twelve years old). At this they were completely astonished. He gave strict orders not to let anyone know about this, and told them to give her something to eat.

One Of History's Top Ten Wake-Up Calls

I like Jesus' response to the professionals' insensitivity. He doesn't argue with them. He simply kicks them out. Only a select group of five people got to see what happened next. Jesus took the young girl by the hand and spoke a beautifully tender wake-up call, recorded in his exact Aramaic words—a sign of Peter's firsthand, ear-witness involvement. Literally rendered, Jesus said, "Lamb, get up."

And marvelously, she did.

IT'S GREEK TO ME

If you are a parent, you'll relate strongly to the reaction of Jairus and his wife: *"they were completely astonished."* The unusually vivid Greek here means out of their minds with amazement, speechless, or as my Irish coworker says, "gob-smacked." We can only assume this emotional overload was due not only to their surprise, but to their joy.

This makes Jesus' next deed even stranger: *"He gave strict orders not to let anyone know about this."* Jesus wanted the five witnesses to withhold the detail that he could revive dead people. It was simply too explosive a fact for the people to handle. Seekers would have focused on miracles, power signs, and sensation—not Jesus' real message of God's kingdom. (Later, when Jesus revives a dead man publicly, the act virtually <u>ends his ministry</u>.) He did not mean they could never speak of it; he meant they had to wait until <u>later</u>.

☞ **GO TO:**

John 11:45–54 (ends his ministry)

Mark 9:9 (later)

What Others are Saying:

William L. Lane: Since even the poorest man was required by common custom to hire a minimum of two fluteplayers and one professional mourner in the event of his wife's death, it is probable that one who held the rank of synagogue-ruler would be expected to hire a large number of professional mourners. It was necessary to remove the mourners from the girl's room.[5]

John Fischer: Our worship in the form of astonishment is full of amazement both over who God is and over why, given who he is, he would be interested in being associated with us at all. . . . It's the thing that will cause all of us to proclaim when we reach our final destination and first lay eyes on the glories of heaven, "What could I possibly have done to deserve this?"[6]

WHY A SANDWICH?

> **Mark 5:43** He gave strict orders not to let anyone know about this, and told them to give her something to eat.

What Mark Has Joined Together, Let Not Man Rend Asunder

With this final verse of Mark's second sandwich, we need to pause and consider why he felt he could best convey his message by merging the two stories together. What do we learn by considering them together that we wouldn't learn from considering them individually? A quick comparison of the two healings may reveal Mark's broader theme.

The Story of the Bleeding Woman	The Story of Jairus' Daughter
Features an outcast of society	Features members of the Jewish establishment
Came to Jesus in poverty (5:26)	Came to Jesus in wealth and privilege (5:22)
Sick for twelve years (5:25)	Alive only twelve years (5:42)
Unclean and illegal to touch (Lev. 15:25)	Unclean and illegal to touch (Lev. 21:11)
Incurable	Incurable
Touched Jesus	Touched by Jesus
Healed secretly, brought public	Came publicly, healed in secret
Told by Jesus, "Your faith has healed you"	Told by Jesus, "Don't be afraid, just believe"

Side by side these two healing accounts present contrasts. Many times Mark has shown Jesus helping fringe folk; the bleeding woman is yet another. In sharp distinction we also see Jesus' unquestioning support of Jairus, a distinguished community insider. There are other contrasts, but you'll also see commonalities. In each story, for example, the person was unclean, the misery absolutely incurable, and the touch of Jesus brought instant healing. They show one other common thread, which I think is Mark's big point; the bleeding woman and Jairus both believed in Jesus. They had faith.

Faith is not an end in itself. Faith does not mean forcing a certain outcome. Faith means trusting that Jesus will do the right thing, and continuing to trust he has done the right thing even after people get sick or die or the bank repossesses your house. Faith is not about you. Faith is centered on Jesus.

This is the kind of faith that the bleeding woman and Jairus had. They didn't know what Jesus would do for them. They had hopes, but in neither case did the encounter proceed just the way they had planned. In Jairus's case Jesus' comment to him implies the synagogue leader had as much fear as he did faith. Jairus's amazement shows he didn't have a huge amount of faith, but what little he had was the right kind. This was the mustard-seed faith Jesus had spoken of earlier—not enough to anticipate how glorious the result would be, but enough for the miracle to happen. Enough to let Jesus have his way.

Eugene H. Peterson: Jesus provides both context and content for everyone's life. Spirituality—the attention we give to our souls—turns out in practice (if we let St. Mark shape our practice) to be the attention we give to God revealed in Jesus. The text trains us in such perception and practice. Line after line, page after page   Jesus, Jesus, Jesus. None of us provides the content for our own spirituality; it is given to us; Jesus gives it to us. . . . no exceptions.[7]

Something To Eat

Besides the mistaken notion that faith can force a certain outcome, another subtle error commonly preached on the radio and lived out in churches is the idea that faith and common sense don't work together. How many times have you heard (or said) statements like this:

- "I don't know what job God wants me to have, so I'm going to sit and pray until he brings the right one along."
- "The church doesn't have enough money to build the new sanctuary, but we're going to start anyway and trust that God will provide."
- "Juan has better experience and qualifications for running the men's ministry, but George is a friend and he seems more anointed, so we're going with George."

Sometimes using logic and normal, obvious planning is seen as depending on man instead of depending on God. I'm not claiming you should *never* make statements like those above, but if they reflect your *normal* problem-solving approach, you'll be disappointed most of the time. Jesus demonstrates in this verse that faith and common sense do go together. Yes, he miraculously raised the young lady from the dead; but immediately he told the parents to give her physical nourishment.

Admittedly, people (even Christians) can have an arrogant <u>mindset</u> that is hostile to God. This is probably why when Jesus said to love the Lord with all your heart, he also said to love the Lord with all your <u>mind</u>. People pursuing his command should not assume their own common sense is evil and ungodly. God created both faith and reason; both have their place. Here's a good rule of thumb. Pray and believe in the knowledge that everything depends on God, but work as if everything depends on you.

☞ **GO TO:**

Romans 8:5–8 (mindset)

Mark 12:30 (mind)

Timeless Treasure

While we're on the subject of *"Be not afraid, only believe,"* let's rev up another Power Tool: *the correct interpretation of a passage will be timeless.* Do you believe God loves twenty-first century Americans, but didn't really care about all the people who came before us? Ridiculous! Yet many Christians interpret the Bible that way. For example, preachers of the health-and-wealth Gospel use *"Be not afraid; only believe"* to "prove" that God wants you rich.

POWER TOOL

Look for God's timeless lesson.

Such an interpretation would only be possible in modern suburban America. Their interpretation would mean that Chinese Christians stripped of jobs and homes because of their testimony for Jesus are bad Christians. It would mean the first generation of believers, thrown to lions and burned at the stake for their faith, were not as close to Jesus as we are, because we have BMWs. This is just one example of bad **exegesis**.

We're anxious to apply God's Word to our lives, here and now, but if you grab a phrase and force fit it onto your current situation, if you make a passage mean now something it never meant before, you're no longer following God's <u>eternal</u> message. Before you rush into a misinterpretation of Scripture, use the very first Power Tool: *find out what the passage meant to its first audience.* Next, look for a timeless lesson that is true for all people everywhere, *then* carefully apply it to today. This process will keep you well away from wasting years of time and energy on a mistake.

exegesis: explanation of a text, in this case Scripture

☞ **GO TO:**

Mark 13:31 (eternal)

THE HOMEYS TAKE OFFENSE

> **Mark 6:1–6a** Jesus left there and went to his home-town, accompanied by his disciples. When the Sabbath came, he began to teach in the synagogue, and many who heard him were amazed.
>
> "Where did this man get these things?" they asked. "What's this wisdom that has been given him, that he even does miracles! Isn't this the carpenter? Isn't this Mary's son and the brother of James, Joseph, Judas and Simon? Aren't his sisters here with us?" And they took offense at him.
>
> Jesus said to them, "Only in his hometown, among his relatives and in his own house is a prophet without honor." He could not do any miracles there, except lay his hands on a few sick people and heal them. And he was amazed at their lack of faith.

Why The Prophetic Looked Pathetic

When the first half of Mark's Gospel reaches its conclusion, Mark will record a powerful confession of who Jesus is, but for now he shows only confusion about Jesus' identity. His placement of this account is **poignant**.

A lot has happened since the last time Jesus was rejected in a synagogue. Since then he has gathered twelve apostles and used parables that practically forced people to decide if they were in or out of God's kingdom. He has stopped nasty weather and cast out thousands of demons. By the time he heals a woman who had an incurable disease, then immediately revives a dead girl, anyone who's paying attention has to be thinking, "This Jesus guy *rocks*!"

This is where Mark places the story of Jesus returning to his hometown, Nazareth. After all we've seen Jesus do, the towns-people should give him the keys to the city, declare it "Jesus Day," and carry him around on their shoulders. The *Nazareth Daily Herald* should read "Local Boy Makes Good." We're flabbergasted when his own people disregard him.

At first Jesus impressed the home crowd, who had not seen him since he began his public ministry out of Capernaum. The townspeople were "amazed" and commented on his wisdom and his miracles, but then they started wondering where he got this wisdom and power. He seemed so common. He was a blue collar worker from a no-big-deal family.

poignant: deeply touching; piercing.

☞ **GO TO:**

Mark 3:1–6
(synagogue)

Matthew 2:23
(Nazareth)

T
peo
at h
Jesu

N
ous
out
fait
lou
par
Naz
In r
peo
lack

owns-
azed
ered.

previ-
issed
d the
racu-
hetic
ng to
ogue.
of the
d the

ne so

Da...familiar to them could get all this power. Their preoccupation with this issue means that they never get around to asking the crucial question: What does it all mean? . . . They are not driven so much by a desire to know what is behind Jesus' miracles as by an itch to confirm their private prejudice that he cannot be all that remarkable.[8]

What Others are Saying:

Billy Graham: Unbelief is sin because it is an insult to the truthfulness of God.[9]

KEEP IT REAL—This section offered plenty to think about in terms of personal faith. For what it's worth, here are concepts that hit me while chewing thoughtfully on Mark's second sandwich:

• Mark 5:36. Jesus says to me each day, *"Don't be afraid; just believe."* My heart says to me each day, "Be afraid. Be *very* afraid." Maybe the key to hearing Jesus louder than my timid heart is found in the first part of the verse: *"Ignoring what they said."* Jesus, help me to screen out the bluff and bluster of earthly concerns, and trust you no matter what.

• Mark 5:40–41. Today's worldly culture rewards scoffers. Comedians make millions of dollars belittling and trivializing every person and incident they encounter, while contributing nothing of value themselves. As with the professional mourners, that mindset misses everything that's beautiful, in effect booting themselves out of the room. No wonder God said *"Blessed is the man who does not . . . sit in the seat of mockers. But his delight is in the law of the LORD, and on his law he meditates day and night"* (Psalm 1:1–2). *Thank you for writing that, Lord. Now I really get it.*

Study Questions

1. Who was Jairus, and what did he want from Jesus?
2. What interruption seemed to prevent Jesus from fulfilling Jairus's request?
3. What did the Gerasene demoniac, the bleeding woman, and the daughter of Jairus have in common?
4. Despite the many differences between the bleeding woman and Jairus, what was the important thing they both did?
5. From Jesus' viewpoint, what was amazing about the people of Nazareth?

CHAPTER WRAP-UP

- Jairus, a synagogue leader, asked Jesus to heal his daughter. This required significant faith because other synagogues disapproved of Jesus. (Mark 5:21–24a)

- A woman with an incurable blood disease snuck up, touched Jesus' clothes, and was cured. It was illegal for her to be with people, but Jesus stopped and affirmed her faith, saying it was her faith that had healed her. He completed her healing by restoring her socially and psychologically. (Mark 5:24b–34)

- Jesus' key words to Jairus were, *"Don't be afraid; just believe."* He raised Jairus' daughter from death, but first he drove the unbelievers from the room. (Mark 5:35–43)

- Mark blended the two healing stories into one of his intercalations to demonstrate that regardless of your background, social standing, income level, or anything else, the most important thing is faith in Jesus.

- Faith is not an end in itself. Believing hard that a specific thing will happen is not proper faith. Proper faith is a blanket faith in Jesus himself, granting him room to do whatever he thinks best.

- Faith and common sense are not mutually exclusive. They usually work together. Jesus demonstrated this when he miraculously healed a young girl, but told her parents to give her something to eat. (Mark 5:43)

- The people of Nazareth took offense at Jesus because of his style. He wasn't what they expected in a "prophet." Their shallowness—the fact that style meant more to them than Jesus' wisdom, power, and the content of his teaching—amazed Jesus. (Mark 6:2–6)

Part Three

WHO IS JESUS?

"I know the Pharisees are annoying somtimes, but you didn't have to toilet-papyrus their houses!"

The Bible For Eggheads

The next few chapters of Mark's Gospel seem pretty complex if you're looking to wring out of them every ounce of meaning Mark intended. Interpreters disagree about what system Mark used to organize his material, and about how much it matters.

☞ **GO TO:**

Mark 1:38–39; 3:7–12;
6:6; 6:56
(summary statements)

Mark 6:7–13 (apostles)

Mark 3:13–19
(second time)

Mark 1:4–8, 14
(John the Baptist)

Mark 6:14–29
(return appearance)

Mark 2:23–28; 7:1–23;
8:11–13
(showdowns)

Mark 6:30–44; 8:1–10
(feeds)

holistic: examining
lengthy passages for
patterns

Leading methods of interpretation include:

- Dividing Mark into sections using the <u>summary statements</u> peppered throughout the first half as boundaries for each section. Most of his text is about specific incidents in Jesus' ministry. Whenever the narrative generalizes—for example, *"So he traveled throughout Galilee, preaching in their synagogues and driving out demons"* (Mark 1:39)—it may signal the end of one narrative section and the beginning of another. Noting the summary statements allows us to examine the stories in between them to see why Mark grouped those together.

- Focusing on recurring subjects and themes. Using this approach we would notice in the upcoming section that the role of the <u>apostles</u> comes up for the <u>second time</u>; that <u>John the Baptist</u>, mentioned in the beginning of the book, gets an extensive <u>return appearance</u>; that there are more <u>showdowns</u> with the Pharisees; that Jesus <u>feeds</u> multitudes twice; and so on. Sometimes bringing together all the passages on one subject and studying them as a unit provides insight.

- **Holistic** reading and looking for literary devices. Following this method we'll note another of Mark's sandwiches, and a strange one at that—Jesus dispatching his apostles on their first missionary trip brackets the story of John the Baptist's gruesome death. Looking for literary devices, which we've just seen in the previous chapter on Mark 5:21–6:6, causes us to ask, What extra meaning does Mark intend by making these stories comment upon each other?

Don't let all the interpretive choices intimidate you. To paraphrase Jesus very loosely, interpretive tools were made for man, not man for interpretive tools. Knowing about different approaches like these is great if you hit a dry spell in your personal Bible study. If the Bible seems blah one day, switch to an approach you haven't used for awhile, and you'll usually get some new insights. Until then there's nothing wrong with simply reading the Bible, with or without a systematic approach.

Even a light reading of Mark's next few chapters reveals obvious themes. Confusion about the true identity of Jesus reaches a crescendo as everyone from the disciples to the Pharisees to Palestinian royalty gets in on the guessing game. The Pharisees continually ask for more proof of who Jesus is, yet remain unable or unwilling to grasp whatever Jesus shows them. The disciples, with whom we are meant to identify, embrace Jesus (unlike the Pharisees), yet display a seriously superficial perception of him (like the Pharisees). Nonetheless, even with the disciples' imperfect understanding, Jesus sends them out to spread God's kingdom.

Mark uses the Pharisees and the disciples to warn us there is much more meaning to Jesus than what we see on the surface. Will you get the symbolism in his actions, and understand him better than the befuddled apostles?

MARK 6:6–56
MORE CLUES ABOUT JESUS' SECRET IDENTITY

Let's Get Started

In the sixth chapter of his Gospel, Mark continues presenting Jesus' powerful acts as clues to who Jesus is. He also widens the focus to include more of the disciples' interactions with Jesus. At times they understand him enough to imitate him; at other times they can't understand him, and suffer for it. Through it all Mark uses their bewilderment to make the reader ponder the same question they do: who is this Jesus guy really?

This chapter also includes the only story in Mark's Gospel that does not have Jesus in it. In another example of his literary craftmanship, Mark uses this story to fill in what has happened to John the Baptist. What does that have to do with Jesus? The answers lie ahead . . . so let's get started!

MARK SANDWICH:
THE TWELVE AND HEROD

> **Mark 6:6b–7** Then Jesus went around teaching from village to village. Calling the Twelve to him, he sent them out two by two and gave them authority over evil spirits.

Jesus Spreads The Franchise

The short phrase about Jesus going from village to village could be one of the summary statements that seem to divide the sections of Mark. It is the <u>third time</u> Mark records Jesus taking his act "on tour" through the villages of Galilee. The crowds who welcome Jesus provide sharp contrast to the cold reception he received in his hometown. Perhaps it was because of his hometown's cold reception that for the rest of the book Jesus never enters a synagogue again, nor does he need to. At this point he's so famous people come to him. In fact, he can't get away from them, as we'll see.

Mark already told us Jesus intended the apostles *"to have authority to drive out demons"* (Mark 3:15)—a central aspect of Jesus' ministry in this Gospel. Now the apostles have watched the Master long enough; Jesus shares with them his authority over Satan. He puts them in the "driver's seat."

This act alone establishes Jesus as a unique figure in Jewish history. Characters such as Moses (see GWMB, pages 71–90), Samson (GWMB, pages 121–129), and Elijah (GWMB, pages 130–140) had great power from God, but none of them could pass their anointing to others at will. In fact, when Elisha (GWMB, pages 140–147) asked Elijah to pass on his anointing, <u>Elijah responded</u>, *"You have asked a difficult thing."* It was really up to God, which is exactly Mark's point. Jesus was the Son of God, so he could grant God's authority to anyone he chose. If we had to pinpoint a moment when the church was born, in one sense this is it. From this moment on, Jesus is not the only one who can do God's kingdom work; his followers can too.

You have to be proud of the apostles for one thing; once Jesus told them to spread God's kingdom, they got up and did it, whether they understood Jesus completely or not. Can you and I claim as much?

🖙 **GO TO:**

Mark 1:14, 39; 6:6
(third time)

🖙 **GO TO:**

2 Kings 2:10
(Elijah responded)

Something to Ponder

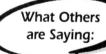

What Others are Saying:

John Henry Newman: God has created me to do Him some definite service; He has committed some work to me which He has not committed to another. I have my mission. Therefore I will trust Him. Whatever, wherever I am, I can never be thrown away. If I am in sickness, my sickness may serve Him; if in perplexity, my perplexity may serve Him; if I am in sorrow, my sorrow may serve Him. My sickness, or perplexity, or sorrow may be necessary causes of some great end, which is quite beyond us. He does nothing in vain.[1]

> **Mark 6:8–11** These were his instructions: "Take nothing for the journey except a staff—no bread, no bag, no money in your belts. Wear sandals but not an extra tunic. Whenever you enter a house, stay there until you leave that town. And if any place will not welcome you or listen to you, shake the dust off your feet when you leave, as a testimony against them."

Your Missionary Manual

Scholars speculate why Jesus gave such restrictive instructions to his first missionaries. He gave them different instructions later. The instructions in these verses were for this time and setting; it would be a mistake to apply them literally today.

This was no luxury junket. The apostles were asked to travel in voluntary poverty. *"No bread"* and *"no money"* meant they could not provide their own meals. "No bag" would translate today into, "don't hold your hat out for spare change," because the kind of bag Jesus referred to was commonly associated with beggars. The apostles were not to beg. *"Not an extra tunic"* meant they would not be able to stay warm at night if they had to sleep outdoors.

Jesus' directions left them heavily dependent on the hospitality of those who received their message. Jesus had already toured the Galilean villages three times, so many villagers would know what the apostles stood for. In a given village the first person to invite the missionaries in would probably be the most open to Jesus' kingdom. Jesus' command to the apostles not to change houses may reflect his desire to reward the most earnest seeker, and to eliminate the hurt feelings and politics generated by shifting houses each time someone offered more comfortable or prestigious quarters.

In light of what happened in Nazareth, Jesus also told them what to do if a town rejected the disciples: *"shake the dust off your feet when you leave, as a testimony against them."* What was that about?

> The Jews of Jesus' day believed that because they were God's people, Israel was more holy than surrounding countries. When pious Jews reentered God's territory after traveling outside of Israel, they customarily removed from their feet and clothing any dust from alien lands. Their goal was to dissociate themselves from the judgment that eventually would fall on the pagan nations.

KEY POINT

The true gospel message forces individuals to decide for or against God.

THE WAYBACK MACHINE

For the disciples Jesus transformed this common custom into the symbolic act of a prophet. Jewish villagers would not expect to see visiting brethren brush the dust of a Jewish town off themselves, as if the village were Gentile. Jews would understand the act to mean they were being consigned to God's judgment. This would force them to reconsider how they had regarded the disciples. In a way this made the disciples' presence like that of Jesus himself, because it forced people to choose for or against God.

What Others are Saying:

Walter W. Wessel: For the Jews heathen dust was defiling. The significance of the act here is to declare the place to be heathen and to make it clear that those who rejected the message must now answer for themselves. . . . The disciples' message, like that of Jesus, brings judgment as well as salvation. This always happens when the gospel is preached.[2]

> **Mark 6:12–13** They went out and preached that people should repent. They drove out many demons and anointed many sick people with oil and healed them.

Talented Amateurs

Okay, I'll just say out loud what I'm thinking. I can't believe it worked. I realize these men had spent time alone with Jesus, getting the parables explained to them, watching his adventures on the Gentile side of Lake Galilee, and so on. But it's a whole other thing for them to do what Jesus did. They preached his message. They did some mighty deeds!

What it proves, though, is not that the Twelve were saints. It proves Jesus' power and authority were so strong that he could work through well-meaning, imperfect amateurs—like you and me.

> **Mark 6:14–16** King Herod heard about this, for Jesus' name had become well known. Some were saying, "John the Baptist has been raised from the dead, and that is why miraculous powers are at work in him."
> Others said, "He is Elijah."
> And still others claimed, "He is a prophet, like one of the prophets of long ago."
> But when Herod heard this, he said, "John, the man I beheaded, has been raised from the dead!"

Got Guilt?

Mark interrupts the account of the apostles' first short-term mission trip, but will <u>return</u> to it briefly. Here he inserts the apparently **incongruous** story of how Herod killed John the Baptist.

Although these verses show how the whole region obsessed about Jesus' identity, you and I are probably more confused about Herod's identity.

"Herod" was not one guy's name. Herod was a family name. The Herodian dynasty, marked by brutish violence, incest, and chariotfuls of betrayal, extended from 40 B.C. to about A.D. 100. Herod the Great had ten wives (including his niece) and left six different wills when he died in 4 B.C. Each will differed regarding which of his **three sons** should inherit the kingdom, so the sons locked themselves into a power struggle for dad's throne that resolved only when Rome gave each of them a portion of their father's kingdom.

The son who ruled over Galilee was Herod Antipas, but he was never actually a king. According to Rome, technically each son was a **tetrarch**. Antipas stole his brother Philip's wife, Herodias. Herodias constantly goaded Antipas to strive for greater glory, so Antipas constantly pestered Rome to promote him to king. When other regional rulers received the title "king" before he did, he got so pushy about the issue that by A.D. 39, an irritated Emperor Caligula stripped Antipas of his rule, banished him to southern France, and gave his kingdom to a rival, Herodias's brother <u>Agrippa</u>.

Because Mark recorded this story years after Herod Antipas lost his power, it may be part of Mark's trademark irony to needle the disreputable ruler by calling him "King Herod." As you'll see, Antipas deserved disrespect.

Fiction Is Stranger Than Truth

Historical background aside, we can now focus on the real meat of the text. Jesus' fame had grown so that everyone from the peasants of Galilee to its ruler was buzzing, wondering who he was. I can see why someone would be reluctant to make the leap and blurt out, "He's God!" but some of their guesses seem even more goofy than the truth.

John the Baptist didn't do any supernatural works. Not one. So why would Herod Antipas suddenly attribute to him the ability to return from the dead and perform miracles? The probable cause

☞ **GO TO:**

Mark 6:30 (return)

THE WAYBACK MACHINE

incongruous: *not conforming to what surrounds it*

three sons: *Antipas, Archelaus, and Philip*

tetrarch: *a governor over one fourth of a province*

☞ **GO TO:**

Acts 25:13–26:32 (Agrippa)

is Herod's haunted, guilty conscience. The next verses reveal why he was probably plagued by guilt.

What Others are Saying:

Matthew Henry: It seems by this, that the rising of a prophet from the dead, to do mighty works, was thought neither impossible nor improbable, and it was now readily suspected when it was not true; but afterward, when it was true concerning Christ, is as obstinately gainsaid and denied. Those who most wilfully disbelieve the truth, are commonly most credulous of errors and fancies.[3]

> **Mark 6:17–23** For Herod himself had given orders to have John arrested, and he had him bound and put in prison. He did this because of Herodias, his brother Philip's wife, whom he had married. For John had been saying to Herod, "It is not lawful for you to have your brother's wife." So Herodias nursed a grudge against John and wanted to kill him. But she was not able to, because Herod feared John and protected him, knowing him to be a righteous and holy man. When Herod heard John, he was greatly puzzled; yet he liked to listen to him.
>
> Finally the opportune time came. On his birthday Herod gave a banquet for his high officials and military commanders and the leading men of Galilee. When the daughter of Herodias came in and danced, she pleased Herod and his dinner guests.
>
> The king said to the girl, "Ask me for anything you want, and I'll give it to you." And he promised her with an oath, "Whatever you ask I will give you, up to half my kingdom."

Happy Birthday From The Gruesome Twosome

History tells us the daughter of Herodias was Salome. Salome, conceived during Herodias's first marriage to Philip, the brother of Antipas, would be the niece of Antipas. (Sorry if this is confusing, but everything related to the Herodian dynasty is convoluted and weird.) It seems unlikely that Salome's dance moved Antipas so deeply because he was big into gymnastics. Presumably, the amoral Herodias sent her teenage daughter to perform erotically for Uncle Herod and all the high officials, military commanders, and leaders of Galilee. Yeesh.

> **Mark 6:24–29** She went out and said to her mother, "What shall I ask for?"
>
> "The head of John the Baptist," she answered.
>
> At once the girl hurried in to the king with the request: "I want you to give me right now the head of John the Baptist on a platter."
>
> The king was greatly distressed, but because of his oaths and his dinner guests, he did not want to refuse her. So he immediately sent an executioner with orders to bring John's head. The man went, beheaded John in the prison, and brought back his head on a platter. He presented it to the girl, and she gave it to her mother. On hearing of this, John's disciples came and took his body and laid it in a tomb.

John And Jesus

So why has Mark wedged this mildly disgusting story here of all places? The story of John's death may be Mark's way of foreshadowing what will happen to Jesus. The parallels are strong:

John the Baptist	Jesus
Innocent of any crime, but offended the civil rulers	Innocent of any crime, but offended the religious rulers
Held in civil prison before his execution	Held in civil prison before his execution
Herodias manipulated Herod to strike at John	Chief priests manipulated Pilate to strike at Jesus
Herod didn't want to kill John, but feared the consequences if he didn't	Pilate didn't want to kill Jesus, but feared the consequences if he didn't
Executed by a civil power	Executed by a civil power
Followers of John claimed the body and buried their leader	Followers of Jesus claimed the body and buried their leader

Mark's unusual placement of this story casts the shadow of the cross over the apostles' victories. The apostles' good work bracketing the misdeeds of Herod Antipas provides another set of contrasts:

Apostles	"King" Herod
Sent in poverty	Ruling in decadent luxury
Selfless	Selfish
Healed people	Killed people
Served Jesus because it was right	Sought Jesus as an entertainment
Brave	Cowardly
Martyred for serving God	Banished for serving self

☞ **GO TO:**

Luke 23:6–12
(entertainment)

Mark's placement of these two stories approaches brilliance. The disciples' work shows us the blessing and victory of following Jesus. John's death reminds us of the cost of following Jesus.

Mark gives us two options. Option 1 shows a cowardly man who has wealth but no character. Option 2 shows brave men who have character but no wealth. Option 1 enjoys earthly power. Option 2 enjoys heavenly power, which may cost us everything. Mark doesn't patronize us with any nonsense about Jesus making our lives easy. He shows us following Jesus can be costly, but it's right. Mark seems to say you can have Option 1 or Option 2, but not both. Choose. Now.

What Others are Saying:

R. C. Sproul: We are not to follow the world's lead but to cut across it and rise above it to a higher calling and style. This is a call to transcendent excellence, not a call to sloppy "out-of-it-ness." Christians who give themselves as living sacrifices and offer their worship in this way are people with a high standard of discipline. They are not satisfied with superficial forms of righteousness. The "saints" are called to a rigorous pursuit of the kingdom of God.[4]

JESUS INVENTS FAST FOOD

My friend Dave, a former biker, didn't become a Christian until age thirty. He's a pastor now, but back when he converted he had many questions about his new faith and about church life. One of the first and foremost was, "What is this thing called a 'potluck' and why do we have to have one every time we get together?" Well, Dave, here's where it all started.

> **Mark 6:30–34** The apostles gathered around Jesus and reported to him all they had done and taught. Then, because so many people were coming and going that they did not even have a chance to eat, he said to them, "Come with me by yourselves to a quiet place and get some rest."
>
> So they went away by themselves in a boat to a solitary place. But many who saw them leaving recognized them and ran on foot from all the towns and got there ahead of them. When Jesus landed and saw a large crowd, he had compassion on them, because they were like sheep without a shepherd. So he began teaching them many things.

A Brief Debriefing

The story about John the Baptist gave us a sense of passing time, and now we return to the account of the sent-out apostles. Mark's **terse** wrap-up gives us little detail of what they accomplished, but instead shows that Jesus and the apostles couldn't even get a few moments of peace to debrief. Mark rushes to the next big incident—one of very few miracles recorded in all four Gospels.

As Mark begins the tale of the miracle picnic, his account implies Jesus took the Twelve to the wilderness as a kind of training retreat. <u>Luke</u> leaves room for the same interpretation. In <u>Matthew</u>, however, it seems like Jesus wanted time away to mourn the death of his cousin. The Gospel of <u>John</u> begins the same story without relating it to anything that happened beforehand. These minor differences bring us to the Power Tool for this chapter: *read the New Testament cross-references.*

This is a rewarding practice any time. For example, you can't fully understand Paul's teaching on what it means to be led by the Holy Spirit until you've read all the passages where he writes about this topic. Reading parallel New Testament passages becomes especially useful when trying to understand the life of Christ. Here's why.

The Life Of Jesus In Full Color And High Definition

You may already know that every magazine or brochure printed in "full color" is, in reality, printed in only four ink colors: cyan, magenta, yellow, and black. Combining those four creates the other hues.

Some printed pieces work okay with sloppy color (the Sunday comics). Other printed works require exacting color (an ad for lipstick shades). The hardest, most unforgiving thing to print is a food ad. The slightest color variation can turn "luscious" into "sickening." If the restaurant's steak and shrimp ad has a slight greenish tinge, the printer has to fix it before people associate the restaurant with food poisoning. But remember, printing doesn't use green; it combines blue and yellow to make green. So is the shrimp-color problem in the blue plate or the yellow plate? The only way to know is to examine blue and yellow individually, adjusting first one, then the other.

Just as these four colors combine to create a fully dimensional picture, the four Gospels combine to create a fully dimensional picture of Jesus. Each one contributes a different "hue":

terse: short, concise, brusque

☞ **GO TO:**

Luke 9:10 (Luke)

Matthew 14:12–13 (Matthew)

John 6:1 (John)

POWER TOOL

Read the New Testament cross-references.

- Matthew emphasizes Hebrew scriptures and customs, and points out various Jewish prophecies that Jesus fulfilled.
- Mark emphasizes the powerful actions of Jesus more than the other writers, as you've been seeing.
- Luke wrote to a Gentile audience, and tells you in his opening paragraph that he is trying to gather the most complete account of Jesus up to that date.
- John focuses on lengthier discourses of Jesus and the deep theological significance of Jesus' words and deeds.

If we breeze through the individual Gospels in order to rush to the full color picture, some of our individual plates may be maladjusted, without our knowing it. We then believe in and worship a distortion—a Jesus who is more green or more magenta than the real Jesus (or worse, a blur), but one we think the Bible describes. If you want to understand Jesus *accurately*, you must first seek to understand each Gospel individually. The best way to do this is to compare and contrast how they treat similar stories. Only then can you assemble a correct picture of what the gospel writers were trying to show us. Remember, only you can help stamp out blue Jesuses.

What Others are Saying:

Eugene H. Peterson: Matthew, Mark, Luke, and John tell the story, each in his own way. Each narrative is distinct and has its own character. . . . we can be encouraged to celebrate each one as it is, and to magnify the features that make it distinct from the others. Instead of melting them down into an ingot of doctrine, we can burnish the features that individualize them. When we do that, our imagination expands, and the resurrection acquires the sharp features and hard surfaces of real life. Through the artistry of the four evangelists, the particularity and detail of local history, the kind we ourselves live in, becomes vivid.[5]

Parallel Picnics

This book deals only with Mark, so I'll be focusing on Mark's version, but I encourage you to read the parallel passages in all four Gospels, carefully noting the subtle differences between each rendition. You'll find the other accounts in Matthew 14:13–21, Luke 9:10–17, and John 6:5–13. May God reward your diligence!

> **Mark 6:35–44** By this time it was late in the day, so his disciples came to him. "This is a remote place," they said, "and it's already very late. Send the people away

so they can go to the surrounding countryside and villages and buy themselves something to eat."

But he answered, "You give them something to eat."

They said to him, "That would take eight months of a man's wages! Are we to go and spend that much on bread and give it to them to eat?"

"How many loaves do you have?" he asked. "Go and see."

When they found out, they said, "Five—and two fish."

Then Jesus directed them to have all the people sit down in groups on the green grass. So they sat down in groups of hundreds and fifties. Taking the five loaves and the two fish and looking up to heaven, he gave thanks and broke the loaves. Then he gave them to his disciples to set before the people. He also divided the two fish among them all. They all ate and were satisfied, and the disciples picked up twelve basketfuls of broken pieces of bread and fish. The number of the men who had eaten was five thousand.

He Must've Super-Sized It

Many scholars refuse to believe this story, because this miracle seems so . . . well, miraculous. Some write that the example Jesus set provoked everyone to break out their lunches and behave generously, and the people were fed because of a "miracle of sharing." Others claim this was a symbolic feeding, where everyone got a nibble, but not a real meal. Hello? Are they reading the same Bible I'm reading? Mark states Jesus *"divided the two fish among them all"* and that *"they all ate and were satisfied."* Nothing unclear there. Furthermore, every gospel writer treats the feeding of the five thousand as a major event in Jesus' ministry—something they would not have done if the incident were merely a nice time.

Mark says Jesus fed an arena's worth of people with five chunks of pita bread and a couple sardines, and he means it. Mark has no problem writing this because he believes Jesus is the same God who made the entire universe out of nothing. If this strains our faith, then strain we must, but there's no purpose in trying to correct Mark. It may be our **prerogative** to disbelieve him, but it is not our prerogative to put words in his mouth. Mark has forced a decision upon his readers—either Jesus is God, or he's not. This is exactly the confrontation Mark intends.

prerogative: *special right or privilege*

A Clash Of Symbols

When we get to Mark 8, we'll see there is more meaning to this miracle than the satisfaction of a crowd's hunger. Mark's wording contains many Old Testament links that point us to further layers of symbolism:

- The Greek word translated *"solitary place"* (6:32) and *"remote place"* (6:35) could also be translated "wilderness." Any Jew reading about a multitude in the wilderness miraculously receiving bread would realize Jesus was taking the place of Moses as the righteous leader of Israel.

- In a lesser yet similar miracle, the prophet <u>Elisha</u> once fed one hundred men with twenty loaves of bread. (Remember, these weren't our modern loaves of sliced bread; this would've been Middle East flat bread.) Mark's Jewish readers would see Jesus did a superior work, proving at the very least he was a prophet extraordinarily blessed by Yahweh.

- The phrase *"they were like sheep without a shepherd"* elicits <u>strong images</u> from Ezekiel. Speaking through Ezekiel long after the death of King David, God <u>promised</u> captive Israel, *"I will place over them one shepherd, my servant David, and he will tend them; he will tend them and be their shepherd. I the LORD will be their God, and my servant David will be prince among them. I the LORD have spoken."* Jesus, a descendant of David acting with the heart of the good shepherd, fulfills the old prophecy. (For a table of Bible references that cite God as a shepherd, see GWLC2, page 79.)

☞ **GO TO:**

2 Kings 4:42–44 (Elisha)

Ezekiel 34 (strong images)

Ezekiel 34:23–24 (promised)

What Others are Saying:

William L. Lane: It is appropriate to see in the feeding of the multitude a fresh affirmation of the promise that the Messiah will feast with men in the wilderness (Isa. 25:6–9). . . . The meal was eschatological to the degree that the people experienced rest in the wilderness and were nurtured by the faithful Shepherd of Israel, but it pointed beyond itself to an uninterrupted fellowship in the Kingdom of God.[6]

THIS WALK IS ABSOLUTELY DIVINE

In this next passage Mark writes about the disciples having an apostrophe. At least that's what my daughter Sarah called it when she was a middleschooler. Eventually she got it straight; they had an **epiphany**. But they didn't get as much out of it as they should've. The way Mark tells it, the disciples were even more confused than Sarah.

epiphany: striking revelation; vision of divinity

> **Mark 6:45–46** Immediately Jesus made his disciples get into the boat and go on ahead of him to Bethsaida, while he dismissed the crowd. After leaving them, he went up on a mountainside to pray.

Mark's Way With Segues

Mark definitely sets a brisk pace. We've barely had time to process the miraculous feeding as he launches into the next miracle with the concise transition, *"Immediately."* This word or a simple "Then . . ." are Mark's favorite segues throughout the book. His use of "immediately" doesn't always mean "just seconds later." He often seems to mean something like, "Next, . . ." but in this case, Mark sets the feeding of the five thousand closely beside the following miracle; he wants us to consider them together.

Notice once again, as <u>earlier</u>, Jesus values prayer with his Father so strongly that when it doesn't fit readily into his schedule, he forces it in.

☞ **GO TO:**

Mark 1:35 (earlier)

> **Mark 6:47–51** When evening came, the boat was in the middle of the lake, and [Jesus] was alone on land. He saw the disciples straining at the oars, because the wind was against them. About the fourth watch of the night he went out to them, walking on the lake. He was about to pass by them, but when they saw him walking on the lake, they thought he was a ghost. They cried out, because they all saw him and were terrified.
>
> Immediately he spoke to them and said, "Take courage! It is I. Don't be afraid."

Row, Row, Row Your Boat, Gently Past The Ghost

In this amazing passage Jesus seems to see his disciples with supernaturally enhanced vision, as he is miles from them in the middle of the night. Rowing into a headwind, the disciples made poor progress crossing the lake (but at least they aren't in danger, as in Jesus' <u>previous sea miracle</u>).

☞ **GO TO:**

Mark 4:35–41 (previous sea miracle)

THE WAYBACK MACHINE

IT'S
GREEK
TO ME

When Jesus decides to catch up with them, it is the *"fourth watch,"* a Roman reckoning of time that determined when the sentries changed shifts. The fourth watch lasted from 3:00 to 6:00 A.M., so the exhausted disciples were rowing in the dead of night.

The text reads, *"He was about to pass by them,"* which is puzzling. Why would Jesus decide to go out to the disciples, then pass them? If he saw them struggling, why would he snub them? The phrase doesn't make sense to us.

For that very reason some scholars of Greek have declared the phrase a mistranslation. They believe the correct rendering should be, "He was passing their way," implying Jesus was walking roughly *toward* the boat. Though that would make the phrase less problematic, the theory has as many detractors as supporters. Maybe the context suggests Mark is up to something else.

Even if Jesus intended to assist the disciples, they sure didn't think he was. Folklore of the time held that demonic specters sometimes rose up from bodies of water at night. Perhaps the disciples have this in mind when every last one of them shouts in terror. Poor guys. This trip began the day before with them seeking a chance to rest, but instead they ministered to thousands. I can understand why they'd be frazzled in the howling, tossing dark at three o'clock in the morning.

Jesus comforts his men with the phrase *ego aimi*—"I am." Again the Greek scholars divide into separate camps. Some say the wording is the same as the familiar statement you use when calling a good friend who knows your voice. You say, "Hi, it's me," and your friend recognizes you. Others hear echoes of Yahweh revealing his <u>name</u> to Moses: "I am who I am." I'm going to side with the Exodus 3:14 crowd. The next verses show why.

☞ **GO TO:**

Exodus 3:14 (name)

> **Mark 6:51–52** Then he climbed into the boat with them, and the wind died down. They were completely amazed, for they had not understood about the loaves; their hearts were hardened.

Understand The Loaves, Or You Could Be Toast

The account of Jesus feeding five thousand and the account of him walking on water seem to be entirely unrelated incidents at first; yet Matthew, Mark, and John tie the two stories together. (Luke omits the sea-walking incident.) I believe Mark gives us a big interpretive hint in tying this story directly to the miracle of the loaves and fish.

Let's stipulate for a moment that the miracle feeding in the wilderness is meant to evoke comparisons between Jesus and Moses. Looking back on Moses leading the Exodus, what are the two stand-out miracles? Certainly one is the daily manna that allowed millions of Jews to survive for forty years. For number two, I vote for the crossing of the Red Sea. It was blown into two halves by a strong wind, allowing the Israelites to walk across on dry ground. Wind . . . walking across the ocean . . . see any similarities to our current story?

There's more. In chapter 6 I detailed how only Yahweh could control the waters—a metaphor of his rulership over the universe's chaos. Now consider what Job said about God: *"He alone stretches out the heavens and treads on the waves of the sea. . . . He performs wonders that cannot be fathomed, miracles that cannot be counted. When he passes me, I cannot see him; when he goes by, I cannot perceive him"* (Job 9:8, 10–11). And as long as we're looking at the theme of <u>God passing</u> people by, check out Exodus 33:18–23.

Okay, are you back from looking that up? Let's combine these elements. Only God can tread the waves. His glory is so great that the only way humans can survive looking at him is to let him pass by, then glimpse his afterglow. When the disciples see Jesus, he identifies himself with the words Yahweh used to identify himself to Moses.

All of it points to Jesus' divinity.

Mark says the disciples didn't understand what Jesus was up to because they didn't understand the loaves. What had the disciples not understood? They saw firsthand Jesus could do tricks with food, but they didn't follow the logic to its conclusion; he could multiply food because he's God, which means he can do anything. Even walk on water. Full of heavenly glory because of his lengthy prayer time, Jesus enacted a divine epiphany right before his disciples' eyes. But it all went right past them, because *"their hearts were hardened."* This evokes another Mosaic reference, because the <u>same phrase</u> is used repeatedly to describe why Pharaoh would not release his Hebrew slaves just before the Exodus.

KEY POINT

Jesus' mighty miracles demonstrated his godhood.

☞ **GO TO:**

1 Kings 19:11 (God passing)

☞ **GO TO:**

Exodus 8:15, 32; 9:12; 10:1, 20, 27; 11:10 (same phrase)

Here is perhaps the coolest part of the story. When Jesus saw that his presence brought panic instead of comfort, he didn't shrug and trudge on. He didn't keep his mind in the heavenlies and pursue some lofty agenda, allowing the disciples to catch up whenever they could. He stopped what he was doing and got in their boat, and the wind calmed.

Could the lofty, intangible God of Moses clamber into the boat with twelve frightened men? No. This was why God became man. By choosing to be with them, Jesus demonstrated not only his divinity, but also the deep love that brought him to this planet—all expressed in one pedestrian act.

N. T. Wright: As part of his human vocation, grasped in faith, sustained in prayer, tested in confrontation, agonized over in further prayer and doubt, and implemented in action, he believed he had to do and be, for Israel and the world, that which according to scripture only YHWH himself could do and be.[7]

Max Lucado: I saw God. The God who can't sit still when the storm is too strong. The God who lets me get frightened enough to need him and then comes close enough for me to see him. The God who uses my storms as his path to come to me. I saw God. It took a storm for me to see him. But I saw him. And I'll never be the same.[8]

DAYS OF POPULARITY

> **Mark 6:53–56** When they had crossed over, they landed at Gennesaret and anchored there. As soon as they got out of the boat, people recognized Jesus. They ran throughout that whole region and carried the sick on mats to wherever they heard he was. And wherever he went—into villages, towns or countryside—they placed the sick in the marketplaces. They begged him to let them touch even the edge of his cloak, and all who touched him were healed.

Off Course, But On Point

Back in verse 45 Jesus dispatched the disciples to Bethsaida. The wind must have blown their boat far off course, for the disciples land at Gennesaret (see illustration, page 135). Having had no

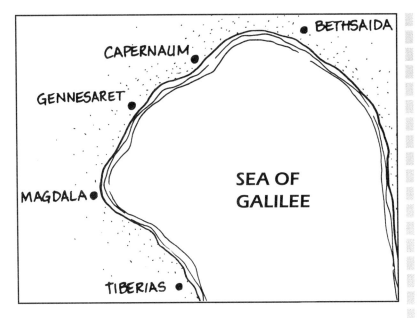

Map of Bethsaida and Gennesaret

The apostles wound up far from their original destination. Jesus had sent them to Bethsaida, but the wind pushed them to Gennesaret. Jesus healed everybody there anyway.

sleep (but a really great workout on the rowing machine), the disciples launch into another full day of trying to keep up with the tireless, compassionate Jesus.

This short passage is another of Mark's summary statements, indicating the end of this group of stories. With people rushing to him everywhere he ventures, Jesus definitely has momentum on his side. Naturally the Pharisees are about to do their best to stop it, but, like Mark, we'll save that for the next chapter on Mark 7:1–8:21.

KEEP IT REAL—Mark unveiled some of his most compelling stories in this chapter. So many lessons, so little space! Here are just a couple:

• Mark 6:37. The apostles had traveled the countryside exercising Jesus' authority to heal people and drive out demons. But when Jesus said, *"You give them something to eat,"* they immediately returned to the old habit of working from their own resources rather than depending on God's resources. When Jesus was through, there were enough leftovers for each disciple to have his own basketful. *Father, help me depend upon you. Even if all I have are five loaves and two fish, you're never bankrupt.*

• Mark 6:48–51. The disciples thought of mountaintops as the place where revelation occurred, so they didn't recognize Jesus when he appeared to them down on the water. *Lord, help me to place no mental limits on where I expect to find you. I don't ever want to mistakenly call something evil simply because you're doing a wonder I've never seen you do before.*

Study Questions

1. Jesus told the apostles that if a town rejected them, they were to shake the dust off their feet, as a testimony against the town (Mark 6:11). Why did he tell them to do this?
2. What were the three leading guesses about who Jesus was? Were any of them correct?
3. What are the two words Mark often uses to transition from one story to the next?
4. Name three Old Testament references evoked by Jesus' miracle feeding of five thousand people in the wilderness.
5. According to Job, God is the only one who can do what?

CHAPTER WRAP-UP

- Mark includes only one story in his Gospel that does not involve Jesus: the story of how Herod killed John the Baptist. Because Mark inserted the story in the middle of his account of Jesus passing authority to the apostles, he may have put it there to remind us of the cost of discipleship, and to foreshadow the death of Jesus. (Mark 6:6–30)

- Mark intends us to take the miraculous feeding of five thousand people literally. However, the account may also have symbolic meanings drawn from the Old Testament to show how Jesus was, like Moses, the one God sent to lead Israel; like Elisha, an extraordinarily anointed prophet; and, as promised by Ezekiel, the good shepherd (Mark 6:31–44). The real meaning of the story, though, is to demonstrate that Jesus was God.

- Jesus' second ocean miracle, walking on the water, also demonstrated that he was God, for the Old Testament says only God can tread the waves (Mark 6:45–52). But the disciples did not yet fully understand who he was.

- Instead of going to their intended destination, Bethsaida, Jesus and the disciples were blown off course to Gennesaret, where Jesus healed the throngs who pursued him. (Mark 6:53–56)

MARK 7:1–8:21
OUT-OF-BOUNDS JESUS

CHAPTER HIGHLIGHTS

- What Makes a Person Unclean?
- Jesus among the Gentiles
- Meaning in the Feedings
- "Do You Still Not Understand?"

Let's Get Started

I happened to be driving to an office in Seattle the night the Grateful Dead played in Seattle Center's Memorial Stadium. You couldn't miss the Dead Heads—legions of fans who dropped their own lives in order to follow the Dead from state to state. Long-haired folks wearing vivid tie-dyed everything (even socks!) filled the streets. Beat-up Volkswagen vans festooned with peace signs and stickers putt–putted along at mellow speeds. (I had to chuckle at one van bearing a psychedelic paint job and a sticker reading, "Who are the Grateful Dead, and why do they keep following me everywhere?") The grocery stores literally sold out of beer as the Dead Heads prepared to party. When the band finally fired up their amps in the outdoor stadium, the city rang with their music for miles around. Cops had to redirect traffic because Dead Heads who were too poor to afford tickets danced in the streets.

This phenomenon is probably the closest modern comparison we could make to the state of Jesus' ministry at the end of Mark 6. He had inspired the popular imagination in a way that lured crowds wherever he went, stopping traffic in the towns, drawing thousands in the country. *"All who touched him were <u>healed</u>"* (Mark 6:56), so folks probably danced in the streets during Jesus' tour too.

Given an ongoing religious sensation of this magnitude, we shouldn't be surprised by the return of the Pharisees. Today Christians tend to boo them as if they were the black-hatted, handlebar-mustached villains in a Victorian melodrama. Though we owe them a debt of gratitude (as I detailed in the chapter on Mark 2:1–3:6), in the following account they live up to their villainous ste-

☞ **GO TO:**

Mark 6:56 (healed)

reotype. Once again bringing in Grand Poobahs from Jerusalem's temple cult, they deliberately try to embarrass Jesus in public.

☞ **GO TO:**

Mark 2:1–3:6 (earlier)

Why did Mark put this story here, when it would fit so readily with the other conflict stories he assembled <u>earlier</u>? Because of the subject matter. The Pharisees accuse Jesus and his disciples of being "unclean." Mark uses the story as a formal introduction to three stories of Jesus playing way outside the bounds of pious Jewish "cleanliness."

Throughout these stories the disciples act increasingly dim-witted and shallow. Jesus doesn't give up on them; instead, he patiently keeps explaining. And explaining. And explaining. Finally even he sounds amazed at their lack of progress, marveling aloud, "Do you still not understand?"

alfresco: *outdoors; open air*

In the next few passages, Jesus calls a woman in need a "dog," pokes his fingers where they don't belong, spits on a sick guy, and dines **alfresco** with thousands of despised Gentiles—all while insisting that his idea of purity is superior to the Pharisees'. How can you resist learning more about the unpredictable Jesus?

WHAT MAKES A PERSON UNCLEAN?

Mark 7:1–5 The Pharisees and some of the teachers of the law who had come from Jerusalem gathered around Jesus and saw some of his disciples eating food with hands that were "unclean," that is, unwashed. (The Pharisees and all the Jews do not eat unless they give their hands a ceremonial washing, holding to the tradition of the elders. When they come from the marketplace they do not eat unless they wash. And they observe many other traditions, such as the washing of cups, pitchers and kettles.)

So the Pharisees and teachers of the law asked Jesus, "Why don't your disciples live according to the tradition of the elders instead of eating their food with 'unclean' hands?"

Killing Ancient Cooties

The Pharisees had little formal power in Israel, so they brought in the big guns. These teachers, bureaucrats from the Jerusalem Temple's legal department, hoped to find fault with Jesus, as they did with anything that had not originated with themselves.

Of all Jesus was saying and doing, the shallow legalists focus on the issue of unclean hands. Jesus has touched a bleeding woman, a dead body, and numerous sick people, all of them "unclean." In every case Jesus did not become infected; rather, the people he touched became purified.

Imagine your church put on a series of revival meetings that was fabulously successful; hundreds of unbelievers converted to Christianity, miraculous healings occurred, divorced couples reunited. Then your denominational headquarters sent some leaders to check out the excitement, and all they paid attention to was a misspelling in the outdoor banner. These temple teachers were that trivial. They did not care about the people being healed or the good news of the reign of God breaking in. All they cared about was *"the tradition of the elders."*

In Greek the word translated here as "unclean" is *koinos*, which means "common." The word relates to a Hebrew term meaning "as is." The legalists weren't accusing the disciples of eating with literal grime or dirt on their hands; they were accusing the disciples of being normal. In the Pharisee's mind "common" was not good enough for God.

IT'S GREEK TO ME

God did command priests who offered sacrifices at the altar to have <u>clean hands</u> and feet. Typical of their superholiness, the Pharisees extended the commandment and tried to apply it not only to temple priests but to everyone, all the time.

The Jews lived in a desert culture, so they wanted to minimize the amount of water "wasted" on this activity. At the same time they wanted to meet the technical definition of having washed one's hands. Centuries of oral tradition developed, specifying whether you should hold your arms so the water trickled up or down them; how to hold your fingers so that water could seep through to the other side of your hand; and so on. By sometime around Jesus' era, the "washing" was done with one little fistful of water taken in the palm and spread around the hand. This ritual rinsing was a nod at God's purity laws, not a genuine cleansing. Its chief value was in demonstrating that you weren't like the pagan non-Jews. It cleaned away little more than imaginary Gentile cooties.

By gathering around Jesus and confronting him publicly about his sloppy followers, the Pharisees and Jerusalem lawyers hoped to demonstrate to the crowd that uncredentialed

THE WAYBACK MACHINE

☞ **GO TO:**

Exodus 30:17–21
(clean hands)

Jesus taught incompetently. They had blurred the line between Scripture, which God authored, and tradition, which humans authored. Jesus is about to show them the difference—and none too gently.

What Others are Saying:

John Fischer: Washing cups, pitchers, and kettles? Who cares? Only the Pharisees. . . . Not only do these traditions separate the Pharisee from the rest of humanity, they allow the Pharisee to deflect the larger issues of love, mercy, and justice by being consumed with irrelevant minutiae. . . . Pharisees erect a god ominous and powerful and bigger than everybody and then go behind the façade and control it from the inside so as to make themselves its high and lofty representatives . . . This is the heart of the system of religion Jesus detests and will ultimately destroy.[1]

> **Mark 7:6–13** He replied, "Isaiah was right when he prophesied about you hypocrites; as it is written:
> "'These people honor me with their lips,
> but their hearts are far from me.
> They worship me in vain;
> their teachings are but rules taught by men.'
> You have let go of the commands of God and are holding on to the traditions of men."
> And he said to them: "You have a fine way of setting aside the commands of God in order to observe your own traditions! For Moses said, 'Honor your father and your mother,' and, 'Anyone who curses his father or mother must be put to death.' But you say that if a man says to his father or mother: 'Whatever help you might otherwise have received from me is Corban' (that is, a gift devoted to God), then you no longer let him do anything for his father or mother. Thus you nullify the word of God by your tradition that you have handed down. And you do many things like that."

The Best Offense Is A Good Reference

Instead of answering his opponents' question, Jesus lobs a trustworthy hand grenade for any religious discussion; he labels the Pharisees "hypocrites"—a Greek term that rose from the theater arts and originally referred to actors, pretenders, and mimics. The surprised Pharisees probably did double takes fast enough to get whiplash.

Jesus backs up his response by quoting a <u>potent reference</u> from Isaiah. The reference condemns not only phony people but anyone who makes up religious rules and places them higher than God's Word. Jesus adds, in effect, "You dudes *totally* live up to this!"

To prove his assertion, Jesus cites an extreme example of their error. He quotes one of the Ten Commandments against them (see WBFM, pages 22–23). This devastating technique pits the Pharisees' own highest authority against them. The principle underlying Jesus' argument was that if a circumstance ever arose where Scripture and oral tradition conflicted, the religious leaders favored oral tradition, thereby placing their own ponderings higher than God's commands. The details underlying Jesus' argument were related to the tradition of corban.

Corban was a technical term related to offerings. If you declared something "corban," in theory it was no longer yours, but God's, and sooner or later you would donate it (or the profits from it) to the Temple. The tradition, however, allowed loopholes and complexities too exhaustive to describe here. Sometimes people declared something "corban" not to give it to God, but to get out of giving it to someone else (such as a creditor). Sometimes people declared something "corban" but waited a l-o-o-o-n-n-g time before actually donating it.

Jesus attacked the position that held a vow of "corban" was utterly unbreakable, even if spoken rashly or if the vow resulted in unforeseen consequences. When Jesus says, *"you no longer let him do anything for his father or mother,"* he means it literally. If you promised to give your money to the Temple, and then your life circumstance changed—say, your mother became ill and ran up large medical bills—the temple officials would not release you from your vow so that you could fulfill your obligation to help your parents. This made the vow more binding than the Ten Commandments.

Don't miss the arrogance of the religious leaders. The interpretation of Torah that said "anything promised to the Temple must come to the Temple," was created by temple employees—government fat cats putting their own comfort ahead of all else, then making it sound legit with religious terminology.

Jesus' final phrase (*"And you do many things like that"*) means this is just one example of the heartless legalism of the scribes and Pharisees.

☞ **GO TO:**

Isaiah 29:13
(potent reference)

THE WAYBACK MACHINE

KEY POINT

Any religious tradition that contradicts Scripture is dispensable.

What Others are Saying:

Dallas Willard: And here also lies the fundamental mistake of the scribe and the Pharisee. They focus on the *actions* that the law requires and make elaborate specifications of exactly what those actions are and of the manner in which they are to be done. They also generate immense social pressure to force conformity of action to the law as they interpret it. They are intensely self-conscious about doing the right thing and about being thought to have done the right thing. But the inner dimensions of their personality, their heart and character, are left to remain contrary to what God has required.[2]

Richard C. Halverson: Tradition can be dangerous. It can not only modify the truth; it can replace it altogether.[3]

> **Mark 7:14–15** Again Jesus called the crowd to him and said, "Listen to me, everyone, and understand this. Nothing outside a man can make him 'unclean' by going into him. Rather, it is what comes out of a man that makes him 'unclean.'"

Jesus Blesses Pepperoni Pizza

☞ **GO TO:**

Mark 7:6, 9, 14, 18, 20 (starts over)

If you read this passage carefully, Mark's introductory phrases make it seem like Jesus' lecture <u>starts over</u> again several times. Textual experts believe Mark gathered teachings of Jesus from different occasions into one dissertation on true purity.

The subject shifts here. The discussion was about the proper place of human traditions. Now it addresses what is true purity before God. Jesus asserts the way a person becomes "unclean" (which is to say, sinful before God) has nothing to do with physical items such as food. "Uncleanness" is a spiritual condition that arises from sinful tendencies in a person's heart, which Jesus will list in verses 21 and 22.

KEY POINT

Sin doesn't come from outside us; it comes from inside us.

This seems like a simple concept to us. Suppose I'm standing in line at Blockbuster to rent an edifying movie like *Babette's Feast,* but the guy in line behind me is renting porn. If he gets jostled and the porn video touches me, that does not make me sinful. The sinful part of pornography comes from within me. If I watch it and my mind and heart lay out a welcome mat for sexual immorality, then I am unclean.

The concept stumps the disciples completely. Raised to follow the dietetic food laws God gave Moses, they had always been taught that consuming nonkosher food separated you from God. They didn't realize Jesus was rewriting the book.

> **Mark 7:17–19** After he had left the crowd and entered the house, his disciples asked him about this parable. "Are you so dull?" he asked. "Don't you see that nothing that enters a man from the outside can make him 'unclean'? For it doesn't go into his heart but into his stomach, and then out of his body." (In saying this, Jesus declared all foods "clean.")

Even Brussels Sprouts?

We can see how confused the disciples were, because they took Jesus aside and asked for an explanation of the "parable." Jesus had not used any metaphors, so he could not explain it any simpler or plainer. His private explanation was nearly a repeat of his public assertion.

Jesus does add one interesting wrinkle, though. The **mishnah** admitted that excrement definitely could be offensive, but taught it was not ritually impure. As Dave Barry writes, I am not making this up. For reasons that totally escape me, rabbis considered poop kosher. So Jesus makes a wry argument, possibly mocking the Pharisee's contradictory tradition; if food has the power to make you unclean, what makes it come out of you clean? (For a fuller discussion of "clean" and "unclean" foods, see GWHN, pages 151–157.)

mishnah: literally, "repetition"; written traditions of the rabbis

Jesus is trying his best to show the disciples God's new reign is not about external style. It's about the state of your heart toward God and fellow humans. God would rather have you <u>eat pork</u> with a heart full of love and mercy, than keep kosher with a heart full of self-righteousness and judgmentalism.

☞ **GO TO:**

Romans 14:17–18 (eat pork)

Richard J. Foster: [The Pharisees'] righteousness consisted in control over externals, often including the manipulation of others. The extent to which we have gone beyond the righteousness of the scribes and the Pharisees is seen in how much our lives demonstrate the internal work of God upon the heart. . . . Our world is hungry for genuinely changed people. Leo Tolstoy observes, "Everyone thinks of changing humanity and nobody thinks of changing himself."[4]

What Others are Saying:

> **Mark 7:20–23** He went on: "What comes out of a man is what makes him 'unclean.' For from within, out of men's hearts, come evil thoughts, sexual immorality, theft, murder, adultery, greed, malice, deceit, lewdness, envy, slander, arrogance and folly. All these evils come from inside and make a man 'unclean.'"

It's A List, Not A Menu

Jesus sharpens his point by detailing his redefinition of "unclean." Even the slowest disciple must have understood Jesus by the time he finished reciting this list of human evil. *Of course* all these things matter more to God than whether you mix meat and dairy products.

KEEP IT REAL—It's fun to sit in the balcony and jeer at the stupid Pharisees and temple lawyers for putting their own traditions ahead of God's Word. Be careful. We do the same. "Where?" you ask. It would be too easy to tell hundreds of stories about church people who violate every "love one another" command in *Scripture* because someone switched to a different *tradition* of worship music. Christians protest and boycott certain sins such as homosexuality or abortion, while remaining tolerant or even actively supportive of <u>greed</u>, which is also a sin.

The truth is we pick and choose the sins we denounce and the sins we commit based on our culture and traditions, just as the Pharisees did. Before we pride ourselves on how closely we follow Scripture, we'd better invest in a reality check and pray that Jesus is not marveling, "Are you so dull?"

☞ **GO TO:**

Luke 12:15; Romans 1:29; Ephesians 5:3; Colossians 3:5 (greed)

JESUS AMONG THE GENTILES

Most Jews thought the Messiah would save them from the Gentiles, yet the Old Testament said Messiah would rule over not only the Jews, but all nations. At this point in Mark, only one man knew what this meant. Thank God, he decided to demonstrate.

> **Mark 7:24–26** Jesus left that place and went to the vicinity of Tyre. He entered a house and did not want anyone to know it; yet he could not keep his presence secret. In fact, as soon as she heard about him, a woman whose little daughter was possessed by an evil spirit came and fell at his feet. The woman was a Greek, born in Syrian Phoenicia. She begged Jesus to drive the demon out of her daughter.

Can Jesus Minister While Tyred?

POWER TOOL

Pay attention to geography.

Jesus' change in location brings us to this section's Power Tool: *pay attention to geography*. Most places in the Bible are unfamiliar to us, so we tend to hurry past them. In doing so we miss a lot of meaning.

In this passage the significance of Tyre is its relation to Israel. Tyre is north of Israel, but not part of Israel. Tyre is Gentile territory. Some things Jesus did there do not make sense unless we realize he was not addressing Jews.

Mark sets as much of his Gospel as he can around the Sea of Galilee. In John's Gospel it seems as though Jesus spent most of his time around Jerusalem. Each writer has a reason for emphasizing the locations he chooses. If we're not paying attention, the extra meaning sails over our heads.

> Josephus, a Jew who lived around the time of Jesus, wrote that people from Tyre were the Jews' "bitterest enemies." Economically Tyre was more successful than Roman-occupied Palestine. Tyre bought much of the <u>food</u> produced in the Galilean region, so in a way Tyre took bread from Jewish peasants. Within the territory of Tyre was a gorgeous, commercially magnificent port city, also called Tyre, filled with Greek architecture and pagan temples (see illustration, page 146).
>
> Though nothing physical marked the boundary between Israel and Tyre, in rulers' minds the border was as unyielding as that between New Mexico and Texas. People in Galilee resented Tyrians because they felt outclassed financially, threatened religiously, and intimidated militarily. Many Jews assumed Tyre wanted to expand its borders by stealing Galilean territory.

THE WAYBACK MACHINE

What Others are Saying:

D. J. Wiseman: Herod I rebuilt the main temple [of Tyre], which would have been standing when our Lord visited the district bordering Tyre and Sidon. People of Tyre heard him speak (Mark 3:8; Luke 6:17), and he cited Tyre as a heathen city which would bear less responsibility than those Galilean towns which constantly witnessed his ministry (Matthew 11:21–22; Luke 10:13–14).[5]

Beware Of Greeks Begging Gifts

Jesus seems to have retreated to Tyre because the frenzied Jesus-mania of Galilee threatened to spin out of control. Mark tells us Jesus tried to keep his presence in Tyre secret, but his fame had grown too great, and who would find him, if not a determined mother with a distressed child?

Map of Tyre and Galilee

Heavily influenced by Hellenism, Tyre and Sidon displayed the sophistication of Greek culture in coinage and architecture. Most Jews, especially those in neighboring Galilee, resented Tyrians.

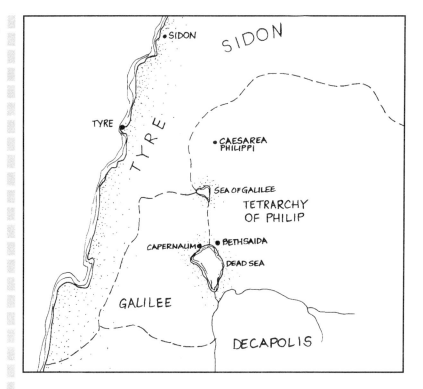

☞ **GO TO:**

Matthew 15:24
(lost sheep)

This persistent Greek woman normally would have no reason to seek out a Jewish Messiah. Obviously, word of Jesus' healing abilities had spread far outside Israel, for the woman not only seeks him but she also travels to him, prostrates herself before him, and begs for his help.

Jesus had ministered to Gentiles before, when he traveled to the region of the Gadarenes and freed a man from a legion of demons, but many Jews despised the people of Tyre. Furthermore, Jesus said he was sent for the <u>lost sheep</u> *of Israel*. What would he do with this objectionable woman throwing herself at his mercy?

> **Mark 7:27–30** "First let the children eat all they want," he told her, "for it is not right to take the children's bread and toss it to their dogs."
>
> "Yes, Lord," she replied, "but even the dogs under the table eat the children's crumbs."
>
> Then he told her, "For such a reply, you may go; the demon has left your daughter."
>
> She went home and found her child lying on the bed, and the demon gone.

Jesus Dispenses Puppy Chow

Jesus' reactions surprised us the last time he visited Gentiles (see the chapter on Mark 4:35–5:20), but that was nothing compared to this. Instead of helping the woman, Jesus refuses. What's more, he refers to Israelites as "children" and to Gentiles as "dogs." This woman is a Gentile, so Jesus is calling her a dog!

There is one softening aspect to his response, though. The Greek term for "dogs" used here is not the word for marauding street dogs that Jews often used when describing non-Jews. The word "dogs" here means "little dogs of the home"—basically, puppies. Maybe Jesus did mean it more kindly than it reads. We weren't there, so all we can do is speculate.

I like this lady. She managed to find Jesus while he was traveling **incognito**. She's the first person since John the Baptist to grasp who Jesus is and refer to him as "Lord." She is also the first to enter into a substantive discussion of Jesus' message on his own terms. With amazing humility, presence of mind, and wit, she accepts Jesus' metaphor, and builds upon it. On top of that, her request is selfless. She weathers his insult nobly and remains focused on the health of her daughter.

Had Jesus already sensed her excellent qualities, and merely sought to test her? Or did her answer truly change his mind? Either way he rewards her persistence, just as he did the men who broke through the roof to enter his presence. *"For such a reply"* he grants her request, and in doing so Jesus proves again he loves non-Jews too.

What kind of reply is *"such a reply"*? Clever? Flexible? Humble? In recounting the same story, Matthew tells us Jesus rewarded <u>her faith</u>. She takes the Lord at his word instead of begging him to go to her house, as did Jairus the synagogue leader. Here is Mark's subversiveness once again; a mere woman, and a Gentile one at that, shows more faith than a Jewish man.

Maya Angelou: Being a woman is hard work. . . . The woman who survives intact and happy must be at once tender and tough. . . . In a time and world where males hold sway and control, the pressure upon women to yield their rights-of-way is tre-

IT'S GREEK TO ME

incognito: with identity concealed

☞ **GO TO:**

Matthew 15:28 (her faith)

Something to Ponder

What Others are Saying:

mendous. And it is under those very circumstances that the woman's toughness must be in evidence. . . . The struggle for equality continues unabated, and the woman warrior who is armed with wit and courage will be among the first to celebrate victory.[6]

Charles Spurgeon: Jesus will surely heal those who believe in him; he knows the best method; and he is to be trusted without reserve.[7]

> **Mark 7:31–35** Then Jesus left the vicinity of Tyre and went through Sidon, down to the Sea of Galilee and into the region of the Decapolis. There some people brought to him a man who was deaf and could hardly talk, and they begged him to place his hand on the man.
>
> After he took him aside, away from the crowd, Jesus put his fingers into the man's ears. Then he spit and touched the man's tongue. He looked up to heaven and with a deep sigh said to him, *"Ephphatha!"* (which means, "Be opened!"). At this, the man's ears were opened, his tongue was loosened and he began to speak plainly.

The Doctor Will Poke You Now

Mark lived in a "pre-map" culture, so his listing of Jesus' travel itinerary seems strange to us. Going from Tyre to Decapolis by way of Sidon is like going from Los Angeles to New Orleans by way of Canada. Mark may be orienting us culturally more than geographically, emphasizing these locales because Gentiles populate them.

☞ GO TO:

Mark 5:20 (fame)

By the time Jesus reaches Decapolis, his <u>fame</u> has preceded him. I love Jesus' response when presented with a man who is both deaf and mute; he leads the man to a private place. This shows tremendous respect for the man, because it treats his problem without turning him into a spectacle. The sort of carnival atmosphere common in today's healing ministries stands in stark contrast with Jesus' low-key, considerate approach.

What follows next, though, seems bizarre. Why does Jesus' poke his fingers into the man's ears? Then he spits and, without first washing his hands, touches the man's tongue. Mark doesn't tell us what Jesus spit at. Ancient peoples widely believed, however, that saliva had healing properties. Jesus probably spit on his own fingers, then used them to touch the man's tongue.

Why? First of all, Jesus can't communicate with the man verbally, because the man can't hear. This healing requires gestures. Second, if a doctor diagnosed your health without taking your temperature, using a stethoscope, or checking your blood pressure, you would doubt the doctor's competence. People in the first century had a similar expectation that their healers would do something purposeful to facilitate healing. Jesus is meeting the man's expectation.

Jesus then <u>looks</u> into heaven, the source of his power, just as he did before breaking the bread when he fed the multitude. He prays to his Father in the form of one poignant sigh. Then he says, "Ephphatha!" (eff-FAH-thah).

☞ **GO TO:**

Mark 6:41 (looks)

Mark tells us that *"At this, the man's ears were opened."* Imagine your ear channels snapping open and all the sounds of the world suddenly pouring in with startling clarity—the breeze whispering over the grass, children playing and giggling in the distance, the murmurs of your nearby friends. No wonder this man instantly found he had something to say!

A. B. Simpson: Christ never performed miracles as spectacles for the gaping crowd, nor does He do it yet. The men that want to parade divine healing as a spectacular attraction belong to another world than that of the lowly Nazarene.[8]

What Others are Saying:

> **Mark 7:36–37** Jesus commanded them not to tell anyone. But the more he did so, the more they kept talking about it. People were overwhelmed with amazement. "He has done everything well," they said. "He even makes the deaf hear and the mute speak."

. . . Although It Was Rumored He Did His Steaks Medium

Despite Jesus' command to keep silent, the witnesses of this healing talked, and *"people were overwhelmed with amazement."* Even so these Gentiles did not completely realize what they were witnessing. They wouldn't have known about the Jewish prophet Isaiah, who seven centuries earlier predicted: *"Say to those with fearful hearts, 'Be strong, do not fear; your God will come, he will come with vengeance; with divine retribution he will come to save you.' Then will the eyes of the blind be opened and the ears of the deaf unstopped. Then will the lame leap like a deer, and the mute tongue shout for joy"* (Isaiah 35:4–6). The astonishing thing about this ancient prophecy was that Jesus was fulfilling it for both Jews and non-Jews. Though the grateful crowd was oblivious to the prophecy, they concluded, *"He has done everything well."*

> **Mark 8:1–10** During those days another large crowd gathered. Since they had nothing to eat, Jesus called his disciples to him and said, "I have compassion for these people; they have already been with me three days and have nothing to eat. If I send them home hungry, they will collapse on the way, because some of them have come a long distance."
>
> His disciples answered, "But where in this remote place can anyone get enough bread to feed them?"
>
> "How many loaves do you have?" Jesus asked.
>
> "Seven," they replied.
>
> He told the crowd to sit down on the ground. When he had taken the seven loaves and given thanks, he broke them and gave them to his disciples to set before the people, and they did so. They had a few small fish as well; he gave thanks for them also and told the disciples to distribute them. The people ate and were satisfied. Afterward the disciples picked up seven basketfuls of broken pieces that were left over. About four thousand men were present. And having sent them away, he got into the boat with his disciples and went to the region of Dalmanutha.

Mark And A Basket Case

In the words of Yogi Bera, "It's déjà vu all over again." Crowd . . . loaves . . . feeding . . . Didn't we just read this passage? Nope; Mark has recorded two miraculous mass feedings. In substance the stories overlap strongly, but a sharp reader can spot a few minor differences. While the first feeding story contains many allusions to Jewish thought and Old Testament passages, the second story has none. In the first story the leftovers filled twelve baskets of the size suited for taking an offering. The second story uses a different Greek word for baskets, found also in <u>Acts</u>; the leftovers filled seven baskets large enough to hold a person. And of course, the number of people who are fed is different.

This last point especially puzzles us. In our culture storytelling follows a pattern where each section tops the previous section until

☞ **GO TO:**

Acts 9:25 (Acts)

you reach a climax at the end. To our eye Mark seems to have goofed by presenting a miracle that uses five loaves and two fish to feed five thousand men, then later recounting a "lesser" miracle that uses seven loaves and a few fish to feed four thousand. In the next section I'll explain why Mark has not goofed.

Middle Eastern minds often attached symbolic significance to numbers. Jesus will forcefully draw the disciples' attention to the numbers of each miracle in a few verses; only then can we see the real meaning of the two miracle picnics.

Mark concludes the account of the second feeding with, *"he got into the boat with his disciples and went to the region of Dalmanutha."* Dalmanutha is not mentioned in any ancient literature we've found. Scholars have made so many guesses about its location, you can have your pick of 101 Dalmanuthas. The next passage has our Jewish buddies the Pharisees returning, so this little phrase seems to conclude Jesus' sojourn among the Gentiles.

MEANING IN THE FEEDINGS

> **Mark 8:11–12** The Pharisees came and began to question Jesus. To test him, they asked him for a sign from heaven. He sighed deeply and said, "Why does this generation ask for a miraculous sign? I tell you the truth, no sign will be given to it."

You Already Have A Sign; It Says "Closed"

The Pharisees had already seen Jesus drive out <u>demons</u> and perform miraculous <u>healings</u>. If they were paying attention, they could have noticed the miraculous feeding of five thousand people in the wilderness. Why ask for another sign now? Mark says bluntly, *"to test him."*

The really hard-hearted part of their request was what they demanded—*"a sign from heaven."* This is a special term from **apocalyptic** literature, having to do with cosmic activity in the sky. They were asking Jesus to prove who he was by doing something like blocking the sun, turning the moon plaid, or making starry constellations spell "LWJD!" (Look What Jesus Did!), but what would be the point? They had already attributed his previous miracles to <u>Satan</u>.

The Pharisees probably thought they had Jesus trapped. They figured he might try to do the miracle and fail, in which case they could ridicule him. Or, if he pulled it off somehow, according to

☞ **GO TO:**

Mark 3:22, 30 (demons)

Mark 2:1–12; 3:1–6 (healings)

Mark 3:22 (Satan)

apocalyptic: *forecasting the ultimate destiny of the world*

☞ **GO TO:**

Deuteronomy 13:1–6
(Moses' law)

Mark 7:34 (same sigh)

Moses' law they could accuse him of preaching the wrong God and have him put to death. But Jesus knew their minds were closed. Instead of taking offense, he seems to pity their narrow-minded, hateful condition; he *"sighed deeply."* It's the <u>same sigh</u> we heard when Jesus felt pity for the deaf and mute man. He asks a question to which he already knows the answer—why do you ask for a sign? Implied answer: so they can pick it apart and excuse themselves from hearing God.

In its second half Mark's Gospel explains at length the deep cost of discipleship. Jesus will soon explain that standing up for God can cost you your life. This philosophy could not be more opposed to the Pharisees' notion that God-followers have all the power, call all the shots, and literally boss the universe around. So when Jesus says, *"no sign will be given to* [this generation]," he really means it. For a sign to be given to a generation, the generation must receive it; Jesus is saying "this generation" has refused to receive his signs.

> Jesus performed many signs, the greatest one being his death and resurrection, but if you're looking for God to jump through your hoops—sorry, Yahweh don't play that way.

KEY POINT

We don't call the shots. God does.

Remember
This . . .

What Others
are Saying:

Eugene H. Peterson: Spirituality is always in danger of self-absorption, of becoming so intrigued with matters of soul that God is treated as a mere accessory to my experience. . . . Spiritual theology is the discipline and art of training us into a full and mature participation in Jesus' story while at the same time preventing us from taking over the story.[9]

> **Mark 8:13–16** Then he left them, got back into the boat and crossed to the other side.
>
> The disciples had forgotten to bring bread, except for one loaf they had with them in the boat. "Be careful," Jesus warned them. "Watch out for the yeast of the Pharisees and that of Herod."
>
> They discussed this with one another and said, "It is because we have no bread."

I Never Metaphor I Didn't Like

euphemisms: *nicer ways of saying something offensive*

Pundits have created many **euphemisms** for saying someone is really stupid, such as:

- "She's a few fries short of a Happy Meal."
- "She forgot to pay her brain bill."
- "His Slinky's kinked."
- "The wheel's spinning, but the hamster's dead."
- "He couldn't pour water out of a boot with instructions on the heel."

I mean no disrespect in saying these expressions could describe the disciples in Mark. I realize these men went on to change the world, did more for Christianity than I'll ever do, and probably look better at their worst than I do. On the other hand, they were also slow. I mean, come on . . . they've seen Jesus miraculously feed over nine thousand people, and they think he's worried about bread for thirteen?

The Hebrew culture commonly used yeast (and its synonym, leaven) as a metaphor alluding to sin and evil. Ancient cultures produced leaven by keeping a chunk of the previous week's dough, storing it just right, and adding juices to make it ferment. Done right, a bit of leaven could make raw dough rise when baked and give bread a pleasing, light texture. Done wrong, leaven could become tainted and poison the rest of the dough. Leaven was dangerous stuff, and a little bit went a long way.

THE WAYBACK MACHINE

While the Pharisees and Herod seem to have little in common, Jesus describes them both as having leaven—a toxic flaw that can infect others. Given the context, this flaw is probably a failure to believe, even after being confronted with the truth. Jesus is warning his disciples not to fall victim to the same lethal attitude.

Living up to the very thing against which Jesus is warning them, the disciples miss the analogy completely. They are too wrapped up in the tiny superficial concerns of the moment.

> **Mark 8:17–21** Aware of their discussion, Jesus asked them: "Why are you talking about having no bread? Do you still not see or understand? Are your hearts hardened? Do you have eyes but fail to see, and ears but fail to hear? And don't you remember? When I broke the five loaves for the five thousand, how many basketfuls of pieces did you pick up?"

> "Twelve," they replied.
> "And when I broke the seven loaves for the four thousand, how many basketfuls of pieces did you pick up?"
> They answered, "Seven."
> He said to them, "Do you still not understand?"

Those Disciples Have Got Some Crust

☞ **GO TO:**

Mark 7:18 (dull)

Isaiah 63:17 (hardened)

Jeremiah 5:21ff.
(Jeremiah)

Jesus has already called the disciples dull, but now gives them their harshest rebuke yet, all in the form of questions. Think back to times your mom scolded you with nothing but questions, and you'll understand the tone ("What's the *matter* with you? If everybody jumped off a cliff, would you do it too? What am I going to do with you?")

Jesus asks the disciples if their hearts are hardened, whether their eyes fail to see, and whether their ears fail to hear. As good Scripture-reading Jews, the disciples would have been painfully aware of the company with whom Jesus was lumping them. All of these questions rise directly from Jeremiah and other Old Testament prophets who condemned Israel for failing to acknowledge the Lord.

Then Jesus forces the disciples to recall the two miraculous feedings they have recently witnessed. Recall that the feeding of the five thousand was in Jewish territory and contained Jewish overtones; the feeding of the four thousand was in Gentile territory and did not contain Jewish overtones. Jesus emphasizes the numbers, but the disciples fail to see their significance.

Jesus has already cued us to be thinking metaphorically, so we may be able to figure out what the numbers mean. The "five loaves" might represent the five books of Torah. "Twelve" to a Jewish mindset would always suggest the twelve tribes of Israel. The miracle becomes an illustration of Jesus fulfilling the laws of Moses so that all of Israel would find spiritual satisfaction. Alternatively, it could be an illustration of Jesus breaking the bread of God's Word to the Jews so that all of Israel is spiritually fed. If you take the bread as being God's Word, it is even possible that the *"one loaf they had with them in the boat"* represents Jesus himself.

The number seven (and seventy) was often linked with Gentiles. Some Jewish interpreters believed the Torah listed seventy nationalities that populated the world after the Flood. Also in Jewish tradition, the Gentiles were not part of God's covenant with the Jews, but were sometimes said to be bound by the covenant with Noah, which was considered to have seven commandments. Another long-standing tradition equated seven with the number

☞ **GO TO:**

Genesis 10:1–32
(seventy)

Genesis 9:1–17 (seven)

of perfection or completeness, as in the seven days of <u>creation</u>, or <u>forgiving</u> seven times.

If we interpret the second feeding according to these symbols, the seven loaves become a symbol of Jesus spiritually feeding the Gentile nations—all the world—and the seven baskets represent the completeness or the perfection of his reign. This makes even more sense when we realize the second feeding comes right after the Gentiles' statement, *"He has done everything well."*

Combined, the two stories may represent Jesus as the answer for the Jews and for all other nations, the Gentiles. This would explain why, in his fast-paced, compressed narrative, Mark included *two* feeding stories.

The passage ends with Jesus' haunting question, *"Do you still not understand?"* Significantly, Mark leaves the question unresolved. It hangs in the air, demanding an answer not only from the disciples, but also from the reader. As the disciples (and we) awkwardly juggle our possible responses, the first half of the book ends.

But the second half will make crystal clear who Jesus really is.

☞ **GO TO:**

Genesis 1 (creation)

Matthew 18:21 (forgiving)

Charles Spurgeon: But his miracles were sermons; they were acted discourses, full of instruction. . . . All his actions were significant; he preached by every movement.[10]

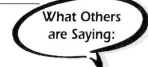
What Others are Saying:

KEEP IT REAL—Got me again, Mark! Will I never make it through one of these chapters unmarked by your powerful pen?

• Mark 7:6–13. The temple lawyers put the well-being of their church higher than the well-being of the people. Sometimes I have gotten so involved with church activities that I have lost all contact with unbelievers. How can the church be salt to the world if we always stay in the shaker? *Help me find your balance, Lord.*

• Mark 7:29–30. *The Greek woman took you at your word. Her faith even impressed you, Lord. Grow me up into her league, please—I could use a break from all this useless worry!*

Study Questions

1. What did the Pharisees mean when they accused the disciples of eating food with hands that were "unclean"?
2. Name some areas you are aware of where you may be placing human tradition on a level equal to or higher than Scripture.
3. Why is it significant that Jesus ministered in Tyre, Sidon, and Decapolis?
4. What kind of "dog" did Jesus call the Greek woman?
5. Why did Mark include two different stories of Jesus miraculously using a little food to feed thousands?

- Jesus and the Pharisees clashed because the Pharisees wanted to see outward purity, while Jesus focused on inner purity—the cleanliness of the heart. He also chastised them for putting their own human thoughts and traditions higher than the commands of God. (Mark 7:1–23)

- After Mark shows that Jesus had a new definition of purity, he details three accounts of Jesus ministering to the "unclean" Gentiles: driving an evil spirit out of a girl because her Greek mother asked with faith; privately healing a man who was deaf and mute; and feeding four thousand people with just seven loaves and a few small fish. (Mark 7:24–8:13)

- Jesus warned his disciples about a toxic character flaw that the Pharisees and Herod both had, symbolized as yeast. Both parties were confronted with God's truth, but refused to believe. When the disciples were slow to get his meaning, Jesus stressed the miraculous feedings they had witnessed, and the numbers in particular. The apostles should have understood that Jesus was God. (Mark 8:14–21)

Part Four

ROAD SCHOLAR JESUS

REVEREND FUN

"So tell me then, Jesus, how hard would it be for a rich camel to enter the Kingdom of God?"

Mark Comes Unhinged

This next section, 8:22 through 10:52, forms the centerpiece of Mark's book. Commentators often call it the "Markan hinge" because in it, Jesus predicts his own fate three times, which changes everything—even the message he preaches.

Mark focused tightly on Jesus in the first half of his book. In the second half he still keeps the focus on Jesus, but pulls out enough to include the disciples. The Master reveals the totally unexpected mission of the Messiah; instead of initiating a military conquest of Rome, the Messiah will somehow redeem Israel by dying. Jesus' flat prediction of death contradicts the expectations of the Twelve so utterly that they go into complete denial, busily acting as if they hadn't heard him. The more he warns them of his coming death, the more they ignore him. Instead, they argue over who will be his right-hand man when he kicks Roman butt.

Peter didn't pull any punches when he recounted these stories to Mark, because Peter ends up looking like a buffoon. In Peter's powerful <u>confession</u> that Jesus is Christ, he gets the words right, but moments later proves he doesn't know what they mean. His misguided words and actions provide an opportunity to explain the pros, the cons, and the true meaning of following Jesus.

☞ **GO TO:**

Mark 8:29 (confession)

Mark 8:22–26; 10:46–52 (too blind)

As the shadow of the cross begins to loom over his narrative, Mark introduces a note of tension; as powerful as Jesus is, can he break through the disciples' dullness and misconceptions before his rapidly approaching death? All this time misunderstanding about his identity and mission has reigned. Can Jesus make the Twelve understand what they really signed up for? When he is absent, will the disciples have grasped enough to continue Jesus' work?

Mark's "hinge" is bracketed between stories of Jesus encountering men who are <u>too blind</u> to see what's right in front of them. Get the hint? If so, you're quicker on the uptake than the disciples. See for yourself.

MARK 8:22–9:29
GLOW-IN-THE-DARK JESUS

- "I See People . . . Like Trees Walking"
- Peter's Great Confession
- The Transfiguration
- Jesus Drives a Demon Out of a Boy

Let's Get Started

In the chapter on Mark 3:13–35 I introduced the Power Tool, *watch for literary devices*. Since then we've studied several of Mark's intercalations (which we've been calling sandwiches or Oreos). But intercalations aren't the only literary device Mark used, so we need to introduce another one: the **inclusio**.

Sometimes gospel writers repeat phrases or actions that either emphasize themes or conclude sections. Scholars of the Gospels call this technique the inclusio. Matthew uses it a lot. In a sense the whole Gospel of Matthew is one big inclusio. Matthew begins with *"they will call him 'Immanuel'—which means, 'God with us'"* (1:23). It ends with Jesus saying, *"And surely I am with you always"* (28:20). Just for good measure, smack in the center of Matthew, Jesus says, *"For where two or three come together in my name, there am I with them"* (18:20). Would you be surprised to find out Matthew's Gospel explores the theme of God coming to be with his people? I didn't think so.

Mark uses inclusios too. At verse 8:22 Mark begins an important section of his Gospel with the story of Jesus healing a blind man. The section ends with Jesus healing another blind man in 10:46–52. What is Mark trying to tell us by using this technique? Good question—one we're about to explore.

Don't worry too much about remembering the technical term. Just remember that when a Bible writer repeats himself in a way that forms a pattern, it's often a good idea to take a closer look at what's in between those repetitions. Come on, I'll show you what I mean.

inclusio: *literary repetition intended to mark sections*

POWER TOOL

Watch for literary devices: inclusio.

NOW WHO'S THE BLIND ONE?

> **Mark 8:22–26** They came to Bethsaida, and some people brought a blind man and begged Jesus to touch him. He took the blind man by the hand and led him outside the village. When he had spit on the man's eyes and put his hands on him, Jesus asked, "Do you see anything?"
>
> He looked up and said, "I see people; they look like trees walking around."
>
> Once more Jesus put his hands on the man's eyes. Then his eyes were opened, his sight was restored, and he saw everything clearly. Jesus sent him home, saying, "Don't go into the village."

Two Touches Of The Master's Hand

☞ GO TO:

John 1:44 (Bethsaida)

Mark 8:18 (blind)

Jesus and the disciples arrive back in <u>Bethsaida</u>—the hometown of Philip, Andrew, and Peter—for an unusual healing. We've seen Jesus heal lots of people before, including <u>blind</u> men. Remarkably, this blind man of Bethsaida is the only person Jesus could not heal at once. All the other sick people Jesus touched (or who touched him) were instantly whole—even dead people. With this man, for the first time Jesus has to ask whether his ministry has been effective.

The answer is, "Partly." The man's condition has gone from total blindness to severely distorted vision. People look like trees. Not to be **dissuaded**, Jesus applies his healing touch again, and the man can see perfectly well.

dissuaded: advised against doing something

Something to Ponder

Why do scholars believe this physical healing comments on the spirituality of the disciples? Primarily because of what comes before and after it in Mark's account. Just before it is Jesus' question to the disciples, *"Do you have eyes but fail to see, and ears but fail to hear?"* (Mark 8:18). After it Peter (speaking for the disciples) demonstrates partial understanding of who Jesus is and partial misunderstanding, like the distorted vision of this blind man. It all fits together too perfectly to be a coincidence, especially when you consider that in the four Gospels, only Mark recorded this story.

PETER'S GREAT CONFESSION
(AND ENSUING GOOF)

> **Mark 8:27–30** Jesus and his disciples went on to the villages around Caesarea Philippi. On the way he asked them, "Who do people say I am?"
>
> They replied, "Some say John the Baptist; others say Elijah; and still others, one of the prophets."
>
> "But what about you?" he asked. "Who do you say I am?"
>
> Peter answered, "You are the Christ."
>
> Jesus warned them not to tell anyone about him.

Half A Confession Is Better Than None

Jesus has led his entourage on a meandering path through Gentile territory and now reverses his geographical direction, sticking primarily to Jewish territory. The journey does not seem to have an intended destination; it seems more intended as something to do while Jesus instructs his disciples. Note that he began this discussion *"on the way,"* and that several more lessons happen "on the way," "on the road," "on his way," or "along the road." In this section "the way" becomes a metaphor for Jesus' teachings, primarily about his own suffering, but also about the need for his followers to deny themselves.

Jesus begins the conversation with a nonthreatening question, and he receives answers to which Mark already exposed us. Characteristic of Jesus, his follow-up question suddenly turns heaven's attention directly onto us: *"But what about you? . . . Who do you say I am?"* With his gaze leveled at us, suddenly we realize that a lot—maybe everything—depends on our response.

For once, big-mouth Peter gets it right. He blurts out, *"You are the Christ."* At this moment in Matthew's account Jesus commends Peter's answer. For centuries pastors and teachers have referred to this as Peter's Great Confession with the equivalent of a big "Yessss!" and a touchdown dance. Curiously, however, Mark and Luke record only one reaction from Jesus; he tells all the disciples to keep his identity to themselves.

☞ **GO TO:**

Mark 8:27; 9:34
(on the way)

Mark 9:33 (on the road)

Mark 10:17
(on his way)

Mark 10:52
(along the road)

Mark 6:14–15
(already exposed)

Matthew 16:13–20
(Matthew's account)

Luke 9:18–21 (Luke)

Peter stood squarely in the mainstream of the era's Jewish thought. When he called Jesus "Christ," he thought he had recognized a political revolutionary. He had the word right, but the meaning wrong. Later Jesus would tell Peter, *"You do not have in mind the things of God, but the things of men."* Jesus realized that virtually no one understood the true nature of the Messiah's role. He did not want people calling him something that meant to them the opposite of what it meant to him, which is why he silenced people that recognized him as the Messiah. He repressed their use of the term "Messiah" to buy more time—time to help them unlearn their religion and relearn the truth.

> **Mark 8:31** He then began to teach them that the Son of Man must suffer many things and be rejected by the elders, chief priests and teachers of the law, and that he must be killed and after three days rise again.

Death And Discipleship

Who is this "Son of Man" Jesus speaks of? It was actually Jesus' favorite way of referring to himself, used fourteen times in Mark. But what did it mean? If he was the Son of God, as Mark told us in the very first verse, how could he be the Son of Man?

Jesus did not invent the phrase. Many Jews knew it and thought of it as another name for the Messiah, because of its use in Daniel 7:13–14 (Check it out!).

This prophesied "Son of Man" would have a great gig. He would share the throne with God and rule over everyone everywhere in an everlasting kingdom. The Son of Man would turn the world into one big ol' Jewish colony, the Jews assumed, bringing justice and holiness on behalf of God's people.

If this is what Peter pictured every time Jesus called himself the Son of Man, imagine what an utter disappointment it was when Jesus said the Son of Man must suffer, be rejected, be killed, and rise again.

> **Mark 8:32–33** He spoke plainly about this, and Peter took him aside and began to rebuke him.
>
> But when Jesus turned and looked at his disciples, he rebuked Peter. "Get behind me, Satan!" he said. "You do not have in mind the things of God, but the things of men."

Peter Colors Outside The Lines

When you realize how totally daft Jesus' predictions must've sounded to the disciples, even though we can't excuse Peter's reaction, we can understand it. At least he had the diplomacy to take Jesus aside. But Peter tries to correct Jesus, which introduces a bunch of problems.

Jesus scolds Peter with shocking intensity. In Jesus' culture the phrase translated *"Get behind me"* has the same meaning as "Get out of my sight!" in our culture. What's more, Jesus calls Peter "Satan." Picture Peter, the lumbering brute fisherman, stumbling backwards in complete shock, surprised by Jesus' fierceness. (For more on Peter's hoof-in-mouth disease, see GWMB, pages 241–246.)

IT'S
GREEK
TO ME

Andrew Murray: I thank God for the story of Peter. I do not know a man in the Bible who gives us greater comfort. When we look at his character, so full of failures, and at what Christ made him by the power of the Holy Ghost, there is hope for every one of us. . . . There was Peter in his self-will, trusting his own wisdom, and actually forbidding Christ to go and die. . . . He had left his boats and his nets, but not his old self.[1]

What Others are Saying:

> **Mark 8:34** Then he called the crowd to him along with his disciples and said: "If anyone would come after me, he must deny himself and take up his cross and follow me."

Three Startling Demands

Jesus' strong reaction to Peter's bad advice seems to carry Jesus into this next discussion—the original "come to Jesus" meeting. He begins with sobering demands of his followers; if you want to follow me, Jesus says, you must *"deny yourself"*—the exact opposite of political ambition. Even worse, you must *"take up [your] cross."* Now this phrase would make any Jew think twice. Here's why.

While we understand "take up your cross and follow" as an admonition to put serving Christ ahead of serving our own ambitions, at least initially the disciples would not have heard it that way. Crucifixion was a common form of Roman capital punishment, and I do mean common—it was reserved for the poor and for noncitizens. (Wealthy Romans who committed

THE WAYBACK MACHINE

serious crimes were executed by poisoning. Average Roman citizens were beheaded.)

Crucifixion was the death penalty with an attitude—an unspeakably shameful way to die. Criminals were crucified naked. Crucifixion itself did not kill a person; the spike wounds were too slight. Instead, the condemned hung helplessly for days at a time, weakening from starvation and thirst. The stretched arms caused the rib cage to compress the lungs. The only way to get a deep breath was to ease tension off the arms by straightening the legs, putting weight on the spiked feet. As the condemned person grew weary, he became too feeble to leverage himself up for air. Most crucified people died of eventual suffocation. The process could take days, with nothing to look forward to but exposure to weather, thirst, starvation, infection, and complete helplessness if predatory birds or animals attacked.

The Romans made sure all crucifixions took place near major thoroughfares to make a public example of the condemned person. When quashing rebellions, Romans executed so many men that both sides of the famous Roman roads were lined for miles with the crucified. Josephus recorded an occasion when a Roman governor crucified two thousand men. When the Romans finally sacked Jerusalem in A.D. 70, Josephus claimed Titus crucified so many people, they ran out of wood for crosses.

Every adult Jew who had traveled to Jerusalem in Jesus' lifetime had seen crucifixions firsthand, so when Jesus told his followers to take up their crosses, the imagery would have hit them like a gut punch. Our culture completely lacks an equivalent. In first-century Palestine you didn't go through life carrying a cross. You carried the cross a short way, and then you were killed on it. Perhaps the closest we can get is, "If anyone would come after me, he must march with me to the electric chair," or "If anyone would come after me, she must put her arm out for a lethal injection and follow me." This was worlds removed from the popular expectation of a conquering Messiah—as far removed as it is from our own popular notions of a blessed, happy, prosperous Christian life.

Though Jesus' words, *"deny yourself"* and *"take up [your] cross,"* are sobering, the third demand was, *"follow me."* Jesus did not call his disciples, including us, to do anything he himself did not do. No matter what suffering we endure because of our

To follow Jesus means you must die to self.

Something to Ponder

faith, Jesus is there with us. (The apostle Paul pointed to Christ as an example of sacrificial love; see GWRM, pages 220–221.)

> **Mark 8:35–38** "For whoever wants to save his life will lose it, but whoever loses his life for me and for the gospel will save it. What good is it for a man to gain the whole world, yet forfeit his soul? Or what can a man give in exchange for his soul? If anyone is ashamed of me and my words in this adulterous and sinful generation, the Son of Man will be ashamed of him when he comes in his Father's glory with the holy angels."

He Didn't Say It Would Be Easy

Jesus made it clear his kingdom was not something you joined for personal gain. The first objective of a Jesus-follower is to be with Jesus; Jesus walked the way of death, the way of service, the way of loving the unlovely. The second objective of a follower of Jesus is to do whatever he or she can to bring the reign of God to bear in every situation, bringing as much healing, help, and love to people as we can.

Our modern American version of Christianity allows for wealthy Christian celebrities; pastors bedecked in diamonds, minks, and $2,000 suits; and popular teachings that the Gospel is about God wanting to keep us healthy and rich. How can you get any of that from a Jesus who told his followers to deny self and be willing to die with him?

Frederick Buechner: The story of Jesus is full of darkness as well as of light. . . . It is the story of a mystery we must never assume we understand and that comes to us breathless and broken with unspeakable beauty at the heart of it yet by no means a pretty story though that is the way we're apt to peddle it much of the time. We sand down the rough edges. We play down the obscurities and contradictions. What we can't explain, we explain away. . . . We're apt to tell his story when we tell it at all, to sell his story, for the poetry and panacea of it. . . . Our commission is to tell it in a way that makes it come alive as a story in all its aliveness and to make those who hear it come alive and God knows to make ourselves come alive too.[2]

What Others are Saying:

GO (TRANS)FIGURE

So if committing yourself to the Messiah involves sacrifice and suffering, wouldn't a smart person avoid the whole thing? Jesus spoke against that notion, saying that *"whoever wants to save his life will lose it"* (Mark 8:35)—in other words, a life guided only by self-preservation is not fulfilling, and has disastrous eternal consequences.

Mark likes to set opposing points next to each another, holding them in tension. Now that he's explained the fearful cost of following Jesus, he immediately shows the spectacular glory of following Jesus, hinting at why those who lose their lives for Jesus will find themselves.

> **Mark 9:1–4** And he said to them, "I tell you the truth, some who are standing here will not taste death before they see the kingdom of God come with power."
>
> After six days Jesus took Peter, James and John with him and led them up a high mountain, where they were all alone. There he was transfigured before them. His clothes became dazzling white, whiter than anyone in the world could bleach them. And there appeared before them Elijah and Moses, who were talking with Jesus.

The Original Mountaintop Experience

Mark 9:1 is one of the most hotly debated verses in the whole book. When Jesus says *"some who are standing here will not taste death before they see the kingdom of God come with power,"* we immediately think of the same kind of all-encompassing kingdom that the Twelve expected Jesus to initiate in their lifetimes. But one of Mark's major themes is that Jesus himself *was* the kingdom of God arriving with power. Judging from Mark's placement of the next account, it seems clear he believed what happened in 9:2–8 fulfilled the promise in 9:1.

His account begins with something rare in Mark: a specific amount of time. *"After six days"* helps ground this surreal story in reality; the event he is about to relate really happened.

Also, many scholars believe Mark uses the phrase *"six days"* to link this event to a similar mountaintop revelation that happened to Moses in Exodus 24. Guess how long Moses prepared for this revelation. You got it—six days. Here is a comparison of the two mountaintop experiences.

Mark	Exodus
Jesus takes three disciples up a mountain (Mark 9:2).	Moses takes a bunch of people up a mountain, but only three are named (Exodus 24:1, 9).
Jesus is transfigured and his clothes turn dazzling (Mark 9:2–3).	Moses' skin shines after talking with God (Exodus 34:29).
God's presence comes, veiled by a cloud (Mark 9:7).	God appears in veiled form, in a cloud (Exodus 24:15–16, 18).
A voice speaks from the cloud (Mark 9:7).	A voice speaks from the cloud (Exodus 24:16).
The people are astonished when they see Jesus after he descends from the mountain (Mark 9:15).	The people are afraid to come near Moses after he descends from the mountain (Exodus 35:30).

Mark tells us Jesus was **transfigured**. The Greek word he used is *metamorphothe*, from which we get our word metamorphosis. Anyone who played with Transformers as a child should understand the concept; Jesus changed into his "other" identity.

In the Old Testament, brilliance, shining, and bright light are used as indicators of the <u>glory of God</u>. Luke's record of this seems to set it at <u>night</u>, so Jesus' *"dazzling white"* clothes shining in the darkness must have looked literally awesome.

When you compare what happened in Exodus to what is happening before the disciples here, it's obvious this incident is a **theophany**. The Exodus and Mark stories are similar, but in Mark, Jesus is in the role of God. The veil of his humanity has slipped aside to reveal his divinity.

Why Moses And Elijah?

Two extra characters beam in, *Star Trek*-style. Moses and Elijah speak with Jesus, but Mark does not record what they said, indicating that the important thing is their presence. Moses, in Jewish thought, stood for the old covenant—the law that God had given him, with all its promises and curses. Moses had predicted that a <u>prophet</u> would come to speak God's words to the people. His visit here endorses Jesus as that prophet.

Where Moses represented the law, Elijah represented the prophets and was the prophesied <u>forerunner</u> of the Messiah. Both men had predicted the coming of the Messiah. Now here they are, flanking Jesus, indicating "Here's the guy I told you about."

IT'S
GREEK
TO ME

transfigured: given a new, exalted appearance

theophany: God showing himself visibly

☞ **GO TO:**

Daniel 7:9 (glory of God)

Luke 9:32 (night)

Deuteronomy 18:15–19 (prophet)

Malachi 4:5–6; Mark 1:2 (forerunner)

> **Mark 9:5–6** Peter said to Jesus, "Rabbi, it is good for us to be here. Let us put up three shelters—one for you, one for Moses and one for Elijah." (He did not know what to say, they were so frightened.)

I Don't Know What To Say, And I Can Prove It

One aspect of Mark's irony is that throughout his book, the greater the revelation of God, the fewer the number of people who witness it. Peter, James, and John surely realized they were privileged beyond words to see what they were seeing. Probably after several moments of stammering ("hamina hamina hamina"), Peter suggests building three **tabernacles** to honor Jesus and his, er, distinguished guests.

tabernacles: sanctuaries in tents

THE WAYBACK MACHINE

☞ **GO TO:**

Exodus 33:7
  (Tent of Meeting)

> Tents had religious significance to Jews. Their heritage includes forty years of living in tents while migrating from Egypt to Israel. In addition the Tent of Meeting played a momentous role in the story of the Exodus; it was where people could seek God's guidance.
>   Peter's offer to build tents shows a good but misguided heart. Apparently it doesn't occur to him that if he doesn't know what to say, he doesn't have to say anything; so once again, Peter finds himself dining on his sandals. He may have thought building three Tents of Meeting would give these mighty men of God a place to stay, so the people could take pilgrimages up the mountain and benefit from their wisdom, but his notion has two serious flaws. First he places Jesus, Elijah, and Moses as equals. Secondly he doesn't yet realize that Jesus himself *is* the Tent of Meeting. While on earth, Jesus was the real Tabernacle of God—the temporary dwelling place of Yahweh.

> **Mark 9:7–8** Then a cloud appeared and enveloped them, and a voice came from the cloud: "This is my Son, whom I love. Listen to him!"
>   Suddenly, when they looked around, they no longer saw anyone with them except Jesus.

Today's Forecast: Cloudy, With Speeches

☞ **GO TO:**

Exodus 13:21–22;
  40:34–35 (cloud)

Mark 1:11 (baptism)

Fortunately God enters the picture and clears things up. A cloud floods the scene, evoking thoughts of the Old Testament shekinah glory of God. A voice speaks, endorsing Jesus just as it did at his baptism. This time, though, the approval includes the phrase, *"Listen to him!"* The phrase indicates clearly what Moses was doing there, because it comes directly from his prophecy: *"The LORD your God will raise up for you a prophet like me from among your own brothers. You must listen to him"* (Deuteronomy 18:15). In the broader context of Mark, the voice is telling the disciples that Jesus is exactly right in predicting his own death.

The word used for "listen" is *akoute*, a Greek word that really means "listen *and obey*." God was saying this is my beloved Son—pay attention to him and do what he tells you.

Suddenly, the three disciples found themselves alone with Jesus. Elijah and Moses had faded away. The imagery seems to say Jesus fulfills everything to which the law and the prophets pointed; they will fade away, leaving only him as the path to God. He is so much more than equal to Moses and Elijah.

Peter did not understand what he was seeing at the time, but he understood it later, after Jesus died and was resurrected (see also GWPB, pages 253–254). Take a look at what Peter wrote in 2 Peter 1:16–18.

IT'S
GREEK
TO ME

> **Mark 9:9–10** As they were coming down the mountain, Jesus gave them orders not to tell anyone what they had seen until the Son of Man had risen from the dead. They kept the matter to themselves, discussing what "rising from the dead" meant.

Huh? "Rise Again"?

Jesus can tell Peter, James, and John still do not understand the real mission of the Messiah, so he orders them not to speak of the amazing things they've just seen. For the first time in the whole book, finally someone obeys Jesus' command and keeps silent. (You would too, if God himself had just boomed from a cloud, "Listen to him and obey!") He implies they can speak of it after he has risen from the dead, but they still can't fathom what this means.

Jesus told the disciples three times he would die and then come back to life, but they still didn't get it. I don't think you or I would, either. No matter how much you respect a spiritual leader in your life, if he told you God wanted him to die but come back to life, you would not **credulously** respond, "Wow, good for you!" Critics of the Gospels who think the disciples were gullible may not have looked closely enough at the fact that the Twelve resisted believing Jesus' implausible claims, until after he fulfilled them.

☞ **GO TO:**

Mark 8:31–32; 9:31–32; 10:33–34 (three times)

Remember
This . . .

credulously: *ready to believe without evidence*

Malcolm Muggeridge: At the Transfiguration, when the glory was upon Jesus, the luminosity was too much for the three disciples with him, and they had to shut their eyes. . . . Coming down from the mountain when it was all over, the reaction will have set in. I imagine them then, their footsteps laggardly, and their talk listless, looking closely at Jesus's familiar face and movements, and wondering whether it had really happened—that light, those voices, the words spoken from on high.[3]

> **Mark 9:11–13** And they asked him, "Why do the teachers of the law say that Elijah must come first?"
> Jesus replied, "To be sure, Elijah does come first, and restores all things. Why then is it written that the Son of Man must suffer much and be rejected? But I tell you, Elijah has come, and they have done to him everything they wished, just as it is written about him."

"They Have Done To Him Everything They Wished"

Despite their flawed understanding of "Messiah," after seeing the glory of Jesus the three disciples know deep down he is it, but there's one thing they can't figure out. Elijah was supposed to come before Messiah. They saw Elijah for the first time *after* the Messiah had arrived. Their question translates roughly into, "So whassup with that Elijah thing?"

Jesus' response indicates they took the <u>prophecies</u> too literally. Elijah himself did not come, but someone operating in the spiritual power, fearless attitude, and prophetic authority of Elijah had. *"Elijah has come, and they have done to him everything they wished,"* speaks of poor beheaded John the Baptist. In the Markan hinge's context of repeated predictions of the Son of Man's death, the words *"they have done to him everything they wished"* will soon apply to Jesus as well.

In the midst of his answer, Jesus poses his own question, which Mark leaves unanswered. The prophecies said that when Elijah returned, he would restore *"the hearts of the fathers to their children,"* and vice versa. So if Elijah was supposed to restore all things, why must the Son of Man still *"suffer much and be rejected"*? The answer is that Elijah came, but too many people ignored him. The prophecy of Elijah had an "or else" clause (*"or else I will come and strike the land with a curse"*), showing that God knew Elijah might

☞ **GO TO:**

Malachi 4:4–6
(prophecies)

not succeed. The Son of Man must suffer to remove the curse from God's disobedient, hard-hearted people.

In finishing the transfiguration story on this note, Mark again brings back the theme of the cross. This is the paradox and the tension of following Jesus: self-sacrifice and persecution, mingled with glorious divine revelation. The sacrifices are temporal. The glory will be eternal.

Charles R. Swindoll: Never believe that if you walk by faith you've got the world by the tail. God never promised us a rose garden! Faith does not change my circumstances; faith changes me. Faith may not bring in the tuition check when I need it, but faith will give me what it takes to hang on. . . . Trusting God doesn't alter our circumstances. Perfect trust in Him changes us. It doesn't make life all rosy and beautiful and neat and lovely and financially secure and comfortable.[4]

What Others are Saying:

SOMETHING'S GOTTEN INTO THAT BOY

> **Mark 9:14–15** When they came to the other disciples, they saw a large crowd around them and the teachers of the law arguing with them. As soon as all the people saw Jesus, they were overwhelmed with wonder and ran to greet him.

. . . Meanwhile, Back In The Valley

After the glorious epiphany on the mountaintop, Jesus, Peter, James, and John descend back to regular life. The first thing they encounter is yet another dispute between the temple cult and the followers of Jesus. If this isn't annoying enough, in moments Jesus will be faced with another strong and contemptuous demon. A similar thing happened to Jesus earlier; after he was <u>baptized</u> and the voice of God lovingly approved him, immediately he encountered <u>Satan</u>.

Why would people be *"overwhelmed with wonder"* at seeing Jesus? My best guess is that this is Mark's final parallel to the story of Moses meeting God on the mountain. When Moses came down the mountain, his <u>face shined</u>, reflecting God's glory. It freaked people out so much that Moses had to wear a <u>veil</u> until the glory faded. Similarly, perhaps Jesus displayed

☞ GO TO:

Mark 1:9 (baptized)

Mark 1:12 (Satan)

Exodus 34:29–35 (face shined)

2 Corinthians 3:13–16 (veil)

Something to Ponder

MARK 8:22–9:29—GLOW-IN-THE-DARK JESUS **171**

KEEP IT REAL—As it was with Jesus, so it is with his followers. We may wish to linger far from the concerns of daily life—savoring our mountaintop experiences with God—but our spiritual highs are useless if they never touch down in reality. God blesses us that we may be a blessing to others. Again, Mark shows us that the Christian walk mingles grit and glory.

a touch of afterglow, amazing the crowds. Mark's narrative doesn't say, however, so we can only speculate.

> **Mark 9:16–19** "What are you arguing with them about?" he asked.
>
> A man in the crowd answered, "Teacher, I brought you my son, who is possessed by a spirit that has robbed him of speech. Whenever it seizes him, it throws him to the ground. He foams at the mouth, gnashes his teeth and becomes rigid. I asked your disciples to drive out the spirit, but they could not."
>
> "O unbelieving generation," Jesus replied, "how long shall I stay with you? How long shall I put up with you? Bring the boy to me."

The Non-Exorcists

If you have a heart at all, you have to pity this father and his boy who has been tormented (apparently for years) by a vicious demon. Dad brought his problem to the disciples for help. What did he get? First, no help, and second (as if the first weren't bad enough), an argument. Nothing could be more disheartening to someone in real need than to become the subject of a bitter theological debate.

The teachers of the law, seeking any excuse to discredit Jesus, undoubtedly jumped all over the disciples for their failure at **exorcism**. The disciples' obvious retort might be, "Well, you couldn't do any better!" The disciples look more and more like the scribes and Pharisees as the book progresses. It wasn't long ago that the disciples were able to <u>conquer demons</u>, but now they're as helpless as nonbelievers. The context indicates their failure is due to a shift in their focus. They went from spreading God's kingdom to obsessing about their own importance in that kingdom.

Such an attitude breaks Jesus' heart. His *"how long?"* lament, whether directed at the disciples or at Israel in general, reflects

exorcism: act of freeing someone from a demon

☞ **GO TO:**

Mark 6:13
(conquer demons)

the loneliness and anguish of the one authentic believer on a planet filled with self-centered unbelievers.

Mark Noll: Over the long course of Christian history, the most depressing thing—because repeated so often—has been how tragically far short of Christian ideals we ordinary Christians so regularly fall. Over the long course of Christian history, the most remarkable thing—because it is such a miracle of grace—is how often believers have acted against the pride of life to honor Christ.[5]

What Others are Saying:

> **Mark 9:20–24** So they brought him. When the spirit saw Jesus, it immediately threw the boy into a convulsion. He fell to the ground and rolled around, foaming at the mouth.
>
> Jesus asked the boy's father, "How long has he been like this?"
>
> "From childhood," he answered. "It has often thrown him into fire or water to kill him. But if you can do anything, take pity on us and help us."
>
> "'If you can'?" said Jesus. "Everything is possible for him who believes."
>
> Immediately the boy's father exclaimed, "I do believe; help me overcome my unbelief!"

The Non-Ministers

Demons seem to <u>resist Jesus more</u> and more as Mark progresses. Where previous demons have cried out in fear at the sight of God incarnate, this one purposely harms the boy right in front of Jesus, as if to say, "Muah ha ha! I've got him, and I'm not letting go!" (By now, word may have spread through the demon overground that though their opponent walked the earth, he was not sending them to the Abyss yet.) The display stirs Jesus' compassion.

The disciples are helpless before the power of this demon, plus they've turned the father into the center of an unwanted controversy. Jesus finally shows up, and then what happens? The boy's condition worsens. You can understand why the father's faith sinks. We hear both desperation and resignation in his plea, *"If you can do anything . . . help us."*

Jesus did not let the first part of the man's plea go unnoticed. When Jesus says, *"If you can?"* it sounds sharp, especially followed by the blunt statement, *"Everything is possible for him who believes."* The gist of his mini-rebuke is, "Whether this boy gets

☞ **GO TO:**

Mark 1:23–27; 5:1–20 (resist Jesus more)

KEY POINT

Everything is possible if you have faith in God.

healed has more to do with your faith than it has to do with any limits on my power."

The boy's father seems to grasp this point immediately. His famous answer, *"I do believe! Help me overcome my unbelief!"* has hit a responsive chord in the hearts of countless believers over two millennia.

Jesus' everything-is-possible statement does not mean we can make up weird things for God to do, and he will do them if we believe hard enough. That puts God in the place of serving our human agenda, or makes him a dependable magic add-on, like Peter Pan's pixie dust. Jesus' statement means God wants to move powerfully to establish his kingdom, but can be limited by our lack of faith. Faith serves not our agenda, but God's.

Remember This . . .

> **Mark 9:25–26** When Jesus saw that a crowd was running to the scene, he rebuked the evil spirit. "You deaf and mute spirit," he said, "I command you, come out of him and never enter him again."
>
> The spirit shrieked, convulsed him violently and came out. The boy looked so much like a corpse that many said, "He's dead." But Jesus took him by the hand and lifted him to his feet, and he stood up.

Convulsed, But Not With Laughter

While the unbelief in Nazareth was so purposeful and hard-hearted that it stopped Jesus, this man's unbelief is different. He is doing the best he can, and is repentant that he cannot do better. Thank God, this is enough. Jesus drives the demon out with an unusual double rebuke. The demon not only has to leave but Jesus also forbids it from ever coming back.

Maliciously, the demon shakes the boy one more time before exiting. The boy is set free, but appears dead. The Greek word used here for "dead" is the same word Mark used for the man whose hand was shriveled, or withered. This must have been a ghastly sight for the beleaguered dad. The Greek implies his son appeared shrunken, caved in, and utterly motionless. But Jesus calmly resuscitates the boy.

☞ **GO TO:**

Mark 6:1–6 (unbelief)

Matthew 12:43–45 (coming back)

Mark 3:1 (withered)

IT'S GREEK TO ME

What Others are Saying:

Frederick Buechner: Even at our most believing, I think, we have our serious reservations just as even at our most unbelieving we tend to cast a wistful glance over our shoulders.[6]

> **Mark 9:28–29** After Jesus had gone indoors, his disciples asked him privately, "Why couldn't we drive it out?"
>
> He replied, "This kind can come out only by prayer."

Why We Can't Do It

One of the benefits of being the Twelve was that permanent backstage pass, and I suspect this time they couldn't wait to get Jesus alone. They wanted to know why or how their new toy, authority over demons, had broken.

When Jesus healed the demon-possessed boy, he did not employ some sort of special prayer, like a spell or incantation, to drive the demon out. The *"prayer"* he speaks of is an ongoing prayer relationship with the Father. It comes back to the issue of faith. Much of the rest of the Markan hinge shows the selfish attitude of the disciples as they jockey for position among themselves, trying to grab political power because they think Jesus will institute his kingdom any day now. This competitive spirit has nothing to do with prayerfully seeking the will of God in an attitude of obedience, which was Jesus' attitude and example.

Something to Ponder

Why does the modern church often seem so powerless in the face of need? Because we also worry too much about who will get credit, who has the style God likes most, how we can get noticed or promoted, who gets to lead worship at the big Sunday service instead of hanging out with the preschoolers in the back, and so on. Christianity isn't about that. It's about being with God. The rest is supposed to be the outworking of that prayer relationship, not a substitute for it.

What Others are Saying:

Henri J. M. Nouwen: We have fallen into the temptation of separating ministry from spirituality, service from prayer. Our demons say: "We are too busy to pray, we have too many needs to attend to, too many people to respond to, too many wounds to heal." Prayer is a luxury, something to do during a free hour, a day away from work or on a retreat.[7]

Jim Cymbala: You can tell how popular a church is by who comes on Sunday morning. You can tell how popular the pastor or evangelist is by who comes on Sunday night. But you can tell how popular Jesus is by who comes to the prayer meeting.[8]

KEEP IT REAL—As soon as I saw that the theme of this section was the real cost of discipleship, I knew I was in trouble. But I want obedience . . . *Lord, help my disobedience!*

• Mark 8:34. How long has it been since I seriously sacrificed for Jesus? Sometimes I have done it, and joyfully. But sometimes there are nights when I wouldn't even "sacrifice" a couple hours of TV for Jesus. *Lord, after all you've done for me, how could I ever be slow to give what you ask? Burn these words into my heart: "It's not about me."*

• Mark 8:29; 9:18. Like Peter, I have eagerly mouthed Christian words and high-sounding praise of God, only to find out that I couldn't really walk my talk. *Jesus, the last thing I want to be is someone's reason for not following you. Grow consistency in me, Savior.*

Study Questions

1. What is an inclusio? Why is it relevant to the passages we studied in this section?
2. We just saw a possible solution to the question of why Jesus silenced people whenever they realized he was the Messiah. Why do you think he did that?
3. What did the Old Testament say about the Son of Man?
4. List the three startling demands Jesus makes of his disciples.
5. Why did Moses and Elijah appear at the Transfiguration?

CHAPTER WRAP-UP

• One blind man Jesus healed required a second touch before he could see clearly. Because of the material that follows that story, most scholars believe the story also serves as an analogy for the spiritual dullness of the disciples. (Mark 8:22–26).

• With Peter speaking on their behalf, the disciples now realize Jesus is the Messiah. However, they have a mistaken idea of what Jesus has come to do, leading him to lecture strongly on what it means to follow him: put your ambitions to death, be willing to die if necessary, and go where Jesus goes. Though that sounds harsh, a self-centered life is less fulfilling and has disastrous eternal consequences. (Mark 8:27–38)

• On a mountaintop, Peter, James, and John got to glimpse Jesus in his divine glory, endorsed by Moses, Elijah, and God himself. (Mark 9:1–13)

• The disciples lost authority over demons because they lacked faith, and because they began to focus on their own importance instead of on seeking and serving God. Jesus said that *"Everything is possible for him who believes"* (Mark 9:14–29).

MARK 9:30–10:52
OPTOMETRIST JESUS

CHAPTER HIGHLIGHTS

- Predicting the Passion
- Who's the Greatest?
- Who's the Greatest? (Revisited)
- Blind Man or Bookend?

Let's Get Started

The next verse in Mark begins, *"They left that place and passed through Galilee"* (9:30), and then Jesus predicts his death and resurrection for the second time. Strange as it seems, those two things tie together. Since Peter's breakthrough realization that Jesus is the Christ, the path of Jesus has changed from a meandering, **itinerant** journey around Palestine into a march to Jerusalem. Jesus is going there to die, and he knows it (see map, page 178). The trip **culminates** with his triumphal entry into the city.

During this journey Jesus tries urgently to teach the disciples what it means to follow him. They don't get it, and twice Mark tells us they are <u>afraid</u>. Mark even shows embarrassing behavior from Peter, James, and John, portraying the leading disciples in bright, unflattering light. As some of Jesus' death talk begins to sink in, the disciples gradually transition from jockeying for a position closest to him, to following him at a distance in a sort of petrified parade.

How did you come to follow Jesus? When I first got to know him, I heard a lot of teaching about how Jesus would be my buddy, take care of my every need, and make all my troubles vanish. If you've had a similar picture of what it means to be a Christian, take a deep breath and hang on. We've been seeing a distortion like the "walking trees" back in 8:24. Courtesy of Mark, Jesus is about to say some things that may shock us out of comfy delusions.

itinerant: traveling around, covering a circuit

culminates: reaches a climactic point

☞ **GO TO:**

Mark 9:32; 10:32 (afraid)

As Jesus sensed his ministry was drawing to an end, he stopped wandering northern Palestine and began marching to Jerusalem. Because Passover was nearing, thousands of Jewish pilgrims also flocked to Jerusalem, and Jesus followed their traditional route.

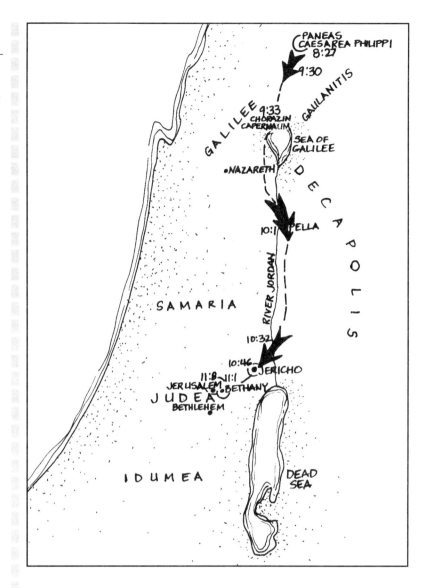

MORE DOPINESS FROM THE DISCIPLES

Mark 9:30–32 They left that place and passed through Galilee. Jesus did not want anyone to know where they were, because he was teaching his disciples. He said to them, "The Son of Man is going to be betrayed into the hands of men. They will kill him, and after three days he will rise." But they did not understand what he meant and were afraid to ask him about it.

Unlearning My Religion

Jesus' focus has changed from *"Let us go <u>somewhere else</u> . . . so I can preach there also,"* to *"Jesus did not want anyone to know where they were, because he was teaching his disciples."* We sense his determination as he labors to correct the Twelve's flawed understanding of his mission. Time is running out, and the disciples' hard heads haven't softened, even before the greatest teacher who ever lived.

For the second time Jesus explains the highlights of what will happen to him. The disciples still can't fit "Son of Man" together with "killed," but ever since Peter got a serious scolding when he tried to correct Jesus, now they're afraid to ask him what he means. Or perhaps they're afraid to ask because they *are* gradually realizing what he means—and it does not sound pretty.

☞ **GO TO:**

Mark 1:38–39
(somewhere else)

> **Mark 9:33–35** They came to Capernaum. When he was in the house, he asked them, "What were you arguing about on the road?" But they kept quiet because on the way they had argued about who was the greatest.
>
> Sitting down, Jesus called the Twelve and said, "If anyone wants to be first, he must be the very last, and the servant of all."

What Jesus Wants His Disciples To Be

Sometimes Jesus asked questions because he really wanted to know something, like when he asked the demon-possessed boy's father, *"How long has he been like this?"* (Mark 9:21). Other times he asked a question to which he already knew the answer. I believe he knew good and well what the disciples had been discussing. They were arguing, so he probably overheard their angry voices. Of all the ridiculous topics for any group to discuss, they had been disputing which of them was the greatest.

Mark, based on Peter's eyewitness account, says Jesus sat down before giving his **discourse**. In our culture the students sit while the teacher or preacher stands. In Jesus' culture it was the opposite. The teacher, who was worthy of respect, sat. To honor him, the students stood. The fact Jesus sat down shows this lecture was important and "official."

Jesus began his talk with a concept that stood the disciples' argument completely on its head; whoever wants to be first

discourse: formal, orderly thoughts on a subject

THE WAYBACK MACHINE

in God's kingdom must be the servant of all. Like Jesus saying, "take up your cross," we think of being the "servant of all" as a metaphor for a humble attitude. But the disciples lived with servants around them every day. They knew firsthand what it meant to be everybody's servant. The servant got all the scut work nobody else wanted. The servant cleaned up after the animals (ew!). The servant was last to eat, last to sleep, first to rise. To put it in our vernacular, being a servant stunk. Yet Jesus said that's who would be most honored in his kingdom.

The room probably filled with the sound of twelve men swallowing very hard.

John MacArthur: Christian discipleship . . . strikes a death-blow to the self-centered false gospels that are so popular in contemporary Christianity. It leaves no room for the gospel of getting, in which God is considered a type of utilitarian genie who jumps to provide a believer's every whim. . . . It undermines the gospel of self-esteem, self-love, and high self-image, which appeals to man's natural narcissism and prostitutes the spirit of humble brokenness and repentance that marks the gospel of the cross. . . . The heart of Christian discipleship is giving before gaining, losing before winning.[1]

> **Mark 9:36–37** He took a little child and had him stand among them. Taking him in his arms, he said to them, "Whoever welcomes one of these little children in my name welcomes me; and whoever welcomes me does not welcome me but the one who sent me."

But Kids Can't Vote!

In both Greek (the language Mark wrote in) and Aramaic (the language Jesus probably taught in), the term "child" can also mean "servant." Jesus is using a child as a visual pun following the phrase *"servant of all."*

☞ **GO TO:**

Mark 10:13–16
(enjoyed children)

Jesus' culture did not view children in a rosy light. While Jesus himself loved and <u>enjoyed children</u>, the reason he placed a child in their midst and said *"welcome one of these"* wasn't because kids were cute. It was because in that time and place, children were powerless.

First-century folks made a living strictly from what they could produce with physical labor, and a child produced nothing. The disciples were jockeying for political position in their version of God's kingdom, and a child had no clout. To the world of ambition and power politics, a child was worthless. But to the loving Father who made each individual, everyone had worth because they bore <u>God's image</u>. That was why Jesus befriended the leper, the bleeding, the paralyzed, the demonized, and the Gentiles. If the disciples were to help usher in God's kingdom, they had to do the same.

☞ **GO TO:**

Genesis 1:27
(God's image)

> **Mark 9:38–41** "Teacher," said John, "we saw a man driving out demons in your name and we told him to stop, because he was not one of us."
>
> "Do not stop him," Jesus said. "No one who does a miracle in my name can in the next moment say anything bad about me, for whoever is not against us is for us. I tell you the truth, anyone who gives you a cup of water in my name because you belong to Christ will certainly not lose his reward."

You Can Do More Good If You Don't Seek The Credit

At first John's question seems like a **non sequitur**. Jesus was talking about welcoming children, and John seems to interrupt like either a braggart or a tattletale, but his question is legitimate. If Jesus says to welcome children *"in my name,"* what should they do about someone who could be abusing Jesus' name?

non sequitur: a response unrelated to anything previously said

Given the disciples' frame of mind, they were probably surprised Jesus did not commend them for their vigilance. Their position is especially ironic because just a few verses back, they were unable to drive out a demon, and now they're stopping someone who can. They want to become Israel's name-brand exorcists, thus making themselves indispensable. In contrast, Jesus would love it if *everyone* could defeat the works of Satan, so he says, *"Do not stop him."*

As Jesus explains his statement further, there are only two sides: "for us" and "against us." When it comes to God's kingdom versus the works of Satan, every individual is part of the problem or part of the solution.

Jesus' example about a *"cup of water"* illustrates that in this battle, the stakes are so high, all acts of obedient service—from a powerful miracle like an exorcism to giving a fellow believer some refreshment—are approved and valued by God. God's economy does not distinguish between "important" acts and "trivial" acts. He sees every obedient act as important.

A Present-Day Equivalent

As a teenager I was a camera operator for a Christian television station. I saw evangelists lie in order to make money; I saw them reverse their doctrinal stand in order to please people of influence; I saw the head of the organization set up fake "miracles" in advance of air time so that it would appear God was blessing his "ministry."

During one season the host of a show encouraged poor widows to skip one dinner a week so that by the end of the month, they could send in the money they had saved by fasting. When the extra money began to arrive, the man sent me to a local store with a check for $1,000 to pick up a fancy clock for his office wall! I asked him if that was the right way to spend the money. He looked at me as if noticing me for the first time and said, "I can see to it that you never work in Christian television again." This is the spirit the disciples had fallen into; they wanted to be the gate-keepers and the great ones, at any cost.

☞ **GO TO:**

Galatians 5:22
(fruit of the Spirit)

KEEP IT REAL—Author Sheila Walsh once told me about a time she sang at a church in the deep South. The concert seemed to go very well, but afterwards an arguing couple approached her in the church lobby. The wife was begging the husband, "Please just hear her out; we really don't know—" The husband interrupted, "There she is! Let's ask her!"

Storming up to Sheila, the man demanded, "Do you believe in the Super Nine All the Time?" Caught off guard, Sheila stammered, "I don't know; I haven't heard the expression before." In angry triumph, the man turned to his wife and crowed, "See? She doesn't! What'd I tell ya?" and tried to leave. But Sheila touched the man's shoulder and pleaded, "Wait; give me a chance! It may be something I believe in but know by different terminology." With the wife and the husband both explaining at the same time, it took Sheila several minutes to realize what these people called the "Super Nine All the Time" was the fruit of the Spirit. Sheila was able to affirm that she believed in the Super Nine All the Time—much to the wife's relief and to the husband's apparent disappointment.

I often think of Sheila's story when I realize I've become so fond of favorite terms, methods, styles, or emphases that I'm convinced my little group pleases God the most. I can become preoccupied with my own little kingdom when I'm supposed to be advancing God's kingdom—in all its multifaceted glory.

> **Mark 9:42–48** "And if anyone causes one of these little ones who believe in me to sin, it would be better for him to be thrown into the sea with a large millstone tied around his neck. If your hand causes you to sin, cut it off. It is better for you to enter life maimed than with two hands to go into hell, where the fire never goes out. And if your foot causes you to sin, cut it off. It is better for you to enter life crippled than to have two feet and be thrown into hell. And if your eye causes you to sin, pluck it out. It is better for you to enter the kingdom of God with one eye than to have two eyes and be thrown into hell, where
> > "'their worm does not die,
> > and the fire is not quenched.'"

Jesus' Warning

Jesus continues correcting his disciples' Mohammed Ali problem ("I'm the greatest!") by letting them know how seriously God takes it when someone who supposedly represents him causes a weaker believer to sin.

Christ's millstone statement is the first of several **hyperboles** Jesus gives in quick succession. Jewish law forbade <u>self-mutilation</u>, and people with such deficiencies were not allowed in the Temple. Jesus does not mean for the disciples to follow his words literally.

In cases requiring capital punishment back then, judicial officials sometimes showed mercy to convicts by substituting maiming for death. Jesus is saying it would be better to give up something that is not only dear to you, but seems entirely necessary, than to face the wrath of God. For some of us, giving up our dreams of ambition may hurt almost as much as plucking out an eye, but Jesus urges us to do whatever it takes to keep from becoming spiritually pompous.

Jesus is talking only to the Twelve. Most would assume the disciples were on their way to heaven at this point, yet Jesus is warning them they could *"be thrown into hell,"* if they nurse sin in their hearts instead of getting rid of it (see also GWPB, pages 188–189). Jesus' warning does not fit a neat and tidy theology that says, "I went forward and accepted Christ as my Savior on March 3, 1992, so now I'm saved." Philippians 2:12 says to *"work out your salvation with fear and trembling."* Christians often argue about the meaning of such verses, but we would be wiser to heed them.

hyperboles: gross exaggerations

☞ **GO TO:**

Deuteronomy 14:1–2 (self-mutilation)

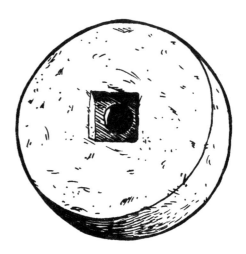

IT'S
GREEK
TO ME

Millstones were tire-shaped rocks used to crush grain into flour (see illustration above). Some millstones were small enough for a woman to operate by herself, but here Jesus' words specify "the millstone of a donkey"—a millstone so large and heavy it required the strength of a harnessed donkey to roll it over the grain. Being *"thrown into the sea"* with such a massive boulder tied around your neck would be more than certain death; it would be overkill.

> **Mark 9:49–50** "Everyone will be salted with fire."
> "Salt is good, but if it loses its saltiness, how can you make it salty again? Have salt in yourselves, and be at peace with each other."

Salt and Fire

There are times when it's fun being a Christian, like when you sing a solo at church and people applaud thunderously. But Jesus said *"Everyone will be salted with fire,"* a paraphrase of the saying *"Every sacrifice will be salted with salt"* (Leviticus 2:13). The word "fire" implies persecution. In other words, every believer in Jesus will suffer for him at some point. If your goal is to look cool, receive acclaim, and wield power, how long will you last when following Jesus costs something?

In verse 50 Jesus puts another spin on the "salt" theme. Using salt as a symbol for everything that is appealing and "tastes good" about true Christian character, he asks, in effect, "If you experience what it's like to be a true follower of mine, then gradually convert your spiritual journey into a self-admiring, self-important, self-glorious racket, what more can I do for you?" The implied answer? Nothing. Once you dull yourself to the convicting work of the Holy Spirit, it's very difficult to become sensitive to it again.

That's why Jesus wraps it up by encouraging the disciples to hang onto good spiritual qualities and *"be at peace with each other."* This brings the discussion full circle, because the reason for the lecture was the disciples' war about who was greatest. There'd be no problem if each man's goal was to serve the others, out of love for God.

Though the Twelve couldn't see it then, eventually they learned the <u>humble life</u> is actually the happiest life. Jesus strongly emphasized this teaching, so we need to make a point of knowing it by heart.

☞ **GO TO:**

1 Peter 3:8–12; 1 John 2:9–10; 3:14 (humble life)

Kathleen Norris: The church . . . is a human institution, full of ordinary people, sinners like me, who say and do cruel, stupid things. But it is also a divinely inspired institution, full of good purpose, which partakes of a unity far greater than the sum of its parts. That is why it is called the body of Christ.[2]

What Others are Saying:

WHO'S THE GREATEST? (REHASHED)

The next few passages continue to answer the question, Who's the greatest? The answer seems to be: Not the spiritual "experts." Not the wealthy. Not the ambitious. Instead, in God's kingdom the helpless can be the greatest.

> **Mark 10:1–4** Jesus then left that place and went into the region of Judea and across the Jordan. Again crowds of people came to him, and as was his custom, he taught them.
>
> Some Pharisees came and tested him by asking, "Is it lawful for a man to divorce his wife?"
>
> "What did Moses command you?" he replied.
>
> They said, "Moses permitted a man to write a certificate of divorce and send her away."

Divorce And The Phrustrated Pharisees

Jesus has traveled into a province ruled by Herod, where the Pharisees have been hanging out with their unlikely partners in crime, the <u>Herodians</u>. When John the Baptist spoke God's word about

☞ **GO TO:**

Mark 3:6; 8:15 (Herodians)

the impropriety of Herod's marriage to Herodias, John was be-headed. I think the Pharisees were trying to trick Jesus into making comments that could be turned inflammatory and reported back to Herod.

Their question was, *"Is it lawful for a man to divorce his wife?"* Had the Pharisees been true spiritual seekers at this point, it would've been a reasonable question to ask. Rabbinic opinions on the subject varied widely. Some thought the only legitimate grounds for divorce was adultery. Others thought a man had the right to divorce his wife if all she did was annoy or embarrass him.

As usual, rather than fall into their clumsily crafted trap, Jesus shifts the burden back to the Pharisees. He asks them, *"What did Moses command you?"* Instead of answering with what Moses commanded, the Pharisees answered with what Moses would let you get away with in a worst-case scenario. Their answer rests on Deuteronomy 24:1–4, which is worth reading if you want a better grasp of this discussion. The intent of Deuteronomy's law was to make sure Israel never got anywhere near wife-swapping.

> **Mark 10:5–11** "It was because your hearts were hard that Moses wrote you this law," Jesus replied. "But at the beginning of creation God 'made them male and female.' 'For this reason a man will leave his father and mother and be united to his wife, and the two will become one flesh.' So they are no longer two, but one. Therefore what God has joined together, let man not separate."
>
> When they were in the house again, the disciples asked Jesus about this. He answered, "Anyone who divorces his wife and marries another woman commits adultery against her."

God: The Inventor Of Marriage

Jesus said Moses wrote "this law" only because he had to deal with the real condition of the human heart. Moses' law set up conditions to prevent divorce from having worse consequences than it already had, but it didn't come close to God's ideal. Jesus cites verses from Genesis 2:23–24, which the Pharisees believed Moses had written, to reveal God's ideal for marriage. He also alluded to Genesis 1:27, so have a look at both references.

Divorce in ancient times was even more cruel than it is now. If a man decided to give his wife a "certificate of divorce," his only obligation was to return her **dowry**. If she had come from a poor family, a man was legally authorized to forget about her and his kids by giving her something as cheap as a goat. Moreover, only husbands could divorce wives. Wives could not divorce husbands.

dowry: money or goods a woman brings into marriage

A first-century Palestinian would have been stunned to hear Jesus speak of a man committing adultery *against his wife*. First-century Palestinians thought adultery was a sin that one man committed against another man—either the husband of the adulterous wife, or the father of the unmarried woman. Women had no rights and didn't count.

Jesus, however, was there to preach the kingdom of God, which has no second-class citizens. His teaching puts women on the equal footing with men that God intended when he created them. And because all Jesus did was cite Scripture, the Pharisees could not use anything he said to get him in trouble with Herod.

KEEP IT REAL—Highly regarded pollster George Barna has reported for some years now that in the United States, the percentage of marriages that end in divorce is as high for Christians as it is for non-Christians. Among certain denominations the percentage of Christian divorces exceeds the percentage of secular divorces. This is a terrible reflection on the spiritual state of the American church. It proves that the worldly perspective of putting your own happiness first (even if it means abandoning people who depend on you) has permeated God's family.

> **Mark 10:12** "And if she divorces her husband and marries another man, she commits adultery."

To Remarry Is To Commit Adultery?

Here Jesus recognizes the right of women to divorce their husbands—a right not recognized in Judaism. Again, Jesus raises the status of women.

For both men and women, Jesus' teaching implies any person who divorces and remarries is committing adultery. This is a bitter pill to swallow. Elsewhere in Scripture, however, Jesus makes an exception to this rule. He says you're not an adulterer if you remarry after divorcing someone because of "marital unfaithfulness."

But what about other extreme cases? What if a person remar-

☞ **GO TO:**

Matthew 19:9 (marital unfaithfulness)

ries after divorcing an alcoholic who beats him or her and the children? Does Jesus think such a person is an adulterer? Honestly, I don't know because Scripture doesn't say, but for Jesus to call such a person an adulterer, I think he would have to act contrary to the spirit of the rest of his teachings.

Divorce is a controversial and emotionally loaded topic. Obviously these few sentences from Jesus are not God's full and exhaustive opinion on the topic. One of the reasons "God hates divorce" (Malachi 2:16) is because it hurts people (see WBFC, pages 299–301). Husbands or wives looking for an easy way out of their vows need to ask God to lead them out of self-centeredness and into the life of servanthood Jesus wants us to have.

On the other hand, leaders and teachers in the church must be careful how they defend their interpretations of God's Word for marriage and divorce. They need to avoid condemning and damaging people in ways God did not intend. In all cases the best way forward is through prayer and sincerely seeking God's wisdom.

What Others are Saying:

Judy Bodmer: [If you divorce your spouse] at first, you might feel relief, but that is short-lived. Tests show that for the first five to six years you will be consumed by moderate to severe anger. Depression, which at its very core is a feeling of failure, will become your companion. One writer called it a private hell. Stress tests rank separation and divorce as the second and third most traumatic events in a person's life. . . . This shouldn't be surprising when you look at the Bible. The word used for [they shall become one] "flesh" is the same word used to describe the attachment of muscle to bone. The pain of tearing living tissue is reflected in the pain of tearing apart a relationship.[3]

> **Mark 10:13–16** People were bringing little children to Jesus to have him touch them, but the disciples rebuked them. When Jesus saw this, he was indignant. He said to them, "Let the little children come to me, and do not hinder them, for the kingdom of God belongs to such as these. I tell you the truth, anyone who will not receive the kingdom of God like a little child will never enter it." And he took the children in his arms, put his hands on them and blessed them.

The Bouncers' Boo-Boo

In the previous passage Jesus confronts humans' warped view of marriage; here he tackles the disciples' reprehensible treatment of children; and the next story is about money. All of these accounts are nestled in the context of what it means to be a disciple of Jesus, so perhaps Mark grouped them together because they reveal human tendencies that are most likely to prevent the disciples (and us) from pursuing Jesus.

This account reminds us of 9:36–37, where Jesus placed a child in the middle of the disciples and said, "Welcome these." And again, despite what Jesus commanded them, the disciples are haughtily scolding people who would "bother" the Master with mere children. No wonder Jesus was indignant!

The point of Jesus' teaching remains the same as with his other statement about children. They have no clout, no rights, never assert power or influence, but are more open to receiving unearned gifts than adults are. The only people who will enter the kingdom of God are those who realize it is a gift they do not deserve.

KEY POINT

You cannot enter the kingdom of God if you don't fully acknowledge God as King.

Something to Ponder

> **Mark 10:17–20** As Jesus started on his way, a man ran up to him and fell on his knees before him. "Good teacher," he asked, "what must I do to inherit eternal life?"
>
> "Why do you call me good?" Jesus answered. "No one is good—except God alone. You know the commandments: 'Do not murder, do not commit adultery, do not steal, do not give false testimony, do not defraud, honor your father and mother.'"
>
> "Teacher," he declared, "all these I have kept since I was a boy."

The Self-Centered Seeker

Jesus is traveling when a <u>rich</u> <u>young</u> <u>ruler</u> dashes up to him and kneels. This humorous gesture, obviously meant to be humble, interrupts Jesus and blocks him from going about his business. The man takes it for granted that the most important thing for Jesus to do is help him.

He greets Jesus with a title more exalted than Jews typically used with one another: *"good teacher."* Jesus questions the title not to deny it, but to see if this young guy realizes what he's say-

☞ **GO TO:**

Mark 10:22 (rich)

Matthew 19:22 (young)

Luke 18:18 (ruler)

ing. I think he wanted the young man to ponder his definition of "good." In a moment we'll see this young man thought "good" included himself. (For more about how Jesus viewed himself, see GWLC, pages 173–177.)

Unlike the Pharisees, who asked Jesus questions so they could tear apart his answers, this young man seems to mean it when he asks, *"What must I do to inherit eternal life?"* The young man's question is based on the assumption that one must *do* something to obtain eternal life, which stands in contrast to what Jesus just taught; to enter the kingdom of God, a person must *receive* it like a little child receives a gift.

It's easy to picture Jesus answering with a bemused smile. *"You know the commandments,"* he answers, and lists a few of them randomly. The rich young ruler's response again strikes a note of both humility and insensitivity. He says he has kept God's commands since he was a boy, referring to when he was bar mitzvahed and thus became accountable for obedience. He seems sincere. Of course, only someone who is seriously out of touch with himself would honestly believe he had not sinned since childhood. Yet this young man must have sensed his shortcomings, or he would not have rushed up to Jesus in the first place.

> **Mark 10:21–24a** Jesus looked at him and loved him. "One thing you lack," he said. "Go, sell everything you have and give to the poor, and you will have treasure in heaven. Then come, follow me."
>
> At this the man's face fell. He went away sad, because he had great wealth.
>
> Jesus looked around and said to his disciples, "How hard it is for the rich to enter the kingdom of God!"
>
> The disciples were amazed at his words.

Tell Me What I Want To Hear, Not What I Need To Hear

As Jesus regarded this kneeling man, the man's face must have reflected a strange combination of seeker and braggart. Was Mr. first-century GQ really asking for insight, or had he assumed eternal life, like everything else in his life, would simply be handed to him? Had he rushed to Jesus out of eagerness to find God or because he thought getting a blessing would be the equivalent of a fast-food transaction?

Jesus saw something in the mixture that appealed to him, and he paid the young man the tremendous compliment of telling him not what he wanted to hear, but what he needed to hear.

Jesus' answer should not be read to emphasize the "give to the poor" part. It should be read to emphasize the "follow me" part. Later rabbinic law actually forbade a Jew from giving away so much of his own wealth that he became a burden on society. Jesus is purposely answering the man's *what must I do?* with an impossible standard. He is trying to show the man that relying on human goodness and resources is insufficient for salvation because, *"No one is good—except God alone."* To enter the kingdom of God, you must put yourself in a place of helplessness and accept God's gift. Following a set of rules will never get you there, but following Jesus will.

Instantly the rich young man gave up. No follow-up question. No "are you sure?" No "help me understand." Giving up his riches was a total deal breaker, proving that his righteousness did not run as deeply as he claimed.

The disciples, meanwhile, are amazed. Given their ambitious state of mind in previous passages, they were probably thinking, *"Dang!* We could have used a major contribution right about now!"

The young ruler stopped the Savior *"as Jesus started on his way."* Remember the context. Jesus is going to Jerusalem to die for our sins. In asking the young man to give his all for the poor, Jesus was asking for nothing more than he himself was in the act of doing. Other religious figures point the way. Jesus leads the way.

Something to Ponder

Philip Yancey: By instinct I feel I must *do something* in order to be accepted. Grace sounds a startling note of contradiction, of liberation, and every day I must pray anew for the ability to hear its message. . . . Jesus' kingdom calls us to another way, one that depends not on our performance but his own. We do not have to achieve but merely follow. He has already earned for us the costly victory of God's acceptance.[4]

What Others are Saying:

> **Mark 10:24b–27** But Jesus said again, "Children, how hard it is to enter the kingdom of God! It is easier for a camel to go through the eye of a needle than for a rich man to enter the kingdom of God."
>
> The disciples were even more amazed, and said to each other, "Who then can be saved?"

> Jesus looked at them and said, "With man this is impossible, but not with God; all things are possible with God."

Imagine How The Camel Must Feel Afterwards

In the face of the disciples' initial amazement, Jesus repeats his statement and amplifies it. They become *"even more amazed"*—words that imply exasperation. Some Jews understood wealth to be a sign of God's <u>blessing</u>. If wealth is a sign of God's favor, and wealthy people can barely enter God's kingdom, how can anyone else enter?

They have not listened closely enough to Jesus. He doesn't have many favorable things to say about <u>money</u>. Besides referring to money as a <u>little thing</u>, Jesus regards money as an obstacle to surrendering to God. Not only that, with the camel metaphor Jesus is saying it's absurdly, ridiculously hard—and afterwards, as C. S. Lewis wrote, "picture how the camel feels, squeezed out / In one long bloody thread from tail to snout."[5]

In fact, by any human means it is impossible for the wealthy to put others first—for Scrooge to wake from his dreams and instantly reverse his greedy nature. *"But not with God; all things are possible with God,"* Jesus says. People often quote this verse out of context to avoid taking responsibility for a lack of preparation. Jesus meant that God can change the <u>hearts</u> of people who otherwise would have been the last to enter his kingdom.

☞ **GO TO:**

Deuteronomy 28:1–14; Job 1:10; Proverbs 10:22 (blessing)

Matthew 6:19–34; Luke 12:13–34; 16:1–15; 19:1–10 (money)

Luke 16:10 (little thing)

Proverbs 21:1 (hearts)

What Others are Saying:

James S. Stewart: [People will] always find ways and means of eluding a religion's stern demands while still calling themselves its followers and signing its creeds and continuing to bear its name; . . . they will always regard the half-allegiance they are prepared to give with a wonderful complacency and satisfaction, feeling that anyone—even God Himself—might be gratified by the interest they show and the patronage they offer; not realising that attitude, which seems so reasonable and respectable, is dealing religion a blow and doing it damage compared with which all the direct, frontal attacks of its open enemies are a mere nothing.[6]

> **Mark 10:28–31** Peter said to him, "We have left everything to follow you!"
> "I tell you the truth," Jesus replied, "no one who has

> left home or brothers or sisters or mother or father or children or fields for me and the gospel will fail to receive a hundred times as much in this present age (homes, brothers, sisters, mothers, children and fields—and with them, persecutions) and in the age to come, eternal life. But many who are first will be last, and the last first."

You'll Have To Move, Mr. Gates; You're In Mother Teresa's Seat

After being called Satan a few passages back, perhaps Peter needed reassurance from Jesus. Despite the selfish tone of Peter's question, he does have a point; the rich young ruler gave up his spiritual aspirations instantly upon finding out their cost. The disciples had faced the same issue and chosen Jesus.

Jesus' response to Peter says you can't outgive God. Anyone who gives up family, field, or house for God has received the much larger <u>family</u>, <u>field</u>, and <u>house</u> of God. The rewards Jesus lists are not to be taken materialistically; many people have given up their home for God, and have not received one hundred homes during their lifetime. In addition, Jesus makes a point of mentioning all the rewards come *"with persecutions."*

"This age" probably refers to the age that began when Jesus came, and the "next age" refers to the age that will begin the second time Jesus comes.

☞ **GO TO:**

Mark 3:31–35 (family)

Mark 4:26–29; Matthew 9:37–38 (field)

John 14:1–4 (house)

> **Mark 10:32–34** They were on their way up to Jerusalem, with Jesus leading the way, and the disciples were astonished, while those who followed were afraid. Again he took the Twelve aside and told them what was going to happen to him. "We are going up to Jerusalem," he said, "and the Son of Man will be betrayed to the chief priests and teachers of the law. They will condemn him to death and will hand him over to the Gentiles, who will mock him and spit on him, flog him and kill him. Three days later he will rise."

The Petrified Parade

Mark's striking narrative reveals the confusion of the disciples. They are *"astonished"* and *"afraid"*—but at least they are still following. In this snapshot we don't get the impression Peter or any of the disciples are walking next to Jesus in fellowship and conversation. We see Jesus alone, dragging his followers behind him by sheer determination to complete the mission his Father gave him.

For the <u>third time</u> Jesus tries to explain to his disciples exactly what will happen when they get to Jerusalem. This prediction is the most detailed, including the facts that he will be delivered to the Romans and mocked, spit upon, and whipped.

☞ **GO TO:**

Mark 8:31; 9:31
(third time)

Something to Ponder

> Jesus knew what was in store for him, but chose it anyway. He knew exactly the kinds of emotional and physical torture Jerusalem held for him. He decided that you and I were worth it, and resolutely marched to his death to redeem us. It just makes me love him all the more.

What Others are Saying:

Philip Yancey: Christian leaders have shown an impulse to pin everything down, to reduce behavior and doctrine to absolutes that could be answered on a True/False test. Strangely, I do not find this tendency in the Bible. Far from it. I find instead the mystery and uncertainty that characterize any relationship, especially a relationship between a perfect God and fallible human beings.[7]

OF BLIND MEN AND BOOKENDS

> **Mark 10:35–38a** Then James and John, the sons of Zebedee, came to him. "Teacher," they said, "we want you to do for us whatever we ask."
> "What do you want me to do for you?" he asked.
> They replied, "Let one of us sit at your right and the other at your left in your glory."
> "You don't know what you are asking," Jesus said.

What Jesus Wants His Disciples To Be, Part 2

What were James and John thinking? After watching Jesus blow away all the verbal traps of his enemies, did they really believe Jesus would fall for, "Promise you'll give us whatever we want"?

Their request is for Jesus to give them the positions of highest honor in his kingdom. It's an ironic request, considering Jesus said the greatest in his kingdom must be the servant of all—not the one who grasps for power and position.

Jesus had just announced to them they were all going to Jerusalem, so James and John may have thought Jesus was about to make his move to take over the Jewish government. They may have been getting their dibs in early.

Jesus, too wise to sign their blank check, first asks what favor they want. He hears them out. When he tells them they have no idea what they're asking, it's an understatement.

> **Mark 10:38b–40** "Can you drink the cup I drink or be baptized with the baptism I am baptized with?"
>
> "We can," they answered.
>
> Jesus said to them, "You will drink the cup I drink and be baptized with the baptism I am baptized with, but to sit at my right or left is not for me to grant. These places belong to those for whom they have been prepared."

A Cup For The Cross-Eyed

Jesus tries to help the sons of Zebedee understand what they're asking. He asks them if they can *"drink the cup"* he drinks. To fully understand Jesus' question, you need to read the Old Testament cross-references and understand what "the cup" was to the Jewish mind. I could give you lots of references, but a few will do: Psalm 75:6–8; Isaiah 51:17–22; Jeremiah 25:15–28; and Ezekiel 23:31–34.

After reading these you will have deeper insight into why Jesus will soon pray, *"Father, . . . Take this cup from me."* What is in this foaming cup that can bring sorrow, shame, convulsions, vomiting, and ruin? The cup contains God's wrath. It is the cup of judgment, which Jesus will guzzle to the bottom, so God won't have to pour it out on Israel, God's people.

When Jesus asks James and John if they can drink the cup he drinks, he is not asking them if they can die for the world's sins. As sinful men, James and John were not capable of this. Jesus used "my cup" to mean "my lot in life," which is a second meaning for "cup" in Hebrew scripture. To "share someone's cup" was an expression for sharing another's fate. Jesus is asking whether James and John are prepared to live a life with more than its share of suffering because of their association with the Messiah. Strongly implicit in Jesus' question is the idea that suffering with Jesus is an indispensable part of later sharing in his glory.

James and John answer without thinking. Their response is so glib, I can't help but hear it in the voice of Goofy: "Yup! Shore we can drink it! Hyuk!"

James and John thought Jesus was about to kick the Romans

☞ **GO TO:**

Mark 14:36 (this cup)

Psalm 16:5–6; 23:5; 116:13 ("cup")

out of Jerusalem and take an earthly throne. In other words, their understanding of what the kingdom of God would look like was very different from what Jesus had in mind. They also did not understand that Jesus operated solely in obedience to God the Father, and would not be the one to determine who receives the most honor in heaven. The two men had accomplished nothing with their request, except to expose their hunger for power. Later, however, <u>John would understand</u> what Jesus struggled so hard to convey.

☞ **GO TO:**

1 John 3:16 (John would understand)

Something to Ponder

Before we smirk too much at James and John, we would do well to put ourselves in their shoes. How would we fare if the whole world was allowed to analyze all our recently submitted requests of Jesus?

What Others are Saying:

Henri J. M. Nouwen: What makes the temptation of power so seemingly irresistible? Maybe it is that power offers an easy substitute for the hard task of love. It seems easier to be God than to love God, easier to control people than to love people . . . Jesus asks, "Do you love me?" We ask, "Can we sit at your right hand and your left hand in your Kingdom?" . . . We have been tempted to replace love with power.[8]

> **Mark 10:41–45** When the ten heard about this, they became indignant with James and John. Jesus called them together and said, "You know that those who are regarded as rulers of the Gentiles lord it over them, and their high officials exercise authority over them. Not so with you. Instead, whoever wants to become great among you must be your servant, and whoever wants to be first must be slave of all. For even the Son of Man did not come to be served, but to serve, and to give his life as a ransom for many."

How To Save People Like Genghis Khan

The other ten disciples did not have any noteworthy reaction to Jesus' third prediction of his own rejection, torture, and death, but they sure had something to say about James' and John's request to be rulers. They were not indignant with the brothers' insensitivity to Jesus. They were indignant because James and John had beat them to the punch. Once again, Jesus sits the Twelve down and tries to impart his upside-down (or right side up) philosophy.

As far as we can tell from Scripture, Jesus had not yet been to a major Roman city, but evidence of Gentile arrogance would have been all around him. Besides the crucifixions I mentioned in the chapter on Mark 8:22–9:29, Jesus would have seen plenty of Roman and Syrian coins. The copper coins used in Herod Philip's territory, for example, showed the head of Augustus with the inscription, "He who deserves adoration." The denarius Jesus used to pay his taxes depicted Caesar Tiberius as the semidivine son of a god and a goddess. The true Son of God understood the pathetic emptiness of these rulers' claims. It must have saddened him to see his disciples yearn for the power to make similar claims.

The worldly philosophy of self-advancement at all costs reaches its logical conclusion in this quote, attributed to Genghis Khan: "A man's greatest work is to break his enemies, to drive them before him, to take from them all the things that have been theirs, to hear the weeping of those who cherished them, to take their horses between his knees and to press in his arms the most desirable of their women."

In the face of this hard-hearted, hellish philosophy, Jesus commands his followers, "Not so with you." Instead, he places his highest stamp of approval on love, which expresses itself in tasks of service. Any act of compassion done as an expression of devotion to Jesus counts as both worship to God and service to the recipient.

Whenever our hearts are confronted with this beautifully high standard, we instinctively know we have blown it. In knee-jerk fashion, we try to shift our feelings of shame with a quick, "Oh yeah? Well what about *you*?" Jesus' response silences us and inspires reverence: "*For even the Son of Man did not come to be served, but to serve, and to give his life as a ransom for many*" (Mark 10:45). When someone gives up being God to come wash your feet, it's pretty hard to find fault with him.

Mark 10:45, quoted above, summarizes all of Mark's Gospel. It's the only verse that states explicitly why Jesus died. If you memorize only one verse from Mark, I recommend this one.

THE WAYBACK MACHINE

☞ **GO TO:**

Mark 12:16 (taxes)

Remember This . . .

☞ **GO TO:**

Philippians 2:5–7 (being God)

IT'S
GREEK
TO ME

Do you know what the word "ransom" means in Greek? It means "ransom." Surprise! It means now what it meant then: to buy someone out of helpless bondage. Back then, you could buy the freedom of an <u>enslaved relative</u>. The person whose liberty was bought then owed his life to whoever paid the bill. This and more is packed into Jesus' decision to <u>ransom</u> us—even those of us who at our core think like Genghis Khan.

What Others
are Saying:

☞ **GO TO:**

Leviticus 25:47–53
(enslaved relative)

Isaiah 53:4–11 (ransom)

C. S. Lewis: Supposing God became a man—suppose our human nature which can suffer and die was amalgamated with God's nature in one person—then that person could help us. He could surrender His will, and suffer and die, because He was man; and He could do it perfectly because He was God. . . . That is the sense in which He pays our debt, and suffers for us what He Himself need not suffer at all.[9]

> **Mark 10:46–48** Then they came to Jericho. As Jesus and his disciples, together with a large crowd, were leaving the city, a blind man, Bartimaeus (that is, the Son of Timaeus), was sitting by the roadside begging. When he heard that it was Jesus of Nazareth, he began to shout, "Jesus, Son of David, have mercy on me!"
>
> Many rebuked him and told him to be quiet, but he shouted all the more, "Son of David, have mercy on me!"

Son Of David Meets Son Of Worth

Jesus, like tens of thousands of Jews, is going to Jerusalem for Passover. The road out of Jericho toward Jerusalem, less than eighteen miles away, would be an ideal location for a beggar. This time of year the traffic was heavy with pilgrims, who might give generously to soothe their consciences before meeting God in his Temple.

A blind beggar such as Bartimaeus, however, was the victim of long-standing <u>prejudice</u> in Jewish culture. To the starstruck crowd who expected Jesus to behave like the *"rulers of the Gentiles,"* Bartimaeus was an annoyance. In response to his pleas for help, this "religious" crowd tells him to shut up.

Bartimaeus shrewdly realized, however, that if people were shushing him, he was probably within earshot of Jesus. He persisted. The more they scolded him, the louder he yelled. He could not know it, but in doing so he put himself in great company. He joined the same club as the four friends of the paralyzed man; the

☞ **GO TO:**

2 Samuel 5:6–8
(prejudice)

GOD'S WORD FOR THE BIBLICALLY-INEPT

woman with the issue of blood; the Syro-Phoenician "dog" woman, and so many more whose desire to meet Jesus brought ridicule from the foolish and reward from Jesus.

Bartimaeus did one other exceptional thing. He called Jesus loudly by a messianic title. No one else in all of Mark calls Jesus "Son of David." Perhaps this is why Jesus noticed the blind man. After all, sitting by the road, Bartimaeus would have been difficult to see through the crowd of pilgrims. His name for Jesus might also explain why people rebuked him. Someone shouting the equivalent of "Yay! The Jewish King!" into a crowd under Roman rule could bring trouble to all of them, especially when the "Son of David" is going to Jerusalem, which used to be David's capital city.

Mark, who rarely names Jesus' patients, tells us this blind beggar is *"Bartimaeus (that is, the son of Timaeus)."* Mark's readers would have known that "bar" means "son of." It's as if he'd written, "His name was George Bush Jr., that is, the son of George Bush Senior." Why the unnecessary wording? (It's straight from the Department of Redundancy Department.) Mark must have wanted us to notice this guy's name. Timaeus is difficult to translate, but its meaning resembles "precious" or "worthy one."

IT'S GREEK TO ME

> **Mark 10:49–52** Jesus stopped and said, "Call him."
>
> So they called to the blind man, "Cheer up! On your feet! He's calling you." Throwing his cloak aside, he jumped to his feet and came to Jesus.
>
> "What do you want me to do for you?" Jesus asked him.
>
> The blind man said, "Rabbi, I want to see."
>
> "Go," said Jesus, "your faith has healed you." Immediately he received his sight and followed Jesus along the road.

Bartimaeus: A Good Role Model

Jesus responds to the call, foreshadowing a change in his policy of silencing those who recognize he is Messiah. Don't miss the detail of Bartimaeus casting his cloak aside. That cloak would have been supremely important to a blind man. By day, he would have spread it before him to collect alms. By night, he would have used it to ward off the chill. It may have been his only possession, but as soon as Jesus called him, he tossed it aside.

This is a man who expects his life to change. He stands in contrast to the rich man who would not give up his possessions to follow God. It also brings our attention to the disciples, who once dropped their nets to follow Jesus, but are now wrapped up in the "cloak" of their own celebrity.

Jesus then asks a question you wouldn't normally ask a blind man: *"What do you want me to do for you?"* It is word for word the same question Jesus asked James and John. They answered with sinful ambition. Bartimaeus answers with humble vulnerability: *"[Teacher], I want to see."*

Because Bartimaeus had the right kind of faith, he received an instant, no-fuss healing. Jesus said, *"Go,"* but tellingly, Bartimaeus chose to come. He followed Jesus *"along the road."* This phrase, repeated in so many ways throughout the Markan hinge, also closes it. The "road" Jesus is on is the servant's road to *"obedience unto death,"* but Bartimaeus gladly follows.

☞ **GO TO:**

Philippians 2:8–9 (obedience unto death)

Something to Ponder

This is the last healing Jesus performs in Mark's Gospel. It forms the other bookend of the inclusio that began with Jesus healing a blind man who required a second touch. This blind man is one of very few who sees by faith that Jesus is the Messiah. He is an example of someone helpless who is nonetheless named "worthy one," cementing everything Jesus said about who will be great in God's kingdom.

Mark intends the physically blind men to comment on the spiritual blindness of the Twelve. This is evident when Jesus asks Bartimaeus the exact same question he asked James and John. Over the course of the Markan hinge, we have seen Jesus' way is a path of death and suffering that will result in resurrection and glory. Those who would share in his glory must humble themselves, love Jesus enough to share his suffering, and imitate him as the one who came *"not to be served, but to serve."*

Mark wants us to know that asking what Jesus can do for you is not central to discipleship. A true disciple's passion is to ask, "What can I do for Jesus?"

What Others are Saying:

Tom Getman: It is not our responsibility "to make people 'Christians'" and get them baptized into a particular denomination, but rather to help people decide to follow Jesus and his radical message. Maybe this is why the New Testament writers only use "Christian" three times but "disciple" on 269 occasions![10]

KEEP IT REAL—Mark 9:36–37. I love to picture myself as a child in Jesus' arms. Spiritually speaking, that really is where I am. That is where all believers are, whether I think much of them or not. *When I look at people who are unappealing to me, Lord, help me to see the part of your image that is in them. I want always to welcome you.*

• Mark 9:42–49. We reassure ourselves, "Jesus didn't mean it literally when he said to cut your hand off if it causes you to sin," and that's true; we shouldn't mutilate ourselves. The trouble is, I often drop the point right there. Jesus obviously meant *something* when he said that. If he didn't mean it literally, what is the figurative equivalent in my life? Do I need to give up listening to gossip? Watching violent or seductive movies? Priding myself in my collection of Bible commentaries? *Show me my sin, Lord, then help me to choose you instead of it.*

Study Questions

1. How many times did Jesus predict his own future in the "Markan hinge" (Mark 8:22–10:52)? What did he say would happen to him?
2. What did the disciples argue about "on the road"? How did Jesus resolve their dispute?
3. What does God think of divorce? What was wrong with the Pharisees' concept of divorce?
4. Jesus asked James and John whether they could drink the "cup" he would drink. What was in the cup?

CHAPTER WRAP-UP

- As Passover neared, Jesus started making his way to Jerusalem, knowing it was his mission to die there. He told the disciples of this three times, but they could not understand him. (Mark 10:32–34; 9:30–32)

- Jesus emphasized the greatest in his kingdom are not those who act important, but those who serve others out of love and receive God's gift of eternal life like little children. (Mark 9:33–50; 10:13–16, 42–45)

- Jesus answered questions about divorce. He explained God's ideal and raised the status of women. (Mark 10:1–12)

- Jesus may require you to give up everything you hold dear in order to follow him. You may suffer persecution, but you will be rich spiritually. (Mark 10:17–31)

- Jesus answers James's and John's request to have the highest places of honor in Christ's kingdom. Jesus tells them those places are not for him to give. (Mark 10:35–45)

- The healing of Bartimaeus shows God can consider spiritual beggars "worthy ones," if they have faith in Jesus. (Mark 10:46–52)

Part Five

TEMPLE TERRORIST JESUS

REVEREND FUN

"It's true that we're selling in the Temple . . . but you should know 10 percent of 'Temple Monopoly' goes to charity."

Jesus In The Big City

After a long, open-yet-secret ministry around Lake Galilee, at last Jesus arrives at the capital of Israel and the center of Judaism it-self—Jerusalem and its magnificent Temple. The arrival marks a new approach for the Son of Man. At last he throws aside the cloak of secrecy he has imposed upon his ministry. He enters Jerusalem not as a pilgrim, but as a king.

Yet is all the secrecy gone? Jesus' symbolic actions in the Big City could be interpreted in several different ways.

THE WAYBACK MACHINE

You'll be able to visualize the rest of Mark's book much better if you understand what Jerusalem would have been like as Jesus rode into it.

No matter where you approached from, you always spoke of going "up" to Jerusalem, because, roughly speaking, it rested on four mountains about 500 meters above sea level. Its height appeared even more dramatic because it had deep ravines on the west, south, and east. You can see why military-minded King David chose it as his citadel—a city set on mountains, bordered by valleys on three sides, would be easier to defend.

Jewish ceremony required every Jewish male to report to Jerusalem three times a year: in the fall (for the Feast of Tabernacles), late spring (Passover), and early summer (Feast of Weeks). At these times hundreds of thousands (and by some estimates, millions) of Jews jammed the city.

Even "off-season" Jerusalem had a population density greater than modern-day Manhattan's, with an estimated 117 people per acre. Most of the common people lived in government-built apartments known as *insula*, mentioned in the chapter on Mark 5:21–6:6. As for privacy, there was none. An average of one private house existed for every twenty-six blocks of "projects." The poorer you were, the higher up you lived in these multi-story apartments. Having no restrooms and living three or four stories up, people commonly used chamber pots, then dumped the contents out the window at night.

The streets were very narrow. What the Romans considered a "big highway" was about fifteen and one-half feet wide (half as wide as the suburban residential street I live on). By the first century Jerusalem had been invaded, plundered, razed, rebuilt, recaptured, re-razed, and re-rebuilt so many times that a map of the streets resembled a spilled bowl of spaghetti. When fires occurred, the crammed housing and narrow streets meant total destruction for large portions of the city. (See illustration, page 205.)

Water was piped only to public fountains, and to the very

rich. Everyone else carried it in jugs and learned to econo-
mize. (They also knew to boil it before drinking it.) Only the
southeastern part of Jerusalem could count on water reliably.
Between the lack of ready baths, the open sewers, all those
animals, and the custom of dumping chamber pots wherever,
the stench of the city could grow overpowering. In the heat
of summer, you could smell Jerusalem for miles.

After dark no one went out alone unless they had a death
wish and a current will. People barricaded themselves indoors

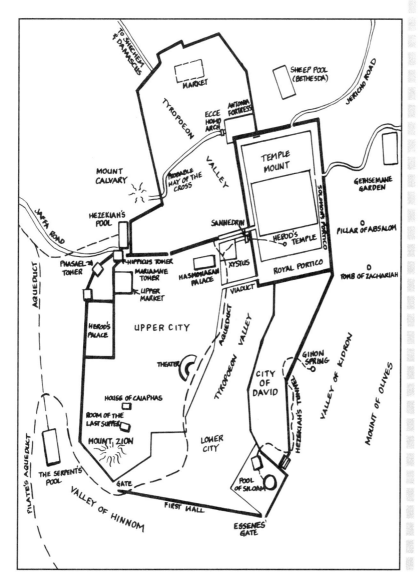

Map of Jerusalem in Jesus' Day

Jerusalem was not situated on a trade route or a port, so the Temple was the city's main industry and tourist attraction. Virtually everyone in town made their living off the Temple, directly or indirectly.

to protect from thieves and corrupt Roman soldiers. If some urgent mission drove you outdoors at night, you gathered as many slaves and friends as you could and made sure they all had torches. In the passages ahead we'll see Jesus and the disciples leave the city before nightfall each day, a good common-sense practice.

Of course, the most prominent attraction in Jerusalem was the magnificent Temple that Herod spent decades building. I'll describe it in the next chapter on Mark 11:1–25.

Jesus Smacked 'Em Right In The Temple

Just as Jesus' arrival in Jerusalem marks a new phase in his ministry, it also marks a change in Mark's narrative. The first half of his book covered years, providing us highlights from Jesus' ministry, organized by theme. Now Mark slows the pace, devoting the rest of his book to the last days in Jesus' life, organized mostly by chronology.

This next section (Mark 11:1–13:37) is about Jesus and the Temple. The Temple was the epitome of Judaism, and Jesus was sent by the Jewish God that the Temple honored, so the two should get along just spiffyriffic, right? Well . . . the way the priests and scribes ran the Temple had decayed to the point it no longer represented God. Jesus did not come to bless the Temple or to celebrate it, but to condemn it. We'll see Jesus object to the Temple in all kinds of ways: through symbolic actions, in pointed debates with the priests, and in blunt predictions of the Temple's utter destruction. (For an excellent overview of this, see GWBI, page 199).

While Jesus' fury with the Temple surprises the people around him, it should not surprise Mark's readers. The more we read, the more we realize that Jesus did not merely disapprove of the Temple. He came to replace it—personally. How could an individual take the place of an entire system of rituals, ceremonies, and sacrifices? How could a man replace an edifice that took decades to build? Mark has the answers . . . so let's dig in!

MARK 11:1–25
CONQUEROR JESUS

CHAPTER HIGHLIGHTS

- Jesus' Royal Entrance
- Jesus Curses a Tree
- Jesus Closes the Temple

Let's Get Started

In the introduction to part 1, I told you about four national symbols that Jews of the first century held dear: Torah, Temple, Territory, and Tribe. Chapter 11 of Mark focuses on the Temple, which represented the presence of God. Jews probably considered the Temple their most significant symbol.

You already know Jews hoped fervently for an end to exile. Part and parcel to this hope was their anticipation of the rebuilding of the Temple, which was a sign of the end of exile. (For a vivid symbolic depiction of this, see Ezekiel 47.) How much did the rebuilding of the Temple mean to the Jews? Here's a hint: We put Malachi at the end of the Old Testament, but before Jesus' time Jews put 2 Chronicles there, even though other books were written later. Why? Because the final verses of 2 Chronicles <u>prophesy</u> that a ruler will rebuild the Temple in Jerusalem. For the four hundred years preceding Jesus' birth, Jews considered rebuilding the Temple God's topmost priority.

The common people mingled the idea of Messiah with the theme of rebuilt Temple until most people believed whoever rebuilt the Temple would *be* the Messiah.

Enter Herod. Though a Roman ruler, Herod had Jewish ancestry and a lust for power. You'll recall how badly he wanted

KEY POINT

The Temple was the central symbol of Judaism.

Something to Ponder

☞ **GO TO:**

2 Chronicles 36:23 (prophesy)

THE WAYBACK MACHINE

to be called "king." He poured resources into rebuilding the Temple partly to keep the rebellious Jews quiet. His deeper motive was to buy the office of Messiah.

Herod began building his Temple in 19 B.C. Appropriately, the priests and Sadducees distrusted his motives. To prove his good will and respect, he had one thousand priests trained as masons, so they could perform the construction themselves. Though the rebuilders finished the bulk of their work in ten years, further construction and refinements continued (probably to keep the most fervently religious Jews peacefully occupied), and the Temple was not officially completed until A.D. 64.

Herod's Temple reflected Herod's grand ambitions. He doubled the foundation size of what had been Solomon's Temple, actually changing the **topography** to do it. The temple area eventually covered the equivalent of thirty-five football fields. The Temple's entire facade was covered with gold and topped with a gold roof, finished with golden spikes to keep birds away. During sunrise the reflection could blind you. On a clear day pilgrims could see the Temple's brilliance from miles away.

This <u>impressed</u> the disciples, but utterly failed to move Jesus. The Temple's outward beauty said nothing about the hearts of those who ran it, and that's where Jesus' problems with the Jewish government began—or, more accurately, that's where they ended. If you think religious leaders <u>got upset</u> when Jesus didn't wash his hands before eating, wait 'til you see what they do when he messes with their precious Temple!

topography: *natural features of a region's landscape*

 GO TO:

Mark 13:1 (impressed)

Mark 7:5 (got upset)

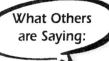

What Others are Saying:

N. T. Wright: Jesus implicitly and explicitly attacked what had become standard symbols of the second-Temple Jewish worldview. . . . I am not saying that Jesus was opposed to the Jewish symbols because he thought them bad, not God-given or whatever. He believed that the time had come for God's kingdom to dawn and that with it a new agenda had emerged diametrically opposed to the agenda that had taken over the symbols of national identity and was hiding all manner of injustices behind them.[1]

WHEN JESUS ACTED LIKE JUDAS

Jesus' arrival in Jerusalem—the prelude to his entrance into the Temple—seems triumphant at first. If you look below the surface, however, you'll see mixed messages. The twin keys to understanding it involve (1) viewing the story as a series of hyperlinks into the Old Testament, and (2) learning a bit of the era's history.

> **Mark 11:1–7** As they approached Jerusalem and came to Bethphage and Bethany at the Mount of Olives, Jesus sent two of his disciples, saying to them, "Go to the village ahead of you, and just as you enter it, you will find a colt tied there, which no one has ever ridden. Untie it and bring it here. If anyone asks you, 'Why are you doing this?' tell him, 'The Lord needs it and will send it back here shortly.'"
>
> They went and found a colt outside in the street, tied at a doorway. As they untied it, some people standing there asked, "What are you doing, untying that colt?" They answered as Jesus had told them to, and the people let them go. When they brought the colt to Jesus and threw their cloaks over it, he sat on it.

Why A Donkey?

The petrified parade has nearly reached its destination as it sweeps into Jerusalem's "bedroom community," Bethany. Bethany is so close to Jerusalem (about a half mile) that on the Sabbath, when Jewish law enforced rest by limiting the distance you could walk, faithful Jews could walk from one to the other.

Jesus pauses in Bethany to do something highly unusual. Though he has walked everywhere else in his ministry, for his entrance into Jerusalem he chooses to ride a colt. (Matthew and John specify it is a donkey.) Borrowing someone's donkey in that day was comparable to borrowing someone's car today. In that economy donkeys cost significant money for the middle-class person, and could be a vital part of how a person made a living.

Mark's account of how Jesus obtained a donkey is surprisingly detailed. Why is this anecdote covered in all four Gospels? Jesus is deliberately fulfilling centuries-old prophecy (see GWGN page 292, and GWDN, pages 249–255). The table which follows shows why I call this story a series of hyperlinks to the Old Testament:

☞ **GO TO:**

Matthew 21:2; John 12:14–15 (donkey)

New Testament Quote	Old Testament Reference	What It Means
"you will find a colt tied there"	Genesis 49:10–11	This prophecy, about a descendant of Judah, is evoked in the picture of the colt tied at a doorway. The very act of untying it symbolized that the prophesied "he to whom it belongs" had arrived at last.
"which no one has ever ridden"	Numbers 19:2; Deuteronomy 21:3; 1 Samuel 6:7	The fact the donkey had not been ridden or harnessed is recorded because this made it suitable for sacred purposes.
"when they brought the colt to Jesus . . . he sat on it"	Zechariah 9:9	Teachers and rabbis had long puzzled over this Scripture: why did the prophets predict that the great and conquering Messiah would come in "gentle and riding on a donkey," instead of on the typical war Stallion?
"and threw their cloaks over it"	2 Kings 9:6–13	The Hebrew scriptures recorded a precedent for honoring a new king in this manner.

> **Mark 11:8–10** Many people spread their cloaks on the road, while others spread branches they had cut in the fields. Those who went ahead and those who followed shouted,
> "Hosanna!"
> "Blessed is he who comes in the name of the Lord!"
> "Blessed is the coming kingdom of our father David!"
> "Hosanna in the highest!"

What A Revoltin' Development

Pilgrims traditionally entered the city on foot, so riding any animal at all was an uppity thing to do. Kings and heroes rode in on spirited **chargers**, though, making Jesus' mount appear about as prideful as a scooter. So why did people go bananas over a country rabbi on a donkey? The answer is that this religious audience knew the prophecy of Zechariah 9:9. They also knew about another person who entered Jerusalem this way. Who was it and why did it matter? Hang in there; I'm about to tell you.

chargers: large, battletrained horses

Even if you learn every verse in the Bible, you're still missing an important chunk of history: the four hundred years between the last verse of the Old Testament and the first verse of the New Testament. If you want to understand the thinking of Jesus' audience, you need at least a passing acquaintance with those years, because they would have been as alive and influential in the folk memory of Jesus' time as the

THE WAYBACK MACHINE

events of the Revolutionary War are in our time. So here, without further ado, are highlights of what happened between the testaments:

- 198 B.C.—The Syrians take Palestine from the Egyptians.
- 168 B.C.—Syrians, under the **megalomaniac** ruler Antiochus Epiphanes, try to wipe out the Jewish religion. Antiochus abolishes the keeping of Torah (making circumcision and Sabbath observance illegal), burns all the copies of it he can find, and purposely defiles the Temple by erecting a statue to Zeus in it and sacrificing pigs.

  megalomaniac: one with an exaggerated sense of self-importance

- 168 B.C.—Individual Jews such as Mattathias (a priest) revolt against Antiochus. Many of them, including Mattathias and his sons, flee to the hills and gather an army of supporters who want to preserve Torah. They fight the Syrians guerrilla style.
- 165 B.C.—Judas Maccabee, spurred by the death of his father Mattathias, manages to regroup Israel and win some initial conflicts with the Syrians. Believing Judas is fulfilling Genesis 49:9, more Jews rally to him and successfully kick the Syrians out of Jerusalem.
- 165 B.C.—The Maccabeans cleanse the Temple and restore true worship. To commemorate their victory, they invent the Feast of Dedication, called Chanukah.
- 165–69 B.C.—Antiochus Epiphanes dies; the Jews successfully defend the Temple against Syrian counterattacks; Judas makes treaties with Rome that lead to nearly a century of Jewish rule in Jerusalem.
- 68 B.C.—War in Palestine. Maccabean supporters lose Jerusalem to Antipater, and the consecutive reigns of the Herods begin.
- A.D. 1—Jesus is born. Note that some elderly people would still be alive who remembered the freedom of worship they enjoyed under the Maccabeans, and their kids would have been raised with the war stories, just as Gen Xers have heard about the Vietnam era.

When Jesus Acted Like Judas

Okay, there's your whirlwind tour of nonbiblical Jewish history. Part of the traditional story of Judas Maccabee's first major victory was that a few thousand Jews defeated over twenty thousand Syrians. As news of the victory spread into Jerusalem, the bad guys evacuated in fear, and the Jews rose up in celebration. By the time Judas reached town, he entered with popular acclaim, and, according to tradition, he entered riding a donkey to fulfill Zechariah 9:9.

I for one would have to be strongly motivated to pull off my jacket and lay it in the dirt for a baby donkey to step on. In this context, though, you can see why Jewish pilgrims to Jerusalem went nuts when Jesus the prophet rode in exactly like the conquering hero almost two hundred years before. This crowd was so exuberant that when they had used up their cloaks, they cut branches to have something to spread before their revolutionary leader. The man who tried to keep his identity secret for so long suddenly revealed it in one of the most powerful images available to his culture.

What Others are Saying:

N. T. Wright: Jesus' symbolic actions inevitably invoked this entire wider context. Jesus was performing *Maccabean* actions, albeit with some radical differences. This explains, among other things, why the High Priestly family . . . found Jesus' action so threatening. It also explains why that action was so inevitably charged with 'royal' overtones.[2]

ambivalence:
simultaneous
contradictory feelings

Philip Yancey: The triumphal entry has about it an aura of **ambivalence**, and . . . what stands out to me now is the slapstick nature of the affair. I imagine a Roman officer galloping up to check on the disturbance. He has attended processions in Rome, where they do it right. The conquering general sits in a chariot of gold, with stallions straining at the reins and wheel spikes flashing in the sunlight. Behind him, officers in polished armor display the banners captured from vanquished armies. At the rear comes a ragtag procession of slaves and prisoners in chains, living proof of what happens to those who defy Rome. In Jesus' triumphal entry, the adoring crowd makes up the ragtag procession: the lame, the blind, the children, the peasants from Galilee and Bethany. When the officer looks for the object of their attention he spies a forlorn figure, *weeping*, riding on no stallion or chariot but on the back of a baby donkey, a borrowed coat draped across its backbone serving as a saddle. . . . What manner of king was this?[3]

☞ **GO TO:**

Luke 19:41 (weeping)

> **Mark 11:11** Jesus entered Jerusalem and went to the temple. He looked around at everything, but since it was already late, he went out to Bethany with the Twelve.

My Disciples Visited The Temple And All I Got Was This Lousy T-Shirt

Did the cheering crowds hail Jesus all the way through town, into the Temple itself? Perhaps not, because this verse mentions only the Twelve. With all the buildup of Jesus' march to Jerusalem and his dramatic entrance into the City of David, it seems strange that his arrival ends so anticlimactically. What people expect is more heroic gestures from Jesus. What they get is tourist travel. Actually, Jesus is acting as an inspector of the building. He was, after all, the son of the Temple's true landlord. Did the building meet with his approval? Jesus delays his report until the next morning.

A casual reading of this verse can leave the impression that Jesus reacted to the Temple like a Galilean yokel, slack-jawed with wonder as he cranes his head to see the golden roof. Mark, writing in Greek, had his choice of a number of verbs that mean "to look around," but he did not choose the one that means "gawking." He chose one that means "scrutinizing critically"—the same <u>look</u> Jesus gave to the Pharisees when they refused to view the Sabbath as a day to do good. Jesus was not there to get a Temple snow globe or a High Priest–autographed **yarmulke**. He wasn't assessing the Temple for its physical impressiveness, but for its spiritual effectiveness. As he left, he was silent about what he thought. His silence was the quiet before the storm.

IT'S GREEK TO ME

☞ **GO TO:**

Mark 3:5 (look)

yarmulke: *skullcap worn by Orthodox Jewish males (pronounced like Yamaha, but with a "k" instead of an "h")*

What Others are Saying:

Matthew Henry: He looked round about upon all things, but as yet said nothing. He let things be as they were for this night, intending the next morning to apply himself to the necessary reformation. We may be confident that God sees all the wickedness that is in the world, though he do not presently reckon for it, nor cast it out.[4]

MARK SANDWICH: FIG, TEMPLE, FIG

> **Mark 11:12–14** The next day as they were leaving Bethany, Jesus was hungry. Seeing in the distance a fig tree in leaf, he went to find out if it had any fruit. When he reached it, he found nothing but leaves, because it was not the season for figs. Then he said to the tree, "May no one ever eat fruit from you again." And his disciples heard him say it.

From Oreos To Fig Newtons

Why would Jesus use his miraculous powers for destruction? Surely Jesus wouldn't have a temper tantrum over a snack (even a healthy one like figs—see GWHN, pages 73–74). Frankly, this passage *never* made sense to me until I learned three things. First I learned that prophets perform symbolic acts, discussed in the chapter on Mark 3:13–35.

Next I learned about literary devices, including Mark's intercalations, or Oreos. The story that begins with these three verses breaks off and resumes in verse 20. That's our cue to look at the material sandwiched inside for a fuller understanding of the story that begins in these three verses.

Finally, I jumped in the Wayback Machine to find out what the fig tree symbolized in the Old Testament.

THE WAYBACK MACHINE

☞ **GO TO:**

Isaiah 34:4; Hosea 2:12; 9:10, 16; Joel 1:7 (figs)

Jeremiah 8:11–13 (fig trees)

Six hundred years before Jesus, another prophet, Jeremiah, had the sad task of confronting Israel with its sin. Jeremiah's message was urgent, because God had revealed to him that if the Jews did not clean up their act, God would allow the ruthless Babylonians to overrun Palestine. Convinced of their favored status as God's chosen people, the Jewish leaders ignored Jeremiah. Jeremiah described the coming judgment like this: *"Yes, this is what the LORD Almighty says: 'I will send the sword, famine and plague against them and I will make them like poor figs that are so bad they cannot be eaten'"* (Jeremiah 29:17).

In fact, the prophets of the Old Testament sprinkled <u>figs</u> and <u>fig trees</u> all through their writings as symbols of God's judgment upon Israel. Check the Go To verses for fuller understanding.

In spring the kind of fig trees that grow near Jerusalem put out their fruit first, then their leaves. By the time the leaves fully show up, the fruit has ripened and gone. Was Jesus, living in an agricultural society all his life, too stupid to know that? Of course not. The most reasonable explanation for his behavior is that he was performing a symbolic act. If the fig tree stands for Israel, we have to ask, What point is Jesus making?

We can't answer that until we consider the "creamy center" of Mark's Oreo: Jesus' outrageous actions in the Temple.

> **Mark 11:15–17** On reaching Jerusalem, Jesus entered the temple area and began driving out those who were buying and selling there. He overturned the tables of the money changers and the benches of those selling doves, and would not allow anyone to carry merchandise through the temple courts. And as he taught them, he said, "Is it not written:
> "'My house will be called
> a house of prayer for all nations'?
> But you have made it 'a den of robbers.'"

Closing The Temple, Or, The Abominable "No" Man

To fully understand this passage, you have to know a basic thing or two about the layout of Herod's Temple, and about Jewish law. Monuments such as Herod's Temple can be veritable engines of emotion; the Romans understood their subjects might work themselves into a religious frenzy in their Temple. So when the Romans allowed Herod to build it, they also built the Antonia Fortress on one corner of it, with a stairway leading directly from the troop's mustering hall into the temple courts. Any <u>riot in the Temple</u> would draw an immediate armed response from centurions. Just to remind everyone who was really in charge, the soldiers stored the high priest's robes in the fortress.

Within the Temple itself, however, the priests hung onto every bit of self-governance they could. They controlled who could come

☞ **GO TO:**

Acts 21:27–32 (riot in the Temple)

balustrade: *a low barrier with vase-shaped supports for the rail*

Temple Courts	Description
Court of the Gentiles	Technically anyone could visit this area, but signs posted all around in both Greek and Latin warned that priests would take no responsibility for the probable death of Gentiles who wandered any farther.
Women's Court	A few steps higher than the Gentile Court, separated from it by a **balustrade**, the Women's Court contained large chests to receive donations for the Temple, and to receive the temple tax required of every adult male annually. This court was as close to the Temple as women—even Jewish women—were allowed to go.
Court of Israel	Raised slightly higher than the Women's Court, for males only—and even they had to be ritually clean. Laymen could go here and no farther. This was where the animal sacrifices occurred.
Priests' Court	Final stop before the Temple itself because usually only priests were allowed in it.

and go, and successfully preserved the holiest places for Jewish use only.

Once inside the compound walls, you still had to walk through several "courts" before you were in the Temple itself. Working our way from the outside in, the courts are listed in the table on page 215.

Only after crossing all these courts could a person get inside the Temple—a structure about fifteen stories tall. Twelve steps led up to a vestibule with gilded walls. Inside, priests served in a room called the Holy Place, which displayed religious emblems such as the showbread and the golden lampstand.

Beyond that room was the ultimate holy spot in Jewish thinking—a room called the Holy of Holies. Because God's holy presence had once dwelt there (and in Jewish thinking, someday would again), only one priest was allowed in the room, on only one day of the year—the Day of Atonement. Eighty-foot-tall curtains embroidered with the finest linen in blue, scarlet, and purple—"wrought with marvelous skill" according to Josephus—separated the Holy of Holies from the sanctuary, the Holy Place.

Admittedly, this is a very brief overview of the Temple, but it gives you some sense of how seriously the Jews felt about the **sanctity** of this property.

☞ **GO TO:**

1 Samuel 21:4;
2 Chronicles 29:18
(showbread)

Exodus 25:31–36
(golden lampstand)

1 Kings 8:10–11;
2 Chronicles 7:1
(holy presence)

sanctity: *holiness that must not be violated*

What Others are Saying:

Encyclopedia Judaica: For the erection of the altar and the ramp by which the priests ascended to it, unhewn stones were quarried from under the virgin ground . . . No iron touched them in the process. While sacrifices were being offered curtains were drawn before the sanctuary and the courts, both so as to enable the worship to continue undisturbed and to conceal the inner portion of the Temple from the eyes of the multitude.[5]

Worship Made Possible By A Generous Grant From Kingsford Briquets

One of the central spots in Herod's Temple was the altar, where the priests sacrificed burnt offerings to cover the sins of the Israelites. The main altar was essentially a giant pile of boulders with a ramp leading up to it. At Passover the head of each family was required to bring a sacrifice for him and his loved ones—if you could afford it, a lamb; if you couldn't, doves. For other sins, sometimes oxen were offered up. Not all sacrifices had to be burned, but many were. Some offerings involved burning incense. Combine the smell of meat and fat burning with the aroma of incense, and a twenty-first century American standing in the first-century Temple would have said it smelled like barbecue.

In the supercharged atmosphere of Palestine, where religion and politics were inseparably wed, crowds always meant lots of noise. The Temple was the center of everything from large business meetings to protests and demonstrations like the ones associated nowadays with the World Trade Organization.

According to a historical note from A.D. 66, Passover that year required the sacrifice of approximately 255,600 lambs. Where did the hundreds of thousands of Jewish pilgrims find animals for their sacrifices? Traditionally, a multitude of vendors set up shops and booths on the Mount of Olives, just outside Jerusalem. Rather than trek across the country dragging a lamb for a hundred miles, it was easier for the average person to buy one upon arriving at the city. The vendors were prepared with thousands upon thousands of lambs and doves, in addition to the grains, garments, scrolls, and other accessories to temple worship.

The **Talmud** forbade doing business on the Temple grounds, but just a few years before this scene, in A.D. 30, the Sanhedrin authorized the buying and selling of sacrificial animals in the Court of the Gentiles (see illustration, page 219). Presented as a convenience to worshipers, this was actually a greedy ploy to fill the temple coffers. By law, each sacrificial lamb had to be without blemish. If you tried to bring your own, the priests would find something wrong with it no matter how perfect it was. For a hefty extra fee, you could purchase one on the temple grounds guaranteed acceptable to Yahweh.

In addition, every adult male had to pay an annual temple tax. The Sanhedrin declared that heathen coinage was not spiritually appropriate for the Temple, so you had to convert your Roman coins into temple coins. The Temple charged a small percentage for making the exchange. The percentage grew as years passed.

Allowing these activities into the Court of the Gentiles transformed the grounds of the Temple into a place where reflective worship was impossible. Suddenly you had thousands of lambs bleating, moaning, and defecating; thousands of doves cooing; the chink of coins changing hands; the clatter of grains being poured onto scales for weighing; the cry of competing merchants trying to draw customers . . . But what did it matter? It was all in the Court of the Gentiles, and Gentiles were dogs anyway.

It *did* matter, because the average Israelite was the one being exploited. He wasn't naïve. He knew the Temple was profiting illegitimately off him and his family, but if he sincerely

THE WAYBACK MACHINE

Talmud: *authoritative writings of Jewish tradition including the Mishnah*

KEY POINT

Greedy Jewish priests corrupted temple worship.

wanted to worship God, he tolerated all the barriers the priests put in his way, much as we pay our Federal taxes while rolling our eyes at the idiotic use they're put to.

I'll Flip You For It

If the last paragraph made your stomach turn, imagine how Jesus felt, the one who came to bring everyone, even the fringe folk, into the kingdom of God. The Temple that was supposed to symbolize the reign of heaven had become a money-making marketing machine, selling God to the poor and excluding the Gentiles. Its existence depended less on God's blessing and more on a lecherous ruler's ego.

Jesus decided it was time to shut it down.

Imagine the chaos when Jesus flipped that first moneychanger's table! Coins flew in all directions, and so did people, chasing those coins. Picture dozens of terrified doves bursting from cages, flapping and fluttering in people's faces. It might be appropriate to picture delight on the faces of many of the common people. Finally, someone was registering a protest against the gouging of the faithful by the so-called spiritual leaders.

Scholars disagree about what exactly Jesus thought he was doing, but his own quotes give us a generous clue: *"Is it not written: 'My house will be called a house of prayer for all nations'? But you have made it 'a den of robbers'"* (Mark 11:17).

☞ **GO TO:**

Isaiah 56:6–7 (written)

Jeremiah 7:1–11 (quoted)

jingoistic: prejudiced, belligerent national pride

To answer Jesus' rhetorical question, yes, it is <u>written</u>. With his heart of compassion for all people, Jesus could not bear to see the one spot where Gentiles were allowed to worship God stolen from them by greed. The Temple that was meant to welcome all sincere Gentile worshipers had become a symbol of **jingoistic** smugness, a rallying spot to denounce any race but the Jews. To Jesus, this was grotesque.

Besides quoting Isaiah, Jesus <u>quoted</u> Jeremiah. Jeremiah had called the people of Judah robbers because of the way they abused the oppressed. From God's viewpoint, they were robbers in their hearts, all day, every day, so *anywhere* they gathered became, by definition, a *"den of robbers."* By invoking this reference, Jesus was not merely rebuking the business practices of the merchants and priests; he was denouncing them as persons.

Something to Ponder

What did Jesus expect to accomplish? Surely he knew that the moment he left, business as usual would resume. Again, we have to see his action as symbolic. Symbolic of what? The quote below offers a big hint.

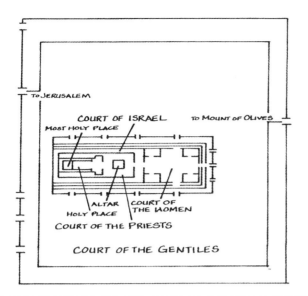

The massive Court of the Gentiles covered the space of almost thirty-five football fields. However, any Gentile who wandered any deeper into the temple complex would be put to death.

N. T. Wright: Why then, specifically, did Jesus banish the traders from the Temple courts? Without the Temple-tax the daily sacrifices could not be supplied. Without the right money the individual worshipers could not buy pure sacrificial animals. Without animals sacrifice could not be offered. Without sacrifice the Temple had—albeit perhaps only for an hour or two—lost its whole **raison d'être**.[6]

What Others are Saying:

raison d'être: French for "reason for being"

> **Mark 11:18–19** The chief priests and the teachers of the law heard this and began looking for a way to kill him, for they feared him, because the whole crowd was amazed at his teaching.
> When evening came, they went out of the city.

Zeal For Your House Has Consumed Me

Religious people have been mad at Jesus before, and even tried to figure out <u>how to kill him</u>. But those were Pharisees, who were like a vigilante group trying to help law enforcement officials. Now Jesus stands in the seat of Jewish power and publicly declares it morally upside down. No one can safely tweak the nose of the powerful high priest, especially when he has hundreds of legalistic minions. Ninety years before—within the folk memory of Jesus' day—thousands of people had died to preserve this temple system, making Jesus' action all the more inflammatory. Jesus' death was actually part of God's plan from before the dawn of time. But humanly speaking, his act of temporarily shutting down

☞ **GO TO:**

Mark 3:6
(how to kill him)

the Temple was the reason the temple cult killed him. John says as much when he writes of this incident, *"His disciples remembered that it is written: 'Zeal for your house will <u>consume</u> me.'"*

Jesus' honest assessment of the "house of God" revealed a situation described centuries before by the prophet <u>Micah</u>. As the representative of God's kingdom, Jesus could not stay silent about the corruption perpetrated in God's name. He was wise, however, to leave Jerusalem each day before nightfall. He knew what would happen under cover of darkness if he stuck around.

☞ **GO TO:**

Psalm 69:9 (consume)

Micah 7:1–3 (Micah)

What Others are Saying:

The Interpreter's Bible: In his clearing out of the traders from the temple Jesus came into conflict with the greatest profit-making power of his time and nation. And it was a deadly conflict. This one act was what led most directly to his trial and condemnation.[7]

> **Mark 11:20–21** In the morning, as they went along, they saw the fig tree withered from the roots. Peter remembered and said to Jesus, "Rabbi, look! The fig tree you cursed has withered!"

Israel Couldn't Give A Fig

Mark completes his narrative sandwich by finishing the story of the fig tree. Did the fig tree learn its lesson after disappointing Jesus the day before? Had it reformed? Obviously not. People often refer to what Jesus did in the Court of the Gentiles as "the cleansing of the Temple," but this misses the point. Jesus wasn't trying to reform the Temple. He was shutting it down. That is the meaning of *"May no one ever eat fruit from you again."* Jesus didn't rebuke the fig tree, then fertilize it; he rebuked it, and it died away. Similarly, the Temple would no longer exist within forty years of Jesus' rebuke. God was done with it.

> **Mark 11:22–25** "Have faith in God," Jesus answered. "I tell you the truth, if anyone says to this mountain, 'Go, throw yourself into the sea,' and does not doubt in his heart but believes that what he says will happen, it will be done for him. Therefore I tell you, whatever you ask for in prayer, believe that you have received it, and it will be yours. And when you stand praying, if you hold anything against anyone, forgive him, so that your Father in heaven may forgive you your sins."

The Incredible Flying Temple

The disciples are amazed at how fast the fig tree died; naturally, Jesus is not surprised. The fig tree represented Israel; it had lots of pretty leaves but offered no nourishment. The pride of Israel was its glorious golden Temple, which focused more on money than on spiritual "fruit."

Something to Ponder

Everyone knows that if you have faith, you can move mountains, right? Well, that's not exactly what Jesus said. He said that if you have faith in God, you can say *"to this mountain"* throw yourself into the sea. What's the difference between *any* mountain and *this* mountain? When Jesus said this, he was standing on the temple mount. *"This"* mountain was the Temple and its entire corrupt system.

When Jesus says faith can move this mountain into the sea and links human forgiveness with God's forgiveness, he is promoting what God wants his worshipers to have—faith and mercy toward others. At the same time Jesus is telling his disciples that the place for dead, formal religion (epitomized by the temple mount) is hell (symbolized by the sea).

What Others are Saying:

N. T. Wright: "This mountain," spoken in Jerusalem, would naturally refer to the Temple mount. The saying is not simply a miscellaneous comment on how prayer and faith can do such things as curse fig trees. It is a very specific word of judgment: the Temple mountain is, figuratively speaking, to be taken up and cast into the sea.[8]

KEEP IT REAL—After seeing Jesus tear into the moneychangers, it's tempting to rail against the materialism and commercialism of American Christians; but ranting against an entire culture wouldn't accomplish as much as reforming myself. I'm the only one I can do something about . . . so once again, it's time to keep it real.

• Mark 11:1–11. Many of the same people who praised Jesus as he rode into Jerusalem shouted for his crucifixion a short time later. This could only be possible because in one situation or the other, they didn't fully understand what they were doing. *Father, let my praise of you be praise indeed, not the kind that fades away or reverses itself if you do something I don't understand.*

• Mark 11:12–25. Given human nature, I assume that somewhere in my own heart, I have unwittingly erected a "Temple"—something that should serve God, but actually uses Christianity to benefit me. *Lord, I don't know when or how the first-century priests lost their sense of duty to you and indulged their own lust for power, but if the same thing is happening in me, I pray you save me from such blindness. Show me my sin, and help me follow you regardless of whether it brings me wealth or influence.*

Study Questions

1. About how long did it take to finish constructing the Temple? (For extra credit: estimate how long the Temple had been in progress when Jesus visited it.)
2. What was the main reason Jesus rode a donkey into Jerusalem?
3. What do figs and the fig tree often symbolize in the Old Testament?
4. Why did Jesus denounce the selling of sacrificial animals and the changing of money within the temple courts?
5. What mountain might Jesus have been speaking of here: *"If anyone says to this mountain, 'Go, throw yourself into the sea,' . . . it will be done for him"* (Mark 11:23)?

CHAPTER WRAP-UP

- In the minds of many first-century Jews, the Messiah would rebuild God's Temple. The Temple itself had many royal overtones as the seat of the Messiah's power.

- Jesus fulfilled prophecy by riding into Jerusalem on a donkey (Zechariah 9:9). Previous Jewish revolutionaries such as Judas Maccabee had also been aware of the prophecy and rode into Jerusalem similarly. Both these truths were in the minds of the public when they cheered Jesus' arrival into Jerusalem. (Mark 11:1–11)

- Jesus cursed the fruitless fig tree not because he had a temper tantrum, but as a prophetic act of God's judgment upon spiritually fruitless Israel, and upon her central symbol, Herod's Temple. (Mark 11:12–14, 20–25)

- When Jesus interrupted the commerce going on in the Court of the Gentiles, it was another prophetically symbolic act. He was showing that God had given up on the corrupt priesthood and was going to shut the Temple down. This message achieved literal fulfillment in A.D. 70, six years after the Temple construction was completed, when Roman troops tore the Temple to bits. (Mark 11:15–19)

- Jesus' comments about prayer and faith have been treated as generic comments about spirituality, but are probably intended to draw the contrast between empty religion and true religion (Mark 11:20–25).

Let's Get Started

One of my all-time favorite movies stars Danny Kaye, who plays a nebbish entertainer named Jocomo in *The Court Jester*. Jocomo bands together with a mob of Robin Hood–style resisters to defeat an evil king. He has little to offer a medieval war party; he can't fight, he isn't strong, and he's not especially brave. But he can sing and joke. The gleefully convoluted plot climaxes when the inept Jocomo duels the greatest swordsman in the land, an evil count played by Basil Rathbone. Luckily, Jocomo has been hypnotized so that he thinks *he* is the greatest swordsman ever. Jocomo turns out to be such a superb fencer that he can look away, yawn, and still parry the count's flashing thrusts.

This theme of the triumphant underdog permeates the next section of Mark, which continues to show us the complex relationship between Jesus and the Temple. In reaction to Jesus' attack on the temple business, pro-Temple special interest groups try to trick this upstart country rabbi into saying something stupid, inflammatory, or suicidal. Whether the party of would-be tricksters is made up of priests, elders, scribes, Pharisees, Herodians, or Sadducees, in each story they approach Jesus as if he is the ignorant one and they are the smart ones.

They seem confident that the technical quandaries they have spent hours crafting will baffle Jesus. Most of the questions are intended to force an impossible choice: If Jesus answers one way, the people will love his answer, but he can be arrested for treason.

If he answers the other way, he will seem to support the Roman government, and thus lose popular support. Jesus' popularity is the only thing keeping the high priests from killing him, because, as David Garland puts it, "they are a savvy lot who do not kick people while they are up."[1]

Like Jocomo, Jesus effortlessly parries their questions and even gives them a taste of their own medicine. How can he do it so easily? Because unlike Jocomo, Jesus doesn't merely *think* he's something special. He is something special. Officials ask questions to prove Jesus is a fraud, but instead the questions end up revealing how corrupt the officials are. Everybody loves it when the outnumbered underdog wins, so let's get started!

WHEN TEMPLE BIGWIGS ATTACK

Jesus' attack on the Temple must have made a big impression on the leadership of the institution, because soon he receives a visit from Jewish dignitaries. They include **chief priests**, **teachers of the law**, and **elders**, all of whom are probably members of the Sanhedrin. They attack Jesus by implying he has no right to do what he's done. He reverses their attack with a simple parable.

chief priests: former high priests and priests with permanent duties in the Temple

teachers of the law: learned legal experts

elders: laymen from the wealthy aristocracy

> **Mark 11:27–28** They arrived again in Jerusalem, and while Jesus was walking in the temple courts, the chief priests, the teachers of the law and the elders came to him. "By what authority are you doing these things?" they asked. "And who gave you authority to do this?"

When Jesus Issued Driver's Licenses

When we read Jesus forgave or healed someone, we take it at face value, but in Jesus' day none of these things happened unless they happened at the Temple. You weren't forgiven until the priest said you were forgiven. You weren't healed until the priest agreed you were healed. When Jesus went around pronouncing people healed, he was doing the cultural equivalent of a hotdog salesman issuing driver's licenses.

By healing and forgiving sins Jesus is acting like a replacement for the Temple—something the temple cult didn't like very much. Then he enters the Temple itself, denounces it, and tears the place up. It's no wonder the chief priests ask him, *"By what authority are you doing these things?"*

> **Mark 11:29–32** Jesus replied, "I will ask you one question. Answer me, and I will tell you by what authority I am doing these things. John's baptism—was it from heaven, or from men? Tell me!"
>
> They discussed it among themselves and said, "If we say, 'From heaven,' he will ask, 'Then why didn't you believe him?' But if we say, 'From men'. . . . " (They feared the people, for everyone held that John really was a prophet.)
>
> So they answered Jesus, "We don't know."
>
> Jesus said, "Neither will I tell you by what authority I am doing these things."

Jesus The Debater

If Jesus answers their question with "God sent me!" they can dismiss him as a raving loon, a self-appointed fanatic, or even a blasphemer. Jesus sees this, so he counters with a question of his own, which was a common style of debate at the time.

His question is brilliant. John forgave sins without involving the Temple, yet everyone understood John was sent by God. The masses loved him during his ministry, and it's likely his martyrdom made him more popular. The answer to "Who authorized John?" (which is what Jesus' question amounts to) is the same as "Who authorized Jesus?"

The resulting huddle of the bigwigs amuses me. Their arrogant attack suddenly turns into a panicky summit meeting. Note that as they consider their response, they don't invest even one second in looking for what is true. They don't want to do God's business or experience the humility God demands, but they do want to appear as if they're spiritual leaders. If they admit John came from God, they've lost the battle because John publicly endorsed Jesus. The best they can muster up is, *"We don't know."*

When Jesus responds, *"Neither will I tell you by what authority I am doing these things,"* he is not refusing to answer for the sake of refusal. The bigwigs already know the answer and won't admit it. When people reach the level of willful self-deception that these "spiritual leaders" had reached, there is <u>no reasoning</u> with them. Jesus' response is the only appropriate one. (For more, see GWBI, page 201.)

☞ **GO TO:**

Proverbs 18:2; 23:9 (no reasoning)

Billy Graham: The Bible is very clear that many have turned away because they listened to Satan's lies and deliberately chose to accept the doctrines of devils rather than the truth of God.[2]

What Others are Saying:

> **Mark 12:1–8** He then began to speak to them in parables: "A man planted a vineyard. He put a wall around it, dug a pit for the winepress and built a watchtower. Then he rented the vineyard to some farmers and went away on a journey. At harvest time he sent a servant to the tenants to collect from them some of the fruit of the vineyard. But they seized him, beat him and sent him away empty-handed. Then he sent another servant to them; they struck this man on the head and treated him shamefully. He sent still another, and that one they killed. He sent many others; some of them they beat, others they killed.
>
> "He had one left to send, a son, whom he loved. He sent him last of all, saying, 'They will respect my son.'
>
> "But the tenants said to one another, 'This is the heir. Come, let's kill him, and the inheritance will be ours.' So they took him and killed him, and threw him out of the vineyard."

Who The Deadbeats Beat Dead

☞ **GO TO:**

Mark 12:12
(religious leaders)

Isaiah 5:7 (vineyard)

Jeremiah 7:25; 25:4;
Amos 3:7; Zechariah
1:6 (servants)

*euphemism: one
expression substituted for
another*

IT'S
GREEK
TO ME

All of Jesus' listeners understand this parable. When Jesus finishes telling it, the <u>religious leaders</u> know immediately they've been zinged, but they may not have understood the parable properly as it was unfolding. The beginning is easy enough: *"A man planted a vineyard."* These scholars of the Hebrew scriptures immediately would think of the parable told in Isaiah 5:1–7. They would recognize the <u>vineyard</u> represents Israel. (Take a moment to read the Isaiah reference. The parallels are striking.)

Furthermore, they would understand that the owner of the vineyard is God, but as members of the ruling elite, initially they would identify themselves with the land owner, not the tenants. They would assume the tenants were the Romans, who dwelt in the land but could never truly own it. But when Jesus describes how the servants of the landlord were treated, his prestigious listeners would gradually realize they are the tenants.

The Old Testament often uses the word "<u>servants</u>" as a **euphemism** for God's prophets. The Greek word translated *"struck on the head"* (verse 4) is very similar to the word for "beheaded." Jesus could be making a veiled reference to John the Baptist here.

After how the tenants treated the landowner's servants, why did he expect the tenants to respect his son? In the culture of the time, there was a vast difference between the respect (or lack thereof) given to a slave and the respect given to a family member of a wealthy household. The owner was not insane or foolish to think his son would receive respect, but he was mistaken.

THE WAYBACK MACHINE

The greedy tenants interpret the presence of the son to mean the owner is dead. Jewish law allowed squatters to claim a dead person's property if no inheritor stepped forward to claim it within a given period of time. If the tenants kill the *"son, whom he loved"* (an expression for an only child), they could guarantee no one else would claim the property.

They not only murder the son; they toss him aside unburied. This was unbelievably offensive in Jewish culture. Our equivalent would be if a murderer killed someone, then urinated on the corpse. Jesus characterizes these tenants as hopelessly foul and callous.

> **Mark 12:9–12** "What then will the owner of the vineyard do? He will come and kill those tenants and give the vineyard to others. Haven't you read this scripture:
> "'The stone the builders rejected
>   has become the capstone;
> the Lord has done this,
>   and it is marvelous in our eyes'?"
> Then they looked for a way to arrest him because they knew he had spoken the parable against them. But they were afraid of the crowd; so they left him and went away.

Twisted Tenants In A Stinging Story

See those first two sentences of the Bible quote above? If there is ever an animated cartoon based on Mark, that's where the priests will turn red and steam will shoot out of their ears. Why? Because in the original story from Isaiah 5, God punished the vineyard itself (in other words, Israel) for failing to produce fruit, but Jesus twists the story so it's not the vineyard's fault; it's the tenants' fault.

When Jesus says, *"He will come and kill those tenants and give the vineyard to others,"* he is telling the priests they caused Israel's corruption and are so irredeemable that God is not going to re-

☞ GO TO:

Ezra 6:16
(second Temple)

Nehemiah 12:27–43
(rebuilt walls)

Mark 8:31 (knows)

capstone: *the central stone that both halves of an arch lean upon*

Something
to Ponder

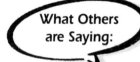

What Others
are Saying:

form them. God is going to snuff them out and find someone better to lead his people.

In case the point isn't clear, Jesus finishes the story with a quote from Psalm 118. Some commentators believe the Jews sang Psalm 118 at the dedication of the second Temple or at the dedication of Jerusalem's rebuilt walls. Given the context of the Psalm, if someone needs a **capstone**, it's because they're erecting a whole new Temple, which means the old one no longer exists. The builders represent the corrupt priests, and the rejected stone is Jesus.

Is all this symbolism too much for the priests, teachers, and elders to sort out? Hardly! They wanted to arrest him on the spot because *"they knew he had spoken the parable against them."*

This parable is an astoundingly brazen thing to say to powerful people, especially since Jesus knows these men represent the very groups that will kill him. Jesus would have offended them less if he had given each of them several stinging slaps to the face. Do you want to know what's even more amazing? After hearing Jesus' warning, the religious leaders immediately march out and behave exactly as his story predicted.

Henri J. M. Nouwen: I often wonder if my knowledge about God has not become my greatest stumbling block to my knowledge of God.[3]

SNARES WITH QUESTION MARKS ON THEM

The verbal exchange between Jesus and the religious leaders seems to start a war of words. Virtually every segment of Jewish leadership lines up to take Jesus down by tempting him to say the wrong thing.

As you read their attempts, you realize these guys were good at this. Their crafty questions, put forth in adroitly manipulated circumstances, must have ended the careers of many wanna-be revolutionaries, but they had never had an opponent like Jesus before. Improvising all the way, Jesus devastates arguments that the Jewish leadership spent hours devising.

> **Mark 12:13–15a** Later they sent some of the Pharisees and Herodians to Jesus to catch him in his words. They came to him and said, "Teacher, we know you are

> a man of integrity. You aren't swayed by men, because you pay no attention to who they are; but you teach the way of God in accordance with the truth. Is it right to pay taxes to Caesar or not? Should we pay or shouldn't we?"

Now This Word From The IRS

The Pharisees believed God would not return powerfully to Israel until the Israelites lived holy lives. The Herodians were practical Jews who believed the best way to further Israel's cause was to ingratiate themselves with their captors, the Romans. The Pharisees considered the Herodians contemptible sellouts who had compromised so much with the pagans that they were no longer on God's side. However, following the maxim that says, "The enemy of my enemy is my friend," the Pharisees and Herodians united in their hatred for Jesus.

They compliment Jesus in complete insincerity, softening him up for the kill. Literally translated, Mark states they hoped to "snare him in the talk." Their snare is this question: *Is it right to pay taxes to Caesar or not?*

IT'S **GREEK** TO ME

The Greek word Mark uses for "tax" is *census*. Different from a property tax, this was a head-count tax, a tax per person that Tiberius Caesar instituted in A.D. 6. Today a nation as broad and diverse as the USA or Canada has one coinage across the entire continent, but in ancient times rulers over small districts could mint their own money and enforce its use within their jurisdiction. Caesar was the top guy, so he decreed his tax to be paid with the denarius, the coin he minted, not with any of the "lesser" coins used throughout Palestine and Syria.

THE WAYBACK MACHINE

Devout Jews would never willingly pay taxes to Caesar for at least two reasons. First, they believed they were God's people, not Caesar's, so he had no right to tax them. Secondly and more importantly, Jews equated paying taxes to Caesar with idolatry, because the coins Caesar required were imprinted with the claim that Caesar was divine, as we saw in the chapter on Mark 9:30–10:52. Some Jews refused to carry, handle, or even look at the denarius, calling it a "portable idol." In short, pious Jews considered everything about the tax detestable.

Herodians made up the other half of the audience asking this tax question. Loyal to the Roman government, they could make sure a refusal to acknowledge Caesar's reign met with severe punishment, including being tossed to the lions.

The Pharisees and Herodians had crafted an exquisitely tricky question. If Jesus said, "Yes, pay taxes," he not only lost the respect of the common people, he virtually renounced being Messiah, as the Messiah's mission was understood to be the liberation of Israel from pagan rule. If he said, "No, the tax is wrong," the Herodians could see to it that he was killed. Either way he answers, they've got him.

> **Mark 12:15b–17** But Jesus knew their hypocrisy. "Why are you trying to trap me?" he asked. "Bring me a denarius and let me look at it." They brought the coin, and he asked them, "Whose portrait is this? And whose inscription?"
>
> "Caesar's," they replied.
>
> Then Jesus said to them, "Give to Caesar what is Caesar's and to God what is God's."
>
> And they were amazed at him.

Two Sides Of The Same Coin

Jesus could have refused to answer on the grounds that their question had no purpose other than sabotage, but Jesus chose to answer. After letting the Pharisees know he's on to their little game, Jesus scores a psychological point with the pious Jews by not having a denarius. His questioners do, or at least they can get one readily.

What does Jesus' highly quotable but mysterious answer mean? The Pharisees got it with crystal clarity. The coin was imprinted with Caesar's image on it, so it belonged to Caesar. Humans, however, are imprinted with <u>God's image</u>, so their entire selves belong to God. In one cutting statement Jesus makes the case that from God's perspective, money is <u>trivial</u>. Caesar can keep his silly idols. What matters is giving every other aspect of your life to God.

This would hit the Pharisees hard because it's a perfect expression of the idealism that was supposed to drive them. They had forgotten about it in the daily grind of striving for power and political infighting.

☞ **GO TO:**

Genesis 1:27 (in God's image)

Mark 10:17–31 (trivial)

What Others are Saying:

The Interpreter's Bible: The Pharisees and Herodians, dripping with oily flattery, . . . thought Jesus naïve, as easy to take in as a yokel from the country. They found him terribly sophisticated. That is not an adjective often applied to Jesus—"sophisticated"— but in one of its primary meanings, "worldly wise," it applies to him as to no one else. He was "worldly wise" in a disconcerting manner. He knew what was in man.[4]

> **Mark 12:18–23** Then the Sadducees, who say there is no resurrection, came to him with a question. "Teacher," they said, "Moses wrote for us that if a man's brother dies and leaves a wife but no children, the man must marry the widow and have children for his brother. Now there were seven brothers. The first one married and died without leaving any children. The second one married the widow, but he also died, leaving no child. It was the same with the third. In fact, none of the seven left any children. Last of all, the woman died too. At the resurrection whose wife will she be, since the seven were married to her?"

"Eschew Obfuscation"

Wait a sec—the Saddu-*who?* I asked this once as a kid in Sunday School. The answer I received was this creaking cliché: "The Sadducees were a group who didn't believe in life after death, so that made them very sad, you see?" This was all I knew about them for decades.

We don't know as much about the Sadducees as we'd like because we've never found any of their writings. What we do know about them was written by other factions who didn't like them, so how reliable are those comments? Here's what we think we know:

- The name Sadducee was derived from Zadakite, meaning followers of <u>Zadok</u>. Zadok was the Jewish high priest in the era of King David and King Solomon. This period was Israel's peak spiritually, politically, and economically, so Zadok's descendants thought of themselves as the truest high priestly line. These priestly families remained aristocracy through the centuries by virtue of their lineage.
- Because they remained political leaders from the time of Solomon forward, by Jesus' lifetime they controlled the

THE WAYBACK MACHINE

☞ **GO TO:**

1 Kings 1:38 (Zadok)

Temple, Jewish finances, and the majority of Israel's land. Basically, Sadducees were the rich ruling class of the Jews—not loved by many Jews, but respected. (Think Kennedys.)

☞ **GO TO:**

John 11:48 (Romans)

- As rich people in control of all the good stuff, they had the most to lose, so they got real cozy with the Romans and with Herod. They called this "being caretakers of God's rule." Most of the other sects thought of them as sellouts.

- The only writing they accepted as Scripture was the **Pentateuch**. This is why they didn't believe in life after death; they hadn't found it in the books of Moses. They also dismissed as laughable the Pharisees' oral interpretation of the law.

Pentateuch: the first five books of the Bible

This last point explains why the hypothetical question they posed to Jesus is so wacky. Have you ever seen the sticker that reads, "Eschew obfuscation"? The joke is that those two words are the most confusing way possible to say, "Avoid confusion." The Sadducees' question is a similar joke. They've dismissed the notion of life after death, so they've made up this question not to learn something, but to mock the whole concept.

> **Mark 12:24–25** Jesus replied, "Are you not in error because you do not know the Scriptures or the power of God? When the dead rise, they will neither marry nor be given in marriage; they will be like the angels in heaven."

Where Error Comes From

☞ **GO TO:**

Deuteronomy 25:5–10 (Mosaic law)

The Sadducees' odd hypothetical question demonstrates a fluent knowledge of Mosaic law. They thought they knew more about Scripture than anyone. They rejected all Bible books except Genesis through Deuteronomy to prevent human error from seeping into the Word of God, yet Jesus tells them they are in error precisely because they don't know Scripture.

Jesus continues correcting the Sadducees by explaining that resurrected life is not a mere continuation of earthly life. Though we may feel disappointed to learn there is no sex (and apparently, no gender) in heaven, the thing that makes sex so great is that it provides us a brief sense of contact, intimacy, and acceptance. In the afterlife we will be completely known yet utterly accepted, not in brief moments, but perpetually. Sex will turn out to be a feeble semblance of what we really yearned for.

KEEP IT REAL—For decades televangelist Jim Bakker preached to large TV audiences that God wanted every Christian to be wealthy. He believed this was a scriptural principal because of 3 John 2: *"Beloved, I wish above all things that thou mayest prosper and be in health, even as thy soul prospereth"* (KJV). After he was convicted of financial fraud and sent to jail, he began reading the Bible—an activity he had been too busy for during his years as a televangelist. Once he examined 3 John closely, he was surprised to find that the verse he had described so many times on TV as a promise was simply a greeting and salutation—the equivalent of opening a letter to your parents with, "Dear Mom and Dad, Hope you're doing well!"

Contrary to what Bakker had taught, the Bible does not guarantee wealth to anyone. It teaches that wealth should not be a consuming goal for Christians. After serving his time Bakker appeared on *Larry King Live* and cautioned believers everywhere not to make the same mistake he had made; he had based his doctrine on what he heard preachers say about the Bible, not on his own careful study of the Bible.

I'm glad you're reading this book because it means you want to study Scripture, but don't put unquestioning faith in any human's interpretation of the Bible, including mine. Be sure you <u>check</u> every assertion against God's Word.

Like the Sadducees and Jim Bakker, we too can fall into error because we *"do not know the scriptures."*

Exciting Excavating

Jesus was being asked tough questions about money, taxes, marriage, the afterlife—all the stuff we care about. If you want God's full advice on these issues, use this section's Power Tool: *look at everything the Bible says on a given topic.* A lot of readily available reference books can help you find your way to relevant passages. Your Christian bookstore can show you several books that list numerous passages on the same subject (for example, faith or finances). Avoid the mistake of the Sadducees, who studied only a fraction of Scripture. Get the whole picture, and increase your odds of understanding God's perspective.

☞ GO TO:

Acts 17:11
(check)

POWER TOOL

Look at all the Bible says on a given topic.

Frederica Mathewes-Green: I was thumbing through a highbrow magazine the other day and came across an interesting essay on the virtue of Hope. But before I'd finished the first page I caught them in an embarrassing blooper. The author stated that hope is ranked alongside faith and love in the 23rd psalm. . . . When it comes to Bible references, too often the court of final

What Others are Saying:

authority is mere fuzzy memory. . . . People would be embarrassed to misquote other great books so badly, yet there's an assumption that the Bible is one of those put-away childish things. . . . The cure for fuzzy memory is refreshed memory; try reading a chapter a night.[5]

> **Mark 12:26–27** "Now about the dead rising—have you not read in the book of Moses, in the account of the bush, how God said to him, 'I am the God of Abraham, the God of Isaac, and the God of Jacob'? He is not the God of the dead, but of the living. You are badly mistaken!"

Dead Rising

At first glance Jesus' scriptural proof for life after death doesn't seem very strong. It seems to rely completely on a verb tense; instead of saying "I *was* the God of Abraham, Isaac, and Jacob," God testified, "I *am* the God of Abraham, Isaac, and Jacob." Though that is part of Jesus' argument, the real strength of his quote is in what it implies.

☞ **GO TO:**

Exodus 3:6 (quote)

The Sadducees understood God was the promise-maker, the steadfast helper, the mighty protector, and the savior of the Jewish patriarchs (Abraham, Isaac, and Jacob). God promised to deliver them and gave them signs of coming deliverance, but if all of God's promises to the patriarchs became null and void as soon as the patriarchs died, what was the point? What was the use of having a cosmic friend who claimed he would protect you from misfortune, but was powerless to protect you from the greater challenge of death?

Everyone within earshot of Jesus would find this concept of God unacceptable and untrue, so Jesus corrected the Sadducees' clumsy understanding of Scripture by quoting from one of the books they accepted. (For more background on Abraham, see GWGN, pages 111–185; on Isaac, see GWGN, pages 189–210; on Jacob, see GWGN, pages 215–246. See also GWMB, pages 13–52.)

What Others are Saying:

Frederica Mathewes-Green: I think the Bible *should* offend women. It should offend men, figure skaters, plumbers, headwaiters, Alaskans, Ethiopians, baton twirlers, Jews and Gentiles. If it's not offending people, it's not doing its job. . . . The Bible, that powerful book, has many effects: it comforts, counsels, instructs, and brings us into the presence of God. . . .We don't know enough to change it. We're not as smart as we think we are.[6]

> **Mark 12:28** One of the teachers of the law came and heard them debating. Noticing that Jesus had given them a good answer, he asked him, "Of all the commandments, which is the most important?"

The Mega-Command

This is going to sound strange, but this verse reminds me of kung fu movies. I love kung fu movies. The more absurd they are, the more I like them. In my kind of martial art film, the actors' lips are out of sync with the overdubbed dialog and the sound effects are overdone so that when an actor pushes his hair out of his eyes, it sounds like a whip crack. Of course, the cheesiest part of all is the premise; kung fu movies make it look as if the ancient Chinese did nothing but argue about what form of combat was superior. With all that chop-socky going on, when did they find time to invent gunpowder and build the Great Wall?

I see a connection between the ancient Chinese and the first-century Jews. Just as any ambitious Chinaman stayed alert to new trends in mortal combat (well, at least in the movies), the religious-minded Jews seemed obsessed with finding new or better ways to understand the laws of God. By Jesus' time the Old Testament laws contained 613 commands. Were some commands more important than others? Was there an organizing principle—some overall point to which all those commands pointed?

This is the intent of the scribe's question to Jesus. He is the first true spiritual seeker in this chapter of Mark. All the other questions were asked by people trying to trap Jesus. This man asked because he noticed Jesus answered legal questions skillfully.

This was a religious conversation held on temple grounds, so they were probably speaking Hebrew, but Mark wrote his Gospel in Greek. In Mark's translation the question becomes, "Which is the mega-command?" *Megas* is the Greek word for the ultimate in anything: the biggest, highest, largest, strongest. In fact, if you imagine the booming <u>voice of God</u> announcing each of his commands to Moses from Mount Horeb, the question could be read, "What is the loudest command?" What is the command that God feels most strongly about?

With 613 commands, how could this question ever be answered? But Jesus doesn't hesitate for a second.

KEY POINT

Ancient Jews tried hard to figure out what mattered most to God. We should, too.

IT'S **GREEK** TO ME

☞ **GO TO:**

Deuteronomy 4:12–13 (voice of God)

> **Mark 12:29–31** "The most important one," answered Jesus, "is this: 'Hear, O Israel, the Lord our God, the Lord is one. Love the Lord your God with all your heart and with all your soul and with all your mind and with all your strength.' The second is this: 'Love your neighbor as yourself.' There is no commandment greater than these."

The Loudest Command

Hillel, a famous rabbi who died during Jesus' childhood, had boiled all the law down to this: "What you yourself hate, do not do to your neighbor: this is the whole law, the rest is commentary." While this wisdom was widely accepted, oddly, it doesn't mention God. In comparison, Jesus' answer focuses on God. Hillel viewed the law as rules for getting along with others. Jesus viewed the law as a vehicle for worshiping the Father. True worship came from a heart of love. Here was how people should love God:

- With all your *kardia* (heart): the center of your feelings
- With all your *psuche* (soul): your spirit
- With all your *dianoia* (mind): deep thought, understanding, imagination
- With all your *ischus* (strength): all the ability, force, or might you can muster

Breaking his answer into four components is what someone from the Western world would do, but the Middle Eastern mind didn't work that way. Jesus meant the answer to be taken in total. In other words, the chief commandment is to love God as hard as you can, with everything you've got.

Jesus adds an answer similar to Hillel's, making "loving your neighbor" secondary to loving God. He was asked, What is the first command? He answered with the first and second commands because they are inseparable. If you love God with every aspect of your being, you will naturally love others.

What Others are Saying:

Saint Augustine: This virtue consists in nothing else but in loving what is worthy of love . . . We are made better by approaching closer to him than whom nothing is better. We go to him not by walking, but by loving. We will have him more present to us in proportion as we are able to purify the love by which we draw near to him . . . we go to him not by the motion of our feet but by our conduct. Conduct is not usually discerned by what one knows but by what one loves; good or bad love makes good or bad conduct.[7]

> **Mark 12:32–34** "Well said, teacher," the man replied. "You are right in saying that God is one and there is no other but him. To love him with all your heart, with all your understanding and with all your strength, and to love your neighbor as yourself is more important than all burnt offerings and sacrifices."
>
> When Jesus saw that he had answered wisely, he said to him, "You are not far from the kingdom of God." And from then on no one dared ask him any more questions.

Mutual Admiration Society

In a Gospel where hardly anyone understands Jesus, it's refreshing to read about somebody who grasps his teaching readily. In Mark's context of the dispute between the temple leaders and Jesus, the big news here is the scribe realizes the **burnt offerings** and **sacrifices** are not ends in themselves. They were meant to point people <u>toward God</u>.

Throughout these passages temple leaders try to demonstrate that Jesus is off-kilter. Many of them think they are doing God and the people a favor by exposing Jesus as a loon, but in these multiple exchanges Jesus proves his teaching is more orthodox than theirs. What religious Jew could argue against loving God with your whole being?

The temple leaders publicly lost every round to Jesus and were forcefully shown errors in their beliefs, so they had double motivation to back off. As we'll see, however, while they stopped asking technical questions, they did not stop opposing Jesus.

burnt offerings: indicates a gift that is totally consumed by flame

sacrifices: indicates a gift that is partly burned, partly given to the priest, and partly eaten by the worshiper

☞ **GO TO:**

1 Samuel 15:22 (toward God)

Os Guinness: God calls people to himself, but this call is no casual suggestion. He is so awe inspiring and his summons so commanding that only one response is appropriate—a response as total and universal as the authority of the Caller. . . . everyone, everywhere, and in everything should think, speak, live, and act entirely for him.[8]

What Others are Saying:

NOW JESUS ASKS THE QUESTIONS

The temple cult has jousted with Jesus and scored nothing. Now that Jesus has silenced them, he can get a word in edgewise. He takes a shot at correcting the popular notion of what the Messiah's purpose is and points out the kind of worship the Temple should promote.

> **Mark 12:35–37** While Jesus was teaching in the temple courts, he asked, "How is it that the teachers of the law say that the Christ is the son of David? David himself, speaking by the Holy Spirit, declared:
> "'The Lord said to my Lord:
>   "Sit at my right hand
>   until I put your enemies
>   under your feet.'"
> David himself calls him 'Lord.' How then can he be his son?"
>   The large crowd listened to him with delight.

I Couldn't Help Noticing That You Like Riddles

The temple leaders seem to enjoy puzzling over complexities within the Hebrew scriptures, so Jesus poses a question of his own. In Hebrew culture a father *never* referred to his son as "Lord"—a term of great respect for another person. Reverence flowed the other way, from son to father. Jesus' riddle is this: if the Messiah is the son (descendant) of David, why does David refer to him as Lord?

He intends for the crowd to deduce the Messiah is divine. The Messiah deserved David's worship because the Messiah is David's God, but the crowd misunderstands. They assume the answer is that the Messiah's kingdom will be even grander than King David's, politically and militarily. Though they listen with delight, it is the same <u>pleasure</u> Herod experienced when listening to John the Baptist, shortly before beheading him. The delighted temple crowd, and the crowd that acclaimed Jesus as the son of David when he rode into Jerusalem, will soon transform into a crowd demanding his execution.

☞ **GO TO:**

Mark 6:20 (pleasure)

A WIDOW DEMONSTRATES PROPER RELIGION

> **Mark 12:38–40** As he taught, Jesus said, "Watch out for the teachers of the law. They like to walk around in flowing robes and be greeted in the marketplaces, and have the most important seats in the synagogues and the places of honor at banquets. They devour widows' houses and for a show make lengthy prayers. Such men will be punished most severely."

If Lawyers Ran Churches

Here Jesus denounces *"the teachers of the law."* Clearly, Jesus is moving from the defensive to the offensive. After this lecture no one could doubt Jesus had broken ties with the temple establishment.

Jesus' beef with the teachers has two parts: the way they stroked their own egos, and the way they took advantage of the less powerful. Their *"flowing robes"* were made of white linen, the color white symbolizing spiritual purity, and were to be worn while performing temple duties. The teachers of the law had taken to wearing them in public, out in Jerusalem's marketplace. There was not a single religious duty that required wearing the robes outside the Temple. The only reason for wearing them outside was to say, "Look at me, everybody! I'm really spiritual and important!"

The *"teachers of the law"* to whom Jesus refers are also known as scribes. Scribes were full-time experts in the laws of Moses, which touched on every aspect of a Jew's life. If your church kept a large staff of attorneys available to help members with their financial, legal, and business affairs, with an eye toward the church's interests, those lawyers would be like the scribes. Scribes performed all kinds of duties that included acting as bankers and helping with wills.

They were supposed to live on donations from the people. In actuality, they handled all these business affairs in ways that benefited themselves handsomely. As long as they cut the Temple into the deal, the priests overlooked any abuses.

"They devour widows' houses" refers to a particular corruption whereby scribes stole from widows. Jewish fathers often created trust funds to help support their daughters when their husbands died. A scribe would be trusted to administer the fund, doling out money to the daughter regularly, like a pension. The less trustworthy scribes would find ways to keep most of the money for themselves while convincing the widow she was getting all that was due her.

It's one thing to be a crook. It's worse to be a crook while claiming you represent God. No wonder *"such men will be punished most severely"*! When you begin to assemble the pieces in Mark's temple section—the corrupt moneychangers, the greedy priests, the mocking Sadducees, the embezzling scribes—you understand why God decided to flatten the place. This short passage helps create a transition to Mark 13, where Jesus discusses how and when the Temple will be wiped out.

THE WAYBACK MACHINE

KEY POINT

God will punish those who use his name to cover crime.

> **Mark 12:41–44** Jesus sat down opposite the place where the offerings were put and watched the crowd putting their money into the temple treasury. Many rich people threw in large amounts. But a poor widow came and put in two very small copper coins, worth only a fraction of a penny.
>
> Calling his disciples to him, Jesus said, "I tell you the truth, this poor widow has put more into the treasury than all the others. They all gave out of their wealth; but she, out of her poverty, put in everything— all she had to live on."

The Widow's Might

"The place where the offerings were put" was the Court of Women. Faithful Jews placed their temple taxes, plus any extra donations they felt like giving, in thirteen offering receptacles that lined the court. These trumpet-shaped receptacles resembled the **shofar**, with a wide mouth funneling down into the chest.

shofar: ram's-horn battle trumpet

☞ **GO TO:**

Matthew 6:2 (clatter)

Notice that many people were *"putting their money into the temple treasury,"* but the rich people *"threw in"* their offerings. Throwing coins in would make a greater <u>clatter</u> and racket than merely putting them in. It was just one more example of the me-first, God-last, show-offy worship that permeated Herod's Temple.

Jesus points out a woman who donated two lepta, the teeniest, least valuable coin circulating then (shown in GWWB, page 297). Two of them together were worth approximately one quarter of a cent in our money. Standing before a massive edifice faced in marble and plated in gold, what was the point of giving such an insignificant amount?

Jesus loved the woman's offering because it was *"all she had."* She stands in stark contrast to the showy religious leaders who were milking the system to their own advantage. But there's more; as he watches the woman, he is two days away from sacrificing his life for us. When we give our all to God, our behavior is worthy of our Savior and model, Jesus.

Something to Ponder

Interestingly, Jesus *commends* her donation even though he *condemned* the institution to which she gave it. Many times we don't give to God because we don't think an organization will make good use of our money. Jesus' approval of this woman's gift points out this is not a valid reason to withhold donations.

Besides praising the widow who gave little, later he'll praise a woman who gives <u>much</u>. Sometimes the size and even the use of the offering doesn't matter. What matters is that our hearts love God enough to worship him sacrificially.

☞ **GO TO:**

Mark 14:3–9 (much)

KEEP IT REAL—Watching Jesus deal with hypocrites cuts two ways. On one hand, I love to see him pop their pompous bubble and expose the garbage they cover with God's robes. On the other hand, I can not truly claim I've never participated with them. My best recourse is to throw myself at Jesus' mercy.

• Mark 12:24–27. Like the Sadducees, I probably overestimate my grasp of both Scripture and the power of God. Though I diligently study and consider Scripture, the fact that my understanding grows over the years proves that at any given moment my understanding is incomplete. *Your majestic power and depth are more than I can completely understand, Ancient of Days. Help me not ever to become arrogant, thinking I know it all.*

• Mark 12:38–40. Like the teachers of the law, we all are in danger of doing religious works for show. No, we don't have linen robes, but we do have bold Christian T-shirts. We don't fight for the seat of honor at banquets, but we do feel proud about heading up the pastoral search committee. Am I just as enthused about my unseen help as I am about work that gains recognition? *If not, Lord, my heart needs you to replace the spirit of the scribes with the Spirit of God.*

Study Questions

1. In Mark 12:27–33, why didn't Jesus answer the question from the priests, scribes, and elders about who authorized him to act the way he was acting?
2. What was a key difference between Isaiah's vineyard story and Jesus' vineyard story?
3. In the saying, *"Give to Caesar what is Caesar's and to God what is God's,"* what is Caesar's, and what is God's? Why?
4. Who were the Sadducees?
5. Jesus rebuked the scribes generally, but told one scribe that he was *"not far from the kingdom of God."* How did that scribe earn Jesus' compliment?

CHAPTER WRAP-UP

• Members of the Sanhedrin asked Jesus a *procedural* question: who authorized him to attack the temple business and to teach the people? Jesus responded by asking them who authorized John the Baptist, because the answers to both questions were the same. The Sanhedrin members refused to answer. (Mark 11:27–33)

- Jesus told the parable of the vineyard tenants, a story that portrayed the religious leaders as hard-hearted murderers and the cause of Israel's problems. The leaders resented the story, yet fulfilled it to the letter. (Mark 12:1–12)

- Pharisees and Herodians asked Jesus a *political* question, about whether it was proper to pay taxes to Caesar. Jesus' response meant the tax was unimportant; it's important to give your entire being to God. (Mark 12:13–17)

- Sadducees asked Jesus a *theological* question: if a woman married seven times, who would be her husband in heaven? Though the Sadducees were Israel's political aristocracy, Jesus scolded them for their ignorance of Scripture and their lack of understanding about God's power. He also told them their question was irrelevant, because marriages do not continue into heaven. (Mark 12:18–27)

- A sincere teacher of the law asked Jesus a *spiritual* question: which was the most important command? The answer is to love God with all you've got. Jesus commended the scribe for realizing that a heart relationship with God was more important than outward religious ceremonies. (Mark 12:28–34)

- Jesus asked the crowds a question intended to hint that the Messiah was not only the son of David, but was also divine. The crowd didn't get it. (Mark 12:35–37)

- Jesus warned us to "watch out" for anyone who does religious work to inflate personal ego. As a contrast and an example, he pointed out a widow whose teeny offering was valued by God because it was *"all she had to live on."* (Mark 12:38–44)

MARK 13:1–37
FUTURE JESUS

CHAPTER HIGHLIGHTS

- When Will the Temple Be Destroyed?
- When Will the Son of Man Return?
- What Should I Do about It?

Let's Get Started

Welcome to the most complex and difficult chapter of Mark, one that causes even world-class scholars to toss up their hands and admit, "We can't tell for certain what Jesus means." Mark 13 is the finale of Mark's lengthy section about the conflict between Jesus and the Temple. It begins when four guys ask Jesus when the Temple will be destroyed. Jesus begins addressing them, but ends addressing everyone. His lecture seems to cover not only the Temple, but also the end of human history; the trick is in figuring out which of his sentences refer to which topic.

Many Christians have torn into this passage with fervor, trying to calculate the exact date when Christ will fulfill his promise to return to earth. These date hunters take hints from Mark 13, from several <u>parallel passages</u>, from prophetic <u>Old Testament chapters</u>, and from the Book of Revelation to construct elaborate time lines intended to reveal God's agenda. While I admire the longing to see Jesus that I presume is behind all the chart making and timeline drawing, it is clear in Mark 13 Jesus was not trying to trigger that kind of activity. In fact, his lecture on the future seems designed to *obscure* the time of his coming. Why? Because Jesus wants people to focus on spreading the word of God, not on figuring out the exact time of his return.

This brings me to the Power Tool for this chapter: *let Scripture set the agenda.* One of Jesus' main points in Mark 13 is believers should be alert and not deceived. Ironically, this passage has been used as a springboard into all kinds of deceived interpretations of

☞ **GO TO:**

Matthew 24:1–51; Luke 21:5–30
(parallel passages)

Daniel 7–12; Zechariah 12–14
(Old Testament chapters)

POWER TOOL

Let Scripture set the agenda.

the Bible. Historian Dwight Wilson succinctly summarizes how accurate our "end times" predictions have been so far:

> The current crisis was always identified as a sign of the end, whether it was the Russo-Japanese War, the First World War, the Second World War, the Palestine War, the Suez Crisis, the June War, or the Yom Kippur War. The revival of the Roman Empire has been identified variously as Mussolini's empire, the League of Nations, the United Nations, the European Defense Community, the Common Market, and NATO. Speculation on the Antichrist has included Napoleon, Mussolini, Hitler, and Henry Kissinger. . . . The "kings of the east" have been variously the Turks, the lost tribes of Israel, Japan, India, and China. The supposed restoration of Israel has confused the problem of whether the Jews are to be restored before or after the coming of the Messiah. The restoration of the latter reign has been pinpointed to have begun in 1897, 1917, and 1948. The end of the "times of the Gentiles" has been placed in 1895, 1917, 1948, and 1967.[1]

Our "end times" predictions are often wrong because we do not let the Scriptures themselves set the agenda. We should emphasize what Scripture emphasizes, and de-emphasize what Scripture de-emphasizes. Instead, each of us often brings to the Bible our own private agenda. We try to make it say what our denomination says, what confirms our own notions, or what blasts others and leaves us unscathed. To read properly, we must not judge the Scriptures, but let the Scriptures judge us.

As I walk through Mark 13 with you, I will show you the interpretation that I think is the best supported. It coincides well with the church's historic interpretation of the end times over the centuries, but differs from today's most popular interpretation. (If you'd like to read about that one, you'll find it clearly and skillfully laid out in GWDN and GWRV.) I'm not saying I'm right and others are wrong; I'm saying we're probably all wrong to some extent.

KEY POINT

We can read God's prophecy book, but he is under no obligation to read ours.

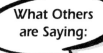

What Others are Saying:

Robert Van Kampen: Sad to say, teachers too often approach prophecy using the method of interpretation that best suits their own biases or circumstances rather than accepting the clear intent of the biblical writer.[2]

David Jeremiah: Rather than spending all your time reading the magazines and trying to figure the nuances of what the future might hold, maybe you should spend at least as much time getting to know Him better. Then when the future becomes the present, you will enjoy a wondrously close relationship with almighty God and you can be walking with the Lord Jesus Christ in strength. No matter what happens.[3]

Dr. Winn Griffin: We never graduate from Bible study until we meet the author face to face.[4]

WHEN WILL THE TEMPLE BE DESTROYED?

> **Mark 13:1–2** As he was leaving the temple, one of his disciples said to him, "Look, Teacher! What massive stones! What magnificent buildings!"
> "Do you see all these great buildings?" replied Jesus. "Not one stone here will be left on another; every one will be thrown down."

Jesus Predicts The Destruction Of EPCOT

I described the Temple to you in the chapter on Mark 11:1–25—eighty feet tall, gold facades, gleaming in the sunlight. . . . turn west at the Mount of Olives, you can't miss it. What I didn't mention is a whole series of smaller buildings connected to the Temple via **colonnaded** courts and a series of enclosures. If you considered "the Temple" to include all its official courts and connected structures, the Temple covered about one-sixth of Jerusalem. No wonder the disciples were impressed.

But Jesus understood what the disciples didn't; the overlords running this first-century EPCOT (Excessively Prideful Community of the Temple) were about to turn all their efforts toward squishing Jesus and his disciples like bugs.

colonnaded: having a series of regularly spaced columns

The disciples would have difficulty picturing the Temple disassembled stone by stone. According to Josephus, the stones measured "about 25 **cubits** in length, 8 in height and 12 in width." A cubit is roughly 18 inches long, so these stones were nearly 40 feet long and 12 feet high. They would weigh tons. What could cause *any* of them to move, much less *all* of them?

Yet Jesus was clear in his assertion. He implied the closure of the Temple by cursing the fig tree and overturning money tables. Now he just comes right out with it—this place is goin' down, hard.

cubits: unit of measurement; the distance from elbow to fingertip

THE WAYBACK MACHINE

David Jeremiah: It was the most spectacular, breathtaking structure imaginable, magnificent by any day's standards . . . and the disciples couldn't grasp the concept that the whole breathtaking complex would soon become a pile of rubble.[5]

> **Mark 13:3–4** As Jesus was sitting on the Mount of Olives opposite the temple, Peter, James, John and Andrew asked him privately, "Tell us, when will these things happen? And what will be the sign that they are all about to be fulfilled?"

The Thing About "These Things"

The four men Jesus called first to be his disciples ask when "these things" will happen. This shows in two ways how much the disciples value the Temple. First of all, when Jesus predicted his own death, they didn't ask him a thing. But when they hear the Temple is in danger, they must know more. Second, notice that Jesus predicted only one thing: the Temple would be dismantled to the last stone. Yet the disciples don't ask about "this thing"; they ask about "these things." This verifies the Temple was the center of the universe for the Jew. In their minds, there was no way God's house could be destroyed unless the whole world went to pieces.

Olivet Discourse: a name for this lecture, given on the Mount of Olives

R. C. Sproul: Jesus begins the **Olivet Discourse** with a statement about every stone of the temple being "thrown down." It is important to note that the entire discourse is provoked by his words about the destruction of the temple. The disciples respond to his prediction by asking about the time-frame for this event. In all three gospels the disciples ask two questions: (1) When will these things be? (2) What will be the sign of their fulfillment?[6]

> **Mark 13:5–8** Jesus said to them: "Watch out that no one deceives you. Many will come in my name, claiming, 'I am he,' and will deceive many. When you hear of wars and rumors of wars, do not be alarmed. Such things must happen, but the end is still to come. Nation will rise against nation, and kingdom against kingdom. There will be earthquakes in various places, and famines. These are the beginning of birth pains."

Be Disciples, Not Dopes

The four disciples asked Jesus what signs would foretell the Temple's destruction, and they probably assumed the Temple's destruction would come with God's judgment on sinful Israel. Jesus gives them several signs not of the end but of the beginning. Things are not going to wrap up as quickly as the disciples assume. The next several comments from Jesus urge the disciples to stay calm during turmoil.

I think I'll name my watchdog Blepo. What's *blepo* (BLEH-poh)? It's the Greek word Mark uses for "Watch out!" or "Watch!" Jesus says <u>over and over</u> in his lecture that his disciples must "watch." It is a call to be vigilant—to be discerning about spiritual things. Jesus is commanding his disciples to avoid being spiritual suckers.

So what kinds of things does a spiritual sucker fall for? Spiritual suckers believe men who say, "I'm the Messiah! I'm back!" Spiritual suckers look at events such as wars and earthquakes, and read too much into them. When Jesus says *"such things must happen,"* he means they represent God's will working itself out in history, but they are not necessarily signs of the end. Rather, *"the end is still to come."*

Jesus says, *"These are the beginning of birth pains."* The Old Testament uses <u>birth pangs</u> to refer to the suffering that God will pour out on Israel so that the nation will be reborn in greater spiritual purity. I think that's what Jesus had in mind here. (For a different interpretation, see GWRV, page 160).

We see the phrase *"beginning of birth pains"* and focus on the words "beginning" and "pain." Jesus probably intends for us to focus on the word "birth." The point is not the pain; the point is that something worthwhile is being born: the age of the Messiah's reign.

George Eldon Ladd: The Old Testament speaks of the birth of a nation through a period of woes (Isa 66:8, Jer 22:23; Hos 13:13; Micah 4:9f.) and from these verses there arose in Judaism the idea that the messianic Kingdom must emerge from a period of suffering that was called the messianic woes or "the birth pangs of the Messiah." This does not mean the woes that the Messiah must suffer, but the woes out of which the messianic age is to be born.[7]

IT'S **GREEK** TO ME

☞ **GO TO:**

Mark 13:5, 9, 33, 35, 37 (over and over)

☞ **GO TO:**

Isaiah 66:7–11; Hosea 13:9–13 (birth pangs)

Something to Ponder

What Others are Saying:

Philip Yancey: "Such things must happen, but the end is still to come." The presence of evil guarantees that the world will be full of strife and that the world will look unredeemed. For a period of time, the kingdom of God must exist alongside an active rebellion against God. God's kingdom advances slowly, humbly, like a secret invasion force operating within the kingdoms ruled by Satan.[8]

> **Mark 13:9–11** "You must be on your guard. You will be handed over to the local councils and flogged in the synagogues. On account of me you will stand before governors and kings as witnesses to them. And the gospel must first be preached to all nations. Whenever you are arrested and brought to trial, do not worry beforehand about what to say. Just say whatever is given you at the time, for it is not you speaking, but the Holy Spirit."

Handed Over On Account Of Me

Jesus began by speaking of troubles that affect people internationally. Next he speaks of troubles that will beset his first-century disciples. The *"local councils"* Jesus speaks of are mini-Sanhedrins. Any city having a Jewish population of at least 120 people could have a Sanhedrin of its own (much like our city councils, which can work as local imitations of the U.S. Congress).

The Jewish leadership felt so threatened by Jesus, not only would they kill him, they would also persecute his followers. The disciples would be cross-examined, flogged, thrown in prison, even martyred. Jesus' focus in these verses is not on their comfort, but on their ability to stand strong and testify. He promises the Holy Spirit will help them do precisely that.

These must have been difficult words for the disciples to absorb. They were just fighting about which of them would nab seats of power next to Jesus. Now he's telling them they will be treated as outlaws because they know him.

*Remember
This . . .*

Some believers take this verse out of context. They interpret the verse to mean studying and otherwise preparing to speak up publicly for Jesus is a bad idea. They think preparing demonstrates a lack of faith in "God's Spirit." That's not the intent of this verse at all. Jesus was speaking specifically to the early Christians about a particular circumstance, whereby these uneducated men would be dragged before world leaders.

The phrase *"the gospel must first be preached to all nations"* may have startled the disciples. When Jesus first sent them out, they went to Jewish <u>villages</u> in Galilee. They saw Jesus minister to a Gentile here and there, but they may not have realized that all Gentiles were welcome to Jesus' kingdom.

When we read *"the gospel must first be preached to all nations,"* we immediately think of a globe with hundreds of nations differentiated by a web of boundaries throughout planet earth. But the disciples had never seen a globe of earth. To them, *"all nations"* meant every nation in the Roman world. If this is what Jesus meant, the disciples brought the Gospel to *"all nations"* as early as A.D. 60. The apostle Paul referred often to the Gospel's <u>worldwide</u> circulation.

THE WAYBACK MACHINE

☞ **GO TO:**

Mark 6:7 (villages)

Romans 1:8; 10:18; 15:18–24; Colossians 1:6 (worldwide)

> **Mark 13:12–13** "Brother will betray brother to death, and a father his child. Children will rebel against their parents and have them put to death. All men will hate you because of me, but he who stands firm to the end will be saved."

Loyalty To The Right Royalty

Jesus is telling his followers that he expects their loyalty to him to be above all other loyalties, including their loyalty to their families. Whether through shrewd analysis of the politics around him or supernatural insight (probably both!), Jesus sees his followers will soon be faced with the decision of denying him or dying.

By the end of the first century, the Roman government turned against Christians. Families were pressured to report anyone who was not loyal to Caesar. Within some Jewish families, loved ones would believe their <u>relatives</u> who followed Jesus had joined an extremist sect and left the faith; some of these family members were capable of fanatical hatred of the ones they perceived as blasphemers. Because of a misunderstanding of what communion was, some mistakenly believed Christians were cannibals! Through all the turmoil believers could cling to the promise that if they kept obeying Jesus, they had a place in heaven.

☞ **GO TO:**

Micah 7:5–8 (relatives)

IT'S
GREEK
TO ME

**Something
to Ponder**

The word for "end" in the phrase *"he who stands firm to the end,"* is *telos*, which in this context refers to the end of a person's life. Anyone who stays true to Jesus until death can count on eternity with God.

Jesus' goal is to prepare his disciples for the difficult times ahead. It must have encouraged them to remember their trials were the fulfillment of Jesus' predictions. Not only did Jesus tell them what to expect, but by dying on the cross, he also gave them a sterling example to follow.

> **Mark 13:14–16** "When you see 'the abomination that causes desolation' standing where it does not belong— let the reader understand—then let those who are in Judea flee to the mountains. Let no one on the roof of his house go down or enter the house to take anything out. Let no one in the field go back to get his cloak.

If Howard Stern Were Pope

Mark 13:14–16 are some of the most difficult verses in Mark's Gospel, so stick with me while I try to unpack them. The key to understanding these verses is in figuring out what Jesus means by *"the <u>abomination</u> that causes desolation."* The phrase comes from the Book of Daniel, to which Mark may be referring when he inserts the words, *"let the reader understand."* (In his culture, "the reader" would have been someone reading the passage out loud to a group.) In Daniel it's clear *"the abomination that causes desolation"* occurs in the Temple.

The first word of the phrase, *bdelygma* ("abomination"), suggests something repugnant to God, and the second, *eremosis* ("desolation"), suggests the abomination will cause the Temple to be deserted—desolate. The **Septuagint**'s translation of Daniel suggests the phrase might be better rendered "the appalling sacrilege." Thus, the phrase seems to refer to a sacrilege in the Temple that is so appalling the Jews abandon it.

What does Jesus say about this *"abomination"*? He says the disciples will see it *"standing where it does not belong."* Now that little word *"it"* makes interpreters pick teams and start fights, but some smart guys make a strong case for translating this word "he."[9]

Everything's clear as can be, right? Hang in there. So far our translation of the phrase looks like this: "the appalling sacrilege

GO TO:

Daniel 9:27; 11:31;
    12:11 (abomination)

*Septuagint: Greek
translation of the Jewish
Scriptures by Jewish
scholars dated 200 B.C.*

standing where he does not belong." Here are three leading theories for what this phrase refers to:

1. The disgusting thing called "he" is a statue, an idol to a false god, erected not merely in the Temple, but in the Holy of Holies. This would be a horrible offense to the God who ordered Jews not to have any gods before him.
2. The disgusting "he" is the <u>Antichrist</u>. The Antichrist is described in the New Testament as a "<u>lawless one</u>" who denies Jesus is Christ and forms an alliance with Satan to organize worldwide resistance against God.
3. The proper translation is not "he," but "it," and "the appalling sacrilege" is almost anything horribly gross and religiously offensive that occurs in the Temple.

Whatever "he" or "it" is, Jesus says that as soon as the disciples see it, they should head for the hills.

☞ **GO TO:**

1 John 2:22 (Antichrist)

2 Thessalonians 2:3, 8 (lawless one)

What did Mark's first readers believe about *"the abomination that causes desolation"*? To answer this question, you'll need some Jewish history.

After Jesus left the earth, the political atmosphere in Palestine got even worse. The **Zealots** pushed for Jewish freedom until A.D. 66 when they convinced Palestinian Jews to initiate a full-scale rebellion.

Fanatically caught up in their cause, the Zealots moved into the Temple and made it their fort. According to Josephus, they treated the Holy of Holies as just another room. They murdered some of their "prisoners of war" in the Temple. Offended by how corrupt the previous temple leaders were, the Zealots satirically ordained a clown named Phanni to be the high priest. (This would be roughly equivalent to U.N. soldiers capturing Vatican City and ordaining Howard Stern to be Pope.) First-century Christians believed Phanni was the appalling sacrilege standing where he did not belong. They did what Jesus told them to do and fled for the hills—not the hills of Judea, but beyond, to a little mountain town called Pella. Unfortunately, other people followed Jewish tradition and stayed in Jerusalem.

In A.D. 70 a Roman general named Titus marched thousands of centurions into Jerusalem and slaughtered the Jews that remained. In a hopeless last stand, the Zealots took shelter in Herod's massive Temple. Titus was too smart to send his

THE WAYBACK MACHINE

Zealots: *Jewish sect that believed in using violence to end Jewish exile*

soldiers through the easily defensible doors of the Temple, so he set fire to the place. The centurions stoked the fire so hot it made the marble stones crumble and the golden roof melt into the masonry. All the Zealots perished. Afterwards, Jesus' prophecy that *"not one stone here will be left on another"* was fulfilled literally; the Romans pried every stone apart to obtain the melted gold.

Roman soldiers then set up flags in the ruins of the Temple and made sacrifices to their gods. Some commentators believe the act of burning the Temple and making pagan sacrifices in it was the *"abomination that causes desolation."*

Something to Ponder

Today it's popular to interpret these verses as a reference to the Antichrist and to the end of the world. I used to hold that position too. When I did, these questions stumped me:

- If Jesus was warning all of us, why did he specify *"those who are in Judea"*?
- The Bible says when the world ends, there will be no place to <u>hide</u>—so what would be the point of fleeing?

What Others are Saying:

☞ **GO TO:**

Revelation 6:15–17 (hide)

Eusebius: The whole body, however, of the church at Jerusalem . . . removed from the city and lived at a certain town beyond the Jordan called Pella. Here, those who believed in Christ removed from Jerusalem, as if holy men had entirely abandoned the royal city itself and the whole land of Judea. The divine justice, for their crimes against Christ and his apostles, finally overtook the Jews, totally destroying the whole generation.[10]

> **Mark 13:17–20** How dreadful it will be in those days for pregnant women and nursing mothers! Pray that this will not take place in winter, because those will be days of distress unequaled from the beginning, when God created the world, until now—and never to be equaled again. If the Lord had not cut short those days, no one would survive. But for the sake of the elect, whom he has chosen, he has shortened them."

What About "Distress Unequaled"?

It's important to remember Jesus is a Jew speaking to Jews. Throughout the Hebrew scriptures, prophecies of God's judgment are expressed in this same kind of earth-shattering, <u>radical language</u>. Time and again prophets predicted God's people would be wiped out in ways unequaled in history.

When the fulfillment of these prophecies is recorded in the Old Testament, it's easy to see the prophecies were stated in exaggerated terms. The armies involved were not, in fact, the most awesome armies in history, the stars did not literally fall out of the sky, the mountains did not melt, the people did not suffer in ways no one else had, and so on. These were prophetic figures of speech, and no Jew would have taken them literally.

The exaggerated language was meant to convey how significant these events were within God's overall plan. The events certainly felt apocalyptic to Jews who met their deaths in the fulfillment of these prophecies, but no scholar takes these Old Testament prophecies in a strictly literal sense.

When Jesus prophesied horrible punishment for the Jews, I believe he used the same kind of language Old Testament prophets used to prophesy the same thing. Jesus did nothing more or less than speak the language of his culture.

☞ **GO TO:**

Micah 1:1–5; Jeremiah 30:4–7; Joel 2:2 (radical language)

If you were to travel back in time and tell a first-century Jew to quit pulling your leg, he would tell you you're nuts because he isn't holding your leg in the first place. Why? Because the figure of speech you used is not a part of his culture. I, however, would understand you perfectly. When we read Jesus' prophetic words, it's as if Jesus has traveled forward in time and is using figures of speech with which we are unfamiliar. We run the risk of interpreting his language in ways that none of his contemporaries would have.

IT'S
GREEK
TO ME

> **Mark 13:21–23** "At that time if anyone says to you, 'Look, here is the Christ!' or, 'Look, there he is!' do not believe it. For false Christs and false prophets will appear and perform signs and miracles to deceive the elect—if that were possible. So be on your guard; I have told you everything ahead of time."

Forewarned Is Forearmed

So far Jesus has prophesied conflict between nations and the believers' hasty withdrawal from Jerusalem. During this kind of chaos, you can always count on *"false prophets"* who grab for power. In fact,

☞ **GO TO:**

Acts 5:34–37
(false prophets)

as Jesus was prophesying, there were some <u>false prophets</u> doing just that. Jesus warns his disciples not to fall for their ploys. In the following verses he explains his return will be plain to his followers.

WHEN WILL THE WORLD END?

At the beginning of Mark 13 Jesus told his disciples the Temple would be destroyed. They asked him what signs would precede the Temple's destruction, and he told them. Jesus knew, however, the disciples would assume the end of the Temple meant the end of the world, so he addresses their assumption.

> **Mark 13:24–27** "But in those days, following that distress,
> "'the sun will be darkened,
>   and the moon will not give its light;
> the stars will fall from the sky,
>   and the heavenly bodies will be shaken.'
> "At that time men will see the Son of Man coming in clouds with great power and glory. And he will send his angels and gather his elect from the four winds, from the ends of the earth to the ends of the heavens."

Today's Weather: Cloudy, With Showers Of Glory

As Jesus finishes detailing the destruction of Jerusalem, he uses the transitional phrase, *"in those days, following that distress."* Note that Jesus does not give a specific time. The disciples believed he meant immediately *"following that distress"* (that is, immediately after the Temple is destroyed), but Jesus didn't say that.

Jesus snatches a <u>quote</u> from Isaiah that describes God's wrath and judgment on the heathen nations of Babylon and Edom. Both nations received their prophesied punishment, but obviously the stars did not fall from the sky and the sky did not roll up like a scroll, as Isaiah predicted. This language is a poetic way of saying, "this changed everything" or, "after this nothing was ever the same." Other Old Testament <u>passages</u> use similar language to describe *"the Day of the Lord"*—a phrase Scripture uses for the end of the world. Jesus cites Isaiah to make it clear that what the disciples had always thought of as *"the Day of the Lord"* would happen when the Son of Man returned.

☞ **GO TO:**

Isaiah 13:10; 34:4
(quote)

Isaiah 24:23; Ezekiel
32:7–8; Joel 2:30–31
(passages)

The Bible gives no indication, however, that the phrase *"the Son of Man coming in clouds with great power"* is a metaphor. In fact, <u>later</u> in Mark Jesus himself seems to take this prediction literally, and so does the apostle <u>John</u>, so we should keep our interpretive options open. Even though the Old Testament prophets did not literally mean it when they said the moon would turn to blood, the Bible relates astronomical <u>disturbances</u> to Christ's Second Coming so repeatedly that some of them may actually happen.

The last part of this passage (*"he will send his angels and gather. . . "*) means when Messiah returns, his glory will no longer be veiled, and neither will the glory of God's chosen people. Israel's great hope for an end to exile will be realized when the Messiah returns, gathering God's people from everywhere. By then *"the elect"* will consist of New Israel—in other words, all those who follow Messiah Jesus, whether Jews or Gentiles.

☞ **GO TO:**

Mark 14:61–62 (later)

Revelation 1:7 (John)

2 Peter 3:3–10 (disturbances)

WHEN FIG TREES TEACH

> **Mark 13:28–31** "Now learn this lesson from the fig tree: As soon as its twigs get tender and its leaves come out, you know that summer is near. Even so, when you see these things happening, you know that it is near, right at the door. I tell you the truth, this generation will certainly not pass away until all these things have happened. Heaven and earth will pass away, but my words will never pass away."

The "It" Generation

There are many interpretations of this passage. One popular rendering from modern times (laid out in GWPB, 185–186) claims the fig tree analogy refers to Israel coming back together as a nation, which happened officially in 1948, and that the "generation" Jesus refers to is whatever generation witnesses this event (allegedly, us).

From a scriptural standpoint, this interpretation is difficult to support for at least two reasons. First, the fig tree analogy does not include any language suggesting Israel's reunification. Secondly, the phrase *"<u>this generation</u>"* occurs numerous times in the Gospels, and it always refers to people living at the same time as Jesus.

☞ **GO TO:**

Matthew 11:16; 12:41–42; Mark 8:12; Luke 7:31; 11:50–51; 17:25 (this generation)

Let's see what Jesus emphasizes. The phrase *"even so"* introduces an explanation of Jesus' fig tree metaphor; the explanation tells us that just as a leafy fig tree means summer is coming, *"these things"* mean *"it"* is coming. Notice that *"these things"* and *"the abomination that causes desolation"* probably refer to the same event or set of events because each is introduced with the phrase *"when you see."*

The simplest, cleanest interpretation, therefore, is that the Israelites should flee when they see the abomination that causes desolation because unheard-of distress ("it") is soon to follow. Jesus says his generation will not pass away until these things happen, and sure enough, "it" did happen.

What Others are Saying:

Expositor's Bible Commentary: The next phrase, *engys estin,* may be translated either "it is near" (NIV) or "he is near." Those who interpret this paragraph (w.28–31) in its entirety to relate to the events surrounding the Fall of Jerusalem usually identify the "it" with the "abomination that causes desolation" (cf. v.14) or the fall of the city itself. If, on the other hand, vv.28–31 are descriptive of the End, then "he is near" would be a more fitting translation, though "it," referring to [Jesus' Second Coming], would also be suitable.[11]

SO WHAT DO I DO ABOUT ALL THIS?

As we near the end of Jesus' lecture about the Temple and the end times, you may feel puzzled. All the possible interpretive options can make your head spin, but remember Jesus didn't say these things so we of the twenty-first century would have a flow chart for the end of time. He said them to encourage and strengthen his first-century disciples.

> **Mark 13:32–36** "No one knows about that day or hour, not even the angels in heaven, nor the Son, but only the Father. Be on guard! Be alert! You do not know when that time will come. It's like a man going away: He leaves his house and puts his servants in charge, each with his assigned task, and tells the one at the door to keep watch.
>
> Therefore keep watch because you do not know when the owner of the house will come back—whether in the evening, or at midnight, or when the rooster crows, or at dawn. If he comes suddenly, do not let him find you sleeping. What I say to you, I say to everyone: 'Watch!'"

Constant Vigilance!

Referring once again to when the Son of Man will return, Jesus emphasizes that *"no one knows about that day or hour."* You can't predict the date of Jesus' return without ignoring the entire point of this passage. Jesus tells his disciples to remain spiritually alert because they *do not know* when the Master will return.

What does Jesus want us to do with the information in this speech? He tells us pretty clearly, if you tune in to his commands sprinkled throughout the passage. Here they are:

Verse	What Jesus Commands His Disciples to Do
v. 5	Watch out.
v. 7	Do not be alarmed.
v. 9	Be on your guard.
v. 11	Do not worry beforehand about what to say.
v. 11	Say whatever is given you in that moment.
v. 18	Pray that this will not take place in winter.
v. 21	If anyone says to you, 'Look, here is the Christ!' . . . do not believe it.
v. 23	Be on your guard.
v. 28	Learn this lesson.
v. 33	Be on guard!
v. 33	Be alert!
v. 35	Keep watch.
v. 37	Watch!

☞ **GO TO:**

Acts 1:6–11 (cloud)

 KEEP IT REAL—In a brief parable, Jesus describes his followers as *"servants in charge, each with his assigned task."* When Jesus tells us *"Watch out! . . . Do not be alarmed . . . Be on guard! Be alert!"* he is telling us each to get on with our *"assigned task,"* and not to be distracted by the world's turmoil. It's wrong to interpret his words in a way that justifies constant guessing about the end times.

Just before Jesus left our planet, he told his disciples to be his witnesses throughout the earth. Then he ascended into the sky and was hidden by a <u>cloud</u>. The disciples kept staring up until *"two men dressed in white"* asked them, *"Why do you stand here looking into the sky?"* Today, we sometimes suffer from the same mixed-up priorities. The job Jesus assigned us, which is to spread news of his kingdom throughout the earth, is not completed. Until it is, we shouldn't spend too much time staring slack-jawed at the clouds and impatiently at our watches. Instead, each of us needs to find out what our assigned task is and do it.

What Others are Saying:

David Jeremiah: Christians need to believe what the Lord said about no human knowing the date or the time. If you are not willing to believe what Christ said about that, then why would you believe *anything* He said about His return?[12]

Philip Yancey: Nothing pleased Jesus more than the successes of his disciples; nothing disturbed him more than their failures. He had come to earth with the goal of leaving again, after transferring his mission to others. The angels' gentle rebuke might as well have been his own: "Why do you stand here looking into the sky?"[13]

C. S. Lewis: He is going to land in force; we know not when. But we can guess why He is delaying: He wants to give us the chance of joining His side freely. . . . But I wonder whether people who ask God to interfere openly and directly in our world quite realise what it will be like when He does. When that happens, it is the end of the world. When the author walks on to the stage the play is over.[14]

KEEP IT REAL—Mark 13:9–13. More than ever in modern times, Christians are dying for their faith in Europe, China, Africa; even in the United States, if you count the shooting at Columbine High. When I was a young Christian, I think I would've readily died for Jesus. Now, as a family man and card-carrying member of the middle class, I can't state with certainty that I would. *Jesus, please kill my love for comfort and luxury, and renew my love for you.*

• Mark 13:35–37. What does Jesus mean by *"If he comes suddenly, do not let him find you sleeping"*? Maybe it's the same thing as that dulled state I get in when I watch too much TV, listen to too many MP3s, spend too much time assessing which DVDs to buy, and generally invest a lot of time in distractions from my *"assigned task."* *I hear your wake-up call, Master. Slap the sleep out of my eyes and help me get back to your work.*

Study Questions

1. What kind of dog is a blepo dog? And what's that got to do with anything?
2. What are some signs that are *not* signs of the end?
3. When Mark interjects, *"Let the reader understand,"* what is he probably referring to?
4. If prophecies about the sun going dark, the moon losing its light, and the stars falling out of the sky are not taken literally, then what would they mean?

5. Which generation does Jesus mean when he refers to *"this generation"* in Mark 13:30?

CHAPTER WRAP-UP

- Mark 13 completes Mark's lengthy section about how Jesus interacted with the Temple (Mark 11–13). The chapter begins with four disciples asking two questions: when will the Temple be destroyed, and what signs will come before its destruction? (Mark 13:1–4)

- According to some scholars (and me), this is a good reason to conclude Mark 13:5–23 is about the destruction of the Temple and Jerusalem; 13:24–27 refers to the Second Coming of Christ; 13:28–32 returns to the destruction of the Temple; and 13:32–37 returns to the Second Coming.

- First-century Christians believed when the Zealots satirically ordained a clown as the high priest, they had seen *"the abomination that causes desolation"* that Jesus warned about. They moved out of Jerusalem *en masse* between A.D. 66 and 68. In A.D. 70 Titus destroyed the Temple, leaving no stone upon another, as Jesus predicted. These and other historical events are the main reasons many scholars believe Mark 13:14–23 has already been fulfilled.

- In the Old Testament, predictions of astronomical chaos were intended poetically, not literally. So when Christ comes again, many of the predictions about the sun giving out, the stars vanishing, and other kinds of astronomical disturbances may not occur literally. However, the Bible does make it clear that Christ will come again. (Mark 13:24–27)

- Some scholars interpret the "parable of the fig tree" to mean the Israelites who saw *"the abomination that causes desolation"* should expect a time of great Jewish persecution and distress was soon to come. The same scholars believe the generation of Jews alive in Jesus' day would not die out before his prediction was fulfilled. (Mark 13:28–31)

- Jesus' real point in this lecture was not to make his followers guess about the precise time he would return. He was rather trying to strengthen and encourage the disciples in advance, because he knew persecution was coming for them on account of their relationship with him. He ended the lecture with a strong command to keep spreading the kingdom of God. (Mark 13:32–37)

Part Six

PASSIONATE JESUS

REVEREND FUN

"I said I want to anoint his head with nard, not with a nerd!"

Keep Your Seatbelt Fastened

Brace yourself for intense drama as we reach the final section of Mark's gritty Gospel. All the threads Mark spins earlier in the book come together in the final twenty-four hours of Jesus' life. The Son of Man is about to experience both unimaginable agony and unspeakable victory. Curiously, Mark depicts the agony without pulling any punches, while he depicts victory with restraint.

The final section of Mark is principally about the murder of Jesus. What Jesus goes through is so emotionally extreme that it is known as the "passion" of Christ. Mark 14 shows the Jewish role in this event; Mark 15 shows the Gentile role; and Mark 16 shows God's role.

Along the way Mark treats us to another of his trademark sandwiches; vivid narration; heartbreaking pathos; and, possibly, an Alfred Hitchcock–style cameo of himself. If you've enjoyed the story so far, the best is yet to come . . . so let's get started!

MARK 14:1–42
BOY SCOUT JESUS

Let's Get Started

In Mark 14 Jesus is getting prepared. The theme of Jesus' fore-knowledge runs through the chapter, evident in almost every scene. Jesus knew he would be <u>betrayed</u>. He knew he was about to <u>die</u>. He knew the Twelve would <u>desert</u> him. He knew he would <u>live again</u>. He knew he would <u>return on clouds</u> of glory.

Mark shows us that Jesus prepared his heart, his mind, and his resolve for the hardest night of his life. Jesus didn't run or compromise or try to pass the buck. He did what needed doing. With forty-eight hours left to live, he prepared for his own burial and for his disciples to carry on the mission in his absence. He prepared his heart before the Father. Then he shouldered his burden—*our* burden—and carried it like the royalty he was. Come on, you just have to see this.

☞ **GO TO:**

Mark 14:18 (betrayed)

Mark 14:8 (die)

Mark 14:27 (desert)

Mark 14:25, 28 (live again)

Mark 14:62 (return on clouds)

MARK SANDWICH: CONSPIRATORS AND WORSHIPERS

By now you should feel like a veteran at interpreting Mark's sandwiches. Once again showing his affection for stark contrasts, Mark places men who hated Jesus excessively around a woman who loved him extravagantly.

> **Mark 14:1–2** Now the Passover and the Feast of Unleavened Bread were only two days away, and the chief priests and the teachers of the law were looking for some sly way to arrest Jesus and kill him. "But not during the Feast," they said, "or the people may riot."

Some Sly Way

Passover, the beginning of the Jewish year, commemorated the time when the death angel of the Lord spared the firstborn sons of Hebrews while killing the firstborn sons of Egyptians. The Jews celebrated Passover and the Feast of Unleavened Bread together, which made for a week-long celebration. On the first and last day of the week, they offered sacrifices. In between, they did no servile work. Our closest cultural equivalent might be the week between Christmas and the New Year.

Sounds like a big party, right? Unfortunately, it didn't quite work out that way. Obligated by custom and by law to come to Jerusalem for Passover, Jews increased the city's population by five times during Passover week. It was always marked by demonstrations and minor power struggles, with emotional crowds primed and ready to explode.

In the beginning of Mark 14 the men who want Jesus dead must be very careful. If they accidentally create a public martyr, it would be like lighting a match in a fireworks factory.

Minor religious leaders have muttered <u>threats</u> against Jesus since early in Mark, but now the people with real power and cunning have plans for Jesus. It's like being placed on the federal government's Most Wanted list. These powermongers know that once they target Jesus, the result is certain. It's just a matter of time.

☞ **GO TO:**

Mark 3:6 (threats)

What Others are Saying:

John MacArthur: The historian Josephus estimated that more than a quarter-million sacrificial lambs would be slain in Jerusalem during a typical Passover season. On average, ten people would partake of one lamb, suggesting that the Jewish population in Jerusalem during Passover could swell to between 2.5 and 3 million. . . . From the conspirators' perspective, it was the worst time to seize Jesus, if they wanted to do it quietly.[1]

> **Mark 14:3–5** While he was in Bethany, reclining at the table in the home of a man known as Simon the Leper, a woman came with an alabaster jar of very expensive

> perfume, made of pure nard. She broke the jar and poured the perfume on his head.
>
> Some of those present were saying indignantly to one another, "Why this waste of perfume? It could have been sold for more than a year's wages and the money given to the poor." And they rebuked her harshly.

Freaks, Geeks, And Nard

Although it seems weird to us, back then it was <u>common</u> for a host to anoint his guests with oil during a meal. In the gritty, parched Middle Eastern deserts, the oil refreshed and moisturized sun-damaged skin and hair.

☞ **GO TO:**

Psalm 23:5; Luke 7:46 (common)

John 12:1–7 (John's account)

Nevertheless, this tale does start on a strange note. Given Jewish health laws (already discussed in chapter on Mark 7:1–8:21), how could a leper host a social dinner? Lepers were unclean freaks, cast out from society. Scholars speculate that perhaps Jesus had healed Simon, who then gave the dinner in the Savior's honor.

The nameless woman (she's not Mary; <u>John's account</u> is a different event) took "anointing" to new heights. The jar Mark describes is worthy of being a family heirloom. Precious alabaster jars like this one were sealed in such a way that they could only be used once, because opening them required breaking them.

Nard was a thick oil extracted from a plant that grew primarily in India, genetically related to ginseng. In Israel it was expensive, imported stuff. The New International Version tries to help our understanding by saying that the nard "*could have been sold for more than a year's wages.*" Actually, the Greek says the perfume was worth more than three hundred denarii. How much is that? Here's a hint: when the disciples were trying to estimate the cost to <u>feed five thousand</u> people, they said it would require two hundred denarii. Next time you buy lunch for over seven thousand of your closest friends, look at the total bill. That's how much this nard was worth.

IT'S **GREEK** TO ME

☞ **GO TO:**

Mark 6:37 (feed five thousand)

Helping the poor with a donation was a Passover custom, but the disciples took their criticism of this woman too far. The word for "*rebuked her harshly*" is ordinarily used to refer to a roar or the snort of a horse. They hated this woman's sacrifice, but Jesus jumps to her defense.

This woman irretrievably poured a family heirloom—the equivalent of someone's life savings—down the drain, just to achieve one beautiful moment of adoration for Jesus. Is he worth that kind of extravagant love to you?

> **Mark 14:6–9** "Leave her alone," said Jesus. "Why are you bothering her? She has done a beautiful thing to me. The poor you will always have with you, and you can help them any time you want. But you will not always have me. She did what she could. She poured perfume on my body beforehand to prepare for my burial. I tell you the truth, wherever the gospel is preached throughout the world, what she has done will also be told, in memory of her."

The Poor Versus The Beautiful

Jesus will soon pour out his precious blood for the sins of the world, and he is touched by the woman's similar gesture. She pours out her most costly possession. His words, *"She did what she could"* remind us of his words about the <u>widow</u> giving her fraction of a penny in the Temple: *"she [gave] all she had to live on."* Jesus deeply appreciates our sacrifices for him.

Look at all the things Jesus knows in advance. He knows he is about to die. He knows his message will be preached throughout the world, not just among Jews. He knows we will still be speaking of this woman today.

As it turned out, Jesus never was anointed with spices for burial, though that was the custom of his day. It was too late to anoint him on the afternoon he died, and an attempt to do it later failed (for a very good reason). Jesus seems to know this lady's perfume is the only anointing he will get.

Jesus' defense of the woman should not be taken as an expression of disrespect for poor people. I've heard Christians quote, "Oh well, 'the poor you will have with you always'" to justify neglecting the underprivileged. Remember that Jesus immediately said, *"and you can help them any time you want."* We <u>should assist</u> the poor. This story is an unusual circumstance; what made the woman's gift appropriate was the approaching hour of Jesus' death.

☞ **GO TO:**

Mark 12:44 (widow)

☞ **GO TO:**

Deuteronomy 15:7–11 (should assist)

KEEP IT REAL—Did the woman know that in Old Testament days this type of anointing signaled the inauguration of a new <u>king</u>? Maybe not. Did she know Jesus was about to die? Probably not. Did she give sacrificially to get fame? Certainly not. Clearly, she was motivated by love. Many times we feel the Holy Spirit encourage us to do things that don't seem to make much sense. We should listen to those promptings, and obey, giving our actions as a love sacrifice to Jesus. Like this woman, we have very little knowledge about how God will fit our actions into his intricate plans. Our smallest obedient gesture may have huge significance when viewed from above.

> **Mark 14:10–11** Then Judas Iscariot, one of the Twelve, went to the chief priests to betray Jesus to them. They were delighted to hear this and promised to give him money. So he watched for an opportunity to hand him over.

☞ **GO TO:**

2 Kings 9:1–13;
1 Samuel 10:1; 16:1,
12–13 (king)

Evil Men's Delight

Judas provided the one thing the powerful priests lacked: insider information on the comings and goings of Jesus. But how could he let himself do it? After spending years as Jesus' companion, after seeing Jesus defend the defenseless and heal the hopeless, how could Judas betray him to the hard-hearted, hypocritical temple leaders?

Jesus Christ, Superstar, among many modern works, tries to make Judas look like the good guy and God the bad guy. Some commentators ascribe noble motives to Judas—he thought Jesus was powerful enough to be the Messiah but was too shy, so he gave him a push . . . you know, just helping Jesus grow as a person. This heap of nonsense brings us to the Power Tool for this section: *study a character.*

Though the stained glass windows of many of our churches present Bible characters as two-dimensional icons with halos hovering over them (or is that a golden Frisbee?), they were actually living and complex people. The same things that motivate us, motivated them: fear, greed, lust, love of family, love of God, and so on. By gaining insight into them, we gain insight into ourselves. A marvelous way to peer into the heart of a Bible story is to find out everything you can about one particular character. Here we want to find out what motivated Judas, so we should look up every scripture reference on Judas. To get you started, here they are:

POWER TOOL

Study a character.

Shows Judas	Describes Judas
Matthew 26:14–16, 25	Matthew 10:4
Matthew 26:47–49	Mark 3:19
Matthew 27:3–5	Luke 6:16
Mark 14:10–11	John 6:71
Mark 14:44–46	John 13:2
Luke 22:1–6	Acts 1:15–19, 25
Luke 22:47–48	
John 12:4–6	
John 13:21–30	
John 18:1–5	

Check 'em out, and see what motivated Judas according to his friends and eyewitnesses. If you enjoy this form of study, a concordance would make it easier. Better still, most Bible study software enables you to type in a person's name and, in a split second, see a list of every verse that mentions the name. Seeing the Bible through a participant's eyes takes Scripture beyond abstract doctrine and makes it come alive.

Wrapping Up Mark's Sandwich

Mark wedges the beautiful worship of the nameless woman in between the conspiracy plans of Jesus' killers. What are we to make of this?

For one thing we see a stark contrast between the nameless woman's choices and Judas's choices. They both met Jesus personally; they reacted very differently. Modern commentators like to present Judas as a helpless pawn of God's will. Mark's sandwich shows Judas made a deliberate, intentional choice, while showing us the alternate choice he could have made.

Perhaps more importantly, Mark wants us to make a choice. His sandwich tells us, "Some people adore Jesus; some people despise him." The implicit question is, Which side are you on?

What Others are Saying:

Anne Graham Lotz: Your choice to either receive or reject the Lord Jesus Christ will determine where you spend eternity. You can: resist the choice, ignore the choice, put off making the choice, deny you have the choice, assume you have made the choice, close this book and forget about the choice, ridicule the choice, but *you are compelled to make a choice*! All of the above attitudes are actually indirect choices to reject. There is no middle ground. . . . Won't you make sure, right now without another moment passing, that you have truly received Him by faith and are a genuine child of God?[2]

PREPARED FOR DEPARTURE

> **Mark 14:12–16** On the first day of the Feast of Un-leavened Bread, when it was customary to sacrifice the Passover lamb, Jesus' disciples asked him, "Where do you want us to go and make preparations for you to eat the Passover?"
>
> So he sent two of his disciples, telling them, "Go into the city, and a man carrying a jar of water will meet you. Follow him. Say to the owner of the house he enters, 'The Teacher asks: Where is my guest room, where I may eat the Passover with my disciples?' He will show you a large upper room, furnished and ready. Make preparations for us there."
>
> The disciples left, went into the city and found things just as Jesus had told them. So they prepared the Pass-over.

And Just To Be Safe, Wear Your Bullet-Proof Yarmulke

Finding a dining room where thirteen people could eat the Pass-over meal should have been a routine, easy task, like when you call the local pizza place to book the banquet room for your soc-cer team. Instead, the disciples rent the room by meeting a man who is doing what was then woman's work—fetching water. They make the arrangements without mentioning Jesus' name, just as Jesus does not name the owner of the house.

All this is the cultural equivalent of spy movies in which the hero must look for a man wearing a green carnation, mumble, "The thrush flies at midnight," and listen for the counter-pass-word. The elaborate cloak-and-dagger process of getting the room shows Jesus understood dangerous people were seeking to kill him, but the Passover meal had to be eaten within Jerusalem's city walls, so he did what he could to accomplish this safely.

This passage also shows Jesus' foreknowledge. He knows ex-actly where to go, what to do, and what will happen. Mark wants us to know that when Jesus is arrested like a common criminal, he is not a mere victim. He is operating according to a preor-dained master plan, every step of the way.

KEY POINT

Though Jesus did not seek to hasten his death, he did die intentionally.

> **Mark 14:17–21** When evening came, Jesus arrived with the Twelve. While they were reclining at the table eating, he said, "I tell you the truth, one of you will betray me—one who is eating with me."
>
> They were saddened, and one by one they said to him, "Surely not I?"
>
> "It is one of the Twelve," he replied, "one who dips bread into the bowl with me. The Son of Man will go just as it is written about him. But woe to that man who betrays the Son of Man! It would be better for him if he had not been born."

Suddenly I'm Not Hungry

Normally, the Passover meal is festive, but part way through this one, Jesus tells the Twelve one of them is a traitor. *"They were saddened,"* the text says. Mark has charted the descent of the Twelve from eager, ready followers of Jesus to half-disillusioned, fearful wimps who wonder why they're here. When Jesus says *"one of you will betray me,"* every man in the room thinks the traitor could be himself.

THE WAYBACK MACHINE

The Passover meal was a time of special remembrance for a people who were the beneficiaries of God's special favor and who were bonded together because of it. In John's Gospel Jesus gives Judas a sop—a piece of bread dipped in the main dish from which all ate (see GWJN, page 188). It was a sign of friendship, which should have touched Judas's heart. In the midst of the warmth and intimacy of this Passover meal, Judas's crime stands out as unbelievably heartless. (For more about Judas, see GWLC2, pages 195–196.)

Jesus' reference to *"one who dips bread into the bowl with me"* evokes Psalm 41, which says in verse 9, *"Even my close friend, whom I trusted, he who shared my bread, has lifted up his heel against me."* King David wrote the psalm when seriously ill, sensing that his enemies hoped the illness would kill him. Psalm 41 ends with David assuring himself that God would vindicate him. Jesus knows God will vindicate him, which is why he expresses sorrow and pity for his betrayor.

Not only are Jesus' actions during his final days messianic actions. The way he performs these actions evokes overtones of the Messiah as Son of David.

> **Mark 14:22** While they were eating, Jesus took bread, gave thanks and broke it, and gave it to his disciples, saying, "Take it; this is my body."

The First Communion Meal Ever

One of the great traditions of the Passover meal is that the head of the family gives a *haggadah*—a running commentary on the symbolism of each food and ritual throughout the meal. These comments were reverently scripted, memorized, and passed down through the generations to keep the sacred meaning of Passover intact. According to tradition, at this point Jesus would have lifted up the **matzoh** and prayed, "Praise be Thou, O Lord our God, King of the Universe, who causes bread to come forth from the earth." This may be what Mark alludes to when he says, *"Jesus took bread, gave thanks and broke it."*

matzoh: flat, unleavened bread; resembles a cracker (pronounced MAHT-suh)

Traditionally, three matzoh were set before the leader; some rabbis thought they represented Abraham, Isaac, and Jacob. Many Christians think of them as representing the Father, the Son, and the Holy Spirit, because the leader was to break the middle one (representing the Son). Ancient Semites believed when a group of people partook of one loaf of bread, it created unity.

As Jesus broke the middle matzoh, he said, in effect, "This is me." Jews were to conduct the Passover meal without diverting from tradition, so it must have startled the Twelve when Jesus did this, essentially reinterpreting one of the symbols. In saying "this is me" and then "eat it," Jesus was showing his disciples that somehow, mysteriously, they would all participate in his death. In ways they could not know yet, Jesus' followers would be identified with the breaking of Jesus' body.

Andy Bond: Recalling that the second matzoh is symbolic of Jesus, it is important to realize that it is this matzoh that was broken, just as Jesus was broken on the cross. Modern matzoh is striped and pierced; in Isaiah 53:5 the Messiah is talked about as being "pierced for our transgressions" and that "with His stripes we are healed."[3]

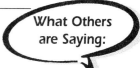

What Others are Saying:

> **Mark 14:23–26** Then he took the cup, gave thanks and offered it to them, and they all drank from it.
> "This is my blood of the covenant, which is poured out for many," he said to them. "I tell you the truth, I

> will not drink again of the fruit of the vine until that day when I drink it anew in the kingdom of God."
>
> When they had sung a hymn, they went out to the Mount of Olives.

A Promise Sealed With Blood

☞ **GO TO:**

Exodus 6:6–7
(fourfold promise)

The ritual Passover meal has four cups, associated with God's <u>fourfold promise</u> of redemption for the Jews: *"I will bring you out . . . I will free you from being slaves . . . I will redeem you with an outstretched arm . . . I will take you as my own people, and I will be your God."* Almost the entire meal passed between the breaking of bread and the third cup, the cup of redemption, which Jesus holds up now. Traditionally, the leader pronounced a prayer of thanksgiving that ended with these words: "May the All-merciful One make us worthy of the days of the Messiah and of the life of the world to come. He brings the salvation of his king. He shows covenant-faithfulness to his Anointed, to David and to his seed forever. He makes peace in his heavenly places. May he secure peace for us and for all Israel. And say you, Amen."

The prayer said over the "Messiah cup" (another name for the cup of redemption) included an unusual list of prophecies: the Messiah would make peace in heavenly places, bring salvation, and fulfill the covenant God had made with David. (God had promised a descendant of David would reign <u>forever</u>.) After everyone had drunk from this cup, Jesus adds, *"This is my blood of the covenant, which is poured out for many."* In other words, "the blood of my coming death fulfills the requirements of the <u>new covenant</u>, for everybody." Jesus' death would fulfill the prophecies of the Messiah cup.

☞ **GO TO:**

2 Samuel 7:12–17
(forever)

Jeremiah 31:31–34
(new covenant)

Psalms 116–118 (Hallel)

Jesus refuses to drink the fourth Passover cup, which was associated with God gathering and fellowshipping with his people. He is going to wait and drink it when all that it implies comes true—when God's kingdom age finally begins (see GWRV, pages 282–284).

Jesus' refusal to administer the final cup shortened the Passover meal. Normally celebrants sat around the table fellowshipping and reflecting on the works of God until midnight. This party *"sang a hymn"* and went out. Traditionally, Passover participants sang the <u>Hallel</u> psalms. "Hallel" comes from the Hebrew word meaning "praise." The leader sang the psalms, and the celebrants answered with a hallelujah. Know-

THE WAYBACK MACHINE

ing what was about to come, it must have encouraged Jesus to sing words like the following:

- *"For you, O Lord, have delivered my soul from death, my eyes from tears, my feet from stumbling, that I may walk before the Lord in the land of the living"* (Psalm 116:8–9).

- *"The Lord is with me; I will not be afraid. What can man do to me? The Lord is with me; he is my helper. I will look in triumph on my enemies. It is better to take refuge in the Lord than to trust in man"* (Psalm 118:6–8).

- *"The stone the builders rejected has become the capstone; the Lord has done this, and it is marvelous in our eyes. This is the day the Lord has made; let us rejoice and be glad in it. . . . O Lord, grant us success"* (Psalm 118:22–25).

What was this meal like for the pitiful disciples? First they find out one of them is a traitor; then Jesus strangely reinterprets the meaning of the matzoh; and then he tells them the wine they just drank is human blood. (Is that why Jesus waited until *after* they had drunk to introduce this new symbol?) He mystifies them with references to his coming death. Obviously, the meal made a huge impact on the Twelve, but they wouldn't understand its meaning until later.

Something to Ponder

Morna D. Hooker: No Jew could have regarded the drinking of blood with anything but horror, for the blood represented the life of an animal and belonged to the Lord. The blood of any sacrifice was poured out as an offering, and animals killed for human consumption must be drained of all blood before being eaten. . . . The final clause is couched in sacrificial language: the blood of Jesus is poured out, i.e., his life is offered up to God, for the sake of many. How his death benefits them is not explained . . . but in view of the Passover setting of the story, Mark may well have the Passover lamb in mind and so be thinking of the death of Jesus as the redemptive act which brings the new community of God's people into existence.[4]

What Others are Saying:

> **Mark 14:27–28** "You will all fall away," Jesus told them, "for it is written:
> "'I will strike the shepherd,
> and the sheep will be scattered.'
> But after I have risen, I will go ahead of you into Galilee."

Scandalized, Scattered, Schooled

☞ **GO TO:**

Mark 4:17 (before)

Zechariah 13:7 (quotes)

"You will all be *skandalizo*," Jesus told them. It's the Greek root from which we get "scandalized." Mark used it <u>before</u>, when describing how seed sown in rocky soil grows up briefly, but falls away. Likewise, the disciples will *"fall away"* in mere hours, when they see their shepherd about to be stricken.

Jesus knows all his chosen men will fall away, so why is he so calm? Perhaps it is in part because Jesus knows from his study of Scripture what will happen. When he says *"it is written,"* he then <u>quotes</u> the Old Testament prophet Zechariah. The circumstances in this chapter are strongly tied to Zechariah 9–14, as the following table shows. Though Jesus faces dire circumstances, Scripture tells him all is going according to God's plan, which means it will end well. Apparently Jesus was comforted by the reliability of the Bible, just as we can and should be.

Phrase or Event	Mark Reference	Zechariah Reference
My blood of the covenant	Mark 14:24	Zechariah 9:11
That day, the kingdom of God	Mark 14:25	Zechariah 14:4, 9
The Mount of Olives	Mark 14:26	Zechariah 14:4
Strike the shepherd	Mark 14:27	Zechariah 13:7
Restoration of the sheep	Mark 14:28	Zechariah 13:8–9

Jesus is certain the disciples will desert him. He is equally certain he will regather them. When Jesus says, *"after I have risen, I will go ahead of you into Galilee,"* he does not mean Jesus will race them to Galilee and get there first. It means that in Galilee, he will again lead them around and school them, just as he has in the past.

> **Mark 14:29–31** Peter declared, "Even if all fall away, I will not."
>
> "I tell you the truth," Jesus answered, "today—yes, tonight—before the rooster crows twice you yourself will disown me three times."
>
> But Peter insisted emphatically, "Even if I have to die with you, I will never disown you." And all the others said the same.

Maybe This Passage Has Two Roosters Crowing

Here are eleven men, each of whom inwardly feared he would betray Jesus and now swears to die on Jesus' behalf. Undoubtedly, they meant it when they said it. But when the moment comes, they won't be able to walk their talk. This is one more proof that Christianity doesn't depend on our ability to follow, but on Jesus' ability to lead.

Peter (who, by the way, is one of the most fascinating character studies in the Bible) tries to put himself above all the others. His misguided boasting almost amuses us; the one who told Jesus the Messiah wouldn't have to <u>suffer</u> now embraces the suffering not only for the Messiah, but for himself too. He is trying to learn, but I think Peter is saying the right thing mostly to look cool, not because he really understands what it means to be the servant of all. Peter probably thinks the *"even if I have to die with you"* part has a nice brave ring to it, but is not a choice he will actually have to make. Jesus gives it to him straight; Peter will face just such a decision in a matter of hours.

☞ **GO TO:**

Mark 8:31–33 (suffer)

PREPARING TO DIE

With this final prophetic warning, Jesus has done all he can to prepare the disciples for getting along without him. Knowing the horrendous trial to come, he now focuses on preparing his heart before God. As the clock passes midnight, Jesus enters the last day of his life (summarized in GWBI, page 204).

> **Mark 14:32–36** They went to a place called Gethsemane, and Jesus said to his disciples, "Sit here while I pray." He took Peter, James and John along with him, and he began to be deeply distressed and troubled. "My soul is overwhelmed with sorrow to the point of death," he said to them. "Stay here and keep watch."
>
> Going a little farther, he fell to the ground and prayed that if possible the hour might pass from him. *"Abba, Father,"* he said, "everything is possible for you. Take this cup from me. Yet not what I will, but what you will."

A Goblet Of Grief

Why is Jesus nearly dead from grief? His prayer tells us; he is sorry to face *"the cup."* In the chapter on Mark 11:1–25 we examined *"the cup"* in depth and learned that it is God's wrathful judgment. The man who never sinned is about to take upon himself everyone's sins. The man who spent every moment of his life in intimate harmony with the Father will, for the first time in eternity, be separated from God's holiness. It is not the physical torture of the cross that crushes Jesus' heart, but the certainty of breaking fellowship with the Father whom he knows so intimately, he calls him "abba"—daddy.

This is the moment when the full cost of his obedience becomes real and immediate to Jesus. Sometimes this chalice of death was <u>avoided</u> in the Old Testament, and so he prays for that possibility. Yet even in his darkest moment he insists on submitting to God's will.

☞ **GO TO:**

Isaiah 51:17–23
(avoided)

> **Mark 14:37–40** Then he returned to his disciples and found them sleeping. "Simon," he said to Peter, "are you asleep? Could you not keep watch for one hour? Watch and pray so that you will not fall into temptation. The spirit is willing, but the body is weak."
>
> Once more he went away and prayed the same thing. When he came back, he again found them sleeping, because their eyes were heavy. They did not know what to say to him.

You're Weaker Than You Think

Jesus finished Mark 13 by sternly warning his disciples to keep watch. Here they are, dozing on the job, dully unaware of the momentous events taking place right before their heavy lids. Peter had just sworn he would stand with Jesus even if nobody else did. Now, as Jesus points out to him, he can't stay on watch for even one hour.

While readers usually assume Jesus felt hurt because his buddies wouldn't pray with him, a detached reading of this passage suggests things may have been the other way around—that Jesus was worried about his friends, not himself. He already knew they were going to desert him. He already knew they didn't understand the necessity of his death. He undoubtedly knew better than to count on them; he had already had eight of them stay behind.

He didn't ask Peter, James, and John to pray with him; he told them to watch. When they fail, does Jesus say, "Come on, guys, I need your support right now"? No. He says, *"Watch and pray so that* you *will not fall into temptation."* (Temptation in Mark usually means pressure to be untrue to God.) I am simply stunned to see a man in the height of agony still selfless enough to keep checking on his vulnerable friends. For their part, the same three guys who did not know what to say during the transfiguration are equally tongue-tied now about their own uselessness.

Jesus says the spirit is willing, but what spirit is he talking about? It could be the human spirit, but more likely, it's the <u>Holy Spirit</u>.

☞ **GO TO:**

Psalm 51:11–12
(Holy Spirit)

> **Mark 14:41–42** Returning the third time, he said to them, "Are you still sleeping and resting? Enough! The hour has come. Look, the Son of Man is betrayed into the hands of sinners. Rise! Let us go! Here comes my betrayer!"

Slapping The Snooze Bar One Time Too Many

The "threepeat" of Jesus waking the disciples, only to find them sleeping, may foreshadow Peter's triple denial. The number three indicates how thoroughly they had let Jesus down. Jesus' question, *"Are you still sleeping?"* is not meant tenderly. He is rebuking them.

The word "Enough!" could also be translated, "It is settled" or "The account is closed." We don't know how long Jesus spent wrestling in prayer between visits to this narcoleptic trio, but at some point he reached inner resolution about facing his fate. He had prayed that *"if possible the hour might pass from him."* Now he says, "It is settled. The hour has come." With majestic courage and dignity, Jesus accepts his God-ordained fate so willingly that he heads *toward* his betrayer and, literally, a night from hell.

IT'S
GREEK
TO ME

KEEP IT REAL—Critics who have accused the Gospels of being made-up fairy tales have some hard things to explain in this chapter. No one trying to fabricate a new religion would show disciples that were so petty, so clueless, so inept. Mark (and Peter) have kept their portrayals very honest and authentic.

• Mark 14:6. *"Leave her alone,"* said Jesus. . . . *"She has done a beautiful thing to me."* The disciples thought the woman had done something stupid, but Jesus declared her sacrificial deed beautiful. Often I find myself equally clueless about what Jesus does and doesn't like. *I want to love what you love, and hate what you hate, Lord. Help me to spend time with you so that I share your sensibilities, not the world's.*

• Mark 14:28, 38. Jesus never stopped caring about and looking out for his followers even when he knew they were about to act like cowardly oath-breakers. Seeing the specific examples here helps me get a grip on the abstract concept that God loves me unconditionally. *Father, I rejoice that you choose to see me not as I am, but as I will be in heaven!*

Study Questions

1. What made the woman's outrageously expensive gift of nard appropriate?
2. The priests and elders were powerful people; why didn't they just kill Jesus? Who was Jesus' betrayer? What did the betrayer provide that the priests needed?
3. Cite four examples where Mark displays Jesus' foreknowledge of events.
4. What did Jesus say the Passover bread represented? What did the Passover wine represent?
5. Jesus said, *"My soul is overwhelmed with sorrow to the point of death."* Why was that so?

CHAPTER WRAP-UP

- Mark 14 begins with a Markan sandwich that contrasts evil men conspiring to kill Jesus with a woman who loved Jesus deeply. It implies that your own opinion of Jesus must fall in one camp or the other. (Mark 14:1–10)

- The first communion meal was actually a Passover meal. Jesus followed the traditional feast, except he reinterpreted the matzoh as a symbol for his own body. Of the four Passover cups of wine, he called the third one *"my blood of the covenant, which is poured out for many"* and refused to drink the fourth cup until the kingdom of God fully reigns. (Mark 14:12–26)

- Jesus continued loving and caring for his disciples even when he knew they would desert him. (Mark 14:27–31)

- Jesus prayed he wouldn't have to face God's wrath because there was an Old Testament precedent that sometimes *"the cup"* could be removed. He never wavered, however, from submitting his will to God's will. Once he knew for certain there was no escaping the cross, he gave himself to it willingly. (Mark 14:32–37)

MARK 14:43–15:15
PRISONER JESUS

Let's Get Started

The influential Sanhedrin has set its trap, thanks to insider information from the greedy traitor, Judas. Their goal is to assassinate Jesus quietly. Their method is to find Jesus guilty of a capital felony so that they can kill him "legally." Throwing dirt and shame all over his reputation should head off any popular move to call him a martyr. Their problem is that because they rule under the Roman government, they are not authorized to kill anyone. Ever. So, how can they use the legal system to get Jesus executed?

It won't be easy, but when it comes to working the system, no one matches the temple leaders. They will have to find Jesus guilty of a crime worthy of death under their own laws, then turn him over to the Romans to do the wet work. The Roman authorities, however, think the Jewish religion is amusing nonsense. They might not agree to execute a Jewish **blasphemer**, yet the Jewish high priest has a strategy for dealing with this too.

blasphemer: one who insults or disdains God

Normally the victim of all this governmental scheming and injustice would panic, but Jesus is no normal victim. He knows the Sanhedrin's most devious calculations only work as God allows. Like a little paper boat on the mighty current of God's will, Jesus lets events carry him to his destiny. He does not resist; he does not talk back. All the same, Jesus is in for a long, painful night.

JESUS GETS BUSTED

> **Mark 14:43–46** Just as he was speaking, Judas, one of the Twelve, appeared. With him was a crowd armed with swords and clubs, sent from the chief priests, the teachers of the law, and the elders.
>
> Now the betrayer had arranged a signal with them: "The one I kiss is the man; arrest him and lead him away under guard." Going at once to Jesus, Judas said, "Rabbi!" and kissed him. The men seized Jesus and arrested him.

The Most Infamous Kiss In History

In our era of mass media, it's hard for us to remember what life was like without television, billboards, and national magazines. Today, a miracle-worker like Jesus would appear in everything from *Weekly World News* to *Scientific American*, with accompanying photos. Back then, anyone who had not attended one of Jesus' lectures wouldn't know what he looked like. Telling the temple police, "Well, he's a Jewish fellow with long hair and a beard" wouldn't narrow things down much. Judas provided not only the timing for the most secluded arrest possible; he also identified Jesus by a prearranged signal.

THE WAYBACK MACHINE

☞ **GO TO:**

Luke 7:38 (kissed)

IT'S
GREEK
TO ME

Americans pucker up primarily as a sign of affection, but other cultures have many additional uses for a kiss. In Jesus' culture a kiss could signify respect. Slaves kissed their masters' feet to show deep esteem; disciples sometimes kissed the hem of their teacher's garment to display their devotion and commitment (a practice that continues to this day among Christians in the Orthodox church). A kiss on the face signified friendship and personal affection. Students commonly offered a kiss to their rabbi.

Judas's kiss is *kataphileo*, which means he <u>kissed</u> Jesus earnestly, intensively, or repeatedly. In other words Judas displayed extraordinary affection for Jesus during the moment of betrayal. Was Judas already regretting his deed? Or was he simply making sure the police knew whom to arrest in the darkness under the olive trees of Gethsemane? Either way, using the kiss as a signal was intended to keep everything friendly until the last possible moment.

Mark includes a list of guys who sent the arrest force as well as a description of how they're armed to let us know this is a squad of temple police. Ignorant of Jesus' teachings on peace and servanthood, these troops are prepared to take on a large contingent of violent rebels—a fact that must have intimidated the disciples as they realized their own puny might compared to the resources of the Sanhedrin.

John MacArthur: Judas evidently knew no shame. He could have chosen any signal for identifying Christ to his fellow conspirators. He deliberately chose one that compounded his own guilt with the most diabolical kind of hypocrisy. He seems to have deliberately drawn out his kissing in order to detain Jesus as long as possible, to be sure that the soldiers had time to apprehend Him.[1]

> **Mark 14:47–50** Then one of those standing near drew his sword and struck the servant of the high priest, cutting off his ear.
>
> "Am I leading a rebellion," said Jesus, "that you have come out with swords and clubs to capture me? Every day I was with you, teaching in the temple courts, and you did not arrest me. But the Scriptures must be fulfilled." Then everyone deserted him and fled.

The Shortest Battle In History

Chaos starts to break out in the dark garden, but Jesus heads it off. His mild objection to the temple squad's method for arresting him is as close as he ever gets to protesting the injustice he is about to endure. With his observation that *"the Scriptures must be fulfilled,"* he surrenders—not only to the temple police, but to the Father's will.

The disciple's attempt at armed <u>resistance</u> seems clumsy and unfocused. The ambivalent disciples don't seem to know how they should act or even how they *want* to act. If Jesus had tried to rally them together, they may have fought more. But when he gives in, alluding to the Zechariah passage we discussed in the last chapter, their nerve fails them utterly. They dash in all directions like cockroaches when the light snaps on.

☞ **GO TO:**

John 18:10–11
(resistance)

> **Mark 14:51–52** A young man, wearing nothing but a linen garment, was following Jesus. When they seized him, he fled naked, leaving his garment behind.

Mark's Gratuitous Nude Scene

For centuries commentators have indulged their imaginations in trying to explain this mysterious incident that only Mark records. Early church fathers believed the *"young man"* (a term for a man between the ages of twenty-four and forty) was Mark himself. Mark did live in <u>Jerusalem</u>, but otherwise we're not sure why second-century Christians assumed this.

A theory I enjoy as much for its drama as for its plausibility is related to the possibility that the Last Supper was held in Mark's home. Following this theory, Judas leads the arrest party first to Mark's house but arrives too late. Jesus and the disciples have already left, and Mark is in his pajamas, ready for sleep. Mark sees what Judas and his gang are up to, so he tries to run ahead of them and warn Jesus in Gethsemane, but he arrives too late.

Mark records almost nothing without some theological purpose. Another theory of why these two verses exist arises from studying the term *"young man."* In the **Jewish Apocrypha**, the Septuagint, and the writings of Josephus, the term refers to exceptionally strong, valiant, faithful, and wise men. Mark may have recorded this individual's plight to show the complete breakdown of support for Jesus; even the mighty ran like wimps. This thought evokes an Old Testament <u>reference</u> that describes a day of judgment so terrible that *"'even the bravest warriors will flee naked on that day,' declares the LORD."*

☞ **GO TO:**

Acts 12:12 (Jerusalem)

IT'S
GREEK
TO ME

Jewish Apocrypha: Jewish teachings that were not in the Old Testament

☞ **GO TO:**

Amos 2:16 (reference)

SUPREME INJUSTICE
FROM THE SUPREME COURT

> **Mark 14:53–54** They took Jesus to the high priest, and all the chief priests, elders and teachers of the law came together. Peter followed him at a distance, right into the courtyard of the high priest. There he sat with the guards and warmed himself at the fire.

Wily Trial While Denials Compile

Mark begins his account of Jesus' trial with the Sanhedrin meeting at Caiaphas's house. The Sanhedrin was not supposed to meet at night, nor on a feast day (the day of Passover was considered a feast day). They probably used a private venue because they didn't want the public to know they were violating Jewish law.

The other Gospels indicate the high priest <u>Caiaphas</u> was behind almost all temple resistance against Jesus. He hired Judas and was a major player in this fake trial. Caiaphas was one wily customer. He managed to hang on to the office of high priest for nineteen turbulent years (A.D. 18–37) when the average term was four.

☞ **GO TO:**

John 18:14 (Caiaphas)

Mark seems to interrupt himself in this passage by mentioning Peter, but actually he's using another of his skillful literary devices. This equivalent of cinematic crosscutting tells us what Peter does several verses later takes place at the same time as this trial, not after it. Mark's masterful construction deepens the heartache we feel for Jesus. He is on trial for his life, and in that very same moment his most ardent disciple is swearing he doesn't know Jesus. In fact, Peter is warming himself at the fire of Jesus' most committed enemy.

Translation Elation

In much of this "Passion" section, Mark intends for us to feel the emotional impact of the Sanhedrin's hypocrisy, Peter's calamity, the soldiers' cruelty, and Jesus' dignity. An excellent way for you to grasp it emotionally is to use this chapter's Power Tool: *reread the passage in a translation you aren't familiar with.*

POWER TOOL

Reread the passage in an unfamiliar translation.

To get the emotional impact of a passage, I like to read *The Message,* a paraphrase of the Bible written by Eugene Peterson. The *New Living Translation* also does a good job of conveying a passage's underlying emotion. If I want to slow myself down to consider what I'm reading more closely, I switch to the difficult but beautiful King James Version. If you're already used to those, you might try the highly literal, word-for-word rendering of the New American Standard Bible. Mark does strange and interesting things with Greek verbs, shifting back and forth from past to present tense to add immediacy. Instead of writing, "They came to a place called Gethsemane, and Jesus took Peter, James, and John with him," Mark shifts into, "They come to a place called Gethsemane, and Jesus takes Peter, James, and John with him." Only the NASB notes these changes of tense.

There are too many fine translations for me to list more than the few examples above. Pick any good translation (or ask your pastor for advice) and reread familiar passages for fresh insight into the Word.

> **Mark 14:55–61a** The chief priests and the whole Sanhedrin were looking for evidence against Jesus so that they could put him to death, but they did not find any. Many testified falsely against him, but their statements did not agree.
>
> Then some stood up and gave this false testimony against him: "We heard him say, 'I will destroy this manmade temple and in three days will build another, not made by man.'" Yet even then their testimony did not agree.
>
> Then the high priest stood up before them and asked Jesus, "Are you not going to answer? What is this testimony that these men are bringing against you?" But Jesus remained silent and gave no answer.

Kangaroo Court

Mark tells us bluntly that this court didn't convene to weigh evidence impartially. It was a kangaroo court, held specifically to find a way to kill Jesus. However, after brilliantly orchestrating the capture of Jesus, Caiaphas mishandles the trial.

In first-century Jewish law, witnesses functioned both as witnesses and as prosecutors of the accused. Each witness told his story apart from the other witnesses. If the accounts of two witnesses agreed, the Sanhedrin could convict, but the two accounts had to agree down to the most trivial details. Only now does Caiaphas discover the problem with arresting an innocent man; it's difficult to find two people who lie alike.

Jewish law required the accused to respond to the witnesses. If someone stood in court and spun a long story about all the crimes you allegedly committed, wouldn't you leap at the chance to stick up for yourself? Not Jesus. He knows how this trial will end, regardless of what he says, so he says nothing.

This simple deed hinders the trial. The evidence doesn't add up to anything, and the defendant hasn't said anything the Sanhedrin can pounce on, so Caiaphas is stuck. He takes charge of interrogating the witness, hoping to break the logjam, but his first effort gains nothing.

KEY POINT

In trying innocent Jesus as a lawbreaker, the Sanhedrin broke many of its own laws.

GOD'S WORD FOR THE BIBLICALLY-INEPT

What Others are Saying:

Larry W. Hurtado: Literally, "many gave false witness," alluding to Exodus 20:16, the commandment against bearing false witness. Here the witnesses are themselves shown to be breaking the OT law.[2]

> **Mark 14:61b–62** Again the high priest asked him, "Are you the Christ, the Son of the Blessed One?"
>
> "I am," said Jesus. "And you will see the Son of Man sitting at the right hand of the Mighty One and coming on the clouds of heaven."

End Of The Clark Kent Savior

Caiaphas hates what Jesus has been doing, but he has studied the Galilean well enough to know what Jesus thinks of himself. He asks a more direct question. What Caiaphas wants is for Jesus to admit being Messiah, so the Sanhedrin can have him killed. The phrasing of the high priest's question piously sidesteps any mention of God, which is ironic when you consider Caiaphas is scheming to kill an innocent man.

The question is posed, and now Jesus is the only one who can help the Sanhedrin win their case against him. If he denies being Messiah, he can save his life. But at last, after years of holding back and keeping his real identity a secret, Jesus comes out with a straight answer: *"I am."* Mark opened his Gospel saying Jesus is the Son of God, but in its context this moment is one of fantastic revelation.

Judaism expected the Messiah to arrive with strong credentials demonstrating his identity, but Jesus has no proof of his claim. To most Jews, the idea of Messiah standing helpless before his foes was unthinkable. To the contrary, if a man stood helpless before his enemies, this proved he was not the Messiah. The rest of Jesus' response is a combination of Old Testament <u>descriptions</u> about the Messiah, which addresses Caiaphas's misconceptions. He says, in effect, "I won't prove who I am right now, but in the future you'll get more proof than you bargained for."

☞ GO TO:

Psalm 110:1; Daniel 7:3; Isaiah 52:8 (descriptions)

What Others are Saying:

Anne Graham Lotz: Every person waited breathlessly to hear how He would answer the bottom-line, no-holds-barred question. . . . Knowing with absolute clarity that His answer would give His accusers the charge they had been searching for . . . Jesus, Who had stood silently through the verbal flogging, answered. And His answer shook the world to its foundation: "Yes."[3]

> **Mark 14:63–65** The high priest tore his clothes. "Why do we need any more witnesses?" he asked. "You have heard the blasphemy. What do you think?"
>
> They all condemned him as worthy of death. Then some began to spit at him; they blindfolded him, struck him with their fists, and said, "Prophesy!" And the guards took him and beat him.

Jesus Wins One For The Prosecution

☞ **GO TO:**

Genesis 37:34; Joshua 7:6; Esther 4:1 (grief)

Leviticus 24:13–16 (blasphemy)

Isaiah 11:2–4 (passage)

Caiaphas tore his clothes (the traditional gesture of excessive grief) to dramatize how outrageous it was for Jesus to claim a position equal to God. Caiaphas accuses Jesus of blasphemy, but really Caiaphas is the one blaspheming because he is condemning the Son of God.

The Sanhedrin thinks it's okay to abuse Jesus physically because that was their culture's way of punishing criminals. They blindfold Jesus and beat him. Because they had misinterpreted a Scripture passage, they think the Messiah should be able to recognize people by smell. The Sanhedrin members thought they were proving further that Jesus was not the Messiah because he failed to identify who hit him.

PETER LEARNS THE COLD HARD TRUTH

> **Mark 14:66–68** While Peter was below in the courtyard, one of the servant girls of the high priest came by. When she saw Peter warming himself, she looked closely at him.
>
> "You also were with that Nazarene, Jesus," she said.
>
> But he denied it. "I don't know or understand what you're talking about," he said, and went out into the entryway.

Peter Peters Out

Mark left a narrative thread hanging in verse 54, showing Peter's torn heart. He had fled Gethsemane, but some magnetic force drew him back toward Jesus. Now Mark takes up the thread again.

Peter, a country fisherman in the big city, finds it impossible to blend in with the classy household of Caiaphas, so why is he here at all? Peter's love for the friend he failed drew him to this place.

He's waiting for some hint of what's happened to Jesus, but fear keeps him jumpy and ready to flee again.

As Jesus courageously faces the questions of the most powerful Jews in Israel, tense Peter collapses before the questions of a powerless servant girl. He lies to her about knowing Jesus and tries to escape her searching stare.

IT'S
GREEK
TO ME

In Greek, Peter's denial reads, "I do not know what you are saying." This was a common way within rabbinical law to make a formal, legal denial. Sadly, Peter's first denial of Christ is thorough and emphatic.

> **Mark 14:69–72** When the servant girl saw him there, she said again to those standing around, "This fellow is one of them." Again he denied it.
>
> After a little while, those standing near said to Peter, "Surely you are one of them, for you are a Galilean."
>
> He began to call down curses on himself, and he swore to them, "I don't know this man you're talking about."
>
> Immediately the rooster crowed the second time. Then Peter remembered the word Jesus had spoken to him: "Before the rooster crows twice you will disown me three times." And he broke down and wept.

Cue The Rooster

Peter's attempt to get away from the alert servant girl proves useless. When she encounters him again, she not only asks the same pointed questions; she involves other household servants. Peter denies Jesus for the second time.

Leaving now would expose him as a liar. He tries to bluff his way through, hanging out and conversing with the others, but his <u>country accent</u> blows his cover. Someone puts two and two together, thinking, "What is a hick from Galilee doing in Jerusalem, unless he's related to the hick from Galilee standing trial inside?" Confidently, this person asserts, *"Surely you are one of them."* Peter panics, and reinforces his denial with curses.

☞ **GO TO:**

Matthew 26:73
(country accent)

While the NIV renders the text, *"He began to call down curses on himself,"* the statement is left without an object in the Greek. In other words, the text doesn't specify whom Peter was cursing: himself, or his audience. He might have said,

IT'S
GREEK
TO ME

"May lightning strike me if I'm lying!" or he might have said "You're fools if you believe her!"

In the middle of his short-lived acting career, Peter hears the rooster crow for the second time (which, incidentally, puts the time between 1:30 and 3:00 in the morning by Roman reckoning). The realization of what he's done shoots through him like a rush of ice water, and Peter learns the cold hard truth; he is nowhere near the man he said he would be. He has just failed the best friend he ever had. There is no harder knowledge than self-knowledge, and Peter bursts into tears. Was he crying at his own failure? Or was he crying because Jesus already told him this would happen, yet continued to love him?

Something to Ponder

Mark stops the story here, but obviously Peter's behavior told the servants and guards that one of Jesus' followers stood before them. What did they do about it? Apparently nothing, because Peter remained a free man. This means there had been no real need to lie about knowing Jesus. Judas betrayed Jesus for money; Peter did it for nothing.

What Others are Saying:

John MacArthur: All the good intentions in the world do not equal real virtue. . . . Peter's braggadocio proved only his folly, not his faithfulness. Genuine allegiance to Christ is best shown by being faithful under fire from the enemies of the gospel, not by a lot of swaggering, blustering words spoken to one's fellow believers.[4]

ONE GOVERNOR, TWO "SONS OF THE FATHER"

> **Mark 15:1–5** Very early in the morning, the chief priests, with the elders, the teachers of the law and the whole Sanhedrin, reached a decision. They bound Jesus, led him away and handed him over to Pilate.
>
> "Are you the king of the Jews?" asked Pilate.
>
> "Yes, it is as you say," Jesus replied.
>
> The chief priests accused him of many things. So again Pilate asked him, "Aren't you going to answer? See how many things they are accusing you of."
>
> But Jesus still made no reply, and Pilate was amazed.

Accused And Silent

The Sanhedrin stayed up all night framing Jesus, knowing the Roman bureaucrats began their work at dawn to take most of the day off. To ensure Jesus' speedy execution, they had to be first in line at the governor's residence, before Pilate's schedule filled up. They took Jesus to the **praetorium** *"very early in the morning."*

The march across town, from Caiaphas to Pilate, also marches Jesus from Jewish law into completely different Roman laws. The Sanhedrin have convicted Jesus of blaspheming, but as far as the Romans are concerned, blasphemy isn't a crime. Recognizing this, the Sanhedrin secularize the term "Messiah" into "king of the Jews"—a term no Roman governor could ignore. This changes the accusation against Jesus from the religious crime of blasphemy to the political crime of high treason. Ironically, the Jews who have condemned Jesus for *failing* to be Messiah now want Rome to condemn him for *being* Messiah. But first they have to get past Pilate.

From A.D. 26 to 35, Pontius Pilate ruled the region as its prefect. Ranking just beneath the Roman senators, a prefect governed small areas that required careful supervision. They functioned like troubleshooters for the Roman government, dispatched to handle rowdy regions. Though they had little property and a small sphere of influence, within their regions they had wide latitude. Compared to the Sanhedrin's cumbersome consensus method, prefects handled criminal proceedings with remarkable efficiency. The prefect heard all the evidence and asked questions until he felt he had heard the matter thoroughly. He then declared his conclusion and the sentence, and the sentence was carried out instantly.

History records Pilate despised the Jews and governed them harshly. Once he grabbed some temple money to pay for a new city aqueduct, then refused to hear protests from the temple leaders. He was shrewd enough to see that while Jesus had not committed a crime against Rome, he had somehow provoked the anger of the Sanhedrin. His attempts to release Jesus probably came not from sympathy, but from a desire to frustrate the Sanhedrin and remind them who was boss.

When asked *"Are you the king of the Jews?"* Jesus responded with a phrase that is difficult to translate. The NIV translates it, *"Yes, it is as you say,"* but such a clear admission would

☞ **GO TO:**

Mark 15:16 (praetorium)

praetorium: *reinforced, fortress-like palace*

THE WAYBACK MACHINE

IT'S **GREEK** TO ME

have ended the trial instantly. Its meaning was closer to, "If you say so," or "Whatever you say."

Jesus was not being sullen, like a teenager rolling her eyes and saying, "Whatever!" He was hinting at the huge difference between what Pilate meant by the phrase "king of the Jews" and what Jesus meant by it. The other Gospels provide a lot of <u>explanation</u> that Mark omits. Mark is focused on telling the essentials—the parts that will help readers understand why Jesus' death buys salvation for every person.

☞ **GO TO:**

John 18:33–38
(explanation)

Remember
This . . .

Mark didn't flinch a bit in chapter 14 when he described how the Jews orchestrated Jesus' murder. Because of this, some have called Mark anti-Semitic in portraying the Jews as Christ-killers. Such an accusation distorts Mark's point entirely. In chapter 15 Gentiles get the same unvarnished treatment, and through Pilate are equally guilty. To Mark, who was probably Jewish himself, the blame for Jesus' death was not a Jew vs. Gentile issue. If you could ask Mark who killed Jesus, he would look you in the eye and say, "I did. He was crucified because of my sin." Mark's message is that the blame for Jesus' murder extends to anyone who has fallen short of perfection.

What Others
are Saying:

John MacArthur: Pilate was in a serious political predicament with Christ on trial before him. He had no legitimate grounds on which to execute Jesus, and yet he could not afford to anger the Jewish leaders over an issue they quite clearly regarded as urgent. . . . Pilate . . . didn't need any more bad press going back to Rome.[5]

> **Mark 15:6–7** Now it was the custom at the Feast to release a prisoner whom the people requested. A man called Barabbas was in prison with the insurrectionists who had committed murder in the uprising.

One Man's Murderer Is Another Man's Freedom Fighter

Barabbas was a worthless thief and cutthroat, right? Actually, that's pretty unlikely, given his name and the technical term Mark uses to describe him.

"Bar Abba" means "son of the father," a name commonly taken

by rabbis. He is in prison as a *lestai*, a term for religious guerrilla fighters in league with the Zealots. Many of the *lestas* were former Pharisees who had grown so radical that they turned to violence to help purify the land. They sometimes resorted to banditry to finance their revolution, making them a strange cross between a Pharisee militia and a Robin Hood–style band of thieves. If Barabbas had killed somebody, it would have been "murder" to the Romans, but to the Jews it would have been a blow for freedom against tyrannical oppressors. In other words, Barabbas was probably about the same kind of murderer as Ethan Allen or George Washington.

Mark mentions him here to set the stage for what comes next.

> **Mark 15:8–15** The crowd came up and asked Pilate to do for them what he usually did.
>
> "Do you want me to release to you the king of the Jews?" asked Pilate, knowing it was out of envy that the chief priests had handed Jesus over to him. But the chief priests stirred up the crowd to have Pilate release Barabbas instead.
>
> "What shall I do, then, with the one you call the king of the Jews?" Pilate asked them.
>
> "Crucify him!" they shouted.
>
> "Why? What crime has he committed?" asked Pilate. But they shouted all the louder, "Crucify him!"
>
> Wanting to satisfy the crowd, Pilate released Barabbas to them. He had Jesus flogged, and handed him over to be crucified.

"Son Of The Father" Or Son Of God?

Pilate had a custom of releasing one Jewish prisoner at Passover. Trying to ruin the Sanhedrin's plans while pretending to serve the people, Pilate offers to free Jesus.

The temple leaders have anticipated this strategy and have prepared the crowd to demand freedom for Barabbas instead. It wouldn't have been hard; the Jews hated Pilate as much as he hated them, so as soon as they saw Pilate wanted to release Jesus, most of them would have wanted to release anyone else. As a freedom-fighter rabbi, Barabbas probably had his own political connections—the most likely reason his name floated to the top of the "release" list.

KEY POINT

God used the complex politics between the Jews and the Romans to work out his plan for Jesus.

THE WAYBACK MACHINE

☞ **GO TO:**

Deuteronomy 21:23;
Galatians 3:13
(cursed by God)

**Something
to Ponder**

THE WAYBACK MACHINE

What Others
are Saying:

Under Roman rule, a man convicted of treason could be punished in one of three ways: he could be given to wild animals in the arena; he could be banished to an island, where he would find no rabble to rouse; or he could be crucified. The hateful temple leaders spurred the crowd to demand the harshest of these punishments. They wanted to make certain Jesus died in a way they could verify. Plus, they believed any person crucified was <u>cursed by God</u>. This manner of death would be one more way of "proving" to the populace that Jesus couldn't have been the Messiah.

Caiaphas and his posse wanted Jesus killed because they felt his teaching would undermine the Temple. But by supporting Barabbas and the Zealots they contributed to a program of violence that forty years later provoked the Romans to destroy the Temple. When we cast aside God's rules because they seem to get in the way of what needs doing, we rarely foresee the consequences of what we're really choosing.

Flogging was a normal preliminary to crucifixion, and it was no mere spanking. If you have a weak stomach, brace yourself. I'm going into detail here, so you'll understand what Jesus' love drove him to endure for you and me.

The flogging whip was a leather cat-o'-nine-tails with sharp bits of bone, lead, bronze, or stone knotted into the lashes. The victim was typically doubled over a waist-high pole, but could be thrown to the ground. With each stroke, the separate lashes struck not only the victim's back, but wrapped around his ribs and stomach. On the backstroke, the sharp thongs ripped the flesh to ribbons, often leaving the victim's guts exposed. Roman law did not specify a maximum number of strokes, so many times the flogging itself proved fatal.

Max Lucado: They scourged Jesus. The legionnaire's . . . goal was singular: Beat the accused within an inch of death and then stop. . . . A centurion monitored the prisoner's status. No doubt Jesus was near death when his hands were untied and he slumped to the ground.[6]

KEEP IT REAL—Mark 14:50. Surely this is one of the most heartbreaking verses in Scripture: *"Then everyone deserted him and fled."* Every time I read it, everything inside me cries, "No!" How would history have been rewritten if some of the disciples had stayed true? *I don't know, Lord, but I never want to see you abandoned again. Help me stick with you no matter how dangerous it looks.*

• Mark 14:60–61; 15:3–5. Never has any man's silence been more moving and impressive. Jesus never insulted those who insulted him. Before Pilate, he protected the reputation of his fellow Jews even as those Jews lobbied for his death. *Jesus, as I stay focused on you as my example, I know you'll build that same kind of grace under pressure in me.*

Study Questions

1. How and why did Judas kiss Jesus?
2. Name three things that were wrong about the Sanhedrin's trial of Jesus, according to Jewish law.
3. Who was the key witness whose testimony sealed Jesus' death?
4. In what ways did Peter set himself up for failure as a follower of Jesus?
5. How did Jesus defend himself during both his Jewish trial and his Roman trial?

CHAPTER WRAP-UP

- Jesus was arrested when Judas, a traitor from the Twelve, identified Jesus to the temple soldiers by kissing him. Just as Jesus had predicted, all his disciples abandoned him and ran for their lives. (Mark 14:43–52)

- In an illegal midnight trial, Caiaphas and the Sanhedrin were unable to frame Jesus, due to inept witnesses and Jesus' silence. When asked directly if he was the Messiah, Jesus admitted it, thus helping Caiaphas convict him. But Caiaphas was the one committing blasphemy. (Mark 14:53–65)

- To his shame and sorrow, Peter denied being one of the Twelve three times before the rooster crowed twice, just as Jesus had told him he would. (Mark 14:66–72)

- Pilate could tell Jesus was innocent of treason, but allowed him to be crucified because Pilate couldn't afford to anger the Sanhedrin and the Jerusalem Passover crowds. (Mark 15:1–15)

MARK 15:16–41
SCAPEGOAT JESUS

CHAPTER HIGHLIGHTS

- Soldiers Mock Jesus
- The Crucifixion
- The Death of Jesus

Let's Get Started

This chapter is not easy reading, because the next part of Mark is not easy reading. In fact, you may have noticed Mark generally isn't interested in being "easy." He's more interested in whacking you upside the head and hollering, "Look! God did this for you! What are you gonna do about it?"

Reading what Jesus suffered is nowhere near as dreadful as going through it. The least we can do is take a good, hard look, and then let our hearts fill with awe at what our Savior put himself through to ransom us.

MILITARY HUMOR: AN OXYMORON

Mark 15:16–20 The soldiers led Jesus away into the palace (that is, the Praetorium) and called together the whole company of soldiers. They put a purple robe on him, then twisted together a crown of thorns and set it on him. And they began to call out to him, "Hail, king of the Jews!" Again and again they struck him on the head with a staff and spit on him. Falling on their knees, they paid homage to him. And when they had mocked him, they took off the purple robe and put his own clothes on him. Then they led him out to crucify him.

No-Brow Political Humor, Circa A.D. 30

If tasteful, intelligent humor is highbrow and dopey sit-coms with lots of jokes about bodily functions are lowbrow, then the crude humor of the soldiers is no-brow—completely based on cruelty.

Mark says the soldiers *"called together the whole company."* The term refers to a cohort, which numbered five or six hundred men. Even if those on active duty couldn't take time for a joke, this racist skit took place in front of at least two hundred men, probably double that. Here's what they did:

- *"Put a purple robe on him."* This was typically a garment worn only by royalty. They might have borrowed one of the faded scarlet cloaks of the centurions.
- *"Twisted together a crown of thorns and set it on him."* The jokester who came up with this probably got lots of pats on the back. Roman coinage showed Tiberius Caesar with a wreath of radiant light emanating from his head, implying his glory. The wreath of thorns would have been interpreted as a visual pun, with some of the thorns pointing out like Caesar's rays of light, implying that the glory of the "Jewish Caesar" was far inferior.
- *"They began to call out to him, 'Hail, king of the Jews!'"* Of course they did it sarcastically, to say this pathetic, broken figure is the best the Jews can muster.
- *"They struck him on the head with a staff."* To complete his royal ensemble, the soldiers gave Jesus a crude semblance of a <u>scepter</u>. When they bashed his head with it, they drove the thorns deeper into his scalp.
- *"They . . . spit on him."* This was meant to break Jesus' spirit.
- *"They took off the purple robe and put his own clothes on him."* Depending on how long they mistreated Jesus, the fabric of the purple robe would have soaked into his scourge wounds. Ripping the robe off him would reopen all his wounds.

All through the description of Jesus' crucifixion and death, you can find allusions to Psalm 22 and Isaiah 53. The passage above reminds me of Psalm 22:6, *"But I am a worm and not a man, scorned by men and despised by the people."* Jesus' silence before his abusers evokes Isaiah 53:7: *"He was oppressed and afflicted, yet he did not open his mouth; he was led like a lamb to the slaughter, and as a sheep before her shearers*

☞ **GO TO:**

Matthew 27:29
(scepter)

Something to Ponder

GOD'S WORD FOR THE BIBLICALLY-INEPT

is silent, so he did not open his mouth." Before you proceed in Mark, take a moment to read those two passages about the suffering of the Messiah. Then see if you can count the references Jesus fulfilled.

Max Lucado: Spitting isn't intended to hurt the body—it can't. Spitting is intended to degrade the soul, and it does. What were the soldiers doing? Were they not elevating themselves at the expense of another? They felt big by making Christ look small. . . . Allow the spit of the soldiers to symbolize the filth in our hearts. And then observe what Jesus does with our filth. He carries it to the cross.[1]

What Others are Saying:

THE BRUTAL HUMILIATION OF JESUS

> **Mark 15:21–24** A certain man from Cyrene, Simon, the father of Alexander and Rufus, was passing by on his way in from the country, and they forced him to carry the cross. They brought Jesus to the place called Golgotha (which means The Place of the Skull). Then they offered him wine mixed with myrrh, but he did not take it. And they crucified him. Dividing up his clothes, they cast lots to see what each would get.

The Road To Skull Hill

The Romans had a highly theatrical way of dispensing justice. Here, they march Jesus through crowded ranks of Passover pilgrims to the arbitrarily chosen crucifixion site. In the ultimate example of adding insult to injury, the Romans made the condemned person carry his own cross to the site of execution.

Scholars have long held that the condemned carried only the horizontal beam, but recent evidence suggests victims may have struggled under massive wooden crosses weighing as much as two hundred pounds. After all Jesus has been through, he can't carry his cross (the rough wood would have rested directly on his shredded back). Romans, as conquerors over Palestine, claimed the right to compel any of the natives to perform <u>certain tasks</u> such as carrying heavy stuff from one place to another. Thus, they dragged Simon of Cyrene into the story.

We don't know much about Simon. Cyrene was part of <u>northern Africa</u>, so tradition says Simon was black. Mark mentions

☞ **GO TO:**

Matthew 5:41
(certain tasks)

Acts 2:10
(northern Africa)

☞ **GO TO:**

Romans 16:13 (Rufus)

IT'S
GREEK
TO ME

THE WAYBACK MACHINE

myrrh: *a bitter-tasting resin from certain Arabian trees*

Something to Ponder

☞ **GO TO:**

Mark 14:25 (drink wine)

Psalm 22:16 (crucified)

THE WAYBACK MACHINE

Simon's sons, Alexander and <u>Rufus</u>, as if his first readers knew them. If they did, Simon must have become a believer in Jesus and raised his sons to join the community of Christians in Rome.

Golgotha is Aramaic for "a skull." We don't know if the site got that nickname because it was a low hill, shaped like a skull, or because so many people were executed there that skulls littered the ground. (Most of the crucified were never buried, and animals were allowed to have their bones.) If Jesus was crucified at Golgotha, why do we have so many songs about him dying at Calvary? Calvary is derived from the Latin word *calvaria*, meaning (you guessed it) "skull."

Just as wealthy women of our time often involve themselves in charities and community volunteerism, respected women of Jerusalem organized volunteers to help ease the pain of Jews who were being crucified. They got the idea from one of the Proverbs: *"Give beer to those who are perishing, wine to those who are in anguish; let them drink and forget their poverty and remember their misery no more"* (Proverbs 31:6–7). With the wine, they mixed **myrrh**—a mild narcotic that slightly dulled the senses and induced drowsiness.

The pain of the cross is implied in the word "excruciating," derived from "crucify." Amazingly, Jesus turned down the painkiller. Though battered half senseless, he wanted to be as alert and clearheaded as he could while fulfilling the suffering God had appointed for him. Why? For one thing, he had promised never to <u>drink wine</u> again until he drank it with his disciples in the fully realized kingdom of God. Was there something more behind his refusal? I'll leave that for you to consider.

With restraint and economy of words, Mark says merely, *"They <u>crucified</u> him."* Everyone alive in his day knew all the brutality this implied. This is why the cross did not become an artistic symbol of faith until the fourth century, well after all who had seen a real crucifixion died off.

What was the "official" method of crucifixion? There wasn't one. When thousands of soldiers are ordered to crucify thousands of victims (see the chapter on Mark 8:22–9:29), the goal is to get the job done, not to adhere to a textbook. The centurions used whatever was available to them, so archae-ologists have found many variations of crucifixion. Sometimes the wrists were spiked to the cross-beam; sometimes they were tied. Some crosses had a small platform the victim could partly sit on; most did not. Sometimes the ankles were spiked into the vertical beam; sometimes the heels were spiked together *behind* the vertical beam, so that the victim straddled it. Some-times the cross was a T; sometimes it was an X. Some crosses were no taller than you; some were high as telephone poles.

We don't know the specifics of how Jesus was crucified. We deduce that his cross was a high one, because the soldier who offered him a drink with a <u>sponge</u> could not reach Jesus' mouth without putting the sponge on a spear. The priests' taunt that he should *"come down"* seems to indicate a higher cross.

We also deduce he was <u>naked</u>. This was typical Roman practice, and Mark says the soldiers gambled to see who would get Jesus' <u>clothes</u>, which he was not wearing. Imagine being callous enough to play games while someone mere feet away is dying in agony! It would be like nonchalantly scratching a Lotto ticket while someone across the room is being executed in an electric chair. The fact this victim was the Son of God makes the act even more depraved.

☞ **GO TO:**

Mark 15:36; John 19:29 (sponge)

Mark 15:32 (come down)

Psalm 22:17 (naked)

Psalm 22:18 (clothes)

What Others are Saying:

Philip Yancey: Even after watching scores of movies on the sub-ject, and reading the gospels over and over, I still cannot fathom the indignity, the *shame* endured by God's Son on earth, stripped naked, flogged, spat on, struck in the face, garlanded with thorns.[2]

R. C. Sproul: The most violent expression of God's wrath and justice is seen in the Cross. If ever a person had room to complain of injustice, it was Jesus. He was the only innocent man ever to be punished by God. If we stagger at the wrath of God, let us stagger at the Cross. Here is where our astonishment should be focused.[3]

> **Mark 15:25–27** It was the third hour when they cruci-fied him. The written notice of the charge against him read: THE KING OF THE JEWS. They crucified two robbers with him, one on his right and one on his left.

More Mockery

First-century people reckoned the day started at 6:00 A.M., so Jesus was crucified at 9:00 A.M.

Not every victim of crucifixion had a sign stating his crime, but many did. Typically any ol' slab of wood was covered with white chalk so that dark letters would stand out. Sometimes the letters were burned into the wood; sometimes they were written in charcoal. The victim usually wore the sign around his neck while carrying his cross, though in some cases the prefect would appoint a servant to carry the sign in front of the condemned.

Pilate obviously did not believe Jesus was the king of Israel. When my kids were preschoolers, they didn't always get along with each other. They learned they were never permitted to hit one another, but sometimes sibling rivalry provoked emotions that compelled action. Sarah would glare at her brother Luke, then pick up some object like a paper bag. "This is your face," Sarah would say, then ruthlessly mash the bag. "Oh yeah?" Luke would say, picking up a nearby stuffed animal, "Well this is *you*!" Then he'd pummel the animal's stomach violently. (Each in their twenties now, they've grown into great friends.) Pilate was doing the same thing to the Jews he loathed: "God's people, eh? Well this is your *king*!"

IT'S
GREEK
TO ME

Crucified between thieves? Not exactly. The word translated "*robbers*" is *lestas* and, as we learned with Barabbas, could also be translated "insurrectionists." These "robbers" are most likely the Robin Hood–style Zealots mentioned earlier, probably caught in the same rebellion as Barabbas, who would have been on a cross with them, had Jesus not died in his place.

The Romans executed Jesus as a revolutionary political leader. Jesus, however, described his death as necessary to implement the plan of God. The fact that each detail of Christ's death is predicted in Scripture reminds us it was part of God's will. The cynical Pilate never knew he was part of something far greater than himself—greater even than the Roman Empire.

☞ **GO TO:**

Mark 10:33–34
(his death)

Isaiah 53:12 (detail)

> **Mark 15:29–32** Those who passed by hurled insults at him, shaking their heads and saying, "So! You who are going to destroy the temple and build it in three days, come down from the cross and save yourself!"

> In the same way the chief priests and the teachers of the law mocked him among themselves. "He saved others," they said, "but he can't save himself! Let this Christ, this King of Israel, come down now from the cross, that we may see and believe." Those crucified with him also heaped insults on him.

A Lot Of Ironies In The Fire

Mark, lover of startling contrasts and sharp irony, reaches his pinnacle here. Jesus is being mocked by representatives of all walks of life, from outlaws to common people to highfalutin' priests. In their mockery the chief priests unwittingly speak the true core of God's plan: in order to save others, Jesus cannot save himself.

Here's how Webster defines irony: "incongruity between a situation developed in a drama and the accompanying words or actions that is understood by the audience but not by the characters in the play." Mark's got irony, big time:

- The Sanhedrin roughed up Jesus for being a false prophet at the same time his prophecies (about Peter) were coming true.
- A representative of the vaunted Roman Empire ignorantly but accurately labeled Jesus, "King of the Jews."
- Gentiles (the soldiers) mockingly bowed before Jesus and worshiped him as king, unaware that the Messiah was to receive worship not just from Jews, but from all nations.
- People mocked Jesus' claim that the Temple would be destroyed at the same time Jesus was doing that which rendered temple worship unnecessary.

Anne Graham Lotz: At the time of His greatest physical torture, instead of having someone bathe His head with a cold cloth, instead of having someone lovingly sympathize with Him, instead of having any tender care at all, he was mocked and tempted almost beyond human endurance—by those for whom He was dying![4]

What Others are Saying:

Larry W. Hurtado: If we understand Mark's use of irony here, we can see that he wants his readers to realize that Jesus truly is the king of Israel, the Messiah from God, even though the crucifixion seems to contradict every known form of Jewish expectation about what the path of the Messiah would be when he appeared.[5]

> **Mark 15:33–36** At the sixth hour darkness came over the whole land until the ninth hour. And at the ninth hour Jesus cried out in a loud voice, *"Eloi, Eloi, lama sabachthani?"*—which means, "My God, my God, why have you forsaken me?"
>
> When some of those standing near heard this, they said, "Listen, he's calling Elijah."
>
> One man ran, filled a sponge with wine vinegar, put it on a stick, and offered it to Jesus to drink. "Now leave him alone. Let's see if Elijah comes to take him down," he said.

History's Darkest Moment

At the sixth hour—high noon—the sky turned dark over Judea (*"the whole land"* is different from "the whole world"). Scholars like to debate how this could happen, but the proper question is not how. The proper question is *why*.

The darkness symbolized several profound concepts. As we established in the chapter on Mark 4:35–5:20, only Yahweh controlled forces such as oceans and weather. The darkness came from God. It also showed that what was happening on Skull Hill carried cosmic significance. It fulfilled an electrifying <u>prophecy</u> that on the Day of the Lord, God would *"make the sun go down at noon and darken the earth in broad daylight"* (Amos 8:9), because *"I will make that time like mourning for an only son and the end of it like a bitter day"* (Amos 8:10). The darkness indicated God was mourning for his son!

Just before the original Passover, a plague of darkness came over the land to show the <u>curse</u> of God was upon it. The original Passover foreshadowed this, the real Passover. Jesus was dying as the entire world's Passover Lamb. God restrained the full force of his wrath while people made Passover sacrifices in anticipation of the Messiah. God then poured out all of his anger against sin on Jesus.

The <u>Bible teaches</u> that nothing less was happening on Golgotha than this: all the sins of every human—past, present, and future—were placed on Jesus as he became the innocent scapegoat for the entire human race. God the Son was taking upon himself the punishment that everyone else deserved, so that sin would be justly punished. He stepped forward in our stead to accept the death penalty we earned, so you and I don't get what we deserve. Instead, we get forgiven. Thanks be to God for his inexpressible gift!

At this point in Mark's narrative, Peter is a wandering, anguished

☞ **GO TO:**

Amos 8:9–19
(prophecy)

Exodus 10:21–23
(curse)

Isaiah 53:4–5, 9–10;
2 Corinthians 5:21;
Galatians 3:13
(Bible teaches)

soul, but later he got the point of all this, and wrote, *"It is better, if it is God's will, to suffer for doing good than for doing evil. For Christ died for sins once for all, the righteous for the unrighteous, to bring you to God"* (1 Peter 3:17–18).

Jesus' Cry

After three hours of darkness and six long hours on the cross, anguish wrenches this cry from Jesus' broken heart: *"My God, my God, why have you forsaken me?"* It is the first verse of Psalm 22, which predicts Jesus' suffering and victory. The profound under- lying meaning is that for the first time in his endless existence, the Son of God was cut off from the Father. When Jesus became sin, holy God could no longer look upon him. This was the mo- ment Jesus had dreaded in Gethsemane—the moment he prayed God would allow him to avoid. His timeless intimacy with God stopped. This was the cup of God's wrath. Even knowing it had to be this way, Jesus could hardly bear it.

> The same Galilean accent that caused trouble for Peter creates confusion around Jesus. Bystanders mistake his cry as a prayer to Elijah. Nevertheless his misery must have been stirring, be- cause a soldier from the same company that beat Jesus up felt compelled to offer him wine vinegar. Sour wine doesn't sound very refreshing to us, but it was the drink that soldiers and farm laborers preferred over water. It was cheap, and it satisfied their thirst more effectively than other beverages.

THE WAYBACK MACHINE

What Others are Saying:

R. C. Sproul: [God] would have been diabolical to punish Jesus if Jesus had not first willingly taken on Himself the sins of the world. Once Christ had done that . . . He became the most gro- tesque and vile thing on this planet. With the concentrated load of sin He carried, He became utterly repugnant to the Father. . . . God made Christ accursed for the sin he bore. Herein was God's holy justice perfectly manifest. Yet it was done for us. This "for us" aspect of the Cross is what displays the majesty of its grace. At the same time justice and grace, wrath and mercy. It is too aston- ishing to fathom.[6]

Max Lucado: God, who punishes sin, releases his rightful wrath on your mistakes. Jesus receives the blow. Since Christ is between you and God, you don't. The sin is punished, but you are safe— safe in the shadow of the cross.[7]

THE DAY GOD DIED

Mark probably thought the next three sentences in his Gospel were the most important ones. Each wraps up deep, wide themes he has developed throughout the entire book.

> **Mark 15:37** With a loud cry, Jesus breathed his last.

The Perverse Victory Of God

The four Gospels differ when recording the final words of Jesus. In attempting to harmonize the accounts, many Bible teachers say that this *"loud cry"* of Jesus is the triumphant statement recorded by John: *"It is finished!"* (John 19:30). The most honest translation of this sentence, however, is that Jesus' final cry was inarticulate—a wordless bellow.

The phrase translated *"breathed his last"* indicates a sudden, violent death. The shout and the abrupt expiring of Jesus are extremely unusual for a crucified man. Death by crucifixion was essentially death by suffocation, making loud cries rare. Typically, the victim slipped into a semi-coma for a day or more before gradually perishing. During the first few centuries of Christianity, this cry was interpreted as a victory shout. The suddenness of Jesus' death was interpreted to mean Jesus was in control of when he died. He left because he knew his job was done.

One of the central verses of this Gospel is Mark 10:45: *"For even the Son of Man did not come to be served, but to serve, and to give his life as a ransom for many."* Jesus predicted his death many times, describing it as the fulfillment of Scripture. This is the moment to which Mark's entire book has pointed. It is the reason Jesus came, the act that buys us back from sin—the true triumph of the Messiah. The Messiah came not to conquer the Romans, but to conquer sin and death by dying; this unexpected truth is the strange and perverse victory of God.

What Others are Saying:

Saint Augustine: The Lord took on flesh in the virgin's womb when he wished it. He came forth to humanity when he wished it. He lived in history as long as he wished it. He departed from the flesh when he wished it. This is a sign of power, not of necessity.[8]

> **Mark 15:38** The curtain of the temple was torn in two from top to bottom.

Mark's Cosmic Inclusio

At the moment Jesus died busy priests bustled about their Passover duties in front of a temple curtain that suddenly split itself in two. Mark doesn't specify whether this is the curtain that acted as the front door to the Temple or the curtain separating the Holy Place from the Holy of Holies, but the meaning is the same either way.

If the curtain had torn from the bottom up, a team of humans might have been responsible. But the eighty-foot-tall curtain tore *"from top to bottom,"* proving God did the tearing. God required sacrifices at the Temple so Jews would understand forgiveness of sins is not free. God paid the full price for forgiveness with the death of Christ, which made sacrifices at the Temple no longer necessary. Jesus, the true lamb of God (see GWRV, page 78), was the ultimate sacrifice—the sacrifice to end all sacrifices. God ripped the curtain to show that the way into his presence was now open.

The tearing of the curtain also pointed to the Temple's imminent destruction, which Jesus had <u>predicted</u>.

> Jesus himself became the way to forgiveness, thus Jesus himself replaced the Temple. His presence enters into each of his followers, so Christians everywhere comprise a <u>living Temple</u>.

> Mark uses the word *schizo* to describe the ripping of the curtain. This word appears in Mark only one other time. When Jesus first appeared and was baptized, the sky ripped open and God declared that Jesus was his son. At Jesus' death the barrier to God's presence was ripped open, and a common man declared that Jesus is God's Son. Thus, Mark's entire Gospel could be considered one long inclusio, neatly encapsulating the entire journey of Jesus' ministry. Mark's Greek is crude, but his construction, like his theology, is masterful.

N. T. Wright: [Jesus] would not rebuild the Temple in a physical sense. He would become the place and the means whereby that for which the Temple stood would become a reality. He would become the reality to which the sacrificial system had pointed. He

☞ **GO TO:**

Mark 13:2 (predicted)

2 Corinthians 6:16;
1 Peter 2:5
(living Temple)

Remember This . . .

IT'S
GREEK
TO ME

What Others are Saying:

had regularly, throughout his ministry, acted in a way to bypass the Temple and its system, offering forgiveness to all and sundry on his own authority. He now went to his death, indicating in his last great symbolic action that a way was being opened through which that normally obtained by the sacrificial system was now to be obtained through him.[9]

> **Mark 15:39** And when the centurion, who stood there in front of Jesus, heard his cry and saw how he died, he said, "Surely this man was the Son of God!"

The Secret Identity Public At Last

By Roman custom the centurion standing next to a cross would have been the one who led the detail of soldiers performing the crucifixion. Centurions were promoted from the ranks and each commanded a hundred soldiers. They were battle-hardened veterans capable of leading men in combat.

Such men did not easily go soft at the sight of suffering, as evidenced by the callous way they joked and gambled their way through Jesus' murder. But something about how Jesus died impressed this centurion. He would not have known about the curtain tearing in the Temple, nor does Mark mention the earthquake to which Matthew refers. This soldier saw something in Jesus himself—his dignity, his refusal to lash out, his refusal of painkillers, his quick, purposeful death—that caused the soldier to realize he had been in the presence of a true hero.

☞ **GO TO:**

Matthew 27:51, 54 (earthquake)

IT'S
GREEK
TO ME

In the phrase, *"Surely this man was the Son of God!"* the Greek lacks the word "the." It reads, "Surely this man was son of god." When the centurion said this, he probably had Roman gods in mind; he probably did not mean the phrase the way Christians now take it. The centurion's statement is yet another example of Mark's trademark irony. An ignorant pagan spoke the truth about Jesus.

Something to Ponder

Regardless of how the centurion meant what he said, this is the first time in Mark that a human identifies Jesus as "Son of God." Peter came close in the Markan hinge, but his understanding was fatally flawed. Throughout his Gospel Mark has been leading us to the truth that until you recognize the meaning of Jesus' death, you don't know Jesus at all. Jesus showed everyone with his public execution that establishing the kingdom of God required him to die as a substitute for all of us. Once you understand this you are able to recognize the Son of God as he wants to be recognized. Never again did Jesus tell anyone to keep silent about who he was. Instead, he commanded his followers to <u>tell everyone</u>.

☞ **GO TO:**

Luke 24:46–48
(tell everyone)

Anne Graham Lotz: No one on this side of hell will ever know the loneliness Jesus endured on the Cross—in your place and mine. When we claim the Lamb as our own sacrifice for sin, we will never be separated from God, because Jesus was. Praise His dear Name! He is still Emmanuel—God with us. The sacrifice of the Lamb is absolutely sufficient in itself to take away our sin and reconcile us to God.[10]

What Others are Saying:

> **Mark 15:40–41** Some women were watching from a distance. Among them were Mary Magdalene, Mary the mother of James the younger and of Joses, and Salome. In Galilee these women had followed him and cared for his needs. Many other women who had come up with him to Jerusalem were also there.

Meanwhile, As The Men Ran Like Little Girls . . .

After all the violence, brutality, and cosmic display of the crucifixion, this extra little note about the presence of women seems out of place. But Mark accomplishes a couple of things by including it.

First, Mark presents another of his sharp contrasts. At the threat of persecution, all the men had fled like little girls. The women, treated as lesser by Jewish culture, were the ones who stayed to the bitter end, showing the courage and commitment that the apostles should have shown.

Second, their presence completes Mark's sketch of Jesus as lover of the fringe folk. The account that starts with Jesus touching the untouchable and healing the outcasts ends with representatives of "lesser" classes understanding the entire Gospel before anyone else, as we'll see in a few verses.

Finally, the specific people Mark names were known in the community of believers to whom Mark wrote his book. After all the exceptional things Mark has written, this little postscript says,

KEY POINT

Mark's Gospel highlights many women whom believers can admire.

"And if you think I made this up, just ask Mary. Ask Salome. They were there; they'll tell you."

Though Mark is a secondhand narrator, he knew plenty of first-hand eyewitnesses to Jesus' extraordinary life. This extra note gives his Gospel authenticity that should reassure any doubtful believer. (For more about Mary Magdalene, see GWWB, page 273. For more on Salome, see GWWB, page 275. Mary, mother of Jesus, was there too; see WBFM, pages 285–288.)

Something to Ponder

We can admire all the women highlighted in Mark's Gospel. Whether it's the courage and honesty of the bleeding woman, the persistence of the Syro-Phoenician woman, the generosity of the widow and the woman with nard, or the quiet commitment of the women at the cross, each displays a quality to which any Christian should aspire.

Read And Meditate

POWER TOOL

Meditate on what you read.

The passive mention of the women ends this section on a reflective note, which brings me to the Power Tool for this section: *meditate on the Scripture you read.* In this section we have covered some of the most profound literature ever written. If you dash through it, close your Bible, and immediately say, "Cool, what's next?" you'll miss most of the meaning and depth your heart longs for.

grebes: *fresh-water birds, two-thirds as big as most ducks, capable of swimming underwater for several minutes.*

When I feel harried by everyday life, I visit a nature preserve blocks from my house. It has paths that take you in and around wetlands, a lake, streams, and lawns. If I make a hurried visit, I walk the entire park without seeing any wildlife. Instead, I need to stand still in the middle of it, then let the rhythm of my thoughts slow to the rhythm of nature. When I wait patiently, things I overlooked gradually reveal themselves to me. By waiting quietly, I have seen eagles teaching their young how to fish, baby **grebes** riding on their mother's back, and beavers building a lodge—sights that filled me with adoration for my Creator. Scripture works the same way. It doesn't pander to today's instant-gratification culture. To plumb its depths, you have to <u>ponder</u> it for awhile.

☞ **GO TO:**

Psalm 119:97, 101, 102 (ponder)

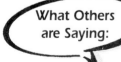

What Others are Saying:

Richard J. Foster: Whereas the study of Scripture centers on exegesis, the meditation of Scripture centers on internalizing and personalizing the passage. The written Word becomes a living word addressed to you. This is not a time for technical studies, or analysis, or even the gathering of material to share with others. Set aside all tendencies toward arrogance and with a humble heart receive the word addressed to you. . . . take a single event, . . . or a few verses, or even a single word and allow it to take root in you.[11]

KEEP IT REAL—As I wrote this chapter on the death of Jesus, repeatedly I was overcome by the depth of his suffering and his supreme selflessness in dying for me. His gift is too great to describe in words. In keeping with the Power Tool of this section, though, I encourage you to think on these things. See what insights into the crucifixion you discover by meditating on these verses before the Lord.

Study Questions

1. About how many soldiers joined in mocking Jesus?
2. Who was Simon of Cyrene?
3. What was mixed into the wine that was offered Jesus? Why the extra ingredient?
4. Describe what "irony" is. Cite examples of where it appears in Mark's account of the Passion of Jesus.

CHAPTER WRAP-UP

- Soldiers beat Jesus, mocked him, and spit on him, but Jesus did not lash back or insult them. Much of this abuse fulfilled prophecies written in Psalm 22 and Isaiah 53. (Mark 15:16–20)

- Jesus was crucified naked at Golgotha (meaning "skull") at nine in the morning on a tall cross, between two Jewish insurrectionists. He refused any painkillers. (Mark 15:21–32)

- As Jesus was dying, the sky turned dark at noon, signifying God was mourning his only son, a curse was on the land, and the sins of the world rested on Jesus—who cried out in despair as holy God turned away from him. (Mark 15:33–36)

- When Jesus died, his substitutionary sacrifice for us made the Temple unnecessary. God signified this by tearing the temple curtain open. (Mark 15:37–38)

- The only way to understand Jesus' mission is to grasp the significance of his death. (Mark 15:39)

- Mark's Gospel holds women in high regard; the women who followed Jesus were braver than the men. (Mark 15:40–41)

MARK 15:42–16:20
THE REAL JESUS

Let's Get Started

After the dramatic death of Jesus, you might suppose we're already past the climax of Mark's powerful Gospel. Don't relax just yet; Mark ends with the strongest bang of all.

Controversy plagues the final eleven verses of Mark, which many scholars believe Mark did not write. Was the extra part added later by an anonymous writer? If so, Mark's Gospel ends on this strange note: *"Trembling and bewildered, the women went out and fled from the tomb. They said nothing to anyone, because they were afraid."* By now we know Mark is anything but a sappy writer, but would he end his magnificent biography like this? As you can see, there is still plenty to explore, so let's get started!

JESUS' BORROWED GRAVE

> **Mark 15:42–43** It was Preparation Day (that is, the day before the Sabbath). So as evening approached, Joseph of Arimathea, a prominent member of the Council, who was himself waiting for the kingdom of God, went boldly to Pilate and asked for Jesus' body.

Third Defector From The Enemy

The Jews of Jerusalem reckoned the Sabbath began at sundown, and burying a dead body on the Sabbath was not allowed. Jewish law also said that dead bodies hanging from crosses could not be

☞ **GO TO:**

Deuteronomy 21:22–
23 (cursed)

Mark 15:34–37
(ninth hour)

John 19:25–27
(witnessed)

Mark 12:28–34
(teacher of the law)

Luke 2:25, 38
(Luke's Gospel)

left out overnight or the land would be <u>cursed</u>. Jesus died shortly after the <u>ninth hour</u> (3:00 P.M.), so Jesus' friends had a narrow window of time in which to bury him.

Jesus' dead body officially belonged to the state, and the state liked to leave bodies out for days to remind citizens of treason's consequences. In some cases if the family stepped forward and asked for the body, it would be granted them. On the other hand, asking for the body of someone convicted of high treason was similar to confessing you were a sympathizer, which was dangerous.

The situation was further complicated because Jesus was captured, tried, convicted, and executed so rapidly his brothers and sisters may not have been aware of what happened; we have no evidence they were even in Jerusalem. Mary the mother of Jesus <u>witnessed</u> what happened, but how can she make a request of Pilate? She's a woman in a culture that disregards women; she's a Jew needing a favor from a government that hates Jews; and she has just witnessed the most shattering sight a mother could dread—hardly a time to fight city hall. The disciples have all run away. Who will take care of the remains of Jesus?

Help comes from the most improbable source: a member of the Sanhedrin, the council that convicted Jesus. Mark has already shown us two unlikely sympathizers who emerged from the enemy camp out of honest respect for Jesus, the <u>teacher of the law</u> who Jesus said was *"not far from the kingdom of God"* and the centurion who recognized that Jesus was Son of God. Now Joseph of Arimathea, a third unlikely ally, steps forward.

IT'S
GREEK
TO ME

Mark gives high praise to Joseph when he attests Joseph *"was himself waiting for the kingdom of God."* The same concept shows up in <u>Luke's Gospel</u> in phrases like, *"He was waiting for the consolation of Israel"* and *"looking forward to the redemption of Jerusalem."* These various wordings describe someone who cared about God's plan for the Jews and was looking forward to the coming of the kingdom of God. Jesus' main message was, "Repent. The kingdom of God is near" (see Mark 1:15), so we can be sure anyone whom Mark describes as *"waiting for the kingdom"* is a good guy.

Where was this good-hearted, godly man when the Sanhedrin framed Jesus and then beat him? We don't know, but if anyone can get away with showing support for a treasonous Jew, it would be a member of the convicting council. Joseph went *"boldly"* to Pilate, and even though he could be exposing himself to the same penalty as Jesus, even though he is not a family member, he asks for permission to bury Jesus.

> **Mark 15:44–46** Pilate was surprised to hear that he was already dead. Summoning the centurion, he asked him if Jesus had already died. When he learned from the centurion that it was so, he gave the body to Joseph. So Joseph bought some linen cloth, took down the body, wrapped it in the linen, and placed it in a tomb cut out of rock. Then he rolled a stone against the entrance of the tomb.

Fabulous All-Expense-Paid Trip To . . . The Cemetery

Now that you know how long a crucified person usually suffered before dying, you can understand why Pilate was surprised to hear Jesus was already dead. What normally took at least two or three days is done in about six hours. Acting outside his normal character, Pilate graciously gives the body up, perhaps indicating he didn't really believe Jesus committed treason.

As a prestigious member of the Sanhedrin, Joseph would've been wealthy. When Mark says Joseph bought cloth, took down the body, and so on, most likely it's meant in the same way a historian might say, "Herod built the Temple." Herod did not spend sixty years as a royal construction worker; but he funded the construction. Likewise, servants would have been the ones to wash and wrap Jesus' body, but it was all done at Joseph's expense.

And what expense! Only a rich man could afford a stone tomb. In Palestine cemeteries of stone tombs were generally found only in rock quarries that had played out. As stone-cutters worked their way back into a hillside, cutting rock, they left niches easily customized into tombs. Most of these tombs had a front chamber. At the back of the front chamber was a rectangular doorway, a mere two feet high, leading into the burial room, which was about seven feet cubed. The burial room had a stone bench—really, more of a shelf—cut into the back wall.

Such tombs were commonly sealed shut with any boulder that was convenient. Only an exceptionally fine tomb had an

THE WAYBACK MACHINE

actual disc-shaped rolling stone. The groove cut in the ground to hold this sealing stone ran downhill toward the tomb entrance, so that it was easy to roll the stone into the closed position. Opening the tomb required rolling the stone uphill, so no one could rob such a grave unless he had several strong helpers. With Jesus placed on the rock shelf in the back of the tomb, and the millstone-shaped rock rolled into position, the King of the Jews had been given the best burial money could buy—and the most secure.

> **Mark 15:47** Mary Magdalene and Mary the mother of Joses saw where he was laid.

Never Underestimate The Power Of Mary Squared

Once again Mark punctuates his account with a reference to women. The two Marys have seen the death of Jesus firsthand. They've seen the burial of Jesus up close. What they see next makes them the best witnesses the church had. Mark has been laying the groundwork, showing you that some people saw the whole story from start to finish.

Something to Ponder

The testimony of women did not count in Jewish law. In order to be "proven" legally, an event had to be witnessed by at least two people, and they had to be men. The fact that the primary witnesses of the Gospel were women attests to the authenticity of Mark's account. If the good news of Jesus had been made up, almost certainly the disciples would have picked themselves as the alleged witnesses—not people of little regard.

THE DAY DEATH WORKED BACKWARDS

In his wonderful allegory about salvation, *The Lion, the Witch, and the Wardrobe*, C. S. Lewis depicts Jesus as a talking lion named Aslan, who willingly gives himself over to death to save a child from the White Witch. After his death, Aslan comes back to life, and explains his amazing return to a quizzical Lucy with these words: "Though the Witch knew the Deep Magic, there is a magic deeper still which she did not know. Her knowledge goes back only to the dawn of Time. But if she could have looked a little further back, into the stillness and the darkness before Time dawned, . . . She would have known that when a willing victim who had committed no treachery was killed in a traitor's stead, . . . Death itself would start working backwards."[1]

Mark ends with a tantalizing snapshot of the day death worked backwards.

> **Mark 16:1–3** When the Sabbath was over, Mary Magdalene, Mary the mother of James, and Salome bought spices so that they might go to anoint Jesus' body. Very early on the first day of the week, just after sunrise, they were on their way to the tomb and they asked each other, "Who will roll the stone away from the entrance of the tomb?"

Three Nice Jewish Girls

Did these faithful women rush to the tomb to see Jesus fulfill his prediction of rising again? Clearly not. They wanted to finish the rituals of burial that the Sabbath had interrupted.

Note that these events happened *"on the first day of the week."* What the women discover next is the main reason Jewish Christians moved their traditional day of worship from the Sabbath (Saturday) to the first day of the week (Sunday).

 KEEP IT REAL—The grief I experienced when my mother died of cancer probably wouldn't equal the grief these women felt at seeing Jesus brutally murdered. But I relate to them in one way. When my mom died, grief wrapped around me like a coarse dark blanket, muffling my thoughts and feelings. I felt like a shrunken soul rattling around in a hollow body, partly removed from the world. Evidently these women felt the same way, for they hadn't thought about how to get into the tomb until they approached it. Grief paralyzed their thought processes.

> **Mark 16:4–6** But when they looked up, they saw that the stone, which was very large, had been rolled away. As they entered the tomb, they saw a young man dressed in a white robe sitting on the right side, and they were alarmed.
>
> "Don't be alarmed," he said. "You are looking for Jesus the Nazarene, who was crucified. He has risen! He is not here. See the place where they laid him."

Young Man + White Robe = ?

Put yourself in the place of these women. You're toiling up the dusty road outside Jerusalem, almost numb with grief, groggy from a sleepless night and a predawn rising. You slap your forehead for not remembering until now that you need someone to open the tomb for you. Concerned, you come around the bend, anxiously looking toward the tomb you saw just the day before yesterday— and the stone has been rolled back. The mouth of the crypt gapes open. What shoots through your mind and heart? *Is this the right tomb? Yes, I know it is. Has one of the Twelve returned to honor Jesus' body?* After the trauma of watching the Romans unleash their very worst on Jesus, you suddenly fear that malice has driven some-one—the Sanhedrin? Pilate? Grave robbers?—to dishonor Jesus even more. *Is his death not enough to satisfy their jealousy?* You exchange worried glances with your friends. Wordlessly, you all walk faster.

IT'S
GREEK
TO ME

☞ **GO TO:**

Mark 14:51–52 (earlier)

Isaiah 1:18 (purity)

Daniel 7:9 (wisdom)

They encounter a *"young man dressed in a white robe."* As we learned <u>earlier</u>, "young man" sometimes referred to an un-usually strong, valiant, faithful, and wise man. The color white was often associated with <u>purity</u>, <u>wisdom</u>, and God's <u>glory</u>. The connotations of the whole phrase indicate this "young man" was really a divine messenger—an angel. He tells them not to be afraid, which is the same <u>thing angels do</u> elsewhere in the Bible.

Understandably, the women are *"alarmed."* The Greek word is very strong—so strong the other gospel writers don't use it. "Alarmed" doesn't translate it properly. Upon hearing that Jesus lives, upon seeing for themselves the empty spot where he once laid, the women are terrified.

What Others are Saying:

Mark 9:3 (glory)

Daniel 10:12; Matthew 1:20; Luke 1:13, 30 (thing angels do)

Hank Hanegraaff: Instead of denying that the tomb was empty, the antagonists of Christ accused his disciples of stealing the body. . . . In the centuries following the resurrection, the fact of the empty tomb was forwarded by Jesus' friends and foes alike. . . . In short, early Christianity simply could not have survived an identifiable tomb containing the corpse of Christ. The enemies of Christ could have easily put an end to the charade by displaying the body . . . the empty tomb is an unassailable reality.[2]

William Lane Craig: When you read the New Testament, there's no doubt that the disciples sincerely believed the truth of the Resurrection, which they proclaimed to their deaths. The idea that the empty tomb is the result of some hoax, conspiracy, or theft is simply dismissed today.[3]

> **Mark 16:7** "But go, tell his disciples and Peter, 'He is going ahead of you into Galilee. There you will see him, just as he told you.'"

Just Like Old Times

The angel has a message for the women to deliver to *"his disciples and Peter."* This phrasing could be read as "his disciples and even that non-disciple, the quitter Peter," but its intent is, "tell his disciples and especially Peter." Almost as amazing as the resurrection itself is the fact that Jesus overlooks and forgives the disciples' cowardly behavior. He looks forward to being with them, to continuing the training they have been so slow to absorb. I love the fact that Peter, who made the biggest claims but denied Christ the most thoroughly, gets a special invitation. Jesus knew Peter's shame, and invites him by name. The later lives of the disciples proved Jesus was right to keep investing time in them. Eventually they got it, and changed the world.

KEY POINT

Jesus freely forgives the shortcomings of his disciples—even today.

As I explained in the chapter on Mark 14:1–42, when the angel says Jesus is *"going ahead"* of his disciples, he means it in much the same way a shepherd goes before his flock. Once again Jesus will lead them, just as he <u>predicted</u> after their Last Supper together.

Where will he lead them? Into Galilee, which is a good sign. In Mark the bad stuff happens in Jerusalem; the good stuff happens in Galilee (see table). The location is a symbolic way of saying, "Guys! I'm back! Let's revisit our old stomping grounds; it'll be just like old times!"

☞ **GO TO:**

Mark 14:28 (predicted)

There's Good Stuff Happening in Galilee!

Mark 1:9	Jesus was from Galilee.
Mark 1:14	Jesus began his ministry in Galilee.
Mark 1:16	Jesus recruited his disciples in Galilee.
Mark 1:28	The whole region of Galilee knew of Jesus.
Mark 1:39	Most of Jesus' ministry occurred in Galilee.

The observation I just made came from the Power Tool, *pay attention to geography*. As my final tip to you on how to interpret Scripture properly for yourself, I encourage you to *combine the*

POWER TOOL

Combine the Power Tools.

Power Tools. Together these tools create a synergy that helps you get to the real meaning of the Word, with fuller understanding. Now you can't use every Power Tool on every verse (How could you do a character study on a passage that has no characters?), but you can usually use several of them. Here's how I used the Power Tools to generate my commentary on this passage:

Verse	Topic	Power Tool Used
16:1–8	What's going on here?	Think in chunks, not verses.
16:1	Who was Mary?	Character study
16:1	What were the spices for?	Use a Bible dictionary.
16:2	What was the first day of the week?	Use a Bible dictionary.
16:5	Who is the "young man in a white robe"?	Check Old Testament cross-references.
16:6	Angels often say "don't be alarmed"	Check Old Testament and New Testament cross-references
16:7	What's the significance of Galilee?	Pay careful attention to geography.
16:8	What's the significance of the women being "alarmed . . . bewildered"?	Notice and study repeated words.
16:1–8	What does the Resurrection mean to me?	Meditate.

None of this is too hard for you. After you're done with Mark, I hope you study another book of the Bible. Try using the Power Tools on it. I think you'll be happily surprised at how much you can get out of the Bible on your own. May your reading be blessed!

What Others are Saying:

Desmond Tutu: Easter means—hope prevails over despair. Jesus reigns as Lord of Lords and King of Kings. . . . Easter says to us that despite everything to the contrary, his will for us will prevail, love will prevail over hate, justice over injustice and oppression, peace over exploitation and bitterness.[4]

MARK'S MYSTERIOUS ENDING

> **Mark 16:8** Trembling and bewildered, the women went out and fled from the tomb. They said nothing to anyone, because they were afraid.

The End (?)

Mark's book ends with surprising abruptness. The women who were already terrified in verse 5, flee in complete, overwhelming dread in verse 8. The End.

Huh? Was that really where Mark stopped writing? By now you have a feel for Mark's style. This ending fits him in several ways:

1. *The abrupt ending matches the abrupt beginning.* While the other gospel writers have long preambles to introduce Jesus, Mark jumps right in with both feet. Mark 1:1 starts with, *"The beginning of the gospel,"* and within eight verses, he's covered all he wants to say about John the Baptizer, Jesus is already an adult, and he's been baptized. The short sharp ending matches the beginning.

2. *Mark leaves many important things unresolved.* Who won the <u>battle</u> between Jesus and Satan? Mark doesn't say; he expects you to figure it out. When Jesus calmed the storm, and the disciples asked one another, "What <u>manner of man</u> is this?" did Mark answer the question? No; he expects you to figure it out. Why did Jesus <u>silence people</u> who called him Messiah? Mark doesn't say; he expects you to figure it out. This unsettling, unresolved ending matches Mark's style.

3. *Mark uses deep fear as the reaction to God's overwhelming presence.* When the divinity of Jesus shines forth most powerfully, Mark shows people reacting in fear. Remember when Jesus shone with glory on the mountain? Peter was <u>afraid</u>. How did the Twelve respond when Jesus acted like Yahweh by controlling the ocean? They were <u>terrified</u>. People were afraid when Jesus cast out a <u>legion of demons</u>, when he walked on <u>water</u>, and so on. The women's fear shows that God did something mighty.

4. *It was common in the literature of the era merely to allude to well-known events.* We read that someone announced Jesus was alive, and we might well ask, "Really? Then what happened?" Mark was writing in Rome, during the lifetimes of these female witnesses, when virtually <u>everyone knew</u> how the story went. Mark can feel free to stop right here. The only other note needed might be, "And the rest is history."

I believe this really is the end of Mark's Gospel. Some scholars believe the real ending was lost. If so, we are remarkably "lucky" to have a book that ends with a complete sentence and with every essential element of the Gospel intact. Though we might wish for Mark to depict the risen savior, we have all we need here to com-

☞ **GO TO:**

Mark 1:13 (battle)

Mark 4:41 (manner of man)

Mark 8:29–30 (silence people)

Mark 9:6 (afraid)

Mark 4:41 (terrified)

Mark 5:15 (legion of demons)

Mark 6:50 (water)

Acts 26:26 (everyone knew)

plete the Gospel. (Many people saw Jesus after his resurrection. They're listed in GWBI, page 211.)

I like his haunting ending, because it drives you back into the book for another look. Of course, we know from the other gospel writers the women eventually overcame their fear and obeyed the command to tell the apostles.

Caution: Weird Passage Ahead

If you open your Bible to Mark 16:9, you'll probably find a note from the publisher that says, "The earliest manuscripts and some other ancient witnesses do not have Mark 16:9–20." This note states part of why most scholars do not consider these verses to be God's Word. I agree with these scholars, so I won't go into the same depth with this passage as I have with the rest of Mark (although I will summarize the passage a little later).

You might be thinking, "Wait a second. If most scholars don't think this passage is God's Word, why is it in the Bible?" Good question. The reason it's there is because the translators of the King James Version, using sixteenth-century knowledge and tradition, accepted it as part of Mark. As our understanding of **manuscript transmission** and ancient Greek has increased, evangelical scholars no longer accept this passage of Mark as being authored by Mark.

Today, publishers include this passage to be sensitive to tradition and to show respect for the work of scholars of previous generations who were well meaning, hard working, and sharp thinking. It would be arrogant to take a passage counted as Scripture for hundreds of years and simply trash it. But because of the well-founded doubts about the origins of this passage, publishers include the note mentioned above to inform you of a fact that may affect your reading of it.

I Knew John Mark, And You're No John Mark

Here's a brief summary of Mark 16:9–20. Back from the dead, Jesus appears to Mary Magdalene, two guys walking in the country, and to the Eleven (so called because Judas is no longer with them). Jesus tells them the signs that will characterize those who are being saved. Then Jesus goes to heaven, where he shares power with God, and the disciples preach the good news throughout the land. (You'll find another account of what Jesus did after his resurrection in part 3 of GWJN.)

KEY POINT

Most scholars today do not believe Mark wrote Mark 16:9–20.

manuscript transmission: how ancient writings are preserved and passed down to us

There are many reasons scholars don't believe Mark wrote this passage. Here are some of them:

- As mentioned in the publisher's note, Mark 16:9–20 is not in the earliest, most reliable copies of Mark we've found. In fact, they don't show up until over two hundred years after Mark lived.

- None of the early church fathers indicate awareness of these verses for the first few centuries of Christianity. They don't quote from them, comment on them, or live by phrases like *"when they drink deadly poison, it will not hurt them"* (verse 18).

- Textually, the vocabulary and style of Greek is not like Mark's.

- Structurally, these verses seem tacked on. The subject changes suddenly (from the women, to Jesus), with no segue whatsoever. Everywhere else, Mark always had a segue, even if it was something very brief like "and then" or "next." Mary Magdalene's already been mentioned three previous times, but she is introduced here like a new character, which doesn't fit Mark's style.

- This passage recommends practices mentioned nowhere else in Scripture that were never part of the life of the early church. None of the believers purposely drank poison or intentionally picked up snakes. The evidence suggests someone from a later period inserted these verses to justify their own beliefs.

Whatever you conclude about whether this passage was written by Mark, we can safely delete it without losing anything significant. Verses 9 through 15 summarize material handled with more depth and detail in the other Gospels. Verses 16 through 18 bring in beliefs that the church did not practice. Verses 19 and 20 are covered elsewhere, especially in the Book of Acts.

Who would add this passage to Mark, and why? We don't know. Our best guess is, the book seemed unfinished to someone who tried to "help" Mark by making it more complete. As for who did it, the evidence suggests it was someone alive around A.D. 200. That's all we know.

SO WHAT?

There you have it. Through faithfulness and persistence, you've studied everything Mark thought was essential to understanding Jesus the Christ. If all this info is still swirling around in your head, maybe I can help it coalesce by recapping some of Mark's major themes.

Mark portrays Jesus as unpredictable. Jesus works at a much higher level than we understand. Any theology that makes him totally understandable and predictable involves some level of self-delusion. Ministry approaches that offer "five powerful concepts" that "end all the uncertainty" don't work, because Jesus is not bound by our concepts any more than he was bound by the Jewish concepts in his era. There is no shortcut around listening for his voice day by day. The kind of faith Mark describes across the sweep of his entire book is this: being a disciple means trusting Jesus, no matter what he does.

Mark spends a lot of time showing various facets of discipleship. Mark's Gospel reveals the Twelve as desperately needing Jesus. They lacked insight, strength, and courage. Sometimes they gave all for the kingdom; sometimes they became pompous and self-centered. None of their inconsistencies threw Jesus off stride. He kept teaching them, forgiving them, and calling them farther along the road. Over time those men became pillars of faith. Jesus still converts losers into conquerors today.

Discipleship is costly. If you're going to follow Jesus, expect your days to mingle pain and glory. Don't fall for a false triumphalism that says a Christian's every waking moment will be wonderful. Some days, you get whipped. Some days, you get beheaded. Sometimes the Pharisees out-argue you. Mark wants us to know that the pain passes. Embarrassment passes. Even death passes. The glory endures.

The story of the death of Jesus also depicts the death of orthodox Judaism. The exclusionary religion of strict rules has been burst like an old wineskin by Jesus' inclusionary way of the heart—a way that offers compassion to outsiders and fringe folk. God's presence has abandoned the corrupt Temple. God's presence now lives in a new Temple, the collective hearts of Jesus' followers. His followers spread God's kingdom, because they know what God's loudest commands are: love him and love one another.

KEEP IT REAL—Jesus showed how to be holy in mean streets. He demonstrated a love that willingly died for us. To be his disciple, I must be willing to take up my cross, too. Out of a sinister maelstrom of plotting, betrayal, and death, new life arose. All of us who commit to Christ can count on enjoying a cup of wine with him in another world, at a feast celebrating a love that is stronger than death—a gritty, persistent love that makes death work backwards.

Hey. . . it's not a secret anymore, okay? I'll tell others if you do!

Study Questions

1. Who was Joseph of Arimathea?
2. What day of the week was it when three nice Jewish girls went to visit Jesus' tomb?
3. Why did the young man specify that his message was also for Peter?
4. Name some reasons why Mark 16:9–20 was probably not written by Mark.

CHAPTER WRAP-UP

- Jesus needed to be buried quickly after his death, because the task couldn't be done on the Sabbath. Joseph of Arimathea got permission from Pilate to bury Jesus, and loaned Jesus an expensive grave. (Mark 15:42–47)

- Women witnessed Jesus' death, burial, and empty tomb. This attests to the authenticity of Mark's account, because if the apostles had decided to lie about Jesus living again, they wouldn't have picked second-class citizens as the primary witnesses. (Mark 16:1–8)

- Most scholars believe the authentic part of Mark ends at 16:8, and the rest was added on later. Scholars still debate whether 16:8 is the real ending, or simply the place where the manuscript got torn. I believe 16:8 is Mark's real ending.

- Jesus fulfilled his promise to live again and rejoin the disciples in Galilee. He's alive today!

APPENDIX A—THE ANSWERS

ANSWERS TO POP QUIZ ON PAGES 19–20

2. Charles Dickens, *A Tale of Two Cities*
3. The Beatles, *Sgt. Pepper's Lonely Hearts Club Band*
4. Shakespeare's *Hamlet*
5. The villain in virtually every episode of *Scooby-Doo*
6. Advertising tag line for Nike
7. Holographic message from Princess Leia in *Star Wars*
8. Radio and TV description of Superman
9. Typical sign-off for *Sesame Street*
10. Dorothy addressing her dog in *The Wizard of Oz*

MARK 1:1–13—WHAT IF GOD WAS ONE OF US?

1. Mark was written for a Roman audience who was unfamiliar with most Jewish customs.
2. *Evangelion* means "good news" or "happy proclamation." The word "gospel" is the English translation of *evangelion*. Only a king could have an *evangelion*, implying that Jesus was a king.
3. Messiah, Anointed One, Christ, and many many others.
4. Possible reasons Jews flocked to hear John include the fact that Jews expected their salvation to come from the desert (and John preached in the desert), and that they expected Elijah to precede the Messiah (and John looked and spoke like Elijah).
5. *Schizo* is a violent word meaning torn, ripped, or split. Mark uses it when Jesus is baptized, and when Jesus dies: first the sky is torn open, later the Temple veil is torn.

MARK 1:14–45—ACTION-FIGURE JESUS

1. Some of the thoughts included in the Jewish concept of *"the day of the Lord"* were: that God would judge and punish the sins of Israel (Joel 1:13–15); that God would judge and punish the countries that mistreated Israel (Isaiah 1:24; 2:12–18); that God would bring salvation, justice, and forgiveness for the truly repentant (Joel 2:28–32; Isaiah 12:1–3); that God would bring the Jews back to the Promised Land and prosper them (Isaiah 61:1–9; Jeremiah 31:10–14); that a descendant of King David would rule (Isaiah 11:1–10; 4:2); and that people of all different nationalities would worship God (Hosea 2:21–23).
2. What Jesus knew about *"the day of the Lord"* that his people didn't, was that *"the day of the Lord"* would come in two parts: first the mercy, later the judgment.

3. Some of Mark's snapshots of the power and authority of Jesus include these incidents: Jesus ordered men to drop everything and follow him, and they did it (Mark 1:18, 20); Jesus taught with mind-blowing authority (1:22, 27); he drove out demons with a word (1:25–26); he healed Simon's mother-in-law of a burning fever (1:31); and he healed all the sick and demonized in an entire village (1:33–34).
4. Mark 1:35 shows how Jesus made a point of praying, even if it was difficult to fit into his schedule.
5. No one with obvious physical handicaps was allowed to worship at the Temple in Jerusalem. The ex-leper could now rejoin society and worship in the Temple.

MARK 2:1–3:12—ANTIESTABLISHMENT JESUS

1. The Pharisees didn't like Jesus forgiving anyone's sin, because only God can forgive sins. They didn't know that Jesus is God.
2. The Pharisees were founded to help all Jews observe the laws of the Torah, so that God might be pleased to end their exile. However, over time they valued their own traditions and interpretations more than Scripture.
3. Jesus ate with non-religious people because, *"The Son of Man came to seek out and to save the lost"* (Luke 19:10).
4. Jesus' presence brought the kingdom of God to earth, initiating a new way of relating to God that Jewish tradition had not addressed before. The ancient customs could not fit with what Jesus was doing.
5. Some parallels between Jesus and David in these stories include: both were on a special mission from God; both were kings who had not been installed in their reigns yet. The comparison indicated that Jesus saw himself as being the *"Son of David"*—the Messiah.

MARK 3:13–35—SHOCKING WORDS OF JESUS, PART ONE

1. Symbolic actions were deeds that prophets did to act out or dramatize a message from God. Some examples are listed in the chart on page 63, but there are many more in both the Old and New Testaments.
2. It was not coincidence that there were twelve tribes of Israel and twelve disciples. Jesus chose twelve men to symbolize the fact that he planned to reconstitute a new

Israel, which had twelve tribes. He called the Twelve "apostles," which means "sent ones" or "messengers."

3. Jesus appointed the apostles to be with him, to preach, and to drive out demons.

4. An intercalation is a literary device where one story is wedged into the middle of another. They are important because when stories are set that way, they are intended to comment upon each other, giving us a different message than we might otherwise notice.

5. "Blasphemy against the Holy Spirit" appears to be the act of defiantly calling God's work the work of Satan when you actually know better.

MARK 4:1–34—SHOCKING WORDS OF JESUS, PART TWO

1. Jesus used parables to try to describe what the kingdom of God is like.

2. Three general guidelines for interpreting parables are:
   A. It couldn't mean what it never meant before, so what did the original audience think of it?
   B. Interpret Scripture using Scriptures that handle the same idea or symbol.
   C. Don't press the parables—not every detail in them is symbolic.
   I agree with these guidelines wholeheartedly!

3. "The word" in Mark 4:14 probably refers to Jesus' pronouncement that the kingdom of God had arrived.

4. "The lamp" could refer to the Messiah, descendant of David (which would be Jesus himself); or it could refer to God's word (1 Kings 11:36; 15:4; Psalm 119:105).

5. The man scattered some seed, but the point of the story is that the crop grew automatically—all by itself. Though humans can help God spread his kingdom, God does the real work using his own timing and methods.

MARK 4:35–5:20—POWER-RANGER JESUS

1. Jesus left the crowd suddenly, without dismissing them. We don't know why. The context makes it reasonable to conjecture that he had reached the limits of his physical energy—he was exhausted.

2. Jesus saved the boat by speaking to the weather, calming the storm and the ocean. The unusual language (in Greek, "Put the muzzle on and keep it on") is the same phrase he used to silence demons in Mark 1:25.

3. Most Jews of the era believed that oceans were a symbol for chaos. Only Yahweh could control the oceans. The fact that Jesus calmed the storm with a word demonstrated that he was God.

4. A Roman legion contained over 6,000 men. The name indicated that many, many demons dwelled within the man of the tombs.

5. Both stories show forces of chaos being overcome by Jesus' authority.

MARK 5:21–6:6—PARTY-POOPER JESUS

1. Jairus, who ruled a synagogue somewhere in Galilee, wanted Jesus to heal his dying daughter (Mark 5:22–23).

2. A woman with an issue of blood touched Jesus' garment and was healed, forcing Jesus to stop and ask who had touched him. During the delay, the daughter of Jairus died. (Mark 5:25–30, 35)

3. All three were utterly incurable by anyone except God (Mark 5:4, 26, 35). All three were brought to wholeness by a single encounter with Jesus (Mark 5:15, 29, 42).

4. They both believed in Jesus enough to receive a miracle.

5. Jesus was amazed at their purposeful lack of faith in him (Mark 6:6).

MARK 6:6–56—MORE CLUES ABOUT JESUS' SECRET IDENTITY

1. This symbolic act demonstrated that a Jewish town was behaving like a Gentile town. The act was probably meant to provoke the people to reconsider the apostles' message.

2. People guessed that Jesus was John the Baptist raised from the dead, Elijah, or a prophet. Since the truth was that Jesus was God, none of the guesses were correct.

3. Mark often segues between stories by simply writing "Immediately" or "Then."

4. God providing manna to Israel in the wilderness (throughout the book of Exodus); Elisha feeding one hundred men with twenty pieces of bread (2 Kings 4:12–44); and the prophet Ezekiel comparing Israel to sheep with no shepherd (Ezekiel 34).

5. Job says God is the only one who *"treads on the waves of the sea . . . He performs wonders that cannot be fathomed, miracles that cannot be counted"* (Job 9:8, 10–11).

MARK 7:1–8:21—OUT-OF-BOUNDS JESUS

1. The Pharisees were not concerned about literal grime. It bothered them that the disciples skipped the ritual rinsing that traditionally made a person clean before God (Mark 7:3–4).

2. This question deals with the personal circumstances of each reader and is intended to provoke thought and discussion; there is no official "right" answer. Any honest answer is right.

3. Tyre, Sidon, and Decapolis were all predominantly Gentile regions. Before Jesus went there, Jews did not expect their Messiah to minister to other races.

4. While most Jews referred to Gentiles as wild street dogs, Jesus used the term meaning a domesticated puppy (Mark 7:27).

5. Mark may have included both stories (Mark 6:30–44, 8:1–10) because one demonstrates Jesus' sufficiency for Jews, while the other demonstrates Jesus' sufficiency for

non-Jews. But he may also have included them both because that's exactly how it happened!

MARK 8:22–9:29—GLOW-IN-THE-DARK JESUS

1. An inclusio is the literary technique of repeating something in order to show where a theme or passage begins and ends. It's relevant here because the center of Mark's book is bracketed by the inclusio of blind men being healed. Inclusios tip us off to how the author of the book wanted the thoughts to be divided.
2. I think Jesus did it because the popular idea of what the Messiah should do was so far from the truth, which only Jesus really understood. If you're studying this book in a group, feel free to kick around some other theories.
3. The Son of Man was a figure who would gloriously rescue Israel, then share rulership forever with God, the Ancient of Days (Daniel 7:13–14).
4. Jesus said, *"If anyone would come after me, he must deny himself and take up his cross and follow me."*
5. The answer to this is subject to debate, but many scholars believe Moses appeared at the Transfiguration (Mark 9:2–13) to represent the fact that Jesus fulfilled the Mosaic law and was the prophet that Moses had predicted in Deuteronomy 18:15–19; and that Elijah was there to represent all the Old Testament prophecies that Jesus fulfilled.

MARK 9:30–10:52—OPTOMETRIST JESUS

1. Jesus predicted his fate three times. The elements of his prediction included that he would go to Jerusalem, be betrayed to the Jewish authorities, be condemned to death, be handed over to the Gentiles, be mocked and tortured, be killed, and three days later rise again (Mark 8:31; 9:31; 10:33–34).
2. The disciples had argued about which of them was the greatest (Mark 9:34). Jesus taught them that, *"If anyone wants to be first, he must be the very last, and the servant of all"* (Mark 9:35).
3. God hates divorce (Malachi 2:15–16). There were many things wrong with the Pharisees' perspective, including the fact that they treated women as property, and sought what Moses would let them get away with instead of seeking God's ideal.
4. Jesus would drink the cup of God's wrath and judgment (Psalm 75:6–8; Isaiah 51:17–22; Jeremiah 25:15–28; Ezekiel 23:31–34; Mark 14:36).

MARK 11:1–25—CONQUEROR JESUS

1. Herod's Temple was under construction from 19 B.C. to A.D. 64—a total of 83 years. The extra credit question is a trick question: the answer is in John 2:20.
2. Jesus was fulfilling the prophecy of Zechariah 9:9.
3. Old Testament writers often used figs, fig trees, and the image of fruitless trees when they wrote of God's judgment upon Israel (Jeremiah 29:17; 8:11–13; Isaiah 34:4;

Hosea 2:12; 9:10, 16; Joel 1:7; Micah 7:1–3).
4. There are many possible answers to this question, but the best-documented answer relies on what Jesus said: *"Is it not written: 'My house will be called a house of prayer for all nations'? But you have made it 'a den of robbers'"* (Mark 11:17). The commerce in the Court of the Gentiles made it impossible for other nations besides Israel to worship in the Temple. In addition, temple policies essentially legalized stealing in the name of God.
5. The context makes a strong case that Jesus was not referring to a metaphorical mountain, but was referring directly to the temple mount upon which he was standing when he uttered the words.

MARK 11:27–12:44—OFFENSIVE JESUS

1. Jesus didn't answer their question because they wouldn't answer the question about who authorized John the Baptist's ministry—and the answer to "Who authorized Jesus?" was the same as the answer to "Who authorized John?" In both cases, the answer is, God Himself.
2. In Isaiah's story, God punished the vineyard for refusing to bear fruit (Isaiah 5:1–7). In Jesus' parable, God punished the *tenants* of the vineyard for not allowing the vineyard to bear fruit. The tenants symbolized Israel's religious leadership (Mark 12:1–12).
3. The coin was imprinted with Caesar's image on it, so it belonged to Caesar. But humans were imprinted with God's image; therefore, your entire self belongs to God (Genesis 1:27).
4. The Sadducees probably began as the followers of King Solomon's high priest, Zadok. In Jesus' time, they were the aristocracy of the Jews: the wealthiest, the largest land owners, and the most politically powerful.
5. The scribe understood that obeying God from the heart means more to God than any amount of outward religious ceremony, such as donating burnt offerings and sacrifices (Mark 12:32–34; 1 Samuel 15:22).

MARK 13:1–37—FUTURE JESUS

1. "Blepo" is Greek for "watch" or "watch out," so a blepo dog is a watch dog. Mark uses "blepo" over and over in Mark 13 because Jesus keeps telling his disciples, "Watch!"
2. Jesus said that wars, rumors of wars, numerous false Messiahs, earthquakes, famines, and nation rising against nation are the *beginning* of birth pains, but *"the end is still to come."* Sloppy interpreters of Scripture have incorrectly listed those as signs of the end (Mark 13:4–8).
3. We theorize that Mark was trying to remind his readers that *"the abomination that causes desolation"* is a phrase found in Daniel 9, 11, and 12.
4. Prophecies of the universe going bonkers were used in

the Old Testament to show the deep theological significance of events. They were often a way of saying "this punishment will totally rock your world!" or "Things will never be the same after this!" Refer to the Go To references in the chapter on Mark 13:1–37 for lots of examples.

5. Scholars debate this topic, but *"this generation"* is used throughout the first three Gospels to refer to the people who were alive when Jesus was alive, so I think it means the same thing in Mark 13:30.

MARK 14:1–42—BOY SCOUT JESUS

1. Nard was a spice used to prepare bodies before burial. Jesus was about to die, and his body would not receive the customary preparation. Jesus sacrificed everything for us, so there's no such thing as us sacrificing too much for Jesus.

2. The priests knew Jesus was popular, and feared that if they killed him, it would spark a riot (Mark 14:1–2). Judas Iscariot betrayed Jesus (Mark 14:10). The priests lacked enough knowledge of Jesus' schedule to nab him when he was relatively isolated, but Judas, an insider, could provide that information (Mark 14:11, 43).

3. When anointed with nard, Jesus knew he would die soon, that the Gospel would be preached for years to come, and that the sacrificially generous woman would be spoken of wherever the Gospel was preached (Mark 14:6–9). When it was time for Passover supper, Jesus knew who the disciples would meet, what to say, and what would happen (Mark 14:13–15). During the meal, Jesus knew that someone would betray him, and who it was (Mark 14:18, 20). The symbols he instituted at the first communion indicate that he knew how he would die. He knew that all the disciples would desert him (Mark 14:27) and that Peter would deny him three times that very night (Mark 14:30).

4. Jesus reinterpreted the Passover matzoh as a symbol for his body, which was broken for us (Mark 14:23). The wine represents his blood and how it bought a new covenant between us and God (Mark 14:24).

5. Jesus grieved because he knew he was going to face *"the cup"* of God's judgment. Having lived since the beginning of time in unity with the Father, he could barely stand the prospect of sin temporarily separating him from fellowship with God (Mark 14:35–36).

MARK 14:43–15:15—PRISONER JESUS

1. Judas kissed Jesus in a repeated, prolonged manner, according to the word Mark used. The kiss told the temple police which man to arrest (Mark 14:44).

2. The Sanhedrin was not supposed to meet at night, was not supposed to meet on a Feast day, and should have met to weigh evidence impartially—but instead, *"were*

looking for evidence against Jesus so that they could put him to death" (Mark 14:55).

3. Caiaphas would have been unable to declare Jesus guilty of blasphemy if Jesus himself had not testified that he was the Messiah (Mark 14:61–64).

4. Peter bragged that he would follow Jesus better than anyone else did (Mark 14:29), but didn't obey Jesus' command to "watch." Instead, he dozed through prayer time, which made him more susceptible to temptation (Mark 14:37–40).

5. This is kind of a trick question. Jesus didn't really defend himself at all—he remained silent and let God's will run its course (Mark 14:60–61; 15:3–5).

MARK 15:16–41—SCAPEGOAT JESUS

1. Mark says they called together the entire cohort, so there could have been up to six hundred soldiers present. A reasonable estimate is two hundred (Mark 15:16).

2. Simon of Cyrene was the man the soldiers forced to carry Jesus' cross (Mark 15:21).

3. Jesus was offered wine mixed with myrrh, which had the narcotic effect of dulling the senses and inducing drowsiness. Amazingly, Jesus rejected it (Mark 15:23).

4. One definition of irony is, "incongruity between a situation developed in a drama and the accompanying words or actions that is understood by the audience but not by the characters in the play." Examples include Caiaphas blaspheming by accusing Jesus of blasphemy (Mark 14:60–65); the Sanhedrin beating Jesus as a false prophet while his prophecies were coming true (Mark 14:65–72); Pilate labeling Jesus "King of the Jews" as an insult when actually it was true (Mark 15:26); and the high priests unwittingly stating the truth of the Gospel while taunting, "He saved others, but he cannot save himself" (Mark 15:31). There are more.

MARK 15:42–16:20—THE REAL JESUS

1. Joseph of Arimathea was a member of the Sanhedrin, the council that convicted Jesus. He was also a wealthy yet brave man who stepped forward to arrange Jesus' burial (Mark 15:43–46).

2. Mary Magdalene, Mary the mother of James, and Salome went to Jesus' grave on the first day of the week—Sunday. This is the reason we worship on Sunday instead of on the Jewish Sabbath, Saturday.

3. Peter had denied Christ, but Jesus wanted him to know he was still invited to be a disciple (Mark 16:7).

4. Reasons cited in this section include: the verses are missing from the earliest, most reliable copies of Mark; none of the early church fathers quoted from those verses; the vocabulary isn't like Mark's; the transition isn't like Mark's; and the verses commend quirky behaviors that the church never followed, such as drinking deadly poison (Mark 16:9–20).

APPENDIX B—THE EXPERTS

Randy Alcorn—Pastor for fourteen years before founding Eternal Perspective Ministries. A popular teacher and speaker who has ministered in more than a dozen countries, Randy is the author of eleven books, including the best-selling novels *Deadline, Dominion,* and *Lord Foulgrin's Letters.*

Maya Angelou—Poet and author of many books including *I Know Why the Caged Bird Sings*, Angelou became the northern coordinator for the Southern Christian Leadership Conference in the sixties at the request of Martin Luther King, Jr. She has written and produced many television programs, received numerous honorary degrees, and served in appointments by Presidents Carter and Ford, and is one of the few women members of the Director's Guild. She is currently a university professor in North Carolina.

Saint Augustine (354–430)—Early Christian church father and philosopher, also known as Saint Augustine of Hippo.

Judy Bodmer—Contributor to the #1 *New York Times* bestseller, *Chicken Soup for the Mother's Soul*, and author of *When Love Dies: How to Help a Hopeless Marriage* and *What's in the Bible for . . . Mothers.* She is past president of the Pacific Northwest Writers Association and is the wife of a pastor on staff at the largest church in Washington state.

Andy Bond—Tutored in Judaism by messianic Jews from Orthodox homes, Bond taught at Congregation Emmaus, the largest messianic congregation in the Pacific Northwest. Recently ordained as a deacon in the Communion of Evangelical Episcopal Churches, he is currently doing postgraduate work at Fuller Theological Seminary.

John Bright—Scholar and prolific author, Bright's writings on the Old Testament are referred to by other scholars, both Christian and Jewish, when attempting to date Old Testament events. His books *A History of Israel* and *The Authority of the Old Testament* are considered must-reads in many seminaries.

Frederick Buechner—Author of more than twenty novels and nonfiction works, including *Godric, The Sacred Journey*, and *Telling Secrets.*

Jim Cymbala—Pastor of The Brooklyn Tabernacle since 1972. His wife, Carol, directs the Grammy Award–winning Brooklyn Tabernacle Choir. Jim has coauthored the best-selling books *Fresh Wind, Fresh Fire* and *Fresh Faith.*

C. H. Dodd (1884–1973)—Professor at Cambridge University, Dodd was also vice-president of the British and Foreign Bible Society, and a founding member of the United Bible Societies. He directed the translation of the Bible into the version called the New English Bible and authored numerous scientific works on the research of the Holy Scriptures.

Eusebius (A.D. 260–340)—The first person to transcribe faithfully the most important existing documents and surviving eyewitness accounts of his day into one comprehensive account of Christianity, covering everything from its inception to about A.D. 330. Because of burnings and persecutions by Rome, a vast number of facts he recorded can be learned from no other ancient source. He is often referred to as "the father of church history."

Gordon D. Fee—Professor of New Testament at Regent College in Vancouver, Canada, and the author of many scholarly works on the Bible.

John Fischer—Graduate of Wheaton College and a pioneering musician and songwriter in the early days of contemporary Christian music. He is now better known as a popular speaker and award-winning author of many books. For years his insightful columns have been a monthly feature in *Contemporary Christian Music* magazine.

Richard J. Foster—A Quaker and the author of five books, including the modern classic *Celebration of Discipline* and *Finding the Heart's True Home*, selected by *Christianity Today* as 1993's Book of the Year and winner of the Gold Medallion Award from the Evangelical Christian Publishers' Association. He is also founder of Renovaré, an infrachurch movement committed to the renewal of the church in all her multifaceted expressions.

David E. Garland—With a Ph.D. from Southern Baptist Theological Seminary, Garland is Professor of Christian Scriptures at George W. Truet Theological Seminary, Baylor University.

Billy Graham—An international crusade, radio, and TV evangelist, Graham has presented the Gospel face-to-face to more people than any man in history. He founded *Christianity Today* and *Decision* magazines, and is the author of many inspirational classics read by millions.

Dr. Winn Griffin—Founder of the Institute of Biblical Studies in Seattle, assisted John Wimber in writing the theology of the Vineyard Movement.

Os Guinness—Earned a D.Phil. from Oxford University and is a writer and senior fellow of the Trinity Forum. A speaker of international renown who served at L'Abri in Switzerland, Dr. Guinness has lived in the United States since 1984 and authored numerous books, including *God in the Dark* and *The Call*.

Richard C. Halverson—One of the best-loved pastors of the twentieth century. As pastor of Fourth Presbyterian Church in Washington, D.C., and later, Chaplain of the U.S. Senate, he has written numerous devotional works, including *Perspectives*, a newsletter that has been ongoing since 1949.

Hank Hanegraaff—Host of the radio program *The Bible Answer Man*, heard daily throughout the United States and Canada. He is also president of the Christian Research Institute and author of award-winning books.

Matthew Henry (1662–1714)—Lover of the Bible, Henry first read aloud from it when he was only three years old. He pastored in churches near London for twenty-seven years. In 1704 he began his *Notes on the New Testament*, which grew into the six-volume *Matthew Henry's Commentary*, for the last 250 years the most widely used of all Bible commentaries.

Morna D. Hooker—The Lady Margaret's Professor of Divinity at The University of Cambridge.

Larry W. Hurtado—Professor of Religion at the University of Manitoba and is the author of numerous articles and books.

David Jeremiah—Best-selling author, the senior pastor of Shadow Mountain Community Church in El Cajon, California, and the chancellor of Christian Heritage College. His internationally syndicated radio program *Turning Point* is broadcast on more than 950 stations.

George Eldon Ladd (1911–1982)—Professor of New Testament Exegesis and Theology at Fuller Theological Seminary, Pasadena, California. He authored many books including what many consider a modern classic, *A Theology of the New Testament*.

William L. Lane—Paul T. Walls Chair in Wesleyan and Biblical Studies at Seattle Pacific University, Seattle, Washington. In addition to numerous articles on New Testament studies, he has written the widely acclaimed commentary *The Gospel of Mark*.

C. S. Lewis—Born in Belfast in 1898, Lewis was Fellow and Tutor in English Literature at Magdalen College, Oxford, and later was Professor of Medieval and Renaissance Literature at Cambridge University, where he remained till his death in 1963. He wrote numerous books of literary criticism and on Christianity, the best known being *The Screwtape Letters*, as well as four novels for adults. The seven books of the *Chronicles of Narnia* were his only works for children.

Anne Graham Lotz—Daughter of the famous evangelist Billy Graham, Lotz founded AnGeL Ministries to revive the hearts of God's people through Anne's live presentations, books, and tapes. Her books have twice won the ECPA Gold Medallion Award.

Max Lucado—Pastor of Oak Hills Church in San Antonio, Texas. He and his wife, Denalyn, have three daughters, Jenna, Andrea, and Sara, and a dog named Salty. He holds a B.A. and M.A. from Abilene Christian University. His numerous best-sellers include *God Came Near*, *And the Angels Were Silent*, *No Wonder They Call Him the Savior*, and *Six Hours One Friday*.

John MacArthur—Pastor and teacher of Grace Community Church in Sun Valley, California. MacArthur is a popular author and speaker whose radio program, *Grace to You*, airs nationwide daily. He has written more than seventy-two books, including several best sellers.

Frederica Mathewes-Green—A highly skilled and prolific writer, Green earned her Theological Studies MA at Virginia Episcopal Seminary. She has been an NPR commentator, a columnist for *Christianity Today*, a book reviewer for the *Los Angeles Times*, a strong voice in the pro-life movement, and senior writer and editor for Big Idea Productions, the makers of "Veggie Tales."

Josh McDowell—Magna cum laude graduate of Talbot Theological Seminary and a member of two national Honor Societies. A traveling representative of Campus Crusade for Christ, he has spoken to more than seven million young people in eighty-four countries, including seven hundred university and college campuses. McDowell has authored or coauthored fifty-two books, including *Evidence that Demands a Verdict*, Volumes 1 and 2.

Henrietta C. Mears—One of the great Bible teachers of the twentieth century. While Christian Education Director at First Presbyterian Church of Hollywood, she built one of the largest Sunday Schools in the world and wrote curriculum that was in such high demand that to publish it, she founded Gospel Light in 1933. Such notable Christian leaders as Richard C. Halverson and Bill Bright were among her students. Miss Mears developed "cradle-to-grave" age-appropriate curriculum, published a new style of vacation Bible school, and lent her support to distributing gospel materials around the world until her death in 1963.

Dean Merrill—Vice-president and publisher of the International Bible Society. The author of ten books, he is the former president of the Evangelical Press Association and a former vice president of Focus on the Family.

Malcolm Muggeridge (1903–1990)—A former Communist who became Christian, Muggeridge was an internationally renowned foreign correspondent for the London *Daily Telegraph*, editor of *Punch* magazine, noted biographer of Mother Teresa of Calcutta, and a leading Christian apologist.

Andrew Murray (1828–1917)—Born in South Africa and sent to study in England at age 10, Murray returned to South Africa as a pastor and evangelist. He led a revival that shook the country. His lifetime effort to deepen the spiritual lives of Christians resulted in profound, timeless writings such as *With Christ in the School of Prayer* and *Absolute Surrender*.

John Henry Newman (1801–1890)—Cardinal-Deacon of St. George in Velabro, a philosopher, man of letters, leader of the Tractarian Movement, and according to *The Catholic Encyclopedia*, the most illustrious of English converts to the Church.

Mark Noll—McManis Professor of Christian Thought at Wheaton College, Noll has served as an editor for the *Reformed Journal* and as a senior editor for *Christianity Today*. He is the author of numerous books, including *A History of Christianity in the United States and Canada* and *The Scandal of the Evangelical Mind*.

Kathleen Norris—Author of numerous *New York Times* best-selling books, including *The Cloister Walk* and *Amazing Grace: A Vocabulary of Faith*. She pastors in South Dakota.

Henri J. M. Nouwen—Catholic priest who taught at the University of Notre Dame, Yale, and Harvard. From 1986 until his death in 1996, he was associated with L'Arche Community in France and Toronto. He has written many noted books, including *The Wounded Healer* and *The Return of the Prodigal Son*.

Eugene H. Peterson—A prolific author, Peterson is best known for his fresh, emotional paraphrase of the Bible, entitled *The Message*. He was Professor of Spiritual Theology at Regent College, Vancouver, British Columbia.

Luci Shaw—Poet, speaker, teacher, editor, and writer, Luci founded Harold Shaw Publishers with her husband. Since then she has served on the faculty of Regent College, Vancouver, Canada, and produced numerous books, some coauthored with her good friend Madeleine L'Engle.

Ronald J. Sider—Author of more than twenty books, including *Rich Christians in an Age of Hunger*, President of Evangelicals for Social Action, and Professor of Theology and Culture at Eastern Baptist Theological Seminary.

A. B. Simpson (1843–1919)—One of the most respected Christian figures in American evangelicalism. A much sought after speaker and pastor, Simpson founded the Christian Missionary Alliance, published over seventy books, edited a weekly magazine for nearly forty years, and wrote many gospel songs and poems.

Gary Smalley—One of the country's foremost experts on relationships. He is the host of numerous popular films and videos. He lives with his wife, Norma.

R. C. Sproul—Theologian, pastor, and teacher, Sproul is chairman of the board of Ligonier Ministries. He teaches at several seminaries, has a daily radio show called "Renewing Your Mind," and preaches at Saint Andrews Chapel near Orlando, Florida. His many books include *Chosen by God*, *Surprised by Suffering*, and *The Holiness of God*.

Charles Spurgeon—One of the world's most prolific preachers, lived from 1834 to 1892. He had already preached more than six hundred times by the age of twenty. He drew such a large congregation with his often humorous sermons that the six-thousand-seat Metropolitan Tabernacle was built for him. At the peak of his career, it was not unusual for him to address over twenty-five thousand people on a Sunday in multiple services, and his sermons were reprinted each week on the front page of the *London Times*.

James S. Stewart—The greatest preacher of the twentieth century according to interdenominational professional magazine, *Preaching*. He was a Scottish preacher and a New Testament professor who also served a two-year term as moderator of the General Assembly of the Church of Scotland in the 1960s.

John R. W. Stott—International preacher, evangelist, and communicator of Scripture. For many years he served as rector of All Souls Church in London, where he carried out an effective urban pastoral ministry. Appointed Chaplain to the Queen for over thirty years, and a leader among evangelicals in Britain, the United States, and around the world, Stott was a principal framer of the landmark Lausanne Covenant (1974). His books have sold millions of copies around the world and in dozens of languages.

Lee Strobel—With a Master of Studies in Law degree from Yale Law School, Strobel was an award-winning journalist at the *Chicago Tribune*. After serving for twelve years as a teaching pastor at Willow Creek Community Church near Chicago, he joined the staff of Saddleback Valley Community Church in Orange County, California. Books he has authored include *The Case for Christ,* which won the 1999 ECPA Gold Medallion Book Award in the category of Missions/Evangelism.

Charles R. Swindoll—President of Dallas Theological Seminary and the host of the nationally syndicated radio program, *Insight for Living.* He has authored more than thirty best-selling books. His practical application of the Bible to everyday living makes God's truths a reality to hurting people. Dr. Swindoll and his wife Cynthia reside in Dallas, Texas, where he serves as senior pastor of Stonebriar Community Church.

Joni Eareckson Tada—Having been tutored in God's Word amidst the bruising reality of quadriplegia for over thirty years, Tada is the author of over twenty books dealing with God's hand in hardship. She serves as president of JAF Ministries, a Christian organization that advances Christ's kingdom among the world's 550 million people with disabilities.

A. W. Tozer (1897–1963)—Born in Pennsylvania, Tozer began pastoring the Alliance Church in Nutter Fort, West Virginia, in 1919. After other pastorships in West Virginia, Ohio, and Indiana, he came to the Southside Alliance Church in Chicago in 1928, where he ministered for over thirty years. Ministering without the benefit of a university or Bible college education, he is known today for his writings—over fifty titles totaling more than 3.2 million copies in print.

John T. Trent—Leading marriage and family counselor and popular speaker.

Desmond Tutu—General Secretary of the South African Council of Churches and an honorary doctor of a number of leading universities in the USA, Britain and Germany, in recognition of his many accomplishments in both theology and civil rights. He was awarded the Nobel Peace Prize in 1984 for his effective and nonviolent leadership in the campaign against apartheid in South Africa.

Robert Van Kampen—Founder of Van Kampen Merrit, an investment banking company that sold to Xerox in the mid-1980s. Today he serves as chairman of six Christian mission and ministry organizations, co-founded two mission agencies, and founded The Scriptorium, an organization whose sole purpose is the scholastic defense of the accuracy and authenticity of the Bible. The Van Kampen Collection is the largest private collection of manuscripts, artifacts, scrolls, and early editions of the Bible in the world today.

Claus Westerman—Theologian, historian, and scholar who has written extensively on the Old Testament.

Dallas Willard—Author of several noted books, including *The Divine Conspiracy*, Willard is a professor at the University of Southern California's School of Philosophy, serving as a visiting Professor at the University of Colorado.

N. T. Wright—Canon Theologian at Westminster Abbey and former Dean of Lichfield Cathedral. He taught New Testament studies for twenty years at Cambridge, McGill, and Oxford Universities. His full-scale works such as *Jesus and the Victory of God* have caused him to be widely regarded as one of the most significant scholars currently studying the historical Jesus.

Philip Yancey—Editor-at-large and columnist for *Christianity Today* magazine. He has written several Gold Medallion Award-winning books, including *Where Is God When It Hurts?*, *Disappointment with God*, *The Gift Nobody Wants*, *What's So Amazing About Grace?*, and *The Jesus I Never Knew.*

Note: To the best of our knowledge, all of the above information is accurate and up to date. In some cases we were unable to obtain biographical information.

—THE STARBURST EDITORS

ENDNOTES

Introduction
1. Henrietta C. Mears, *What the Bible Is All About* (Glendale, CA: Gospel Light, 1953), 12.
2. Josh McDowell, *Evidence that Demands a Verdict* (San Bernardino, CA: Campus Crusade for Christ, 1972), 76.

Part One—Celebrity Jesus
1. John Bright, *The Authority of the Old Testament* (Carlisle, England: Paternoster Publishers, 1997).
2. Gordon D. Fee and Douglas Stuart, *How to Read the Bible for All Its Worth* (Grand Rapids, MI: Zondervan, 1981, 1993), 11.
3. Philip Yancey, *The Jesus I Never Knew* (Grand Rapids, MI: Zondervan, 1995), 57.
4. William Barclay, quoted in Malcolm Muggeridge, *Jesus: the Man Who Lives* (New York: Harper & Row, 1975), 74.
5. N. T. Wright, *The Challenge of Jesus* (Downers Grove, IL: InterVarsity Press, 1999), 21–22.

Mark 1:1–13—What If God Was One of Us?
1. Yancey, *The Jesus I Never Knew*, 52.
2. David E. Garland, *Mark: The NIV Application Commentary* (Grand Rapids, MI: Zondervan, 1996), 42.
3. Billy Graham, *Peace with God* (New York: Doubleday, 1953), 114, 118.
4. William L. Lane, *The Gospel of Mark* (Grand Rapids, MI: Eerdmans, 1974), 49, 50.
5. Philip Comfort, ed., *Life Application Bible Commentary: Mark* (Wheaton, IL.: Tyndale, 1994), 9.
6. Luci Shaw, *Water My Soul* (Grand Rapids, MI: Zondervan, 1998), 104.
7. A. B. Simpson, *The Gospel of Mark* (Harrisburg, PA: Christian Publications), 30–31.
8. Graham, *Peace with God*, 48.

Mark 1:14–45—Action-Figure Jesus
1. Gordon D. Fee, *Paul, the Spirit, and the People of God* (Peabody, MA: Hendrickson Publishers, 1996), 51.
2. John R. W. Stott, *Basic Christianity* (London: InterVarsity Press, 1958), 108–9.
3. C. H. Spurgeon, *12 Sermons on the Love of Christ* (Grand Rapids, MI: Baker Books, 1977), 108.
4. Randy Alcorn, *Lord Foulgrin's Letters* (Sisters, OR: Multnomah, 2000), 279.
5. Ronald J. Sider, *Living Like Jesus* (Grand Rapids, MI: Baker Books, 1999), 60.

6. Comfort, *Life Application Bible Commentary: Mark*, 40.
7. Gary Smalley and John Trent, *The Gift of the Blessing*, quoted in Max Lucado, gen. ed., *The Inspirational Study Bible* (Dallas, TX: Word, 1995), 1134–35.
8. Joni Eareckson Tada, *When God Weeps* (Grand Rapids, MI: Zondervan, 1997), 38.

Mark 2:1–3:12—Antiestablishment Jesus
1. C. S. Lewis, *Mere Christianity* (New York: Macmillan, 1960), 55.
2. Garland, *Mark: The NIV Application Commentary*, 110.
3. Richard J. Foster, *Celebration of Discipline* (San Francisco, CA: HarperSanFrancisco, 1978), 47, 60.
4. Warren Wiersbe, ed., *The Best of A. W. Tozer* (Grand Rapids, MI: Baker Book House, 1978), 120–21.
5. John Fischer, *12 Steps for the Recovering Pharisee (like me)* (Minneapolis, MN: Bethany House, 2000), 14–15, 18.

Mark 3:13–35—Shocking Words of Jesus, Part One
1. Papius, quoted in Eusebius, *Ecclesiastical History* (Kirsopp Lake translation; Cambridge, MA: Harvard University Press, 1926), 3.39.
2. N. T. Wright, *Jesus and the Victory of God* (Minneapolis, MN: Fortress Press, 1996), 300, 532.
3. Yancey, *The Jesus I Never Knew*, 99–100.
4. Dean Merrill, *Sinners in the Hands of an Angry Church* (Grand Rapids, MI: Zondervan, 1997), 148–49.
5. Spurgeon, *12 Sermons on the Love of Christ*, 31.
6. Max Lucado, *A Gentle Thunder* (Dallas, TX: Word, 1995).

Mark 4:1–34—Shocking Words of Jesus, Part Two
1. C. H. Dodd, *The Parables of the Kingdom* (London, 1961), 16.
2. Wright, *Jesus and the Victory of God*, 176.
3. Garland, *Mark: The NIV Application Commentary*, 161.
4. Yancey, *The Jesus I Never Knew*, 242–43.
5. Bill Adler, ed., *The Wit and Wisdom of Billy Graham* (New York: Random House, 1967), 23.
6. Wright, *The Challenge of Jesus*, 52–53.
7. Wiersbe, *The Best of A. W. Tozer*, 15–16.

Mark 4:35–5:20—Power-Ranger Jesus
1. Max Lucado, *In the Eye of the Storm* (Dallas, TX: Word, 1991), 185.
2. Alcorn, *Lord Foulgrin's Letters*, 282.
3. Comfort, *Life Application Bible Commentary: Mark*, 138.

Mark 5:21–6:6—Party-Pooper Jesus
1. Anne Graham Lotz, *Just Give Me Jesus* (Nashville, TN: Word, 2000), 136–137.
2. Andrew Murray, *The Deeper Christian Life and Other Writings* (Nashville, TN: Thomas Nelson Publishers, 2000), 45.
3. Claus Westerman, quoted in Perry B. Yoder and William Swartley, eds., *The Meaning of Peace* (Louisville, KY: Westminster/John Knox Press, 1992), 19.
4. Max Lucado, *When God Whispers Your Name* (Dallas, TX: Word, 1994), 101.
5. Lane, *The Gospel of Mark*, 196.
6. Fischer, *12 Steps for the Recovering Pharisee (like me)*, 138–39.
7. Eugene H. Peterson, *Subversive Spirituality* (Grand Rapids, MI: Eerdmans, 1994), 8.
8. Garland, *Mark: The NIV Application Commentary*, 231.
9. Graham, *Peace with God*, 53.

Mark 6:6–56—More Clues about Jesus' Secret Identity
1. John Henry Newman, *Prayers, Verses, and Devotions*, quoted in *Christianity Today*, May 19, 1997, 36.
2. Frank Gaebelein, ed., *The Expositor's Bible Commentary: Mark* (Grand Rapids, MI: Zondervan, 1984), 667.
3. Matthew Henry, *Matthew Henry's Commentary* (Grand Rapids, MI: Zondervan, 1961), 1377.
4. R. C. Sproul, *The Holiness of God* (Wheaton, IL: Tyndale, 1985), 163–64.
5. Peterson, *Subversive Spirituality*, 101.
6. Lane, *The Gospel of Mark*.
7. Wright, *Jesus and the Victory of God*, 653.
8. Lucado, *In the Eye of the Storm*, 182.

Mark 7:1–8:21—Out-of-Bounds Jesus
1. Fischer, *12 Steps for the Recovering Pharisee (like me)*, 45–46.
2. Dallas Willard, *The Divine Conspiracy* (San Francisco, CA: HarperSanFrancisco, 1998), 143.
3. Richard C. Halverson, *The Living Body*, quoted in *Christianity Today*, June 14, 1999, 84.
4. Foster, *Celebration of Discipline*, 9–11.
5. J. D. Douglas, F. F. Bruce, et al., editors, *New Bible Dictionary* (Leicester, England: InterVarsity Press, 1982), 1228.
6. Maya Angelou, *Wouldn't Take Nothing for My Journey Now* (New York: Bantam, 1994), 6–7.
7. C. H. Spurgeon, *Spurgeon's Sermon Notes* (Peabody, MA: Hendrickson Publishers, 1997), 420.
8. Simpson, *The Gospel of Mark*, 88–89.
9. Peterson, *Subversive Spirituality*, 15.
10. Spurgeon, *12 Sermons on the Love of Christ*, 107.

Mark 8:22–9:29—Glow-in-the-Dark Jesus
1. Murray, *The Deeper Christian Life and Other Writings*, 282–84.
2. Frederick Buechner, *A Room Called Remember: Uncollected Pieces* (San Francisco, CA: HarperSanFrancisco, 1984), 51.
3. Muggeridge, *Jesus: The Man Who Lives*, 78.
4. Charles R. Swindoll, *Perfect Trust* (Nashville, TN: J. Countryman, 2000), 69.
5. Mark Noll, "The Gift of Humility," *Christianity Today*, December 6, 1999, 56.
6. Buechner, *A Room Called Remember: Uncollected Pieces*, x.
7. Henri J. M. Nouwen, *The Living Reminder: Service and Prayer in Memory of Jesus Christ* (New York: Seabury, 1977), 12.
8. Jim Cymbala with Dean Merrill, *Fresh Wind, Fresh Fire* (Grand Rapids, MI: Zondervan, 1997), 28.

Mark 9:30–10:52—Optometrist Jesus
1. John MacArthur, *Mark: The Humanity of Christ* (Nashville, TN: Word Publishing, 2000), 61.
2. Kathleen Norris, *Amazing Grace: A Vocabulary of Faith*, quoted in *Christianity Today*, April 3, 2000, 76.
3. Judy Bodmer, *When Love Dies* (Nashville, TN: Word Publishing, 1999), 8.
4. Philip Yancey, *What's So Amazing About Grace?* (Grand Rapids, MI: Zondervan, 1997), 71–72.
5. C. S. Lewis, *Poems* (New York: Harcourt Brace Jovanovich, 1964), 134.
6. James S. Stewart, *A Man in Christ: The Vital Elements of Paul's Religion* (London: Holder and Stoughton, 1963), 95–96.
7. Philip Yancey, *Reaching for the Invisible God*, quoted in *Christianity Today*, Sept. 4, 2000, 74.
8. Henri J. M. Nouwen, *Mornings with Henri J. M. Nouwen,* quoted in *Christianity Today*, Feb. 8, 1999, 72.
9. Lewis, *Mere Christianity*, 60.
10. Tom Getman, personal correspondence, quoted in *Christianity Today*, March 6, 2000, 86.

Mark 11:1–25—Conqueror Jesus
1. Wright, *The Challenge of Jesus*, 55, 67.
2. Wright, *Jesus and the Victory of God*, 493.
3. Yancey, *The Jesus I Never Knew*, 190.
4. Henry, *Matthew Henry's Commentary*, 1391.
5. *Encyclopedia Judaica*, Vol. XII (Jerusalem, Israel: Keter Publishing House, 1971), 962.
6. Wright, *The Challenge of Jesus*, 66–67.
7. George Arthur Buttrick, ed., *The Interpreter's Bible* (New York: Abingdon, 1951), 829.
8. Wright, *Jesus and the Victory of God*, 422.

Mark 11:27–12:44—Offensive Jesus
1. Garland, *Mark: The NIV Application Commentary*, 443.
2. Billy Graham, *How to Be Born Again* (New York: Inspirational Press, 1977), 190.
3. Henri J. M. Nouwen, *A Cry for Mercy*, quoted in *Christianity Today*, June 14, 1999, 84.
4. Buttrick, *The Interpreter's Bible*, 841.
5. Frederica Mathewes-Green, "Bible Misquotes," broadcast on *All Things Considered*, National Public Radio, October 6, 1997.
6. Frederica Mathewes-Green, "Go Ahead, Offend Me," <http://www.frederica.com> (3 May 2001), Articles.
7. Saint Augustine, quoted in Thomas C. Oden, gen. ed., *Mark: Ancient Christian Commentary on Scripture* (Downers Grove, IL: InterVarsity Press, 1998), 174.
8. Os Guinness, *The Call* (Nashville, TN: Word Publishing, 1998), 30–31.

Mark 13:1–37—Future Jesus
1. Dwight Wilson, *Armageddon Now! The Premillenarian Response to Russia and Israel since 1917* (Grand Rapids: Baker, 1977), 216.
2. Robert Van Kampen, *The Rapture Question Answered: Plain and Simple* (Grand Rapids, MI: Fleming H. Revell, 1997), 24.
3. David Jeremiah, *Jesus' Final Warning* (Nashville, TN: Word Publishing, 1999), 11–12.
4. Dr. Winn Griffin, Institute for Biblical Studies Seattle Catalog, 1996, back cover.
5. Jeremiah, *Jesus' Final Warning*, 14.
6. R. C. Sproul, *The Last Days According to Jesus* (Grand Rapids, MI: Baker Books, 1998), 31.
7. George Eldon Ladd, *A Theology of the New Testament* (Grand Rapids, MI: Eerdman, 1993), 201–2.

8. Yancey, *The Jesus I Never Knew*, 251.
9. See footnote in NIV; David E. Garland, *Mark: NIV Application Commentary* (Grand Rapids, MI: Zondervan, 1996); Terry Frasier, *A Second Look at the Second Coming* (Ben Lomond, CA: Conciliar, 1999); William L. Lane, *The Gospel According to Mark* (Grand Rapids, MI: Eerdmans, 1974); Larry Hurtado, *Mark: New International Bible Commentary* (Peabody, MA: Hendrickson, 1989).
10. Eusebius, *Ecclesiastical History*, 3.5.3, 70.
11. Gaebelein, *The Expositor's Bible Commentary: Mark*, 751.
12. Jeremiah, *Jesus' Final Warning*, 72.
13. Yancey, *The Jesus I Never Knew*, 227.
14. Lewis, *Mere Christianity*, 65.

Mark 14:1–42—Boy Scout Jesus
1. John MacArthur, *The Murder of Jesus* (Nashville, TN: Word Publishing, 2000), 14–15.
2. Lotz, *Just Give Me Jesus*, 34.
3. Andy Bond, *Haggadah for Passover* (Duvall, WA: Brass Weight Productions, 1999), 8.
4. Morna D. Hooker, *The Gospel According to Saint Mark* (London: A & C Black, 1991), 342–43.

Mark 14:43–15:15—Prisoner Jesus
1. MacArthur, *The Murder of Jesus*, 89–90.
2. Larry W. Hurtado, *Mark* (Peabody, MA.: Hendrickson Publishers, 1989), 253.
3. Lotz, *Just Give Me Jesus*, 242.

4. MacArthur, *The Murder of Jesus*, 125.
5. Ibid., 175.
6. Max Lucado, *He Chose the Nails* (Nashville, TN: Word Publishing, 2000), 15–16.

Mark 15:16–41—Scapegoat Jesus
1. Lucado, *He Chose the Nails*, 17, 19.
2. Yancey, *The Jesus I Never Knew*, 199.
3. Sproul, *The Holiness of God*, 121.
4. Lotz, *Just Give Me Jesus*, 271.
5. Hurtado, *Mark*, 266.
6. Sproul, *The Holiness of God*, 121–22.
7. Lucado, *He Chose the Nails*, 114.
8. Saint Augustine, quoted in Oden, *Ancient Christian Commentary on Scripture: Mark*, 234.
9. Wright, *The Challenge of Jesus*, 90
10. Lotz, *Just Give Me Jesus*, 279.
11. Foster, *Celebration of Discipline*, 29.

Mark 15:42–16:20—The Real Jesus
1. C. S. Lewis, *The Lion, the Witch, and the Wardrobe*, quoted in *Christianity Today*, April 6, 1998, 68.
2. Hank Hanegraaff, *Resurrection* (Nashville, TN: Word Publishing, 2000), 34.
3. William Lane Craig, quoted in Strobel, *The Case for Christ*, 212.
4. Desmond Tutu, *Crying in the Wilderness*, quoted in *Christianity Today*, April 5, 1999, 69.

INDEX

Boldface numbers refer to defined (What?) terms in the sidebar.

as representative act, 21
as revolutionary political leader, 300
"Surely this man was the Son of God,"
306
Temple veil torn, 21, 305
(*See also* Crucifixion of Jesus; Resurrec-
tion of Jesus)
Decapolis, 99
deaf man healed, 148–149
Demoniac, **95**
Demon-possessed, **94**–95
Jesus accused of being, 66, 68–69
Demons, **34**–35
cast out of boy, 171–175
characteristics of, 97
disciples given authority over, 119–120, 122
driven out in Jesus' name, 181–182
in Greek woman's daughter, 144–147
increasingly resisting Jesus, 173
Jesus' authority over, 31, 34–37, 95
Jesus granting favor to, 95–96
Legion, 94–99
recognizing Jesus, 14, 22, 31, 34–36, 94–95
Denarius, 229–230
"Deny yourself," 163–164
Desert:
forty days and forty nights, 22–23
Israel led from, 16
John the Baptist in, 16–17
Satan tempting Jesus in, 22–23, 80
Deuteronomy, Book of, 110, 186
Devil (*see* Satan)
Dictionary of Jesus and the Gospels, 97
Diet:
food laws, 142–143
of John the Baptist, 16–18
kosher, 17
Disciples:
backgrounds of, 29–30, 47
competition among, 179–181
as fishermen, 29–30
Jesus transferring mission to, 258
job of, 72
Legion as rejected, 98–99
in Mark's Gospel, 158
as misunderstanding Jesus, 116–117,
132–133, 152–154, 158, 160
Olivet Discourse as for, 256
primary responsibility of, 98
(*See also* Apostles; individual names)
Discipleship, 200
real cost of, 176
Discourse, **179**
Dissuaded, **160**
Divorce, 185–188
among modern-day Christians, 187
God as hating, 188
valid reasons for, 187–188
women, effect on first-century, 187
Dodd, C. H., on parables, 76
Doeg, 53
Dogs, Gentiles called, 146–147, 217
Donkey, Jesus riding, 209–210
Dove(s):
Holy Spirit descending as, 19
symbolism of, 21
as Temple sacrifice, 216
Dowry, **187**

E
Ear, of high priest's servant, 281
Earthquakes, Olivet Discourse prediction, 246
Easter, 318
Edom, 254
Egypt, Jewish slavery in, 16
Elders, **224**
Elijah, 16–18, 120
exempt from death, 17
forerunner of Messiah, 167
Jesus suspected to be, 122, 161
Jesus thought to be calling, 302–303
John the Baptist as, 170–171
at the Transfiguration, 166–171
Elisha, 120
miracle of, 130
Encyclopedia Judaica, on the Temple, 216
End time:
Day of the Lord as, 254
Jesus on, 246–247
prophecy and predictions, 243–244
Enemies of Jesus:
believing Jesus' miracles, 69
Pharisees as, 54–55
religious leaders as (*see* Pharisees;
Religious leaders)
Epiphanes, Antiochus, 211
Epiphany, **131**
Eternal life:
earning, 189
from following Jesus, 193
Jesus describing, 232, 234
rich young ruler, 189–191
Sadducees' disbelief in, 232
Euphemism, **152, 225**
Eusebius, on Romans invading Jerusalem,
252
Evangelion, **12**
Evil (*see* Sin)
Evil spirits (*see* Demons)
Excommunicated, **47**
Exegesis, **111**
Exemplary, **21**
Exodus, Book of, 16–17, 132–133, 168
Transfiguration, parallels in, 166–167
Exorcism, **96, 172**
Explicit, **13**
Expositor's Bible Commentary, on Olivet
Discourse interpretations, 256
Ezekiel, Book of, 207
Ezekiel (prophet), 3, 63, 85, 130
Ezra (priest), 47

F
Factious, **66**
Faith, 107, 110–111, 114, 148, 171, 173
of Bartimaeus, 198–200
of bleeding woman, 105–106
choosing, 268
cross as symbolizing, 298
of Greek (Phoenician) woman,
146–147
"Help my unbelief," 174
of Jairus, 102, 109–110
lack of in Jesus' hometown, 112–113
of Peter, 158
in prayer, 220
what it isn't, 174

Family:
importance of in first century, 72
loyalty to Jesus above, 249
Ten Commandments, Jesus quoting, 140–
141
Family of Jesus, 66–67, 71, 112
Famines, Olivet Discourse prediction, 246
Fasting, **50**
value of, 51–52
Fear:
of bleeding woman, 113
"Don't be afraid; just believe," 101, 106–
107, 111, 113
of Jerusalem-bound disciples, 193–194
in Mark's Gospel, 319
of women at tomb, 318
Feast of Dedication (Chanukah), 211
Feast of Tabernacles, 204
Feast of Unleavened Bread, 264
Feast of Weeks, 204
Fee, Gordon D. and Douglas Stuart, on Bible
for scholar vs. layperson, 2–3
Fee, Gordon D., on end-time expectations, 29
Fig tree, 213–214, 222
Jesus cursing, 220–221
parable of, 255–256
withering of, 220–221
Figurative, **2**
Fire, 184
First-century roof, illustration of, 46
Fischer, John:
on judging others, 55
on Pharisee traditions, 140
on worship and astonishment, 109
Fish:
feeding five thousand, 128–130
feeding four thousand, 150–151
Fishermen, disciples as, 29–30, 65, 90–91
Five thousand, feeding, 128–130
Flogging, 291–292
Flood, the Great, 154
Following Jesus, 30–31, 86, 126
costs and rewards, 163–166, 193
Levi (Matthew), 46–47, 49
Peter, dialogue regarding, 192–193
the rich young ruler, 189–191
"take up your cross and follow," 163–165
(*See also* Apostles; Christians; Disciples)
Forgiveness:
God's, 220–221
Jesus' death paying for, 305
of others, 220–221
our need for, 70
Forgiveness of sin:
baptism and, 18
as divine right only, 43–45
Jesus of paralytic, 43–46
Forty days and forty nights, 22–23
Foster, Richard J.:
on external vs. internal, 143
on fasting, 51–52
on meditation of Scripture, 308–309
Four soils, parable of, 77–78
Four thousand, feeding of, 150–151
Fruit (*see* Fig tree)
Fruit of the Spirit, 182

Lane, William L.:
  on feeding the multitude, 130
  on professional mourners, 108
  on summons to "turn," 17
Last Supper, the, 269–275
  location of, xv
  Mark's home possible site of, 282
Law of Moses (see Moses, law of)
Lawyers, 67
  (See also Sanhedrin)
Laymen, **48**
Leaven, 153
Legion, Jesus healing, 94–99
Leper(s), leprosy, 38–39, 265
  Jesus healing, 37–41
  Simon the Leper, 264–266
Levi (see Matthew)
Lewis, C. S., 314–315
  on camel metaphor, 192
  on God as man, 198
  on Jesus forgiving sin, 45
  on the Second Coming, 258
Life Application Bible Commentary:
  on Christian witness, 99
  on Jesus in Galilee, 37
  on John the Baptist, 18
Lion, the Witch, and the Wardrobe, The, 314–315
Literary devices:
  inclusio, 159
  intercalation, 61–62
Loaves and fishes:
  feeding five thousand (first miracle of), 128–130
  feeding four thousand (second miracle of), 150–151
  Jesus reminding disciples of, 153–154
Locusts and honey, 16–18
Lotz, Anne Graham:
  on Jesus admitting divinity, 285
  on Jesus on the cross, 301
  on meeting others' needs, 102–103
  on receiving or rejecting Jesus, 268
  on sacrifice of Jesus, 307
Love:
  God's for us, 72, 109
  most important commandment, 235–237
  for neighbor as self, 236–237
  ours for God, 82, 110, 235–237
  service as expressing, 197
Lucado, Max:
  on faith, 107
  on flogging, 292
  on God's love for you, 72
  on Jesus bearing your sin, 303
  on seeing God, 134
  on spit of the soldiers, 297
  on storm, Jesus calming, 93
Luke, Gospel of:
  expressing Jesus' mission, 49
  for Gentile audience, 128
  Mark's Gospel contrasted to, 11–12
  (See also Gospels, the four)

M
MacArthur, John:
  on Christian discipleship, 180
  on Judas, 281

  on Peter denying Jesus, 288
  on Pontius Pilate, 290
  on timing of Jesus' capture, 264
Maccabeans, 211–212
Magdala, 33
Malachi, Book of, 16, 27, 207
Manuscript transmission, **320**
Map(s):
  of Bethsaida and Gennesaret, 135
  of Galilee, villages of, 33
  of Jerusalem in Jesus' day, 205
Mark (author of Gospel; John Mark):
  favorite theory regarding, 282
  as (likely) Jew, 290
  as naked young man?, 282
  and Peter, xiv–xvi
Mark, Gospel of, xiv, xvi, 11, 61–62, 73, 305, 322
  anti-Semitic accusations of, 290
  blind man story unique to, 160
  compared/contrasted to other Gospels, 11–12, 60, 127 (See also specific topics and events)
  depicting agony and victory, 262
  divine identity of Jesus in, 14
  elements of, 158
  end of as controversial, 311, 318–321
  Galilee vs. Jerusalem in, 317
  Greek as language of, 180, 283
  the inclusio in, 159
  irony in, 123, 301, 306
  making sense of, 115–117
  "Markan hinge," 157–158
  "Markan sandwich," 61–62
  Mark 13 as misunderstood, 243
  masterful construction of, 305
  as not easy reading, 295
  Old Testament importance in, 15, 20, 130, 209
  one-verse summary, 197, 304
  opening phrase of, 12–13
  Peter as buffoon in, 158
  Peter as source of, xiv–xvi, 61
  purposes of, 12
  Roman audience, as for, 11, 42
  set around Sea of Galilee, 145
  summary, 322
  symbolism in, 130
  theological purpose in, 282
  as well-organized, 89
Marriage:
  adultery (see Adultery)
  and divorce (see Divorce)
  and eternal life, 231–232
  sex, 232–233
Martyr, James (son of Zebedee) as first apostolic, 65
Mary, mother of James and Joses, 307–309
  at tomb of Jesus, 314
Mary, mother of Jesus:
  at crucifixion, 308, 312
  John (son of Zebedee) and, 65
  (See also Family of Jesus)
Mary Magdalene, 307–309
  at tomb of Jesus, 314–317
Mathewes-Green, Frederica:
  on the Bible, 234
  on misquoting the Bible, 233–234

Mattathias, 211
Matthew, Gospel of:
  Mark's Gospel contrasted to, 11–12
  (See also Gospels, the four)
Matthew (Levi), 46–47, 49, 64–65
Matzoh, **271**
McDowell, Josh, on trustworthiness of Scriptures, xv
Mears, Henrietta C., on Old and New Testaments, xii
Measure:
  cubits, 245
  metaphor of, 82
Megalomaniac, **44, 211**
Mercy, of Jesus, 68
Merrill, Dean, on good overcoming evil, 69
Meshiach, **13**
Message, The, by Eugene Peterson, 81, 283
Messiah, 13–15, 21, 301
  "Anointed One," 21
  bridegroom, represented as, 50–51
  crucifixion "proof" against Jesus as, 292
  descendant of David, 81–82
  Elijah as forerunner of, 167
  false, 246–247, 253
  Herod (Antipas) as aspiring, 207–208
  hopes and expectations regarding, 13–14
  Jesus admitting to being, 285
  Jesus' claim as, 52–54, 63–64
  "Messianic secret," 14, 36, 82, 99
  misconceptions regarding, 144, 158, 162, 169, 207
  supposed mission of, 230
  true purpose of, 304
  (See also Jesus Christ)
Messiah cup, 272
"Messianic secret," 14, 36, 82, 99
Metaphor, **82,** 143
  in loaves and fishes miracles, 154
Micah, 220
Millstone, illustration of, 184
Ministry and teaching of Jesus:
  beginning of, significance, 51
  Capernaum as home base, 33
  every act significant, 155
  preparation for, 22–23
  real message of, 108
  "whoever is not against us is for us," 181–182
  (See also specific topics, places, and events)
Minutiae, **53**
Miracles of Elisha, 130
Miracles of Jesus, 149
  authenticity of, 69
  baptism, as after his, 21
  as demonstrating divinity, 90
  few in all four Gospels, 127–128
  Gentiles' reaction to, 149–150
  opponents believing in, 69
  on the Sabbath, 31, 35–36, 54–55
  witnesses forbidden to tell, 149
Miracles of Jesus—healing:
  bleeding woman, 103–106, 109
  blind Bartimaeus, 198–200
  blind man, two-part healing, 160
  deaf mute, 148–149
  demon-possessed boy, 171–175

as enemies of Jesus, 54–55
fasting custom of, 50
God, view of, 54
Herodians, alliance with, 185–186, 229
hypocrisy and superficiality of, 140–143
Jesus and, 116–117
John the Baptist and, 18
lestas, 291
our similarities to, 144
Paul as, 48
questioning Jesus, 228–230
requesting "a sign," 151–152
(*See also* Religious leaders; specific events
    and topics)
Philip, 64–65
    Bethsaida as hometown, 160
Phoenician woman, Jesus healing daughter,
    144–147
Pigs:
    demons entering, 95–96
    sacrificed to Zeus, 211
Pilate, Pontius, 289, 290
    Jesus tried before, 288–293
    and Joseph of Arimathea, 311–313
    Sanhedrin, relationship with, 289, 291
Poignant, **112**
Pompey, **3**
Pontius Pilate (*see* Pilate, Pontius)
Poor, right treatment of, 266
Power:
    Herod (Antipas)'s lust for, 207–208
    the temptation of, 196
Power of Jesus, 25–26, 89, 105, 119, 304
    displays of, 78
    prayer and, 35
    working through disciples, 122
    (*See also* Authority of Jesus; specific
        events)
Praetorium, **289**
Prayer:
    attitudes toward, 175
    and effective Bible study, xvii
    faith in, 220
    at Gethsemane, 275–277
    to heal demon-possessed boy, 175
    of Jesus, 37, 131, 149, 275–277
    Jesus teaching, 220–221
    Temple as house of, 217
Preacher, Jesus as, 36, 155
    (*See also* Ministry and Teaching of Jesus)
Prefect, Pontius Pilate as, 289
Preparation Day, 311
Prerogative, **129**
Priest(s):
    Caiaphas, 283
    chief priests, 224
    greed of, 217
    Phanni ordained by Zealots, 251
    Temple, 215–216
    (*See also* Religious leaders)
Priest's Court, 215
Promised Land, 17
Prophecy, 8
    end-time, 243–244, 252–253
    Messianic, 13–15, 21
    Triumphal Entry as fulfilling, 209–210, 222
    (*See also* individual events, topics, and
        Old Testament Books)

Prophet(s), 3, 62
    called "servants," 226
    false, 253–254
    false, Jesus accused of being, 301
    fig tree symbolism, 214
    Isaiah (*see* Isaiah)
    Jesus as, 13, 122, 130, 167
    John the Baptist as, 16–19, 225
    symbolic actions of, 62–63, 214
    without honor in own home, 112
    (*See also* individual names and Old
        Testament Books)
Prophets (books), **16**–17
Protracted, **35**
Psalms, Book of, 20, 270, 303
    allusions to, 296
    "He who has shared my bread," 270
    Jesus quoting, 228
Purity, 138–140, 142
    (*See also* Cleanliness)
Purple robe, 295–296

Q
Qumran community, 14, 17

R
Rabbi, **32**
Raison détre, **219**
Redemption, **28**
Religion:
    church and state in, 43
    empty vs. true, 221, 222
    of first-century Jews, 43
    (*See also* Christianity)
Religious leaders, 43, 224
    corruption of, 239
    as enemies of Jesus, 219, 223–224, 227–
        228
    Jairus as, 102
    Jesus' conflicts with, 43–57 (58), 58
    Jesus' question for, 238
    parable of the Vineyard tenants, 226–228
    plotting against Jesus, 279
    (*See also* Pharisees; Priests; Sadducees;
        Sanhedrin; Scribes; individual topics,
        places, and events)
Repentance, **15**
Representative acts, 21
Resurrection, 124, 169
    to eternal life, 234
    of Jairus' daughter, 106–108
Resurrection of Jesus, 315–316
    Jesus predicting, 178
    Mark's Gospel not spelling out, 319–320
    witnesses to, 320
Revelation, Book of, 243
Riches (*see* Wealth)
Rich young ruler, 189–191
Robbers:
    crucified with Jesus, 299–300
    Temple moneychangers called, 215, 218
Roman Empire, 4–5
    coins of, 197
    as conquering nation, 8–9
    Herod ruling under, 207–208
    Israel ruled by, 3, 43
    Jewish faith, opinion of, 279
    Jews' wish to overthrow, 84

    living conditions under, 103
    as pagan, 16
    persecuting early Christians, 249
    Pontius Pilate as prefect, 289
    Sadducees and, 232
    taxation practices, 229–230
    Temple, destroying, 252
    Titus (emperor), 251–252
Roman(s):
    in Capernaum, 32
    characteristics of, 11
    Mark's Gospel written for, 11, 42
    viewed as "dogs," 47
Roof:
    first-century, illustration of, 46
    paralytic brought through, 43–46
Rooster, crowing of, 287
Rufus, 297–298

S
Sabbath, **36**
    burial customs and rules, 311
    David eating consecrated bread, 52–53
    Jesus regarding, 52–55
    miracles performed on, 31, 35–36, 54–55
    observance of, 211
    Pharisees' rules regarding, 48, 52–55
    Preparation Day, 311
    Sunday, changed to by Jewish Christians,
        315
Sacrifice(s), **237**
    financial, 240–241
    for Jesus, 266
    Jesus as ultimate, 305–307
    Passover lamb, 269
    Temple, 215–217
Sadducees, 231–232
    John the Baptist and, 18
    questioning Jesus, 231–232
    (*See also* Pharisees)
Salome (at death of Jesus), 307–309
Salome (Herodias's daughter), 124–126
Salt, 181
Salvation, 183–185, 191–192
    bought by Jesus' death, 290
    Christian character, 184–185
    God's gift to us, 302
    as only through Jesus, 19
    reason for, 72
Samson, 120
1 Samuel, Book of, 20, 110
2 Samuel, Book of, 81
Sanctity, **216**
Sanhedrin, **43**, 67–68
    authority of Jesus, questioning, 224–225
    Joseph of Arimathea, 311–313
    Pontius Pilate, relationship with, 289, 291
    punishment given by, 286
    Temple, reaction to Jesus' attack on, 224
    (*See also* Arrest of Jesus; Trial of Jesus)
Satan:
    and Antichrist, 251
    Christians and, 70
    "Get thee behind me, Satan," 162–163
    Jesus as superior to, 22, 68–69, 120
    tempting Jesus, 22–23
Saved, 183 (*See also* Salvation)
Schizo, 21, 305

Books by Starburst Publishers®
(Partial listing—full list available on request)

The *God's Word for the Biblically-Inept*™ series is already a best-seller with over 100,000 books sold! Designed to make reading the Bible easy, educational, and fun! This series of verse-by-verse Bible studies, topical studies, and overviews mixes scholarly information from experts with helpful icons, illustrations, sidebars, and time lines. It's the Bible made easy!

Mark—God's Word for the Biblically-Inept™
Scott Pinzon
The shortest of all the Gospels, Mark focuses on Jesus' actions. Following the story of the adult Jesus from the time of his baptism by John the Baptist to his crucifixion and resurrection, readers will learn about the Book of Mark in simple, vivid terms that will bring it to life like never before!
(trade paper)   ISBN 1892016362 $17.99

Acts—God's Word for the Biblically-Inept™
Robert C. Girard
An important book of history, Acts recounts the ascension of Jesus into heaven, the spread of Christianity throughout the Roman Empire, and the rapid growth of the church—despite the persecution of Paul and other apostles. A must-read for anyone interested in learning more about the early days of the church without getting bogged down in complicated language and confusing details.
(trade paper)   ISBN 189201646X $17.99

The Bible—God's Word for the Biblically-Inept™
Larry Richards
An excellent book to start learning the entire Bible. Get the basics or the in-depth information you are seeking with this user-friendly overview. From Creation to Christ to the Millennium, learning the Bible has never been easier.
(trade paper)   ISBN 0914984551 $16.95

Daniel—God's Word for the Biblically-Inept™
Daymond R. Duck
Daniel is a book of prophecy and the key to understanding the mysteries of the Tribulation and end-time events. This verse-by-verse commentary combines humor and scholarship to get at the essentials of Scripture. Perfect for those who want to know the truth about the Antichrist.
(trade paper)   ISBN 0914984489 $16.95

Genesis—God's Word for the Biblically-Inept™
Joyce L. Gibson
Genesis is written to make understanding and learning the Word of God simple and fun! Like the other books in this series, the author breaks the Bible down into bite-sized pieces making it easy to understand and incorporate into your life. Readers will learn about Creation, Adam and Eve, the Flood, Abraham and Isaac, and more.
(trade paper)   ISBN 1892016125 $16.95

Health & Nutrition—God's Word for the Biblically-Inept™
Kathleen O'Bannon Baldinger
The Bible is full of God's rules for good health! Baldinger reveals scientific evidence that proves the diet and health principles outlined in the Bible are the best for total health. Learn about the Bible diet, the food pyramid, and fruits and vegetables from the Bible! Experts include Pamela Smith, Julian Whitaker, Kenneth Cooper, and T. D. Jakes.
(trade paper)   ISBN 0914984055 $16.95

John—God's Word for the Biblically-Inept™
Lin Johnson
From village fisherman to beloved apostle, John was an eyewitness to the teachings and miracles of Christ. Now, readers can join in an easy-to-understand, verse-by-verse journey through the fourth and most unique of all the Gospels. Witness the wonder of Jesus, a man who turned water into wine, healed the blind, walked on water, and raised Lazarus from the dead.
(trade paper)   ISBN 1892016435 $16.95

Life of Christ, Volume 1—God's Word for the Biblically-Inept™
Robert C. Girard
Girard takes the reader on an easy-to-understand journey through the Gospels of Matthew, Mark, Luke, and John, tracing the story of Jesus from his virgin birth to his revolutionary ministry. Learn about Jesus' baptism, the Sermon on the Mount, and his miracles and parables.
(trade paper)   ISBN 1892016230 $16.95

Life of Christ, Volume 2—God's Word for the Biblically-Inept™
Robert C. Girard
Life of Christ, Volume 2, begins with events recorded in Matthew 16. Read about Jesus' transfiguration, his miracles and parables, triumphal ride through Jerusalem, capture in the Garden of Gethsemane, and his trial, crucifixion, resurrection, and ascension. Find out how to be great in the kingdom of God, what Jesus meant when he called himself the light of the world, and what makes up real worship.
(trade paper)   ISBN 1892016397 $16.95

Men of the Bible—God's Word for the Biblically-Inept™
D. Larry Miller
Benefit from the life experiences of the powerful men of the Bible! Learn how the inspirational struggles of men such as Moses, Daniel, Paul, and David parallel the struggles of men today. It will inspire and build Christian character for any reader.
(trade paper)   ISBN 1892016079 $16.95

Prophecies of the Bible—God's Word for the Biblically-Inept™

Daymond R. Duck

God has a plan for this crazy planet, and now understanding it is easier than ever! Best-selling author and end-time prophecy expert Daymond R. Duck explains the complicated prophecies of the Bible in plain English. Duck shows you all there is to know about the end of the age, the New World Order, the Second Coming, and the coming world government. Find out what prophecies have already been fulfilled and what's in store for the future!
(trade paper)   ISBN 1892016222 $16.95

Revelation—God's Word for the Biblically-Inept™

Daymond R. Duck

End-time Bible prophecy expert Daymond R. Duck leads us verse by verse through one of the Bible's most confusing books. Follow the experts as they forge their way through the captivating prophecies of Revelation!
(trade paper)   ISBN 0914984985 $16.95

Romans—God's Word for the Biblically-Inept™

Gib Martin

The best-selling *God's Word for the Biblically-Inept™* series continues to grow! Learn about the apostle Paul, living a righteous life, and more with help from graphics, icons, and chapter summaries.
(trade paper)   ISBN 1892016273 $16.95

Women of the Bible—God's Word for the Biblically-Inept™

Kathy Collard Miller

Finally, a Bible perspective just for women! Gain valuable insight from the successes and struggles of such women as Eve, Esther, Mary, Sarah, and Rebekah. Interesting icons like "Get Close to God," "Build Your Spirit," and "Grow Your Marriage" will make it easy to incorporate God's Word into your daily life.
(trade paper)   ISBN 0914984063 $16.95

The God Things Come in Small Packages series will make you want to blow the dust off your rose-colored glasses, open your eyes, and recount God's blessings! Join best-selling writers LeAnn Weiss, Susan Duke, Caron Loveless, and Judith Carden as they awaken your senses and open your mind to the "little" wonders of God in life's big picture!

God Things Come in Small Packages
(hard cover)   ISBN 1892016281 $12.95
God Things Come in Small Packages for Moms
(hard cover)   ISBN 189201629X $12.95
God Things Come in Small Packages for Friends
(hard cover)   ISBN 1892016346 $12.95
God Things Come in Small Packages for Women
(hard cover)   ISBN 1892016354 $12.95

An Expressive Heart: Stories, Lessons, and Exercises Inspired by Psalms

Edited by Kathy Collard Miller

An intimate book of inspirational lessons from the best-selling editor of the *God's Abundance* collection. Each selection includes a passage from the poetic Book of Psalms, an inspirational story, lesson, quotation, and idea for personal journaling with room to write. The Psalms provide an unmatched guide for anyone who wants to know God better, and *An Expressive Heart* will help you say what's on your heart.
(trade paper)   ISBN 1892016508 $12.99

A Growing Heart: Stories, Lessons, and Exercises Inspired by Proverbs

Edited by Kathy Collard Miller

The profound truths of Proverbs provide wisdom for making good choices in life. Each selection includes a verse from Proverbs, an inspirational story, teachings, quotation, and idea for journaling with room to write. Lessons will guide the reader on topics such as discipline, friendship, love, parenting, wealth, and work.
(trade paper)   ISBN 1892016524 $12.99

Stories of God's Abundance for a More Joyful Life

Compiled by Kathy Collard Miller

Like its successful predecessor, *God's Abundance* (100,000 sold), this book is filled with beautiful, inspirational, real life stories. Those telling their stories of God share Scriptures and insights that readers can apply to their daily lives. Renew your faith in life's small miracles and challenge yourself to allow God to lead the way as you find the source of abundant living for all your relationships.
(trade paper)   ISBN 1892016060 $12.95

God Stories: They're So Amazing, Only God Could Make Them Happen

Donna I. Douglas

Famous individuals share their personal, true-life experiences with God in this beautiful book! Find out how God has touched the lives of top recording artists, professional athletes, and other newsmakers like Jessi Colter, Deana Carter, Ben Vereen, Stephanie Zimbalist, Cindy Morgan, Sheila E., Joe Jacoby, Cheryl Landon, Brett Butler, Clifton Taulbert, Babbie Mason, Michael Medved, Sandi Patty, Charlie Daniels, and more! Their stories are intimate, poignant, and sure to inspire and motivate you as you listen for God's message in your own life!
(cloth)   ISBN 1892016117 $18.95

Since Life Isn't a Game, These Are God's Rules: Finding Joy & Fulfillment in God's Ten Commandments

Kathy Collard Miller

Life is often referred to as a game, but God didn't create us because he was short on game pieces. To succeed in life, you'll need to know God's rules. In this book, Kathy Collard Miller explains the meaning of each of the Ten Commandments with fresh application for today. Each chapter includes Scripture and quotes from some of our most beloved Christian authors including Billy Graham, Patsy Clairmont, Liz Curtis Higgs, and more! Sure to renew your understanding of God's rules.
(cloth)   ISBN 189201615X $17.95

Seasons of a Woman's Heart: A Daybook of Stories and Inspiration
Edited by Lynn D. Morrissey

A woman's heart is complex. This daybook of stories, quotes, Scriptures, and daily reflections will inspire and refresh. Christian women share their heartfelt thoughts on Seasons of Faith, Growth, Guidance, Nurturing, and Victory. Includes Christian writers Kay Arthur, Emilie Barnes, Luci Swindoll, Jill Briscoe, and Florence Littauer.
(cloth)   ISBN 1892016036 $18.95

Treasures of a Woman's Heart: A Daybook of Stories and Inspiration
Edited by Lynn D. Morrissey

Join the best-selling editor of *Seasons of a Woman's Heart* in this touching sequel where she unlocks the treasures of women and glorifies God with Scripture, reflection, and a compilation of stories. Explore heartfelt living with vignettes by Kay Arthur, Elisabeth Elliot, Emilie Barnes, Claire Cloninger, and more.
(cloth)   ISBN 1892016257 $18.95

God's Little Rule Book: Simple Rules to Bring Joy & Happiness to Your Life
Starburst Publishers

Let this little book of God's rules be your personal guide to a more joyful life. Brimming with easily applicable rules, this book is sure to inspire and motivate you! Each rule includes corresponding Scripture and a practical tip that will help to incorporate God's rules into everyday life. Simple enough to fit into a busy schedule, yet powerful enough to be life changing!
(trade paper)   ISBN 1892016168 $6.95

Life's Little Rule Book: Simple Rules to Bring Joy & Happiness to Your Life
Starburst Publishers

Let this little book inspire you to live a happier life! The pages are filled with timeless rules such as, "Learn to cook, you'll always be in demand!" and "Help something grow." Each rule is combined with a reflective quote and a simple suggestion to help the reader incorporate the rule into everyday life.
(trade paper)   ISBN 1892016176 $6.95

Cheap Talk with the Frugal Friends
Angie Zalewski and Deana Ricks

A collection of savvy tips and tricks for stretching the family dollar from celebrity thrifters, Angie Zalewski and Deana Ricks, known as the Frugal Friends by their radio and television audiences. This book features twenty-nine chapters on various topics, including automotive, beauty care, cleaning products, dating, decorating, entertainment, medicine, pet care, and sporting goods. Includes advice on eliminating credit card debt, making extra money, and organizing the home. Finally, a practical way to save money with without compromising convenience or lowering lifestyle standards!
(trade paper)   ISBN 1892016583 $9.99

Stories for the Spirit-Filled Believer
Edited by Cristine Bolley

It's one thing to know that God is real. It is quite another to have profound and on-going experiences that confirm that belief. In this awesome collection of stories, Cristine Bolley compiles the real-life testimonies of believers who have heard God's voice and responded. This volume includes stories from today's most dynamic charismatic personalities: Oral Roberts, Beth Moore, Tommy Tenney, T. D. Jakes, Joyce Meyer, and more. Each selection contains a Scripture verse, true story, and a prayer. Sure to inspire readers to listen for God's voice in their own lives.
(trade paper)   ISBN 1892016540 $13.99

God's Abundance for Women: Devotions for a More Meaningful Life
Compiled by Kathy Collard Miller

Following the success of *God's Abundance*, this book will touch women of all ages as they seek a more meaningful life. Essays from our most beloved Christian authors exemplify how to gain the abundant life that Jesus promised through trusting Him to fulfill our every need. Each story is enhanced with Scripture, quotes, and practical tips providing brief, yet deeply spiritual reading.
(cloth)   ISBN 1892016141 $19.95

More God's Abundance: Joyful Devotions for Every Season
Compiled by Kathy Collard Miller

Editor Kathy Collard Miller responds to the tremendous success of *God's Abundance* with a fresh collection of stories based on God's Word for a simpler life. Includes stories from our most beloved Christian writers, such as Liz Curtis Higgs and Patsy Clairmont, that are combined ideas, tips, quotes, and Scripture.
(cloth)   ISBN 1892016133 $19.95

The Weekly Feeder: A Revolutionary Shopping, Cooking, and Meal-Planning System
Cori Kirkpatrick

A revolutionary meal-planning system, here is a way to make preparing home-cooked dinners more convenient than ever. At the beginning of each week, simply choose one of the eight preplanned menus, tear out the corresponding grocery list, do your shopping, and whip up each fantastic meal in less than 45 minutes! The author's household management tips, equipment checklists, and nutrition information make this system a must for any busy family. Included with every recipe is a personal anecdote from the author emphasizing the importance of good food, a healthy family, and a well-balanced life.
(trade paper)   ISBN 1892016095 $16.95

What's in the Bible for . . .™

From the creators of the **God's Word for the Biblically-Inept™** series comes the innovative **What's in the Bible for . . .™** series. Scripture has certain things to say to certain people, but without a guide, hunting down *all* of what the Bible has to say to you can be overwhelming. Borrowing the user-friendly format of the **God's Word for the Biblically-Inept™** series, this new series spotlights those passages and themes of Scripture that are relevant to particular groups of people. Whether you're young or old, married or single, male or female, this series will simplify the very important process of applying the Bible to your life.

What's in the Bible for . . .™ Couples *Kathy Collard Miller and D. Larry Miller*　　　WBFC
(trade paper)　ISBN　1892016028　**$16.95**

What's in the Bible for . . .™ Women *Georgia Curtis Ling*　　　WBFW
(trade paper)　ISBN　1892016109　**$16.95**

What's in the Bible for . . .™ Mothers *Judy Bodmer*　　　WBFM
(trade paper)　ISBN　　1892016265　　$17.99

•　**Learn more at www.biblicallyinept.com**　•

Purchasing Information

www.starburstpublishers.com

Books are available from your favorite bookstore, either from current stock or special order. To assist bookstores in locating your selection, be sure to give title, author, and ISBN. If unable to purchase from a bookstore, you may order direct from STARBURST PUBLISHERS®. When ordering please enclose full payment plus shipping and handling as follows:

Post Office (4th class)
$4.00 with a purchase of up to $20.00
$5.00 ($20.01–$50.00)
9% of purchase price for purchases of $50.01 and up

Canada
$5.00 (up to $35.00)
15% ($35.01 and up)

United Parcel Service (UPS)
$5.00 (up to $20.00)
$7.00 ($20.01–$50.00)
12% ($50.01 and up)

Overseas
$5.00 (up to $25.00)
20% ($25.01 and up)

Payment in U.S. funds only. Please allow two to four weeks minimum for delivery by USPS (longer for overseas and Canada). Allow two to seven working days for delivery by UPS. Make checks payable to and mail to: **Starburst Publishers**®, P.O. Box 4123, Lancaster, PA 17604. Credit card orders may be placed by calling 1-800-441-1456, Mon–Fri, 8:30 A.M. to 5:30 P.M. Eastern Standard Time. Prices are subject to change without notice. Catalogs are available for a 9 x 12 self-addressed envelope with four first-class stamps.